A HISTORY OF
HABSBURG JEWS,
1670–1918

A HISTORY OF

Habsburg Jews, 1670–1918

William O. McCagg Jr.

INDIANA UNIVERSITY PRESS

Bloomington and Indianapolis

First Midland Book Edition 1992

Manufactured in the United States of America

Library of Congress Cataloging-in-Publication Data
McCagg, William O.
  A history of Habsburg Jews, 1670-1918 / William O. McCagg, Jr.
    p.   cm.
  Bibliography: p.
  Includes index.
  ISBN 0-253-33189-7
    1. Jews—Austria—History. 2. Jews—Austria—Cultural
assimilation. 3. Austria—Ethnic relations. 4. Jews—Hungary—
History. 5. Jews—Hungary—Cultural assimilation. 6. Hungary—
Ethnic relations. I. Title.
DS135.A9M34 1988
943.6'004924—dc19   88-544
  ISBN 0-253-20649-9 (pbk.)

  3 4 5 6 7 96 95 94 93 92

For Louise
without whose support and
loyalty
this book would have been
impossible

CONTENTS

PREFACE

This book has roots that go back to the beginning of my career. It reflects the wartime 1940s in New England, where as a schoolboy I learned French, German, and Baedeker, and fell in love with Prague; Harvard in the early 1950s, where I read Dante in Italian and became an historian; Monterey just after that, where I learnt Czech while gathering abalone and artichokes; Frankfurt, where I read traffic from Eastern Europe and studied the *Bundesbahn Fahrplan*, to my very great advantage; Vienna in November 1956, where I met my first Hungarians; Columbia University in the later 1950s, where Oskar Halecki and Henry Roberts sought to disentangle me from the Cold War, where I learned Magyar and met my wife; Munich in 1960, whence we first penetrated the European east; Lansing, Michigan, where since 1964 I have been privileged to teach about the length and breadth of East European history, acquiring an empire of knowledge which could scarcely have been mine at any frustier place; Budapest where we lived for over a year in the middle 1960s, and where I began to study Jews; and then Jerusalem, Vienna, Budapest, Cambridge, and New York, where over the past two decades I have done my research.

Not only are the book's roots diverse; its shape is the result of many transformations. Originally it was supposed to be a speedily written Austrian pendant to the book *Jewish Nobles and Geniuses in Modern Hungary*, which emerged from our year in Budapest. Three discoveries soon changed the plan. First, I learned in a cold Vienna winter that research methods that work in Budapest may be ineffective farther up the Danube, and that some of the clear perspectives I obtained while living in Hungary needed changing in Austria. This does not mean that my Hungarian friends had twisted things around and missed the truth, nor does it mean that bright flashes of inspiration do not occur to the Viennese. But there are net differences between the outside world and Hungary which required a total reworking of my original plans. And then I learned, second, that not all Jews speak Magyar, German, and English; and third, that not all were modern-minded in the period before 1848. This had really not featured in the Hungarian book, but it necessarily had to figure in a study of Austrian Jews. Such discoveries brought me face to face with a need for prolonged new study of Jewish history, of Judaism, and of the Jewish tongues. To my great embarrassment, I have failed in the latter task; Yiddish and Hebrew still escape me. But it is the decade since 1973 of reading and teaching about the specifically Jewish past that has actually shaped this book.

Despite this twisted history, I hope the book will find readers, because it seems to me from long experience there is a great need for it. A vast amount of detailed literature is available about the Jews in central and eastern Europe, but no book pulls it all together. There are numerous distinguished histories of the German Jews and the Russian/Polish Jews. But to the best of my knowledge no one since the last century has written a general history of the "Jewries in between." They existed as a separate entity, of course, until the end of the Habsburg Reich. Theirs is a very important case history, fuller by far in its social scope than the history of the German, French, Dutch, or English Jews, less painful than the history of the Jews of Russia. Yet because of the vast complexity of the "in-between lands," and presumably also because of the languages and different cultures involved, historians have let those Jewries slip from our collective memory. This is the gap which I hope this book will fill, the need which I hope it will meet. And perhaps my wandering career, which has fortuitously equipped me with skills for the job, will justify my presumption in writing about Jewish history without the central Jewish languages in tongue.

A remark is needed here about diacritical marks and place names. As any student of eastern Europe knows, anarchy faces anyone who seeks to impose uniform spelling on the region. What is "s" in Magyar is "sz" in Polish, "š" in Czech, "sch" in German, and "sh" in English transliteration of the cyrillic letter used by Ukrainians, Bulgarians, and Serbs. Worse, most locations in east central Europe are known by different names in the different local tongues.

With respect to place-name spelling, I have tried in this book to use the version by which a place is currently known to English speakers: thus Bratislava, Brno, Lwow, Cracow. In all four of these cases, and in many others, the violation to purist ears is severe. But there seems no other way.

With respect to diacritical marks, I have used the umlaut, hačka, and acute and grave accents as needed, but have regretfully omitted the distinction between long and short umlaut in Magyar, the dot over various letters in Czech and Polish, the cedillas in Polish and Romanian, and the slashed "l" in Polish.

Other scholars have shown me a great deal of kindness in the many years of research for this book. I feel especially indebted to Gary Cohen, Michael Silber, David Lo Romer, György Bencze, and an anonymous critic for having taken the time to read and comment in detail on various versions of the manuscript, and to Károly Vörös, P. R. Duggan, Zoltán Szász, Donald Lammers, Péter Hanák, Ludwig von Gogolak, Paul Sweet, Gábor Vermes, and Hillel Kieval, who have been extraordinarily liberal over many years in sharing their skills and knowledge with me and in reading and criticizing rough drafts. The late Robert Kann encouraged me a great deal at the beginning of my project with his support. In Budapest Emil Niederhauser and György Ránki were particularly helpful, but I am indebted also to many other old friends and colleagues at the Történettudományi Intézet and elsewhere, for their continued open-handed friendship and hospitality. In Vienna Franz Baltzarek, Nikolaus Vielmetti, Moritz Csaky, Hannes Stekl, Horst Haselsteiner, Eduard März, and Hanns Jäger-Sunstenau were especially helpful to me during long visits. In Israel Jakob Katz, Shmuel Ettinger, Ezra Mendelsohn, Jonathan Frankl, Béla Vágó, and Baruch Yaron lent me greatly appreciated helping hands. A number of conferences greatly helped me over the years in maturing my ideas: Professor Vágó's at the University of Haifa in 1972 and 1978, Professor Todd Endelman's at Indiana University in 1983, Professor Ránki's at Indiana University in 1984, Professors Victor Karady and Yehuda Don's at the Maison de l'Homme in Paris in 1985, and Professor William Wright's at the University of Minnesota in 1986. My esteemed publisher and friend, Stephen Fischer-Galati, arranged two opportunities for me to present papers related to this book at scholarly meetings. To these scholars, and to the others whom I met at their meetings, I owe a particular intellectual debt. And finally I have learned a great deal from often chance conversation or correspondence with my friends, the late Richard Allen, Árpád Ajtony, Lee Congdon, István Deak, Elinor Despalatovic, the late Miklós Érdely, Claude Gandelman, Jonathan Harris, Marion Low, Anne Meyering, Ivor Oxaal, Michael Riff, Marsha Rosenblit, Gordon Stewart, Hédi Tárján, and Peter Vinten-Johannsen.

Despite the help and advice I have received from all these friends and colleagues, responsibility for the text of this book remains entirely my own.

Every scholar learns early in his career that without the quiet help of book guardians, of archival administrations, and of university and institutional colleagues, he would find his work impossible. My deep thanks are due to staffs of the Widener Library at Harvard and the Vienna National and University Libraries above all, but also to those at the Michigan State University, the University of Michigan, Columbia University, Yale University, Hebrew University, and the New York Public and the Vienna City libraries. I encountered ready and much appreciated assistance from the staffs of the Verwaltungsarchiv, the Haus- Hof- und Staatsarchiv and the Finanz Ministerium Archiv in Vienna, the Országos Levéltár in Budapest, and the Historical Archive of the Jewish People in Jerusalem; also at the Leo Baeck and YIVO institutes in New York. I acknowledge here also my appreciation to the directorships of all these institutions for permission to use the treasures in their care.

Very special thanks are due to Mary Jane Gormley and Janet Rabinowitch of the Indiana University Press for their careful and intelligent help with the editing and publication of the book.

My children have put up with a lot of absenteeism because of this book, as has my broader family. Their indulgence has not gone unperceived. My beloved wife, Louise, has put up with a great deal more than absenteeism. She's come along with me on my journeys, sat by me even while I've been writing, she has taken time from her own work because of my temperament, and she has supported me throughout. I can only say thanks with love.

A HISTORY OF
HABSBURG JEWS,
1670–1918

ONE

Introduction

I

In 1666–67, Jews all over Europe were stirred by the news that at Smyrna the Messiah had revealed himself in the person of Shabbetai Zevi. Despite the slow communications of that day, the word spread like wildfire. At Vienna particularly, it is said, Jewish exaltation led men to sell their property and close their businesses in expectation of an imminent mystic return to the Promised Land.[1] Bad news soon followed. Under pressure from the Ottoman Sultan, Shabbetai Zevi (1626–1676) apostatized. But the excitement he caused showed how deeply the Jews of central Europe then lived in a spiritual world of their own, utterly excluding from their lives their Christian neighbors.

Just three years later, another set of events told a similar story about the Christians in Austria. Kaiser Leopold I (1657–1705) was poorer than his great rival, Louis XIV of France, but no less pious; and in June 1669 he showed off his piety to his new young Spanish Habsburg second wife. She had blamed a miscarriage on the presence in Vienna of Jews, who had been banned since 1492 in the land of her birth. The Christian merchants of the capital had frequently petitioned Leopold to rid them of their "pestiferous" rivals, and were just at that time blaming a recent fire in the imperial palace, the Hofburg, on the Jews, and also the drowning of a Christian woman in the Jewish quarter. Leopold decided that these were pressing reasons for him to "cleanse" his residential city of 3,000 or 4,000 Jewish souls, the fourth largest urban Ashkenazi Jewish community in Europe at the time.[2] First, therefore, he expelled the poor, the most visibly burdensome. Then in August 1669 he ordered out all but the very rich. In February 1670 he commanded even them to leave Vienna within four months, and finally in April 1671 he ordered all Jews out of the province of Lower Austria too.[3] The Viennese Christians rejoiced when the Jews left, though these latter had long been resident in their midst and even spoke something like the same Germanic tongue.

These twin events show clearly what a deep chasm existed between Austrian Christians and Jews early in modern times and cast into high relief the phenomenon which will be discussed in this book: the bridging and transformation of the chasm during the process known as modernization. One hundred and eleven years after the expulsion of the Viennese Jews, Kaiser Leopold's great-grandson Joseph signed a Rescript of Toleration, placing the Jews in his dominions under substantially the same law that ruled the Christians. A few years after that, in 1789, Joseph issued the first patent of nobility given as a matter of policy in Austria to a confessional Jew: this symbolized what a broad social integration of Jewish and Christian Austrians was then beginning. By the middle of the nineteenth century, when the legal emancipation of Jewry in central Europe took final form, one could speak in the major cities of an "Austrian-Jewish cultural symbiosis," as if it were reality. By 1914 Habsburg Jewry was producing a famous array of distinguished "Austrian" cultural figures who have shaped our time: Freud, for one; Wittgenstein and Kafka; the musicians Mahler and Schönberg; and the "Hungarian" latter-day developers of nuclear weaponry—John von Neumann, Leo Szilard, Edward Teller.[4]

A chasm still separated Austria's Jews and Christians in and after 1914, and not only because outside the cities there were still considerable Jewish and Christian populations living according to tradition. In the nineteenth century, the Empire had witnessed some of the earliest outbursts of modern, secular anti-Semitism; and its capital, Vienna, had become the only western metropolis where anti-Semitism was the ideology of a ruling political party. At the end of the century, a Habsburg citizen, Theodor Herzl, took the critical steps leading to the establishment of modern political Zionism. But everywhere in the Danube Monarchy the walls between Christian and Jew were falling, and the chasm was very different by 1914 from what it had been in 1666 and 1670. Indeed, Habsburg Jewry had become a bellwether of sorts for European Jewry as a whole. In Britain about 1914 there were some 250,000 Jews, in France about 100,000, in the German Reich about 617,000; but in Austria-Hungary in 1910 there were 2,246,000, a figure that was significant alongside the 6 million Jews then in the Russian Empire.[5] One could predict (as the Social-Democrat Otto Bauer did in a well-known study published in 1907) that if this vast body of Jews kept on modernizing itself, following the model of the small communities on the Atlantic shores, then all of European Jewry would do so.[6]

II

In 1843 Karl Marx wrote an essay drawing crude analogies between the concentration of the Jews in the commercial professions down through the ages and the embourgeoisement then overtaking the "Christian" world.[7] In one respect he had a point, and the great German sociologist Werner Sombart had no less a point seventy years later when he associated the Jews with modern capitalism.[8] They recalled that for reasons deep in history the Jews were concentrated in certain professions and might consequently be categorized according to their social class. Both men were wildly wrong in the exaggerated conclusions they drew from their data; they

wholly missed perceiving that the Jews were overwhelmingly a "poor urban" and "impoverished middle" class, not a prosperous bourgeoisie; and
they missed the important fact that the Jewish professional complexion was
changing considerably as the decades passed. Still, until well after 1918 in
central Europe the Jews, increasingly urban in domicile and modern in
profession, were viewed as "bourgeois" par excellence. Through study of
the Jews under Habsburg rule, accordingly, historians not only may but
must approach what one might call the "all-Empire" or "Imperial bourgeoisie." And now to make our point: this is the reason for a major peculiarity of this book. Its focus is much more on Jews who were assimilated,
or who tried to be so, on the Jewish core of the Habsburg bourgeoisie,
than on those who stayed the same—who were supporters of their own
Tradition.

The importance of trying to study the "all-Empire bourgeoisie" is self-
evident. Marxists or non-Marxists, historians tend today to describe the
moving force of European history in the past two centuries as "modernization." There is no agreement among them as to what exactly "modernization" is.[9] Some see it as basically an economic process which, emanating
from the west, transformed the base on which society rests. Others perceive
a societal or cultural transformation as paramount, premising that each
region "modernized" according to its own peculiarities. Yet others emphasize the secular, scientific, rationalist concerns which characterized the
western Enlightenment. In our view modernization is best described in
holistic terms, as a confrontation experienced by all peoples during the past
three centuries, a confrontation between ancient ways of life and the nexus
of the European revolution—a confrontation that became ever more pur-
poseful and ever more one-sided as Europe's power, economic, political,
and cultural, grew. We acknowledge with all authorities that the new urban
and educated middle classes of the past two centuries have everywhere
been the central bearers and initiators of the struggle.

Are the "assimilee" Jews the best medium available for studying the
Habsburg all-Empire bourgeoisie? Many historians today duck the issue
by holding that there really was no such thing—that the old Empire contained only a very thin plutocratic or bureaucratic central bourgeois stratum, and that for the rest there were only the various national bourgeoisies
which existed in such very differently developed segments as to defy unified historical treatment.[10] Other historians approach the subject through
study of the German middle class, above all, and this is certainly advantageous since the Habsburg Empire was considered until the end "a German state."[11] But there is a problem embedded in this approach: the
Germans were exceptional in the sense that they shared in the society of
the Emperor and the great aristocrats, whereas all the other peoples were
in effect "subjects." The Germans were no more "just middle class" than
they were the whole middle class. Hence the virtue of studying the subject
through the Jews. These last were in no way the whole middle class, but

at least they were a consistently bourgeois element, more or less equally distributed from Eger [Cheb] in central Germany to Kronstadt [Brasov], the gateway to Bucharest and the Black Sea, from Brody on the Russian frontier to Split [Spalato] on the Mediterranean and Hohenems at the foot of the Swiss Alps.

Rigid insistence on parallels between Jews and bourgeois is not in question here. Basically we are presenting the history of a single nation, and as one may intimate already, a very complex and ramified nation. One cannot overstress the persistent cultural differentness and social apartness of most Jews in the pre-1918 world of central Europe. But since inescapably we must become involved in bourgeois studies, it has seemed useful from the start to break with the exclusively Jewish frameworks usual in Jewish national history. What follows is not just a history of the Habsburg Jews, but a mirror of the Habsburg middle class.

III

For many centuries the Jews regarded themselves as a "nation" in Europe, despite the specifically religious ties that bound them together, and of course they were so considered by others too. Yet long before the Habsburg Empire disappeared in 1918 the Jewish "nation" in a sense dissolved itself. By 1860, to be specific, the Jews of western and central Europe had consented, as the price of their "emancipation" from discriminatory legislation, to being listed in the censuses of the various countries in which they lived not as a linguistic national group, but only as a "confessional" group. In the far east of Europe, in the Russian Empire where until 1906 there was no constitution, the "national" character of Jewry remained relatively more intact; and in the 1890s even in the west a modern (that is, secular) national movement emerged among the Jews. But the overriding tendency of European Jewish history in the nineteenth century was one of national "self"-demolition.

The contrast in this respect between the Jews and other national groups was especially pronounced in the Habsburg context, where the nineteenth century was a time of "nation-building." In case after case there one finds that "modernizers" formed a political alliance with the leadership of this or that linguistic group, with the result that a "nation" found (or "refound") its "soul." Among the Jews, however, "modernists" and "traditionalists" trod divergent paths, often hostile paths. Consistently for over a century the leading modernist Jews deplored and attacked their ancient "identity." In 1907 that same Otto Bauer we mentioned above even gave elaborate ideological expression to the "self"-denial trend: his tract formally recommended that Socialism do its utmost to "save" the Jews from the Zionist movement that was just then developing.[12]

Ultimately the most important justification of our focus on assimilationists in this book has to do with this process of Jewish "self"-denial. A major difficulty faces anyone who probes it (or who probes Jewish "self-hatred," as it is often too narrowly labelled).[13] A great many Jewish communities in Europe have disappeared or been drastically reduced in our time because of a disaster: the eruption of modern anti-Semitism and the Holocaust. Historical discussion of Jewish disappearance is, therefore, in Europe almost inseparable from discussion of the Holocaust; and in Holocaust studies there is really only one answer. The Jews of Europe were attacked, assaulted, mercilessly murdered. Frequently they resisted; sometimes they did not. But in these latter cases there can be no discussion of why, because of the appalling truth that the Jews were Hitler's absolute victims. It is just too awful to discuss in this context the widespread "self"-denying aspirations of modern Jewish history.

The problem is inescapable, however, no matter how sensitive; and hence the value of studying the Habsburg Jewish case of assimilation. Habsburg Jewry did not disappear in the Holocaust, but before it, as a result of the collapse of the Habsburg state in 1918. Morally, that is a much easier subject to handle than the Holocaust, for it does not matter which side one is on; all have their virtues. Nor does it matter if one claims that the Jews had a hand in that cataclysm. There is no indecency in investigating whether Jewish self-hatred (or German, Magyar, or Czech self-hatred, for that matter)[14] contributed in some way to the old Empire's demise. Indeed, as the Viennese writer Karl Kraus put the matter at the start of the war, the Habsburg Empire even before the catastrophes was perceptibly a "Research Institute about the Ending of the World"![15]

In this book we do not perceive unwisdom in national "self"-denial. We premise, in fact, that there is no one of us today who is free from the assimilationist urge; it is not even a negative thing for most of us, though it involves dangers and agony both for individuals and for groups. Assimilation is the price most of us are willing to pay today for comfort. We ask what else the Jewish nation could have done in modern Europe, apart from "self"-denial, when it was faced with the challenge of modernization, yet had no land (as other nations had) and possessed an ancient "self" that stood directly in the path of change. What would any nation do in such a situation? What in fact did the other nations do, if not destroy their old identities—their old "selves"—while entering the modern period?

But our objective here is to come to grips with the central "self"-denial theme of modern Jewish history. Our questions are directed not only at the problems: what kind of Jewish group survival was feasible in modern times? what kind was desirable? but also at the questions: what did "self"-denial do to the modern Jews? what was the variety of its effects?

And finally let us mention one more peculiarity of the book. What follows is an essay in social history, but frequently, because of our interest in "self"-denial as a phenomenon, we will focus not only on the masses of the Habsburg Jewish community but often also on prominent individuals—on biographies as opposed to statistics. What is more, we will not attempt to tell the "whole story," but will concentrate very often on the psychologically "leading sectors." This approach, we hope, will make possible a much deeper understanding of the central phenomenon of "self"-denial than would coverage without individual detail.

IV

What is a "Jew"? What is an "Austrian"? It is useful to reply to these basic methodological questions of our study by citing some special results of the modernization process we will be discussing. Let us look first at the Jews. For many centuries before 1918 one defined Jewishness as membership in a religious grouping. The Jews themselves lived by an inherited law which not only encouraged separatism but subjected deviants to penalties and treated apostates as dead. By some Jewish interpretations a convert out of Judaism was then a physical impossibility. In Christian legal terms also, a Jew existed because of his religion. Under Christian law a Jew ceased to be subject to discrimination if he converted to Christianity. With time, however, exceptions emerged. Converts became much more common. They had children, sometimes by the progeny of ancient Christian families, but sometimes by other converts; and the question arose whether these latter in particular were not Jewish. Further, it grew evident with time that defectors from the Jewish religion might be opting not for another religion but against religion in general. Did they cease to be Jews? For such reasons new "organic" or "racial" norms came into use. Difficulties abounded even so. The intricate calculus of Hitler's Nürnberg laws is witness to how much trouble even racists had in coming up with a satisfactory practical definition of who was a Jew. But the old religious definition nonetheless lapsed.

Because of this definitional change recent approaches to the problem of Jewishness have tended to avoid norms altogether.[16] Scholars have premised, in the first place, that in history nothing is stable, all cultural cores change and evolve; and that if Jewry survives today as an entity, it is no longer the entity it was in 1670, the year the story of this book begins. Beyond this, one acknowledges today that even formal religious defection by a Jewish-born individual need not mean that that individual ceases to be a Jew. The converted (or otherwise "assimilating") individual becomes a borderline case, not (as in the past) a person considered dead. The historian, the sociologist, and the psychologist can study this converted individual to see what in his or her background opened the way for adaptation and change; and what in his or her convert condition lent to preservation of an older identity. The main problem in defining who is a Jew ceases now to be concealment of the renegades and becomes one of how to delimit what Pareto called "residuals." In the following study we will solve that particular problem through arbitrary reliance on a second-generation limit.

In defining "Austrians" similar considerations are useful.[17] Originally, back in 1670, there was a normative definition here too. An "Austrian" was then for all practical purposes a "Christian subject of the Austrian Habsburgs." Later on, however, the Christians, earlier than the Jews, began to accept new secular definitions of themselves. They continued to see themselves as Austrian in point of citizenship, but began in point of "nationhood" to be Germans, Czechs, Poles, Magyars, Rumanians, Croats, Slovaks, or Ruthenians, according to their tongue. In the nineteenth century a massive dichotomy emerged between these secular definitions, on the one side of citizenship and on the other side of nationality. The dichotomy increased as "Austria" changed, as the Austrian Empire became "Austria-Hungary" in 1867 and then as Austria became just one among an array of new little central European successor states after 1918.

Further, the more "Austria" ceased to be a comprehensive societal definition for the inhabitants of Danubian Europe, the more the national definitions became strong. On the one hand, city people of every background began to adopt the tongues and customs of the localities in which they lived, reinforcing the local identities with ideological rationalizations. On the other hand, if only to keep free of the new people, "natives" turned to more and more exaggerated "organic" distinctions of nationality; they distinguished, as we would express it today, between "assimilation" and mere "acculturation," and accused the newcomers of the latter.[18] The "real" Magyars, for example, turned out to be not just the *ecumene* of Magyar-speakers, but the nobility that ruled polyglot Greater Hungary, a social element that was perceived as "born." Correspondingly, the "real" Ruthenian turned out to be not just an Orthodox Christian of east Slavic dialect, but a soul endowed from birth with a full-fledged language, and with "feeling" and "thinking" different from that of a Jew. Long before the dissolution of old Austria, every variety of acquired characteristic had come in practice to be considered part of this, that, or another subject nation's "essence." One even began to hear retroactively about the "Yugoslavs" and "Czechoslovaks" of the eighteenth century and earlier times, because the past was quite literally being rewritten according to the location of modern national frontiers.

Recent students of central Europe have ducked these difficulties by avoiding normative definitions. They have tended to acknowledge that so long as the old Habsburg state existed, everyone under Habsburg rule was an "Austrian," regardless of ethnic or linguistic nationality. Within this general definition, however, one acknowledges that there was a constant struggle over whether an ethnic "self"-identification could outbalance the "Austrian" one; and that in the end the ethnic groups won. The norms here become irrelevant; the pull and tug is supreme. This is approximately the view we will adopt in this book. Inconsistencies will abound in the following pages because to avoid prolixity we will frequently contrapose the words "Jew" and "Austrian" in the same sentence without specifying that in this case we are referring to "Austrian citizens of Jewish religion," on the one hand, and "Christian Austrian citizens," on the other. But in an essay in historical sociology, such inconsistencies are inevitable, and in some part perhaps even desirable, for they remind the reader that essentially we are dealing with cultural cores that change.

PART I

Choosing a Road,
1670–1800

TWO

The First Decisions

I

When the Habsburg Empire came to its end in the early twentieth century, there were Jews resident in every part of it. This had not always been so, however, and in the century after Leopold I's expulsion of the Jews from his capital, Habsburg Jewry was effectively constricted to the three Lands of the Bohemian Crown, Bohemia, Moravia, and Silesia.[1] In the Alpine provinces (modern-day Austria) Jews were then allowed only in the tiny Vorarlberg town of Hohenems. In Trieste and nearby Gorizia and Grado there were tiny Ashkenazi Jewish communities. The Habsburgs had not yet acquired Venice, Dalmatia, and Bosnia where there were small Sephardic communities which at a later date constituted a Habsburg Jewry of the south. And in vast Hungary, which in the eighteenth century became the Habsburg territorial anchor on the Danube, such Jews as remained after the late medieval expulsions had been victims of 150 years of Turkish wars.[2]

Substantial numbers of Sephardim had come into the Hungarian towns in the late sixteenth century under Turkish rule, but these seem on the whole to have retreated after 1688 with the Sultan's armies. By 1700 only a few ancient Jewish communities survived along the Moravian frontier, in today's Burgenland. After the Habsburg reconquest, because of the general depopulation, the royal authorities allowed Jewish immigration. Some of the refugees from Vienna thereupon ended up at Bratislava [Pozsony/ Pressburg], contributing to a new community there. During the eighteenth century many more Jews immigrated to Hungary from Bohemia and Moravia, but until late in the century these could still be considered as having one foot at home.

It is difficult to estimate how large Habsburg Jewry (in other words, Jewry under the Bohemian Crown) was in that century.[3] Modern censuses were not taken and, even if they had been, the Jews would surely have avoided being counted out of fear of the tax-collector. But we do have some rough figures. About 1635 it was estimated that there were some 14,000 Jewish "tax-payers" in Bohemia outside Prague, and some 7,800 in that city itself. By 1700 the Jewish population of the capital had mushroomed to over 11,000, comprising perhaps a fourth of the civic population, and making Prague the largest urban Ashkenazi Jewish community in Europe.[4]

Just after 1700 fire and plague set back the Prague community severely. Further, in 1726 Kaiser Karl VI decided to limit the Jews of the Bohemian Crown. He declared that alongside some 10,000 Jews in Prague, 30,–40,000 would be allowed to live in rural Bohemia, and some 20,–25,000 in Moravia, but no more. He defined these numbers in terms of families, and ordered that no Jewish male who could not find a "place" among these families would be allowed to marry. In the 1740s the Prague community was reduced yet further by a temporary expulsion. Thereafter, however, although the *Familiantengesetz* ceilings remained in place until 1848, there was a slow growth (mainly in the countryside) so that by 1754 there were some 41,000 Jews in the conjoined Bohemian lands and by 1785, 68,794. In Hungary meanwhile by 1785 the overflow of marriageable Bohemian and Moravian Jews led to a quadrupling of the Jewish population to about 80,000 in 1785.

All told, therefore, Habsburg Jewry may have comprised 150,000 souls by the third quarter of the eighteenth century. At that time this was a very substantial population. In all France there were not 40,000 Jews at the time of the Revolution; in England and Holland, far fewer. There had been no Jews in Prussia in the seventeenth century due to expulsions, and in the eighteenth, apart from some thousands in formerly Austrian Silesia, there was only a privileged community of 2,–3,000 at Berlin.

II

How and why did Bohemian (that is, Habsburg) Jewry take its first steps towards "modernity?" A word about a distinctive historical and social "backwardness" of the environment allows a first response.[5] The Bohemian Crownlands were demographically and economically the brightest jewels in the Habsburg heritage. They were fertile. The surrounding mountains were well supplied with ores. Communications with Vienna were good, and with northern Germany via the Elbe and the Oder they were excellent. Prague, until almost 1700, was the first city in the Empire. But these and the other central and east European lands governed by the Habsburgs had very different traditions and very different institutions in the "absolutist" seventeenth and eighteenth centuries from those of western Europe.

In the distant past, no doubt, the crowns had been strong there. Later they followed the model of the great Polish-Lithuanian Commonwealth, where in the early modern period the kings sold privileges to the Estates in order to fund dynastic achievements and frontier wars, and where after 1505 the throne could issue no new laws without approval of the Estates. In Germany the decay of the crown powers commenced early and stemmed from the over-extension of the great medieval German monarchy. In Bohemia the crown was stripped of its powers during the fifteenth century by a Hussite nobility fearful of Catholic revanche. In Hungary the crown was weakened deliberately in the late fifteenth century by a Catholic nobility already long privileged and fearful of royal absolutism. All this diminution of royal power was compounded by the Protestant Reformation and the exigencies of the Turkish wars. Meanwhile, by parallel process, the east European nobilities emerged as a radical challenge to the thrones. By 1500, because of the power of the nobles, even the structure of the estates system was generally different in central Europe from that of the west, where traditionally the first estate was the clergy, the second the nobility, and the "third," the towns and common people. In the east almost universally the second estate was composed only of the magnates, the great barons, whereas the "third" had become the organ of the lesser nobility or gentry, often to the virtual exclusion of the towns and commons.

In addition to this imbalance in the institutional development of eastern Europe in the late middle ages, there had emerged a massive social imbalance which drastically limited the wealth of society.[6] In the west, one may generalize, the new capitalist economy of the sixteenth century had tended to strengthen urban conglomerations, to diversify society, to encourage the movement of people out of their traditional village homes, above all to ensure in the countryside a permanent loosening of seigneurial bonds. Eastward from the Elbe, however, the new economy did the opposite. It tended to encourage not the growth of cities and trade and industry, but that of large-scale commercial agriculture on great baronial estates. It led to the weakening, not strengthening, of the towns; above all to a vast increase in seigneurial exploitation of the peasantry, and to an overall retreat from a money economy in rural areas. This "second serfdom," as it is called, arrived in different regions in very different ways. In the Kingdom of Hungary the economic processes had advanced so far by 1500 that peasant rebellions were breaking out, fearsome jacqueries which were put down with great violence and which resulted in legislation literally reading the peasantry out of the estates system. In Hungary the Turkish invasion of 1526 in some ways represented a reprieve for the peasantry. In Bohemia, on the other hand, the Hussite religious rebellion had weakened the social fabric, but the decisive steps toward second serfdom came late in the sixteenth century and during the devastating Thirty Years War (1618–48).

In all, though Habsburg rulers such as Leopold I lived in an "absolutist" age, their administrative systems and their wealth were simply not comparable to those of the great western absolutist monarchs, or (administratively) to the emergent Prussian regime in northern Germany. Even in Bohemia, where after a gentry-led rebellion in 1618 the Habsburgs drastically limited the constitutional powers of the nobility, the presence of the second serfdom meant that bureaucratic royal control and royal justice were decisively excluded from the landlord estates. In fact, one can well argue that the major administrative achievements that occurred in central Europe under the Habsburgs in the seventeenth century were not the work of the Vienna government but of private corporations and persons. The greatest burden by far, for example, in the resubjugation and reconversion of Bohemia was borne by the Jesuit Order, a private corporation of sorts which glorified the Habsburg rulers, but "reeducated"—that is, re-Catholicized—their subjects without much regard to specific royal control. Meanwhile, generals such as Tilly, Wallenstein, Montecuccoli, and later Prince Eugen of Savoy organized the great imperial armies as private contractors. In Bohemia and in Hungary local administrative power was placed to an ever-increasing extent in the hands of great territorial magnates—the Eszterhazys, Batthyányis, Károlyis in Hungary, the Lobkowitzes, Dietrichsteins, Schwarzenbergs, and Kollowrats in Bohemia, private persons all who ruled their estates as if they were independent.

The Bohemian Crownland Jews existed thus around 1700 in an environment of singularly dispersed power; and not unsurprisingly they possessed complex institutions of self-government, which originated as they had in Poland and some of the German lands in the Middle Ages.[7] From the fourteenth century on, Bohemia, Moravia, and Silesia each had an officially recognized "Chief Rabbi" or *Oberlandesrabbiner* to arbitrate in judicial matters, and then a *Deputation* of wealthy "representatives" set up to supervise the collection of the annual Jewish tax or "contribution" to the throne. The leader of the *Deputation* was a *Primator*, whose duty it was to mediate communications between the Jewish communities, on the one hand, and the Crown and Estates on the other. In Moravia, where the comparatively few Jews lived compactly in larger communities, often on princely estates, this system survived until the nineteenth century. But in Bohemia there was a further change. Here 30,–40,000 "rural" Jews (the *Landesjuden*) lived far from Prague, in as many as 800 villages of the south and center of the kingdom, a residual probably of the one-time multiplicity of small gentry-owned landholdings there. This broad distribution made for administrative difficulties. About 1659, therefore, the Crown instituted a separate Jewish *Deputation* for the "rural" Jews, headed by a separate *Landesprimator* (and later flanked these officials for a time with separate "rural" *Landesoberrabbiner*).

In the seventeenth century this structure proved increasingly able to preserve and accumulate privileges and exemptions for the Jews. One notable result was that the Bohemian Jews were not restricted to the money business and to trading, as were most of the Jews in Germany. They were allowed to make their living, especially in the villages, in *Handwerk* or petty manufacturing (albeit most of their production was aimed at Jewish consumption, and gave no direct competition to the guildsmen of the towns).[8] Another result was that in Moravia, though Jews were not allowed to live at Brno [Brünn], the capital, as they were in Prague, they were permitted to consolidate tight self-ruled settlements in various smaller places—at Nikolsburg, Boskowitz, Trebitsch, Prossnitz, Ungarisch Brod, and Kremsier, for example—where they lived in relative comfort. Was Bohemian Jewry wealthy by consequence of its organization and group privileges? Certainly not. As elsewhere in Europe, from Avignon to Wilno, the humble in the Jewish communities had to live virtually from hand to mouth, eking out what they could from peddling and trading what they could, barred by Christian regulations from more profitable paths of life, hounded from many places, always having to be wary lest inscrutable authority attack them. Whether life was here for most Jews as wretched as for the notorious *Luftmenschen* who lived virtually off nothing in Galicia and central Poland in the later nineteenth century, we do not know. But one may recall that most Bohemian Jews lived in the peasant villages. As late as the 1770s bad harvests there meant that even the Christian population starved.[9] It is unimaginable that in hard times the Jews fared much better. At Prague, moreover, in that age when no city was healthy to live in, the Jews were confined to the most insalubrious part of the town.

Still, the Jews of the Bohemian lands did enjoy a certain autonomy within the Christian world in early modern times. In this they were more like the Jews of the Polish Commonwealth than the Jews of the west. This was a fundamental factor in their behavior when faced with the challenge of modernization: they were not just individuals, they were something like a nation. And to this one may add a factor which distinguished them from the self-governing Polish Jews too. Just as in Germany, political conditions in the seventeenth century enabled some Bohemian Jews to see the concrete possibilities of better living. In Germany in the period of the Thirty Years War the late medieval rejectionist atmosphere around the Jews had changed. The wars reduced capitalist Christian Germany, city after flourishing city, to ruin. Jews alongside the Christians suffered badly. But Christian business-people were bound on the whole to one place, and once ruined stayed ruined. The Jews perforce were used to moving; perforce also they had the know-how and the bravery to face conditions on the roads. They tended to have more connections outside Germany, in places where economic conditions had been less disturbed by the wars, and where capital remained intact. The Jews survived the wars also because everywhere in the Germanies they were considered an external social order, subject to special taxes, and consequently the princes tended to protect them from the wars so as to preserve the tax.[10] By mid-seventeenth century, because of such factors, Jewish entrepreneurs were welcome in many German principalities, and were given the special title *Hoffaktor* as a reward for performing essential economic tasks.[11] In 1670, characteristically, when Leopold I expelled his Jews from Vienna, they did not have to flee to Poland (as in the late Middle Ages) to find refuge. The Hohenzollern Elector of Brandenburg was happy to invite some of them to his lands. Later on, the magnates of western Hungary likewise invited refugee Jews from Vienna to settle in towns upon their vast estates, and to bring commerce with them. Things were looking up.

III

A strictly outside initiative played a major part in launching Bohemian Jewry onto a modernist path. This was the Habsburg House itself, which in the eighteenth century underwent quite suddenly a radical change in attitude towards socio-economic questions.[12]

The eastern Habsburgs, the rulers of Austria, had made one great stab at establishing a central Danubian governmental structure prior to 1700. In 1526, after the battle of Mohács admitted the Ottoman Turks into the heart of Hungary, Ferdinand of Habsburg, the brother of the Emperor Charles V, inherited the thrones of Hungary and Bohemia. He was a man of wholly different mettle from the compliant Jagiellonian monarchs who had theretofore ruled much of eastern Europe, and from his own administratively incompetent Habsburg ancestors. During his long and effective reign he set up an Austrian Court Council [*Hofrat*] and within it a Privy Council [*Geheimrat*] in which he could consult professional advisers. He established an Austrian Defense Ministry of sorts [*Hofkriegsrat*] and an Austrian Treasury [*Hofkammer*]. In general Ferdinand actively sought to insulate the affairs of the lands his family owned on the Danube from those of Germany, where the throne was elective; and he made a number of decisive inroads on the independent administrative structures of Bohemia and Hungary.

These consolidation measures were paralleled, however, by a conspicuous diffusion of Habsburg power in other directions. Habsburg Spain, of course, wasted the wealth from her vast new overseas empire by seeking hegemony in Europe and by defending the old order Church against the Protestant Reformation. In Austria not only did the House seek to re-Catholicize Bohemia and all Germany simultaneously, but while seeking to defend all Europe from the Turk, it supported the distant interests of cousinly Spain. In addition, with few exceptions, Ferdinand's successors on the thrones of central Europe were negligent of the administrative goals he had envisaged. They thought little of administration, and even allowed their Alpine territorial inheritance to be distributed among various heirs.

The Habsburgs of the seventeenth century in particular proved to be weak administrators. They became apostles of a fanatical counter-reformation in central Europe. After defeating the rebellion in Bohemia in 1620, Ferdinand II followed up the victory by expelling Hussitism from that kingdom, an act tantamount to expulsion of the bulk of the lesser nobility, and by subjecting Bohemia to a substantially new law. But wholly unable to impose their claims on Hungary, the Vienna Habsburgs in 1606 signed treaties that in effect acknowledged the independence of Transylvania from the crown. After 1620 they certainly subjugated the Bohemian estates; but they came nowhere near integrating the administration of that kingdom with their Austrian House administration. In 1648 it was the Vienna Habsburgs who effectively surrendered the rights of the Imperial throne to administrative power in the German Reich. All in all, the Habsburgs of the early modern centuries were no Hohenzollerns, skillful administrators driven by exigency and military acumen to consolidate a modern state. It is not surprising that Leopold I decided in 1670 demonstratively to expel the Jews of his residential city, even though they paid their taxes and were important to his financial well-being. His House was indifferent to the muscle-building that could make modern government work.

This indifference was characteristic of the baroque era. Louis XIV revoked the Edict of Nantes in 1685, expelling the industrious French Protestants, though in many respects he was an active backer of the commercial advancement of his kingdom. In Poland, in Italy, and in Spain, no less than in Bohemia, the Jesuits and other Catholic orders organized vast and systematic campaigns of theatrical proselytism which were not particularly contributory to the prosperity of the rulers. Even in the Protestant and middle-class Netherlands the art of the age emphasized display, dramatic effect, panache over sober virtue. But in Austria more than elsewhere, perhaps because the general poverty of the region contrasted so with the lofty mission of the rulers, baroque concerns seem to have captured the mind. It was in Vienna, more than anywhere else in Europe, that the Jesuits brought their theatrical undertakings to high perfection, staging public dramas featuring hundreds of actors with scenes simultaneously in heaven, on earth, and down in hell, depicting the resurrection of the dead, earthquakes, flashes of lightning, battles between dwarfs and flocks of cranes, the Tiber filled with martyrs' blood, Rome burning, and other such marvels designed to edify the faithful and convince the Kaiser of his glory.[13] The characteristic figure of Leopoldine Vienna was the preacher Abraham a Sancta Clara, who had great command of the German language, enormous respect for form and Catholic glory, but practically no concern with the rational meaning of his sermons—a man who spoke rubbish most convincingly.[14]

But now to drive the point home, in the decades after Leopold I circumstances drove the Austrian Habsburgs to attempt a massive reversal of stance.

The first of these circumstances was really Kaiser Leopold's own experience with a Jew. By 1674, shortly after he expelled the Jewish population from Vienna, the exigencies of war compelled this Catholic paladin to find some money fast. Consequently, he began to contract with Jewish army provisioners in the Reich, and to let some of them visit his court at Vienna. One of these was a 44-year-old adventurer from Heidelberg named Samuel Oppenheimer.[15] Oppenheimer turned out to be a man of vast projects, of extraordinary bursts of energy, a financier capable of playing for gigantic stakes against both his princely debtors and his network of sub-contractors and creditors in the Reich. By 1677 he was playing such a large role in the provisioning of the imperial armies on the Rhine that Leopold gave him the formal title *Hoffaktor*. By the end of the French war, in 1680, Oppenheimer was one of the Army's most trusted suppliers, and had been granted the extraordinary exception of settling in Vienna with this family, and even of enjoying the free practice of his religion there.

Hereupon events precipitated Oppenheimer to even greater privilege.

By 1680 the Kaiser owed him 100,000 florins, a sum equivalent to about one-fifth of what the Turkish wars of the next decade would cost each year. The Treasury contained no funds for this, its largest bill. Leopold procrastinated and delayed, and early in 1683 imprisoned Oppenheimer on charges of usury and other sins. But meanwhile, to deter the Kaiser from interference in Germany, the French king had inspired the Turkish sultan to send an army against Vienna. In the middle of the year, therefore, as the siege of the city grew imminent, Leopold released his Court Jew from prison, guaranteed the debts of the past, and then contracted for huge new quantities of supplies for the beleaguered city. This was only the start of the adventure. By 1701, when Leopold embarked on his last great war with Louis XIV, the War of the Spanish Succession, Oppenheimer not only had large responsibilities for feeding the armies and procuring guns but was deeply involved in the entire administration of the Imperial Treasury. He was something approaching a private manager of the Habsburg Government insofar as finance was concerned. His position was anything but secure. In 1700 his house in Vienna was looted by a mob, and he was the object of continuous conspiracies. But he, a Jew, had played an objectively enormous role in enabling Leopold to expel the Turks from Hungary, and bore the title of Imperial *Oberkriegsfaktor*.[16] When he died in 1703, the Hofkammer tried to treat its enormous debts to him as "usury," and thus unpayable.[17] It failed: sixty years of litigation resulted. This dismal result was one factor in forcing the Kaiser's House to acknowledge modern practical concerns—to reform.

Perhaps because the Oppenheimer crisis coincided with the reconquest of Hungary (1699) and even with a territorial expansion into the Balkans, Vienna did not at first come up with all the rationalistic vigor that had been expressed a few years earlier in H. W. von Hornigk's treatise *Österreich über Alles, wenn es nur will*. Leopold's elder son and successor, Joseph I (1705–11), took some first steps towards a more rational financial system at Vienna, establishing a *Wiener Stadtbank* in 1706.[18] Leopold's second son, Karl VI (1711–40), opened a free port at Trieste to further the commerce of his dominions, and in 1716 signed a treaty with the sultan that provided Austrian merchants with reciprocal privileges of trading anywhere in the Ottoman dominions. Later on Karl tried to establish a tobacco monopoly to increase taxes, and more or less informally allowed the reintroduction of a Jewish money-lending settlement at Vienna. But in the Kaisers' own eyes, the major reform of this era was Karl VI's pursuit of a "pragmatic sanction" assuring the integrity of his inheritance, even in the case that a woman was the heir. This first "constitution" of the Habsburg Empire minimally affected administrative practice. Even the treaty with the Turks proved a mistake: the Austrian merchants on the whole proved quite incapable of trading with the sharp indigenes of the sultan's dominions, whereas the Greek and Jewish subjects of that Asiatic potentate proved both bold enough and unscrupulous enough to take over not just the long-distance trade between the Balkans and Vienna but the entire local trade of liberated Hungary. All through the eighteenth century the very word for "trader" in Hungary was "*görög*" or "Greek"; and the Turkish Jews had a full freedom of residence and religious practice in the Habsburg capital that was conspicuously denied to native Habsburg Jews.[19]

When Karl VI died in 1740, however, far greater challenges led his daughter and heir, Maria Theresia (1740–80), into more effective reforms— in fact, into systematic state-building. On the morrow of her father's death, the new young king in Prussia, Frederick II, "the Great," simply denounced the Pragmatic Sanction and seized Silesia, one of the Empress's wealthiest lands. For the first eight years of her reign she had to fight quite literally for the right to her inheritance. After this war, and during and after her second great "seven years" war with Frederick (1756–63), she not only sought belatedly to consolidate a strong centralized state on western models at Vienna, but also undertook in myriad ways the modernization of her people. This "enlightened despot" was a Catholic bigot in no way entirely free of the arrogance of her forebears, but she reformed her army, favored literacy, founded higher schools for bureaucrats and soldiers alike, abolished torture, expelled the Jesuits, extended the tentacles of her administration for the first time into the villages of the western parts of her possessions, challenged the "feudal nexus," and gathered at her court a great galaxy of learned modern-minded advisors from all over Europe to help her in her task.

Maria Theresia did not care for Jews. Early in her reign she nearly expelled all the thousands of Jews of Bohemia on suspicion that they had abetted Frederick the Great, and for a year she did expel them from Prague. She was the last ruler of old Europe thus to expel Jews.[20] At a later date, according to an old tale, when she was forced to receive a wealthy Jew, Israel Hönig, in private audience, she sat behind a linen screen as if somehow to avoid contamination.[21] Toward the end of her reign she would still on occasion write:

> I know of no worse plague for the state than this [the Jewish] nation. . . . With fraud, usury, and money contracts the [Jews] reduce people to beggary, they practice all sorts of dirty dealing which other, honorable men avoid.[22]

But with her mercantilist commercial policies and her rationalizing administrative enterprise she affected in significant fashion the lives even of these pariahs among her subjects. Towards the end of her reign she made it possible, for example, for Trieste Jews to travel almost without regard to the local prohibitions, and to stay at will in the capital.[23] She relaxed the restrictions on the few Jews and their households who lived in Vienna.[24] The great break with the restrictive legislation of the past came just after her death in 1780, but it was her great reform effort above all that changed the Habsburg Jewish world. Now for the first time there actually were royal agents in most of the Habsburg dominions on the Danube to whom a Jew could appeal against the harrying of local officials. Now for the first time a government at Vienna seemed seriously interested in the commercial and financial activities which the Jews had thanklessly pursued for centuries. The timeless autonomy under princely privilege, which had been the condition of Bohemian Jewry in the past, could now give way insensibly, gently, gently, to a time-conscious subjection to a modern state, which was the modern path Bohemian Jewry chose.

I V

Jews from Bohemia did not, as a rule, attain the flashing heights where Samuel Oppenheimer trod. Jakob Bassevi (1570–1634), a Jewish war-contractor from Prague, figured largely in the early history of the German *Hoffaktorentum* (he was banker to the great autonomous Imperial general, Wallenstein) but even in the eighteenth century the emperors recruited their military provisioners and court bankers mainly from Germany.[25] The famous Simson Wertheimer, Oppenheimer's successor and Prince Eugen's financier, was characteristic of these.[26]

In Bohemia a different type of rich Jew emerged during the period of Jewish transition into state subjection, and played a vital role in channeling modern ideas from the Christian into the Jewish world. Of these, the archetype was Joachim Popper (1720–95), the last *Primator* of the Bohemian rural Jews.[27]

The Popper family originated at Bresnitz [Březnice], a market locality on a south Bohemian domaine owned by a Count Kollowrat, Baron of Ujazd and Loksan, one of the very few Slavic aristocratic families remaining in Bohemia after the expulsions of the 1620s. The Kollowrats were not the grandest of the Bohemian grandees, but they did their share of palace-building and lavish living, and accordingly had periodic need for cash. The Popper family began its rise to eminence as village Jews who rendered services to the castle on the hill; and Joachim was in his day the greatest money-lender to the aristocracy in the whole of Bohemia. The Poppers flourished in the loan business, because they were able to develop a broad network of credit relationships; they then used these relationships, as indeed did the German military contractors, to expand into trade. Because they had connections and could obtain cash, they were able to purchase and transport the produce of the land and forests.

From the 1680s on there is a record of regular visits by Poppers from Bresnitz to the great Leipzig fairs, the foci of northern Germany's commerce. And this brought them into other sorts of business. In the 1720s Wolf Popper (Joachim's father) visited Leipzig in partnership with a certain Löbl Hönig of Kuttenplan [Chodová Planá], a locality the other side of Plzen from Bresnitz. Hönig was the founder of a clan which made its breakthrough to wealth in mid-century by participating in the collection of the tobacco tax for the government.[28] Wolf Popper made his by collecting the Jewish *Leibmaut*, or body tax, among the Bohemian rural Jews. By the end of the 1720s he was already *Primator*, an office which gave him the privilege of living in Prague, and which he bequeathed to his son forty years later. During the Prussian and Bavarian occupation of Bohemia in 1742, Wolf Popper "rescued" the treasury of the Bohemian Jews from the invaders, and "saved" it for Austrian exploitation. One is reminded of how Amschel Rothschild "rescued" the Prince of Hesse's treasure from Napoleon at Kassel half a century later, but used the funds to his great personal profit while they were in his hands.[29] In Prague Popper very greatly expanded his business, and when he died in 1767 his wealth was substantial.

Young Joachim Popper had meanwhile engaged in similar activities. During the Seven Years War (1756–63) he took part in the military contracting. In 1765 he was a major partner in the first all-monarchial ten-year tobacco farm granted to Jews. By the 1780s, his money business was sufficient to inspire him to open a branch of his *Wechselstube* [Money Exchange House] in Vienna. But he was not just a dealer in money. Perhaps it was relevant that during the eighteenth century a Count Kollowrat was regularly a member of the Bohemian Commercial Commission, which more than any other organ of Maria Theresia's state assisted the founding of factories on aristocratic estates.[30] When in 1790 Popper petitioned for ennoblement, he boasted that he had played a critical role in helping Bohemian industry. He had exported glassware and linen, and in trying to stem the tide of money flowing out of the kingdom for luxury goods, he had founded a "whale-bone factory" for making stays and bustles.

The Hoffaktoren rose out of Jewish society in Germany in the seventeenth century, because war had forced the leaders of German Christian society to demand more modern economic services than that society could provide. Thriving amidst violence, the Hoffaktoren became the first Ashkenazi Jews to do violence to Jewish Tradition. They early on picked up Christian habits and Christian costume, as well as Christian tongues and attitudes (albeit perhaps seldom Christian scholarly knowledge), and all this they transmitted back into the Jewish communities.[31] The Bohemian "tobacco and *Leibmaut* Jews" did the same in the eighteenth century for the core component of Habsburg Jewry.

There were perhaps a dozen such "very wealthy" families; one may name the Dobruschkas, who obtained a unique right to live in Brno, and the Baruchs of Königswart [Kynžvart] alongside the Hönigs and Poppers among those whose village origin was notable, and the Duschenes, Fraenkl, and Kuh families from Prague. None of them was as flashy as the great German contractors who gravitated to Vienna. They tended to be much closer to the Bohemian aristocracy than to the Habsburg House; their business interests were on the whole specific to Bohemia, though some expanded into Galicia after the partition of Poland; and as the leaders of the Jewish autonomous organizations (and as collectors of Leibmaut) they maintained deep roots in Jewish society. But their role was comparable to the enlightening one of the Hoffaktoren, and this is why they are mentionable here. When the opportunity came in 1781, Joachim Popper was the first Prague Jew to move out of the *Judenstadt* to live among Christians. Salomon Dobruschka had even earlier obtained a permit to live in Jewless Brno. Dobruschka's sons were among the first Habsburg Jews to convert in order to obtain nobility. Löbl Hönig's son was the first to obtain it without conversion. Popper was the second. And where they trod, others were not slow to follow.

V

Alongside the Habsburg House reformers and the "tobacco Jews," the cultural Enlightenment of western Christian society had a strong impact on eighteenth-century Bohemian Jewry, opening it to modern ideas. This happened especially at Prague, which was still in the eighteenth century one of Christian Europe's greatest cities, with its legendary hundred church spires, its spacious castle which occasionally housed the imperial court, its graceful gardens, its ancient university, and its bustling commerce. Almost inevitably in such an environment Jews became sensitive to the changing world around them, to new currents, new attitudes. Despite an interruption caused by the temporary expulsion of 1744–45 and by the great fire in the *Judenstadt* in 1754, this city was in Maria Theresia's reign *the* center where the Ashkenazi were most susceptible to the new ideas of the west.[32]

One should not imagine that the Prague Jewish Enlightenment reached the levels of "westernization" attained further north, at Moses Mendelssohn's Berlin. At Prague by the end of Maria Theresia's reign there were Jewish doctors trained at German universities practicing (a Dr. Jonas Jeitteles and a Dr. Abraham Kisch) as well as a stratum of Jews who were dressing like Christians and who could converse on subjects of Christian learning. Jeitteles in particular corresponded with Enlighteners elsewhere in Europe, and published books on medical topics that were widely read in his profession. But he was no Moses Mendelssohn—no precocious scholar emerging from a traditional Jewish background, learning the tongues and scientific methods of the European new age, construing philosophical syntheses that seemed convincing to Christian philosophers, winning the adulation of a Christian poet such as G. E. Lessing.[33] Alongside Jewish Berlin's active contribution to the western Enlightenment, what happened in Jewish Prague was modest indeed.

Nonetheless, there was a Prague Jewish Enlightenment, and it flourished because of a peculiar circumstance within the autonomous framework of Prague Jewry. In Maria Theresia's day the chief rabbi of the Prague community was Ezekiel Landau, a renowned Talmudist, a relentless warrior against Sabbatianism (the following of Shabbetai Zevi), and he initially assumed an open stance on matters of Jewish Enlightenment. It was in the absence of his disapproval that Mendelssohn's early (pre-1783) work, at least, gained a wide reading by students from all over central and eastern Europe who had come to study in Prague.[34]

How could this be? How could a distinguished orthodox rabbi act somehow as a transmitter of Enlightened ideas? The answer is surely in part that Jewish Tradition then was not yet what it became in the nineteenth century. Perhaps one may say that in Landau's day it bound personal piety, avid adherence to the devotional law, and respect for Jewish learning to a philosophical flexibility recalling the naive ecumenism of pre-Reformation Roman Christianity. It was no doubt extremely dogmatic, closed to outside ideas, but it was also extremely diverse and contentious, and not insensitive to new scientific uses of the mind.[35] Further, the "orthodox" then recognized a major foe within Judaism that was not *Haskalah*, the Enlightenment; this was "heresy," which for the most part meant Sabbatianism, false Messianism. Even the *Mitnaggedim*, the self-styled "opponents" who assumed the lead in Polish-Lithuanian Jewry in the late eighteenth century, were not initially opposed to Haskalah: they opposed Hasidism and its pietist emphasis. Only later did they come to distrust the reformers from the west. Landau's priorities were similar.

At a certain date Landau did take a stand against Berlin. In the 1780s, when Mendelssohn's translation of the Pentateuch appeared and the Berlin Jewish intellectuals began to circulate vast projects for reeducating Jewry, Landau directly and (more often) indirectly rejected the proposed changes, seeking to limit the infiltration of new ideas from the north. But meanwhile much damage had been done; and to balance this image of the Prague Chief Rabbi fulminating against Mendelssohn, one must recall another factor. In the Jewish world, the Prague-based Haskalah may have made almost more difference than that in Berlin, because its roots were in Jewish, not Christian institutions. The Berlin community where Mendelssohn worked lacked Jewish schools. Prague was famous for its schools, the *yeshivot* presided over by *Oberrabbiner* David Oppenheim early in the eighteenth century. Landau himself attracted students from all over the Tradition-bound Jewry of the east. Scholars such as Salomon Maimon or Herz Homberg who came to work with Mendelssohn tended to break all links with the east. Those such as Aaron Chorin who worked with Landau came away still pious Jews. Studying in Prague, they often became no less fundamentally "infected" with western ideas than were the Mendelssohnians. In the 1780s they tended, because of Landau's conservatism, to be more restrained. Later on in life, as we shall see in later chapters, they taught and applied what they had learned.

V I

A final factor that led Habsburg Jewry to take a modern path, and which eased that path, is the most difficult to evaluate. This was the meteoric career at Maria Theresia's court of Josef von Sonnenfels (1732–1817), the grandson of a Grand Rabbi of Berlin.[36]

Sonnenfels was the scion of a man of many tongues who under the name "Aloys Wiener" had converted in 1740 to Christianity, who became then a preceptor of oriental languages in various Vienna schools, and who for unspecified services to the crown in 1746 got himself ennobled. The son after many youthful adventures studied law at Vienna, and in 1763 won a competition for a newly-established Vienna University lectureship in *Kammeralwissenschaft*, a teaching area that today we would call "public administration." He was a good speaker, very versatile; he was imaginative and had a positive genius for categorizing matters, even those with which he was not perfectly conversant. The Empress intended his chair to be the keystone of the educational system for the bureaucrats of her new state. She even labelled the position as one in *Polizei-und-Kammeralwissenschaft*, which implied moral training as well as economics and statistics. She did not want just policemen, as the chair-title suggests to the modern ear, but agents who would care for her heritage on the basis of high modern principles, obediently despotic *philosophes*. In this professorship Sonnenfels became one of the more important and conspicuous figures of Maria Theresia's Austria.

Sonnenfels was important above all for his teaching. He used his opportunity to attack with very great vigor the ancient and parochial institutions of the provinces in which he had grown up. His field of interest was perhaps most of all economics. Here he became virtually an apostle of centralism as a means for furthering the mercantile interests of the state.[37] He spoke out against the myriad internal customs frontiers that still inhibited Austria's commerce. He was equally opposed to the guilds, which regulated all trade and manufacturing on the local level. He was against the economic powers of the noble landlords, and for the lightening or even abolition of the legal serfdom of the rural population. His great ambition—to produce a new modern industrial code for Austria—was never realized. But his ideas, spelled out in the lectures that he delivered and then published in the 1770s, affected the thinking of generations of Austrian bureaucrats, and through them he deeply marked the economic practice of the state.

Sonnenfels lectured also on juridical matters and here he had considerably more specific influence. As early as 1776 he seems to have been pivotal in persuading the Empress to initiate one famous reform: the abolition of torture in her dominions. Later on he was put in charge of other judicial undertakings. In 1790–92 Sonnenfels wrote the original drafts of a new basic regulation of Austrian higher education. Under Franz I he became editor of the Austrian Criminal Code, completed in 1803, and of the Civil Code of 1811, two of the greatest products of the so-called "Josephian" regime.[38] As the foremost propagandist of Maria Theresia's reformer team, Sonnenfels even managed to coin the phrase that epitomized the underlying sentiment of all its members. In his youth he edited a journal entitled *Mann ohne Vorurtheil* [Man without Prejudice]. "An enlightened people," as he explained the title, "obeys because it wants to; a people blind with prejudice does so because it must."[39] For a century and more thereafter this was the guideline which progressive Austrians used in their reforming work, and the ideal to which they aspired.

We will have more to say about Sonnenfels in a later chapter. To make our point here, however, suffice it to say that all his life he was known as a born Jew, though a convert. His father, a teacher of Hebrew, was alive and prominent in Vienna until the mid-1770s, and he himself was known to read that language.[40] Even in his old age he lent himself to the government as an authority on Jewish customs.[41] His prominence therefore had at least one clear effect. On the Christian side it further bridged the chasm of hostility with which Austria had long surrounded the Jews. In this respect one might well label him a Mendelssohn of the South—a figure who by his sheer intelligence and "virtue" demonstrated to his Christian contemporaries that a Jew could be human, capable not just of improvement, but of true Enlightenment.

The problem of assessing Sonnenfels's role lies on the other side of the chasm, on the Jewish side, where of course as a convert he could in no way be compared to Mendelssohn. Does this pariah status mean, however, that he had no impact? This is the question, and perhaps one may come up with the following answer. Whereas German Jews, because of Mendelssohn, would for generations after him embrace Enlightenment virtually without hesitation, making a nigh religious cult of westernizing themselves, perhaps one may say that the Habsburg Jews looking at Sonnenfels had to accept greater caution. Perhaps for them it could not escape notice that Enlightenment might mean apostasy—the outright abandonment of Jewish Tradition.

VII

Which were the most important of these several factors which led to the bridging of the chasm between Christian and Jew in Austria?—which allowed Bohemian Crownland Jewry, the dominant element in Habsburg Jewry in early modern times, to embark on the great cultural, economic, and social transformation we call modernization? Above all, probably, the existence of an autonomous urban organization in a feudal landscape, and then the attitude of the Christian state. The Jewish organization here centered in a city greater than any other in the Germanies, and it did not collapse under its own weight in the eighteenth century (as did that in Poland) but acted as a channel for widely transmitting modern attitudes in a Jewish society that was much larger than in Germany. And the state played a considerably more systematic role in precipitating Jewish change here than in either Germany or Poland, very subtly yet dynamically preparing the Jews for citizenship (as opposed to alien privilege). The other factors we have listed were doubtless significant. Little could have happened, for example, had economic conditions been as grim here as they were in Poland in the century after the "deluge." It helped immensely also that the early Jewish modernizers were less a coinage of war here than in Germany, more a product of the east European world of serfs and magnates, indigenous, more moderate, less revolutionary—however one wishes to express it. But the key differences regarded the power of the state and the Jewish roots.

And now the other critical question which any historian of modern Jewry must face: was there a fairer prospect of Jewish success at modernization here than in Germany or in Poland? In one respect one may venture straightaway: Certainly not! The arbitrary ruling house, hoary with age, and the great magnates of central Europe in the late eighteenth century were in no way prepared to accept Jews as equals, whatever their occasional individual "enlightenment" and susceptibility to pragmatic arguments. Right down to the end of our story in this book the snobbish exclusiveness of the Court denied Jews here the fulness of mobility in civic society that they attained in western Europe. And the exclusion was more damaging here than in Germany proper, because the Court and the magnates remained more important. Still, there were differences. In some ways, for example, the Austrian Court was more receptive to "collaborator Jews" than the Prussian one. It certainly ennobled more of them! Further, as we will repeatedly see in later chapters, the exclusion in Austria was applied rigidly to Christians also; indeed it constituted a strong assimilating factor between Jews and Christian middle classes. In Germany it applied mainly to Jews. The snobbery of the aristocracy had positive as well as negative significance for the Austrian Jews.

And much more important, one can well argue that there was a prospect here that the Jewish community might hold together, with no small elite proceeding into civic comfort (as in England or France or Germany) while the great body of Jewry stayed unchanged. In 1770 the Bohemian-Land Jewish masses were not involved in the pursuit of modern ways. In the mass, they were indeed barely conscious of such things. But the masses were here of much more manageable size than those to the east in Poland, and the stallions of modernity were harnessed to them. In such senses, at the start of the road to Jewish modernization in the Habsburg Empire, the prospects were good.

THREE

"Self"-Denial Begins

I

In 1772 the Habsburgs annexed from Poland a huge territory north of the Carpathians. They dubbed it the "Kingdom of Galicia and Ludomeria," to fit a title that for centuries had been emptily attached to the Hungarian Crown. With it came a vast increment to Habsburg Jewry. Pre-partition Poland was the very heartland of the Ashkenazim, the Yiddish-speaking core of European Jews. In the Bohemian Lands in the 1780s there were about 70,000 Jews and in Hungary about 80,000, but in Galicia just after the occupation the Austrian authorities actually registered 171,851, and in 1785 they counted 215,447. According to modern estimates, the Jews probably comprised about 9% of the population in the new kingdom as a whole. In the eastern region around the capital, Lwow [Lemberg, Lviv], they were probably about 17%.[1] How did this vast increment affect the fate of Habsburg Jewry at the start of its modernization? This is the basic question of the present chapter.

II

Even a cursory review of the qualities of Galician Jewry suggests some answers. Galician and Bohemian Jewry were contiguous geographically. For centuries there had been regular correspondence and intermarriage between them. In point of ritual and scholarship they were in many ways indistinguishable. But in point of separatism the eastern Jews were quite different.[2] In the late Middle Ages when Jews were being expelled from their homes in Germany, Poland-Lithuania had extended them a welcome, and had given them much more extensive home rule than they had enjoyed in the Holy Roman Empire. Ruling themselves far from the Christian urban centers of the west, there had simply been no pressure upon them to open their intellectual horizons to the outside, such as there was daily in crowded Amsterdam, Frankfurt, or Prague. They had consequently developed a singularly hermetic social nexus, much more insular than anything among the Jews of the west.

In addition, the Polish Jews were poor. The seventeenth century had brought Poland terrible wars of long duration, beginning in the very year

(1648) that witnessed the end of the thirty years calamity in Germany. This violent "deluge" of invasions stopped all commerce, laid fields and cities waste, interrupted the free action of the state, and subjected all elements of the population to great tribulation. But as we have seen in Germany, whence most of the Jews had been expelled late in the Middle Ages, the wars had in some ways bettered the situation of the few remaining, and had also produced a wealthy class of valued financiers, military contractors, and provisioners of the courts. In Poland, by contrast, the wars ruined the Jews along with the entire population. Here, where they were highly organized, they were too accessible as a source of tribute for Polish authorities and foreign invaders alike to permit their accumulation of capital; and they were too numerous to avoid being the brunt of popular resentment.

In the middle of the eighteenth century the Jews of Poland began to lose even their organs of self-government, which in any case had become cruelly oligarchic and burdened with debt. In 1764 the Polish Diet abolished the Jewish "Council of Four Lands," the peak of the autonomist system. The decay of Jewry's position was the worse because Poland herself was declining. The mass of the Christian populations, Polish-speaking or Ukrainian-speaking as they might be, had long since sunk under a serfdom much more onerous than in the western Habsburg lands. The Polish state, already a puppet of its militarily vigorous neighbours, would shortly cease to exist. By the late eighteenth century all the Poles alike were trapped, one might say. There was hardly a channel by which an individual among them could change his lot, yet hardly a one who could not crave something better.

In the face of these circumstances, one might well suggest we revise our optimistic calculation in the preceding chapter about the prospects for Habsburg Jewry's modernization. With the huge increment of 1772, the road to modernity was clearly bound to be stonier than we at first perceived. Yet the annexation of Galicia was not the only great event that affected the fate of Habsburg Jewry late in the eighteenth century, and before leaping to a reassessment, let us call to mind another development that made the Habsburg Jewish future seem not more difficult, but brighter. This followed on the death of Maria Theresia in November 1780 and the accession of her son and co-Emperor, Joseph II (1780–90).

Joseph came to the throne bursting with desire to accelerate the enlightened reforms his mother had begun.[3] It took time to prepare suitable decrees, but to signal his intentions right at the start he relaxed the censorship. In October 1781 he published his first great programmatic edict, extending religious toleration to the leading non-Catholic Christian sects of his dominions, the Lutherans, the Calvinists, and the Greek Orthodox.[4] In November 1781 he decreed the end of *Leibeigenschaft* or serfdom. Then with a concatenation of decrees he abolished most of the monasteries, reorganized the central administrative system, completely recast the judicial system, imposed a new prohibitive tariff on manifold imported goods, regulated marriages and funerals and hundreds of other aspects of daily life, and tried to centralize all the crownlands (including Hungary) into an empire ruled from Vienna by bureaucrats of German speech. Occupying a point of precedence in this legislation were directives affecting the Jews; first a "Rescript" dated 1 October 1781, stating the Kaiser's intentions; then a series of patents, or laws, for the more important crownlands.[5] Though each of the new Jewish laws was different, in general the Kaiser expressly abolished the humiliating "body tax" [*Leibmaut*] hitherto levied on Austrian Jews; he gave them the right to attend schools, to enter professions, to found factories—even a certain equality with other subjects before the law.

Often it is suggested that Joseph's Jewish legislation was no great thing; that the Kaiser was, if not anti-Jewish, at the very least intent on "bettering" the Jews by stripping them of qualities that were of the essence of "Jewishness"; that in the long run he was intent on "Christianizing" them.[6] To some extent this is certainly true. Joseph stated his intentions most clearly in a draft edict he submitted to the Imperial Council [*Staatsrat*] on 13 May 1781. He there indicated that the social isolation of the Jews, and above all their linguistic separatism, made it difficult to "improve their condition" or to make them useful to the state. For this reason he assailed the old laws that bound the Jews into their separatism, insisted that they drop the use of Hebrew in public documents, and encouraged them to wear "Christian" costumes, acquire a German education, and otherwise enter the Austrian body social. His was certainly a project for demolishing a great deal of what for centuries had been considered the major defenses of the Jewish nation. Further, the Kaiser was far from aloof to antipathy towards Jewry. Over the summer of 1781 the members of the provincial governments and the Staatsrat examined the benevolent draft edict in private, and then submitted opinions which reflected the broad range of religious and economic prejudices that pervaded the Austrian bureaucracy. Joseph replied to them with a hodge-podge Rescript. His opening words denied any wish to extend the Jewish Nation in the Crownlands, or to introduce it where it was not tolerated. He wanted simply to make Jewry useful to the state where it now was and in that measure alone. Overall the reply was distinctly negative and unfriendly. Yet this was the document that Joseph saw fit to publish to all the world as his introduction to his reform! And the Rescript left intact the most oppressive legal restriction on the Jews, the various local residence restrictions. All told, these and other Imperial legislation of the 1780s stopped very far short of a complete Jewish emancipation.

Nonetheless, Joseph's work unmistakably constituted the first great generalized attack in modern European history by a Christian ruler against the medieval restrictions that burdened Jewish life. And now to approach our point, there is some evidence that Joseph embarked on this course of reform in part at least because of his awareness of the Jewish problem in Galicia. He had visited that region twice before coming to the throne, most recently in the summer of 1780.[7] In addition, while he was in France in 1777, there had been an active literary debate going on about Poland's Jewry. The Physiocrats in general advocated then the transfer of the Polish Jewish population from commercial into agricultural occupations, both for their own betterment and for Poland's. The Abbé Mably argued the same, but for a different reason: he wanted to get the Jews out of the Polish urban economy because he felt it could not be productive with them there. Such utilitarianism was taken over wholesale into the Imperial Jewish legislation of 1781 and after, as was the project for pushing Jews into agriculture.[8]

All this suggests a "Polish" explanation of Joseph's actions. Further, when he first broached the Jewish problem with his draft edict in May 1781, he had a Polish foreign policy reason of sorts for doing so. In the last years of the old reign, he had committed himself to a project for exchanging the southern Netherlands (modern Belgium), a far-lying family possession he had never visited, for nearby Bavaria, thus consolidating territorially the dominions of his House. In 1778–79 Frederick of Prussia, his one-time idol and his mother's nemesis, had forcibly blocked that project. Joseph thereupon decided to press the matter by diplomacy, and specifically by obtaining support from Catherine of Russia in the east. To this end he traveled to Russia in the summer of 1780, and when he gained the throne late in that year, he sought to engage the Tsaritsa in an alliance against the Turks. Galicia was on the road both to Russia and to the theatres of military operation with the Turks. In May 1781 he was eagerly awaiting her response.[9]

Arguments can be marshaled against this "Polish" explanation of Joseph's Jewish legislation. For example, it may be pointed out that Galicia did not directly need a new Jewish law in 1781. In 1776 Maria Theresia had issued a comprehensive *Judenordnung* for the province, introducing a new self-administrative system; and in effect through most of his reign Joseph only repaired that. He did not issue his own *Judenpatent* on Galicia until 1789, just before his death. Furthermore, it has been claimed that it was not Galician exigency but a specific promptor who led Joseph to pay attention to the Jews in 1780–81. A popular candidate has been Christian Wilhelm von Dohm, an enlightened Prussian official, a friend of Moses Mendelssohn, who in 1781 actually published a book about the civic betterment [*bürgerliche Verbesserung*] of the Jews. Dohm's book echoed what we may call the "Judeophile" ideas of Mendelssohn's circle in the Prussian capital, and argued along lines similar to some of those of Joseph's decree. It made a vast impression on European public opinion when it appeared, and from an early date was closely associated in Enlightened minds with Joseph's roughly coincident legislation.[10] Other popular theories make the "revolutionary Kaiser" indebted for his involvement in Jewish affairs either to Josef von Sonnenfels or to a group of prominent Viennese Jews.[11]

Yet to counter all these arguments against a "Galician" explanation of Joseph's Jewish legislation, one needs only cite a major difference between

Joseph's work and other contemporary efforts to improve the condition of
the Jews. In the famous eighteenth-century discussion in Prussia, for example, the discussion launched by Lessing in the 1760s and carried on in
the 1770s between Mendelssohn and those who wished him to convert,
the issue was not how to "improve" the Jews as a nation. The issue was
first whether or not their religion inevitably tainted its individual followers,
and later (after several individuals had been generally accepted as virtuous
by Christian standards) whether or not cosmetic improvements of the religion could not "bring out" its essential grandeur. Increasingly in that
discussion the idea of a Jewish nation was discarded. The Jewish question
was treated as simply a religious question, and Jews were perceived as just
individuals, fortuitously involved in a traditional national-religious
union.[12] So also in France! There as late as 1790–91 a passionate debate
still raged about whether the Jews were foreigners or not; but the "im-
provers," the "enlightened" revolutionaries, perceived them as followers
of a religion, as individuals, not as a nation. It was on that theoretical basis
that the "emancipation" of the Jews in France took place. The actual, sociological situation of the Jews in France was ignored, which led to practical
inconveniences. It was a great embarrassment to French Liberalism later
on, and a great insult to the French Jews, when Napoleon "corrected" the
situation with his so-called "infamous" laws.

In his Rescript of 1781 Joseph II persistently called the Jews a "nation."
Political vocabularies were not so clear-cut in the eighteenth century as
today. Joseph probably thought the word "nation" to be not too different
from "membership of a religious corporation." Still his wording is a sign
that from the summit of power he was concretely aware of the practical
sociological aspects of the Jewish question in his dominions.[13]

All told, therefore, the annexation of Galicia did not just create new
and weighty objective problems for Habsburg Jewry on its path to modernization. It brought benefits too, in the sense that it helped spark in the
Christian political environment an important and pioneering effort to simplify the tasks that the modernization of Habsburg Jewry would entail. In
broad perspective the annexation did not create a break in the course of
Jewry's modernization in the Habsburg Empire so much as it brought about
an increase in the dimension and tensions of the undertaking. The fate of
Habsburg Jewry now ceased to be just a Bohemian affair and became the
question of European interest, which it would remain until after 1918. Here
one could now study whether or not, with state aid, vast multitudes of the
Ashkenazim would break out of their past into the modern world.

III

The years after the Galician annexation did bring one major break with the
Habsburg Jewish past, however, that calls for discussion. Regardless of
what Joseph II thought by the word "nation," European modernizer Chris-

tians and Jews after 1781 fell increasingly into the habit of seeing Jews as "just a religious group." Though the Habsburg Government referred still to a "Jewish nation" until after 1850, Joseph's Rescript was a late marker of that usage. Why was this? Why did Jewish identity choice become so urgent at just this time? Was it, as Heine would suggest, just social opportunism, or worse, economic greed, that led modern Jews now to throw down the banners of their old nation, and to assimilate? Was it, as Zionists would even later propose, some sort of blindness, a group delusion in Jewish elites brought on by Christian pressure? We may get the beginnings of an answer from the career of a Polish-born Jew who came to the Habsburg Empire because of the annexation of Galicia.

Jakob Frank, one of the most adventurous Jews of the time, and certainly the most cryptic, was born in 1728 in the southeastern corner of old Poland, in the province of Podolia, part of which later came under Austrian rule.[14] It is said that his parents were poor, and that this background accounts for his career. But equally important was a peculiarity of his native province. From 1672 until 1699 it had been lost by Poland to the Ottoman Turks. The experience had led to separation of all the local religious groupings from the established institutions of their faiths—from the Christian churches and the Jewish councils alike—and to a blossoming of religious sectarianism. Russian Christianity was particularly ebullient with sects in Podolia. Jewry gave birth there, just in the decades when Frank was growing up, to a preacher who downplayed the grim rigidity of obedience to the Law. This was the famous Israel, the *Baal Shem Tov* [Teacher of the Good Word] or *BEShT*, the founder of Hasidism; even less is known about his life than about Frank's, but his personal example and promise of spiritual escape split the world of eastern Jewry in twain.

In Jakob Frank's youth his father moved to Bucharest, the capital of Wallachia (which was at that time a Turkish fief assigned to Greek rulers). There Frank experienced a specifically sectarian influence. He mingled with Sephardic Jews, Ladino-speaking descendants of the fifteenth-century exodus of Jews from Spain; among them the teaching of the great Jewish false Messiah, Shabbetai Zevi, remained strong. They had a tendency to explain away Shabbetai's apostasy by taking literally some of the doctrines of Godly immanence and transcendence embedded in late medieval Jewish mysticism, and the idea of redemption through sin. They saw Shabbetai's embrace of Islam less as the end of his mission than as the beginning of a higher sort of crypto-Judaism, made the more inspiring through its syncretism of the first and the third religions of the Jewish book (that is, Judaism and Islam).

In 1755, when he was about thirty, Jakob Frank returned to his birthplace in Podolia and began to teach that he himself was the Messiah. Though he appealed to the same universally poor and downtrodden population to whom the *Baal Shem Tov* had spoken earlier, Frank was no Hasid, and his emphasis was on a social escape from the prison of Polish Jewry which contrasted with the spiritualism of the *BEShT*. Not only did Frank elevate his own person and his own authority in a fashion entirely antithetical to the teaching of the Hasidim; he also clad himself grandly in Turkish garb with Polish gentry embellishments. He organized erotic rituals which shocked the pious. He put great emphasis on public display and on military discipline among his followers. This in particular contrasted with the lack of discipline and the free display of emotion that characterized the Hasidim. Finally, whereas the Hasidim encouraged a "happiness" here on earth, brought about by a change of inner attitude among poorer Jews, yet did not (at least at first) challenge Jewish Tradition directly, Jakob Frank encouraged upward social mobility here on earth as the road to happiness; he aspired to a political, aristocratic style of life; and he made a frontal assault in this connection on the legal authority of the traditional Jewish self-governmental councils, the *kahals*.[15]

In January 1756 Jewish leaders of the town of Lanckorona near Lwow denounced Frank to the Polish authorities. He was disturbing the Jews, they said, and he was mocking even Christian beliefs. He responded with outrageous daring. In his turn he denounced the rabbis, with the result that a public disputation about the character of the Talmud was held in a Christian forum in June 1757. The judgment fell against the rabbis, and to the horror of all pious and traditional Jews many copies of the Talmud were seized and burned. Meanwhile Frank had fled to Turkish-ruled Moldavia and there converted formally out of Judaism into Islam, freeing himself finally from the legal authority of the Polish Jews. To his followers he apparently represented this apostasy as an improvement on his messianic stance, as a step upwards toward greater realization of a transcendent relation with God. In 1758 he then returned to Poland and embarked on an ultimate assault on Jewish authority in that land. This time he not only denounced the Talmud; he also threw the "blood libel" at the traditional Jews, and he promised the Polish authorities that he and all the other Jews would convert to the Roman Catholic faith if traditional Jewish authority was condemned and destroyed. In the aftermath of this offer, another public disputation was held. Though the Jews and their learning survived, many of the Frankists kept their word and demonstratively entered the Catholic fold. What is more, some sixty of them sought and within a few years obtained titles of nobility from the Polish crown, apparently aspiring thus to initiate the acquisition by Jews of land.[16]

Under normal circumstances Frank's second apostasy in 1759 might have been the end of his career. The rabbis of Poland were by then more then justified in execrating him. The Christian Poles were learning that he was still secretly acting as a messianic Jew, and even that he might follow up his conversion by trying to have himself crowned their king and by having his neophyte following become their ennobled—and thus landed—élite. They imprisoned him in 1760 at the fortress monastery of Czesto-chówa. But then in 1768 Catherine the Great's armies passed through south-

eastern Poland on their way to war with the Turks; in 1772, in part
to protect the Russian military rear, a first partition of the great Polish-
Lithuanian Commonwealth took place; and in the disturbances attendant
upon the partition, Jakob Frank escaped. He proceeded first to Warsaw,
then in 1773 to the home of a wealthy relative, Schöndl Dobruschka, who
lived in Austrian Moravia at Brno.[17] There he embarked on a new venture.

At the Austrian frontier Frank evidently presented himself as a "merchant and neophyte," but once in Brno he became decidedly more grand.
He claimed now to possess estates at Smyrna in Anatolia. He organized a
court of sorts. He dressed his followers as if they were his private army,
and he allowed rumor to spread that he might be the murdered tsar, Peter
II, the husband of Catherine the Great; and likewise that his daughter,
Eva, was "in truth" the offspring of Peter's predecessor, the Tsaritsa Elisabeth. These rumors may have been convincing even to the knowledgeable
authorities: Frank is supposed to have visited Vienna in March 1775 to be
"consulted" by Maria Theresia about conditions in the province of Bukowina, which her son was then urging her to annex. It is said that Joseph
II became Frank's "protector," and received him in Brno in November
1781.[18]

In assessing this fantastic record, which Gershom Scholem has termed
"one of the most frightening phenomena in the whole of Jewish history,"[19]
one cannot but be struck by its areligious aspect. Frank tried to "secularize"
the Jews, we would say today. His promise was materialistic. He evoked
an earthly impulse among all Jews to follow him. He rejected the religious
tradition of Jewry. In this sense, his movement was probably as near to
an outburst of what today we would call "Jewish secular nationalism" as
was possible under eighteenth-century conditions. All the more reason to
recognize its limits, of which the most obvious was that Frank did not break
completely with the Jewish religion but inserted himself into it. He called
himself the Jewish Messiah, and his claims against the Talmud were based
on the supposed powers of the Messiah. In this he was wholly traditional;
and indeed, had he not been "orthodox" in this sense—had he preached
only upward mobility, material release, and a secular national redemption
for the Jews—it seems self-evident that he would have attracted no following whatever. Only because a Messiah could legitimately release the
Jews from their religiously bound world did Frank acquire a hold. And
even so 1759 showed that he was the leader not of the Jewish masses, as
we might call them today, but only of an elite of individuals. The nation
did not follow him, but stayed behind.

The little we know about Frank's mission among the Jews of Moravia
and Bohemia emphasizes the failure of his nationalist effort, and indeed
the massive impracticality of any positive Jewish nationalist effort in his
time. We know first that not long after his arrival some wealthy Jews with
connections in Brno began to show interest in ennoblement, just as had
the Polish Frankists. One was Benjamin Hönig, the younger son of Löbl

Hönig, the wealthy "tobacco and *Leibmaut*" Bohemian Jew mentioned in the preceding chapter, a close associate of Schöndl Dobruschka's husband. In 1775 young Hönig (then resident in the Dobruschka house) converted and assumed, without any royal authorization whatsoever, the titled name "von Bienenfeld."[20] Next came Wolf Eybeschütz, the son of Jonathan Eybeschütz (c. 1690–1764), a famed scholar-rabbi at Altona in Holstein, who had been notorious in German Jewry in mid-century as a suspect Sabbatian. Wolf himself was decidedly a rogue who had made his fortune contracting war supplies with various German courts. In 1776 he petitioned the Kaiser for nobility without mentioning he was a Jew, and for a time tricked the Court into granting him his wish.[21] Almost at the same moment Karl Abraham Wetzlar, an army contractor and tax-farmer, converted and requested nobility. He was reputed to be the wealthiest businessman of Vienna, and was about to embark on an extensive business enterprise in Poland. After much struggle, he got himself ennobled.[22] Finally in 1777 Schöndl Dobruschka's children, having converted, requested noble rank, hinting that if the plea were granted a host of their servants would convert too.[23]

These conversions and attempts at ennoblement were of some consequence: the individuals involved were prominent and in the long run set the precedent for a century of Jewish bourgeois ennoblements in the Habsburg Empire. From their circle there even emerged a mythology whereby ennobled Jews would form a fresh pillar of the Imperial state— new class of sorts.[24] Yet it is obvious that their success did not amount to much in the 1770s. It was nowhere near what Frank's followers had achieved twenty years earlier at the Polish Court. The failure may account for a marked divergence between Austrian and Polish Frankism about 1780: thenceforth, the Austrians eschewed conversion.[25] It may also explain why Frank himself apparently now turned to another "messianic" path for attaining a new external order for the Jews: to Freemasonry, which was just then thriving, and which may have strongly influenced Joseph II in his early reforms.

As we will see below, this too failed. By 1785 Joseph had had enough of Masons. In December of that year he issued a sneering decree saying he was fully aware of their so-called secrets and tired of their conspiracies.[26] He commanded an immediate reorganization of Austrian Masonry, and then in January 1786 withdrew his protection from Frank, commanding him to leave Brno. Through Masonic connections Frank arranged a new seat for his court at the castle of the Ysenberger family at Offenbach outside Frankfurt am Main.[27] There he continued to hold court, albeit in straitened circumstances, until he died late in 1791. He received visitors from Poland and Bohemia. He presided over rituals and maintained sharp discipline among his followers. But the era of his great projects was past, his political life was over, and he left no monument.

Jakob Frank, one may freely admit, was not a universally known, much less respected, figure in his time. In the Habsburg Empire his influence even among the Jews was confined to an elite in Brno, Prague, and Vienna, a tiny if influential group; and few people had any perspective at all in his time upon his career. Yet, to refer back now to the theme of this chapter, Frank's record sheds considerable light on the question of why, within a few years of the Galician annexation and Joseph II's Rescript regarding the Jewish "nation," the Habsburg Jews were falling in with the general European trend of regarding Jews just as a religious grouping—as individuals without special nationality of their own. In effect a "nationally affirmative" political option was not in that day available to the Jews, nor even within their conception. Frank's career is not the only one to make this point: from Spinoza in seventeenth-century Amsterdam to Solomon Maimon in late eighteenth-century Berlin, there was a steady and growing number of educated Jews who sought to become simply secular, or atheistic, outside the Law. All ended up completely isolated as did Frank, banned among their own people, shunned also by the Christians. For Jews who desired a secular existence then, the only option was cleavage to some non-Jewish nation, and denial of one's "self."

IV

For many Jews in the decades after 1772, certain non-Jewish paths to modernity came to seem especially worthwhile, distracting them subtly from the national cause. The early part of the career of Josef von Sonnenfels suggests one of these.

Until Sonnenfels was ten, he lived in a characteristic central-European milieu, a muddy village of southern Moravia where the peasants, who were serfs, spoke dialects, sometimes German, sometimes Slavic, but never a language of dictionaries which might today be recognizable as proper German or proper Slovak, much less as modern Czech. To add to the confusion, the Jews spoke Yiddish. Sonnenfels' infancy, one may quip, was dominated by linguistic confusion and mud.[28] Nor did the Babel-like character of his surroundings change greatly when he moved with his father to Vienna in 1744, although because of the palaces and the churches, because of the presence of the court in the capital, he now witnessed a much grander outward world. Vienna's aristocratic upper crust spoke Italian and French and wrote a German bastardized with foreign terms. The Church used Latin, as did the government in communications with such provincials as the Hungarians, but this was a Latin corrupted by centuries of misuse. The business stratum of Vienna conversed in Greek, Italian, *Reichsdeutsch* or *Schweitzerdeutsch*, French, Yiddish, or even English, depending whence the speaker came. The lowest classes spoke a German dialect not unaffected by Slavic and Magyar, but different even from the muddled German of nearby Moravia and of the western Hungarian lands.

In 1749, at the age of 16, driven by poverty, Sonnenfels embarked on a military career. During five peacetime years he traveled over the Habsburg provinces, learning their manifold tongues from other recruits (as he later recalled), from camp-girls, from inn-keepers, and from peasants, witnessing their social inequities from the bottom up. It was not until 1754 that he managed to get excused from his army commitments, and returned to Vienna to study law.

Small wonder that after these experiences Josef von Sonnenfels, even while at the university of Vienna during the later 1750s, became a language reformer. It was not that he disliked linquistic diversity; in his maturity he claimed to speak nine tongues with relish! But central European conditions left him exposed to the lure of purity, and just then a classical, high-German literary revival was sweeping the German north. The bright young Germans of the day were dedicating themselves to preserving and improving the German "mother" tongue. This was where the excitement was in German literature then. In 1751 Sonnenfels became programmatic spokesman for a *deutsche Gesellschaft* at Vienna. Soon he was publishing journals through which to "elevate" both the language and the culture of Vienna into German standards, and one of these, a weekly modeled on Addison's *Spectator* and published from 1765–67 with the title *Mann ohne Vorurtheil* [Man without Prejudice], was the vehicle for a particular literary crusade for which he is best remembered.

Vienna's theatrical life was then dominated by two genres. On the one hand was opera, sung almost exclusively in Italian or French. On the other hand was court comedy in French, and a coarse, originally Italian, "native" comedy for the "masses"—the extemporized Harlequin, or *Hanswürst*, in the Viennese dialect. Sonnenfels now pressed the view in public and at court that an imperial German capital should have a "native" opera in the language of the *Reich*, and a dignified and morally elevating German national drama in the German classic style. According to Sonnenfels, both the foreign dramas and the *Hanswürst* in the native dialect must go.

The ground was ready for a theatre reform in Vienna. But it was the public discussion during the 1760s and early 1770s, to which Sonnenfels was a major contributor, that endowed the German theatre in Vienna with its later leadership in the German-speaking world. The German national theatre (the *Burgtheater*) for which Vienna was later famous appeared in 1776, when Joseph II commanded that the *Hoftheater* performances should be only in German. And all through the revolutionary Kaiser's reign, Germanization was pursued as state policy, not only in the theatres but in the new schools.

Often enough it is remembered that Sonnenfels' linguistic leadership had important consequences for the Austrian cultural identity. Because of the cultural reform at Vienna in the mid-eighteenth century, at whose root stood Sonnenfels, educated Austrians came to speak the same German tongue as do the Germans of Berlin, Munich, or Cologne, and to consider themselves as belonging not to a world of dialects and bastard Latin, Italian, and French, but to German culture. Far less frequently recalled is the rationality and fashionability of the Germanist movement in its day. Yet for our subject, this is what was really important. There was no question of "nationalism" here: German romantic "nationalism" would not be invented for another twenty or thirty years after 1780, and to be "just German"—not "cosmopolitan" and European—was considered "un-German." In question, rather, was a universal escape from the impurities of the centuries, escape from the mud and dialects of the village world into an environment in which Man asserted his intelligence over Nature. This escape was not just commanded from above, although Joseph II and Sonnenfels both did quite a bit of commanding. The intellectuals of the day in Germany and Austria saw it as dictated by the disorder surrounding them in the only field where they possessed power: language.

Now to come to the point: for Jews who encountered the movement, Germanism was in no way the opposite of being "Jewish," though it guided them to a new way of life. To speak German was not a divorce from their past so much as a general, non-sectarian cleaning up of the world. Indeed, the case for German was the more persuasive because Sonnenfels, an "ex-Jew," was so prominent in pressing for it in the Austrian lands; and because there was a ready-made place for Jews, a people who spoke an irregular "jargon" derived from German. Yiddish was a ready candidate for "purification!" And then coincident with Joseph II's decree, Mendelssohn, the Jewish "philosophe," cemented the modern-Jewish marriage with German by publishing his translation of the Torah. For fashion-minded Jews of central Europe, German then became a nigh holy tongue, a vehicle for specifically religious expression second only to Hebrew.[29]

V

Nor was Germanism the only great popular craze sweeping the central European Jewish world, subtly tugging people away from their "Jewishness" in the decades after 1772. A democratic vogue was also current: a cult of "improvement" and "betterment" of society from below and not, as in the past, from above. And there is no better suggestion of its subtle effect on Jews than the career of Moses Dobruschka of Brno, who was a cousin of Jakob Frank.

Born in 1753, the son of the prominent tobacco farmer Salomon Dobruschka mentioned earlier, Dobruschka grew up amidst conditions that contrasted with those of most Jews. The Dobruschka household was luxurious; it was also rampant with dissident religious ideas, specifically Sabbatian heresy. Further, religious heterodoxy was common in this family long before Frank arrived at Brno in 1773. Moses' elder brother converted in 1769 to become an army officer. In consequence Moses, the intellectual of the family, received not only a German-language education while a child but also a strong dose of esoteric cabalism.

Moses and most of his eleven siblings converted just after their father's death in 1774, on which occasion he changed his name to Thomas Schönfeld (the first of several name changes that sprinkle this tale). Yet it was not til many years later that in private he began to deny he was a Jew and to attack religion altogether. Evidently he felt in these early years that somehow outward religion may be unimportant, that inner conviction is what may count.[30] And in his cultural activity at this point he was not unlike other Jewish modernists of his time: he was above all a poet and enthusiastic Germanist. By 1778, the year of his ennoblement, Dobruschka-Schönfeld was sufficiently known as such to be listed in a famous compendium entitled *Das gelehrte Österreich* that summed up the achievements of the Austrian intellectual Enlightenment. Then, however, a certain leakage into politics occurred.

Moving to Vienna, Dobruschka-Schönfeld won employment as assistant to Michael Denis, a translator of the famous forged epic of "Ossian" into German, who enjoyed alongside Klopstock enormous popularity as a German bard.[31] Denis was at the center of a circle of intellectuals who had been Jesuits until the dissolution of their order in Austria by Maria Theresia in 1773. They had been used to a discipline at once spiritual and strong. They were not averse to finding a new "home," and were discovering one in Masonry.[32] In the half century since the establishment of the Masonic movement in England in 1717, its universalist social promise, its ideological tolerance, its secrecy, even its persecution by religious authorities, had led to a great popularity throughout Europe. Masonry is said to have appealed to the rising bourgeoisie because it gave newcomers entrée to power; yet it did not offend the aristocrats because the leveling took place behind the scenes. Masonry is said to have appealed to the irreligious, because it rejected clerical hierarchies and all established church ritual, yet it did not offend believers because it acknowledged a universal God and stood in general on a Christian foundation. In sum, explanations of its popularity abound and need not detain us here save as background for the developments of the 1770s, which were a breakdown of unity in the movement and a wild proliferation of new lodges founded (on the whole) by a new generation of intellectuals seeking explanations more complex, more spiritual than those that had satisfied their elders. The *Illuminati*, founded in 1776 in Bavaria, are a good example. Although they were more directly revolutionary then most Masons, they were absolutely characteristic of the sort of spontaneous local growth which Masonry was just then undergoing in the heady atmosphere of the late Enlightenment.

Through his contacts with Denis, evidently, Dobruschka-Schönfeld became a Mason, and then in the excitement of the start of Joseph's reign, early in 1781, he engaged in a remarkable bit of mystification. Though only 27, he became a founding member of a new Masonic lodge, "The Order of the Asiatic Bretheren" (or, as its members boasted, "*Die Ritter vom wahrem Licht*" [Knights of the true Light]) whose peculiarity was a willingness as a matter of policy to accept Jews as members.[33] Other lodges had long since accepted individual Jews, but nowhere as a matter of policy. The new lodge was made possible in part because Joseph had abolished the old organizational framework of central European Masonry which had been centered at Berlin, but in part also because Dobruschka-Schönfeld and his colleagues produced the (wholly false) idea that they were representatives of a league of Masons in the Ottoman Empire—a lost tribe, as it were— and moreover that this Asiatic League was possessed of more ancient and higher insights into Truth and the Divine Will than the European Masons themselves. Had obfuscation not been of the essence of Masonry (and perhaps of Enlightenment also) in that day, had the Masons not been fascinated above all with minting myths about their own ancient history, the Asiatic Lodge could hardly have gotten off the ground. But in that happiest of years, 1781, it throve in Vienna, and Dobruschka-Schönfeld's involvement became decisive because his co-founders almost immediately left the city to spread their message in Germany. He was left as official ideologist of the Asiatic Lodge, and was made responsible for drawing up its statutes.

For three years Dobruschka-Schönfeld now enjoyed great prestige because he was the only one in the lodge who had actual knowledge of the Cabala and the Jewish learning from which the "True Light" was supposed to be drawn. He devised a syncretic structure neither Christian nor Jewish, mixing the symbols and the theosophy of both to create a platform on which practicing Jews and practicing Christians could come together through (minor) ritual sinning by both. Not least of all, he introduced a set of pseudo-cabalistic notions for use by his co-founders. Whether and how deeply Jakob Frank was in on this enterprise, we do not know, though we have reports that Dobruschka-Schönfeld was very close to the "Messiah" and that he took Viennese recruits to the Order to Brno for initiation in these early years.[34] Clear only is the fact that Dobruschka-Schönfeld was now highly political, combining his crypto-Jewishness with broadly conspiratorial efforts to gain influence in high places, advancing even to the steps of the throne, aspiring to change society radically through manipulations from behind the scenes.

High hopes often end in disaster. By 1784 Dobruschka-Schönfeld's manipulation of the Asiatic Lodge in Vienna was at the peak of its success. All sorts of important people, including the great bankers Nathan Arnstein and Bernhard Eskeles, the city's most prominent confessional Jews, were signing up. Then late in 1785, as noted earlier, the Kaiser attacked Austrian Freemasonry. Within weeks the movement withered. Most of its more distinguished members retired from the field. Within the year the center of the Asiatic Lodge was removed from Vienna to Schleswig. Its whole later history transpired in Germany, not Austria. In the wake of debacle, Schönfeld remained at Vienna. Initially he returned to poetry and even published a martial paean dedicated to Joseph on the occasion of the latter's involvement in the anti-Turkish war. He also took up the trade of his fathers and made a fortune contracting to furnish supplies for Joseph's armies in the Balkans. After Joseph's death, he was somehow close enough to the circle of the new Kaiser, Leopold II, to travel with the court to the Pillnitz "summit" meeting of the enemies of the revolution in France. But meanwhile that great event had not only changed the government of France, but also had radicalized Schönfeld's ideas. A few years earlier, with Teutonic ardor, he had called on German poetry to outshine the dull verses of France. Now he was prepared to attack Germany for its despotism.[35]

Instead of returning from Pillnitz to Vienna late in 1791, he stopped at Offenbach, where Jakob Frank had just died. He was reportedly offered the leadership of the Frankist movement, but rejected it. Thence he proceeded to Strassburg, there to take part in the great social upheaval that had by then assured the Jews a new status in France, wholly free of the prejudice and discrimination of old. When the wars began in the spring of 1792, Schönfeld, with his wife, a brother, and a sister, moved to Paris itself. There he changed his name to Junius Frey, returned to poetry, and once again went about constructing an organizational network through which to manipulate the world into favoring the Jewish nation.

We do not really know what happened in the end.[36] In his last years at Vienna Schönfeld had evidently dealt much with money. It was said that in Paris he could not keep his hands clean. Certainly in his search for influence over the Revolution, he allied himself with the Gironde and married his sister to Chabot, a prominent member of the Convention. His new friends were not only themselves involved in questionable financial schemes but they were suspect for political reasons in the eyes of Robespierre. Whether because he joined them or because he received too many large remittances from abroad, Schönfeld in November 1793 ended up in prison. Thence in 1794 he passed together with his brother, his new brother-in-law, and Danton into the embrace of Madame Guillotine.

As a Jewish rich man's son and heretic, Moses Dobruschka was anything but typical even of the small modernist elite in Habsburg Jewry in his day, much less of the masses of traditional Jews. Until very recently the full extent of his career has not even been known. He seemed a negligible figure. Yet his very exceptionality tells us a lot about the tragedy of central European Jewish history. For he was objectively very important, the only Austrian—to put the matter bluntly—to participate actively in the central turmoil of Europe's modern revolution, the upheaval at Paris. That that particular Austrian should also have been a Jew reflects and adumbrates a central phenomenon to be discussed in this book. He shows how even in the eighteenth century modernist Habsburg Jewry took on the burden of Christian Austrian history as well as its own. His career may strike us as corrupt, deceitful, even sleazy at times, but think of the immense dual role he acted out! Who would not have seemed corrupt and deceitful, juggling so many glittering balls?

Dobruschka's career also tells us much about a central phenomenon of this chapter: the tugs to which the democratic movement of the time subjected all central European Jews. As Gershom Scholem has said, despite Dobruschka's political transformation, his relation to Jewishness remained singularly constant. His orthodoxy was suspect from the beginning, his apostasy was suspect til the end. His constant relationship to Jewishness seems the ultimate sign of how little there was in the democratic craze of the late eighteenth century of confrontation with Jewish nationality. Like the Germanism which preceded it, this vogue was less a negation of the Jewish past than an optimistic assertion of Humanity's will to do better. It was a universalist movement in the broad world of European civilization which acted as a powerful lure to the modern-minded of any confession and all.

VI

Did the annexation of Galicia in 1772 make Habsburg Jewry's prospects for modernization different from what they had been before, and less favorable? In the abstract, surely yes! The huge increment of impoverished and introspective Galician Jews meant that the sheer task of modernizing was now very much greater. Habsburg Jewry was no longer even unified, no longer just Bohemian. In significant ways the whole process of modernization now had to begin again.

Yet in context the prospect seems rather different and far less dark, for almost at the same moment as the Galician annexation, the whole environment of Habsburg Jewry was transformed. Joseph II's great intervention against anti-Jewish laws was symptomatic; Christian and Jewish Europe alike just now experienced a nigh millennial shift in mood. The chasm between the religious groups was closing, platforms were emerging for common activity, fora for communication. On the Christian side, secular rationalism was severely curtailing, if not eliminating altogether, the possibility of religious crusading against "Christ-killer" Jewries, the type of ceremonial bloodletting that had characterized western civilization since the 1090s at least. On the Jewish side, ever more evidence was surfacing to make continued introspective nationalism seem futile. Deplorable as we may think Jewish "self"-denial today, it became in the late eighteenth century not only attractive but seemingly necessary to secular-minded Jews. The ancient walls around Jewry were thus undermined, made fragile. And meanwhile popular fads were sweeping the educated classes of central Europe, Jewish and Christian alike, into very vigorous modernizing enterprises: on the one hand, the Germanist linguistic reform, on the other the social betterment movement that culminated in the revolution in France. These factors all made the tasks of Habsburg Jewry's modernization easier by far than they had been before 1772.

One tends to ask of this moment in modern Jewish history whether it was not all a mistake, whether the rosy-seeming late-eighteenth-century prospects were not all illusion. Gone was the communal unity that had been the unique feature of Habsburg Jewry when it centered at Prague. Not only were hundreds of thousands of Polish Jews now within the imperial frontiers; also the Christian state, centered at Vienna, was increasingly the arbiter of Jewish political affairs. Self control was gone; it was renegades, extremist figures such as the three examined in this chapter, who were now the heralds of central European Jewry's future. Given the record of Christian civilization, who could not foresee that the pendulum would swing back again away from the Judeophilia of the moment into some new sort of hatred of Jews?

Such questions overlook the reality, however, that there was no standing still, no possibility of going back. The issue in Jewish history late in the eighteenth century was not whether Jewry would modernize or not; the issue was how the change would take place, whether it would be smooth or difficult, whether the elite would separate radically from the masses, or whether the whole of Jewish society could proceed peacefully through the narrow gate. In this context our earlier optimistic prognosis about Habsburg Jewry remains valid. Because of the annexation of Galicia, the tasks were much more difficult. The other new developments of the time increased the possibility, however, that a large number of Jews in Austria might proceed swiftly, if not without pain, into the modern world.

PART II

The Great Bourgeois
Experiment,
1800–1850

FOUR

Vienna's Bourgeoisie

I

In Maria Theresia's last years and in the early reign of Joseph II, the political atmosphere of Vienna was similar to that at Berlin or even Paris. Peace was on hand, reform was possible, ideas could be freely expressed. But towards the middle of Joseph II's reign there began a new course. First the revolutionary Kaiser himself reinforced the police and set up a new apparatus for the repression of ideas. Then in 1790 Joseph died, his domains in tumult, his state at war. The Habsburg heritage fell to his brother Leopold, a man of similarly enlightened views but of greater tact and cunning. Leopold executed a political retreat from reform. In the spring of 1792, with order only beginning to return in the Danubian crownlands, Leopold also died, leaving the guidance of the Empire to his son Franz. The consensus of Franz's biographers is that he was a genteel man, prepared by his education for a rational world. In Vienna he was known as Franz der Gute. But almost immediately after mounting the throne, he fell into war with revolutionary France. Right at the start he lost the Netherlands that his family had held for centuries. In 1793 he lost to the Revolution the heads of his uncle by marriage, Louis XVI, and of his aunt, Marie Antoinette. In 1797, deserted by Prussia and Russia, he had to make a first concessionary peace. In the face of these horrors abroad Franz decided to change the atmosphere at home.

He rigidified the police and censorship systems, and increased the corps of spies his predecessors had already employed. Convinced he was surrounded by Jacobin conspiracies, he staged witchhunts for revolutionaries, forced his victims to confess, and then hid them in fearful prisons or executed them so as to prevent the further contagion of his subjects by their ideas. By 1802 he had become so worried about revolutionaries infiltrating his capital that he even considered barring industry and manufacturing in the city because they attracted lower-class people, potential Revolution.[1] And this was only the beginning of Austria's turn "backwards" under this Kaiser.

After Franz's catastrophic defeats by Napoleon in the wars of 1805 and 1809, he employed a new chancellor, Count Clemens von Metternich, to bring him peace of mind no matter what the cost. Metternich's diplomatic

agility enabled Austria to emerge in 1814–15 as one of the victors who
rebuilt Europe. Franz nonetheless insisted on reinsurance. He had his chancellor and his Vienna police chief, Count Sedlnitzky, create a "Chinese
Wall" of censorship and repressive law around his Empire lest subversive
notions trickle in even from the well-censored and well-policed Europe
they had "restored." Again in the 1820s there were secret trials of intellectuals and the prisons at Brno and Munkács [Mukachevo] were once more
filled. They stayed full because the change was not momentary. Franz
himself reigned until 1835. His son Ferdinand was soft-minded, but had
advisors who maintained the same policies until the revolutions overthrew
them and caused Ferdinand's removal from the throne in 1848.

What were the consequences of this turn of events for the Habsburg
Jews? This is the central question of this and the following chapters. As
earlier we will be more partial in our attention to the assimilationist elite
than to the broad traditionalist masses of Jewry. It was the elite, after all,
who were setting the pace and choosing the directions in which Habsburg
Jewry moved in the period of Franciscan tyranny. We will first discuss the
Viennese Jews, a part of Habsburg Jewry which rose to particular prominence in the Franciscan era, though it was very small in numbers. In the
following chapter we will return to Bohemian Jewry and observe the broad
trends of the time. Then in a third chapter we will turn anew to Vienna,
discussing the year of its revolution, 1848. We will observe the extraordinary fact that the tiny Jewish elite of the capital city played a crucial political
role in the greatest popular upheaval that Christian Austria had ever
known.

II

To approach a first interpretion of Franz I's impact upon Habsburg Jewry,
let us recall the early development of the Vienna community.[2] When Maria
Theresia came to the throne in 1740, only 12 Jewish families were allowed
to live regularly in the capital, though some of these had fairly large households and all were allowed to receive visitors from other parts of the
Monarchy and from abroad. Since 1670 Vienna had largely shared the
"cleanliness of Jews" that characterized the Alpine provinces and many
cities of the Bohemian Crownlands. By 1780, however, the number of families was 53, of whom 25 enjoyed a special "toleration," and the total number
of regularly resident Jewish individuals had reached 570.[3] In the ten years
of Joseph II's reign the number of families went up to about 70 and the
registered household members increased to about 840. These figures do
not include the ever-more-numerous transient or visitor Jews in the city.
By the end of the reign, Jews were for the first time since 1670 considered
conspicuous in Vienna.[4] And the community from the start until 1848 had
a unique characteristic which set it off from all other central European
Jewish communities, as well as from the Christian population: it had very

few poor members; it was decisively "bourgeois." In the provinces of course, even in nearby Moravia and Hungary, poverty-stricken Jews abounded, but in the capital they were not allowed. There might be 2 Oppenheimers, 14 Wertheimers, 2 Arnsteins, 2 Simons, 6 Schlesingers, and lots of Lehmans and Sinzheims here, but none of them was poor.

The Vienna Jews were long subject both to their own separatist dress, speech, and religious practice, and to Christian *Judenordnungen* which kept them "in their place" (in other words, off the streets on Sundays, away from religious processions, and so forth). Initially they were also subject to professional restrictions which kept them out of the trade in wares, which provided much of the city with its livelihood. A roster dating from 1763, and bearing 57 names, reveals how tight these restrictions were.[5] All but a handful of these men dealt in credit and money. The others were two *Hoffaktoren* from Germany (Wetzlar and Goslar/Arenfeld), seven jewelers who served the imperial court and the aristocracy, two visiting rabbis from the Burgenland Jewish communities (the Viennese were not allowed to have a rabbi of their own), a private tutor in the Wertheimer house, and a Jewish hospital attendant. Eleven were of unknown profession. This list did not include certain categories of Jews who were regularly in the capital city; for example, the transient traders from Bratislava, the Burgenland, Moravia, Bohemia, and Trieste; the great provincial tobacco contractors such as the Dobruschkas, Poppers, Hönigs, and Baruchs; and the Jewish servants of the wealthy. The Hoffaktoren were the only members of the group identifiably trading in wares.

A new Judenordnung of 1764 brought a first major change in the status of the Viennese Jews by allowing them to trade in domestic (though not imported) manufactured wares. That regulation also dropped a number of the sumptuary restrictions on Jews, marking the start of their outward assimilation into the Christian population. As a result many of the Viennese Jews were soon living in a style very similar to the Christians. In 1781 as we have seen Joseph's Tolerance Rescript actually ordered them to do so, encouraging them to obtain a modern education and to go into manufacturing, and putting them more or less finally on absolute commercial parity with Christian businessmen.

The list of tolerated Viennese Jews from 1789 shows the effect of the new legislation.[6] Among the 74 family heads, 14 still dealt in money and state loans and 10 still traded in jewels (of whom seven also dealt in money), making a total of about one-third of the community still in the old professional mold. But there was now only one Hoffaktor (Samuel Wertheimer), whereas there were 8 "wholesalers" [*Grosshändler*], 15 merchants of one sort or another (wool, leather, silk textiles, fancy goods, and horses) and 4 agents for provincial traders in wares. One member of the group owned a dye-factory. There were 3 doctors, a butcher, a baker, and 11 persons who served the special ritual needs of Jews. By 1804 the trend toward professional diversification of the Vienna Jewish community had so much accelerated that of 119 "tolerated" Jews then living in the city, the number of self-styled "money-dealers" was down from the 33 in 1763 to 6. There were still 10 jewelers and 1 Hoffaktor. But there were 16 *Grosshändler* (32 if one includes their relatives of unspecified profession). There were also 8 merchants specializing in silk wares, 12 in wool and leather products, 12 in other raw produce, 7 in manufactured goods, 2 in distilled products, and 5 in paper. This made a total of 44 in wares, and there were also 4 "Galician assessors" (commission agents for Galician merchants).

Not only did the members of the new Viennese Jewish community diversify professionally in these decades; some of them won a certain social prominence. Exemplary were three business associates whom Kaiser Franz ennobled in 1797; Nathan Arnstein, Bernhard Eskeles, and Salomon Herz. Arnstein's forebear, Isaak Arnsteiner (1682–1744), had come to Austria from Würzburg in Franconia at the turn of the eighteenth century and had originally been closely linked in business with the great imperial Hoffaktor, Simson Wertheimer (though apparently Arnsteiner was not, as is often asserted, Wertheimer's relative).[7] In the 1720s after Wertheimer's death, Isaak Arnsteiner became Hoffaktor to the Empress Elizabeth Christine, wife of Karl VI, and as such gained his family lasting wealth. His son, Adam Isaak (who married a Gomperz from the distinguished Jewish family of Nymwegen in Holland), and his grandson, Nathan Adam (1749–1838), were both distinguished businessmen and soon became Vienna's leading Jewish bankers.

If the Arnsteins represented the business acumen among the older Jewish houses of Vienna, Bernhard Eskeles represented their inbreeding.[8] His ancient German-Polish rabbinical family had connections all over Europe. His father Baruch Eskeles (1691–1753) had been *Landesoberrabbiner* of Moravia, but married the daughter of Simson Wertheimer and after 1740 retired from Nikolsburg to Vienna. There he inherited from his wife a portion of Wertheimer's enormous fortune, and then compounded it in his old age by marrying the daughter of Wertheimer's very wealthy oldest son, Wolff (in other words, his own niece-in-law), and producing by her Bernhard as his only son. Young Bernhard grew up in Amsterdam, whither his mother had gone in second marriage, but returned to Vienna in 1772, a thoroughly enlightened millionaire, to found a bankhouse. In the 1790s he worked very closely with Nathan Arnstein. In 1800, after his ennoblement, Eskeles would marry Cecilia Itzig, Arnstein's sister-in-law from Berlin; in 1804, perhaps to gain security against the perils of the time, the two family firms would merge.

Salomon Herz, the third new non-convert Jewish noble of 1797, was a newcomer to Vienna, but little less socially distinguished.[9] Born in 1743, the son of a rabbi of Hamburg, he married Nathan Arnstein's elder sister in 1765 , and came to the Austrian capital in 1770 as an Arnstein partner. He shines in our context because he was enlightened, religiously indifferent, and socially flashy—perhaps the most conspicuous rich Jew of Vienna.

Further, his son Leopold (1767–1828) was in point of economic speculation and social flashiness not one tittle behind.

Despite these heights of bourgeois elegance, Kaiser Franz treated the Jews of his *Residenzstadt* despicably. In the very first months of his reign he accepted a pessimistic assessment of the growth of Vienna Jewry, and acted to halt it.[10] He set up a *Judenamt* [Jewish Office] to try to slow down immigration and to collect a stamp tax from temporary visitors to the city. A sign soon appeared over its door: "For Jews, Chair-carriers and Cabbies," which was the equivalent of the latter-day notice barring Chinese and dogs from the Shanghai Bund. This office was "provisional," but it survived until 1848, and particularly in the early decades of the reign it combined with the rest of the bureaucracy to harass even the wealthiest Jews of the city with pettifogging nonsense, the more deadly because practically any Jew, high or low, could be ordered to leave the city forthwith. Between 1790 and 1814 the State Chancellery alone issued more than 600 regulations affecting Jews. This sort of treatment did not stop the growth of the Viennese Jewish population. (By 1820 the number of tolerated families was up to 135, and the total present was about 1560, a growth of 180% in 40 years; and these figures exclude of course the converts, who cannot be reckoned, and take no account of foreign Jews, for example the "Turkish Jewish community," or of transients and students.) Whereas Joseph I had meant "tolerance" to open doors, Franz II used the same word to close them, making "toleration" for Jews in Vienna a matter of exception, not of rule.

III

Such needling discrimination was only one facet of how Vienna Jewry fared under Franz I. To approach another let us look now at some significant changes that affected Christian Vienna during the period just reviewed. In 1670 when Leopold II expelled the Jews from Vienna, his "residential city" had been little more than a fortress on the Turkish frontier, a town with a palace and a cathedral, but no excess of trade and a population of well under 50,000. Vienna had then been smaller than the other great Habsburg city, Prague, and not great at all in relation to Paris, London, and the urban conglomerations of the Mediterranean world.[11] By mid-eighteenth century, however, peaceful conditions had made Vienna one of Europe's largest cities with some 175,000 inhabitants (compared to 59,000 in 1754 in Prague). Hereupon the Theresian and Josephian relaxations of the Empire's serf legislation and their other reforms led to further demographic growth. By 1780 there seem to have been some 200,000 civilians in the fortified inner city and "the suburbs within the Line" (that is, inside of today's *Gürtel*). By ten years later there had been a jump of 8% to about 215,000; by 1800 another, to about 230,000. By 1820 there would be about 260,000 civilians in the city, a growth of 33% in 40 years. By 1848 there would be well over 400,000 in the bulging capital. Demographically Vienna would slip during the first half of the nineteenth century from about fourth to about sixth place among Europe's largest cities, bowing to Saint Petersburg and Constantinople, as well as to London, Paris, and Naples. But unquestionably even then she remained in the mainstream of that dynamic, all-European urban growth which in the eighteenth century she had pioneered.

Major changes in the character of Vienna's society accompanied this demographic revolution. Above all, the machinery of government expanded. This meant first of all that once the Turks had been removed from the neighborhood, the great aristocrats of the Bohemian, Austrian, and Hungarian Lands established themselves in the city. As noted earlier these great feudal magnates—the Schwarzenbergs, Liechtensteins, Kinskys, Czernins, Pálffys, Eszterházys, Lobkowitzes—were in many ways the real rulers of the crownlands, the actual administrators and taxers of the great mass of the population. They now built great palaces inside the city walls and summer residences in the inner and outer suburbs, making palace construction for a time a major part of the Vienna economy. They also came and went with their masses of servants and administrators, contributing substantially to the population. In addition the military establishment grew. All through the eighteenth (and also the first half of the nineteenth) century military personnel seem to have comprised about 10% of the capital city's population. Their barracks protruded on the landscape. Feeding the soldiers, supplying them, perhaps above all amusing them became a significant part of the city's life. Third, of course, the central bureaucracy expanded, although not as massively as one would have expected considering the extent of Habsburg rule. Until the 1760s it was more through construction activity (building the *Karlskirche*, expanding the *Hofburg*) and through the employment of servants that the Imperial House, like the great aristocrats, contributed to the growth of Vienna.

Although servants, laborers, and street people multiplied as a result of these factors, the social stratum we would today call "middle class" or "bourgeoisie" was surprisingly not subject to massive growth until mid-eighteenth century. The reason was that a guild system then gripped the city's economy quite as firmly as did the serf system of the countryside.[12] Virtually all urban economic activity, from house-painting and chimney-sweeping to brewing, produce-pickling, and cloth-spinning, was dominated by guilds which regulated every detail of the trade and specified who could participate. As late as 1809 there were 159 guilds in Vienna. Enterprising patricians or immigrants could often in practice get around the guild regulations "by special dispensation." There were a few trades (the armorers, for example, and certain book publishers) which had been "freed" by the crown (or by the university) from the guilds. But because of the guild system Vienna's middle class was in general closed in the mid-eighteenth century to modern entrepreneurial activity.

Change did come, because gradually international commerce picked up and a trading community developed in the city. Even here, however, development was slow, for until the middle of the eighteenth century the foreign trade of Vienna was conducted on the whole by "factors" [*Niederleger*], who came from outside.[13] They were the Greeks and the "Turkish Jews," the Armenians, the Serbs and *Reich* Germans, the Swiss and French Protestants, the Italians and the English who gave Vienna its cosmopolitan polyglot character. They wore their own costumes, lived by their own laws, and went home to die. And as foreigners, needless to say, they were barred by law from any participation in manufacture.

After 1763, Maria Theresia and the Lower Austrian authorities sought to repair the economic damages of the Seven Years War by setting up a mercantilist tariff regime discriminating against foreign goods. This significantly encouraged native entrepreneurship.[14] In the 1770s the imperial mercantilists gave another push. They created a specially privileged status called *Grosshändler*, or "wholesaler," for Austrian businessmen who were willing to become entrepreneurs on a large scale. The members of all Christian ranks, commoners and nobles alike, could become Grosshändler if they had enough wealth; and this status brought immunity from most restrictions on trade. At about the same time ordinances from above "freed" many branches of textile-making and textile-trading, and also raw-produce-trading, from guild regulation. It is the peculiarity of Viennese social and economic history that most of the guilds survived these innovations, and also the codified commercial legislation produced during the late Enlightenment (that is, the regulations of 1791 and 1809). As a result, the Viennese "petite bourgeoisie" remained to a surprising extent unchanged from the early eighteenth century until the last years before 1848.[15] But in the late eighteenth century, quite suddenly, an upper bourgeoisie appeared which had been created—and "liberated"—by recent laws.

There is no simple way to assess how many people belonged to this new element in the Viennese population. By 1797 there were 77 Grosshändler in Vienna. In 1823, a year when the so-called *Grosshändler Gremium* was at its largest, there were 118 member firms.[16] But alongside the Grosshändler there were new-wealthy Christian industrialists in some number in Vienna who had risen to riches by extracting privileges from the treasury to build factories either in the suburbs or (more often) in various parts of Upper and Lower Austria. Further, there were many new-wealthy Christians who became rich as bureaucrats or government agents of one sort or another; and there were some of aristocratic background who needed no special privileges. Although they lived in Vienna, they were under no pressure to declare themselves Grosshändler there; indeed, they were sometimes discouraged from doing so by the surviving legislation separating manufacturing from sales.

Since many members of the new upper bourgeoisie managed to win noble status, it was known very generally by the end of Joseph II's reign as the "second nobility" (later on it became the "second society") to distinguish it at once from the higher, titled aristocracy of the past, and from the older guild-bound and unchanging urban stratum which now became a sort of lower bourgeoisie.[17] Despite this terminology, one should not duck the reality that Austria, having become a modern state quite late in European history, was now even later acquiring a non-feudal leading class.

To perceive the significance of this development for Vienna Jewry, one needs only to look back at the concept of modernization. As mentioned early in this book, scholars disagree about exactly what this process entails—about whether it is basically a cultural, a social, or an economic phenomenon—but universally they acknowledge that it is a process and that it involves the removal of people from traditional communal frameworks into new ones. The ease or difficulty of modernization will depend on the presence or absence of factors facilitating reorientation and reintegration. Hitherto in our account of Habsburg Jewry we have perceived a number of such factors, but virtually all effected economic or cultural reorientation. Practically none promised the Jews any sort of social reintegration after they abandoned the Jewish social frameworks of the past. The Vienna upper bourgeoisie did precisely that: it was a social grouping on the other side of the fence, so to speak, that was not just important but open, flexible, and as new to the Austrian civic landscape as the bourgeois Jews.

A contrast between the development of Jewry in the Austrian capital and that in Berlin suggests the impact of this Christian bourgeois group. In both cities at the end of the eighteenth century, fairly prosperous Jewish communities were aspiring beyond cultural enlightenment for what was later called "assimilation." The cultural environments were nigh identical, but socially the two cities were notably different. Berlin was less than half the size of Vienna. It was also the seat of a mercantilist government, but not of a palace-building aristocracy (nor even of open-handed kings), and the key to her mercantilism was not expenditure and the emancipation of bourgeois enterprise but discipline, thrift, and royal reliance on foreign hirelings and Jews. As a result, on the Christian side there was no social group at Berlin with which Jews could mingle. There was only the old guild *Bürgertum* that remained intact, and then a transient court society of gentry, army officers, bureaucrats and fashionable visitors from all over northern Europe. And whereas towards the end of the century the Vienna Jews comfortably began to mingle with their Christian counterparts, the Berliners then made themselves famous for their alienation!

And now to make our point: the Franciscan regime at Vienna actively encouraged Jewish-Christian integration in the new upper bourgeoisie. Joseph II in 1781 had made it possible for Jews to become Grosshändler. Franz I virtually insisted they become so, if they wished to stay in his city. Joseph had ennobled not only a fair number of Christian middle class businessmen at Vienna but several converted Jews, and in the last months of his life he gave nobility for the first time to a confessional Jew. Franz, for all his conservatism, actively continued this policy, paying special attention, as we have seen, to the Arnstein family.[18] Perhaps these were little signs, but in their light Franz's reign appears decidedly less a repression of the tiny Viennese Jewish elite than it did before.

IV

The French revolutionary wars considerably facilitated the integration of Jews into the new Viennese upper middle class. In part this was because the wars created all sorts of new business opportunities. Because they disrupted the economy of all western Europe, to give but one example, Hermann Todesco, a Jewish cloth merchant from Bratislava who specialized originally in silks, could move to Vienna, expand into other wares, become a leading speculator on the Stock Exchange, invest in the Bohemian cotton factories, and become very wealthy—a more than acceptable partner for Christian entrepreneurs. But it was above all through their impact on Austria's finances that the wars cemented the capital's new society.

Finance, as we have indicated in earlier chapters, had never been an Austrian Habsburg strong point.[19] Their treasury had been administratively unified for the first time only in Maria Theresia's reign, and even then had not had its budgetary, tax, and accounting functions properly articulated from one another. Nor had the treasury been effectively separated in the eighteenth century from the fledgling bank-of-issue, the *Wiener Stadtbank*. The only approximation of a balanced budget had been in 1775 and right after that Maria Theresia's final war (of Bavarian Succession), the Balkan wars of Joseph II, and the disruption of civilian life throughout the empire by Joseph's reforms had caused huge new indebtedness. Still, in 1792, when Franz came to the throne, the 28 million florins of *Bankzettel* or paper currency circulated since 1762 was probably coverable by the quantity of hard money in the government's coffers; and the national debt stood at only 147 millions.[20] Private bankers still held a virtual monopoly on most credit operations, including the transport of coinage for the state and the floating of state loans. But over the century even they had become much more institutionalized (that is, they operated ever less on the basis of personal credit, ever more through relationships of their firms) and less blatantly usurious than Samuel Oppenheimer had been. One may admit that the situation was vastly improved since Oppenheimer's day when the State had been dependent on erratic contributions from the various noble-dominated Estates, and when there had been no Stock Exchange to moderate the interest rates charged on state paper.

By the end of the first Coalition War against the Revolution in 1797, however, Austria's finances were out of control. About 74 millions in paper money were now in circulation. The State had rejected its obligation to redeem the Bankzettel on demand, and the national debt stood at 580 millions (including 116 millions owed abroad) despite direct subsidies received from England. Hitherto the treasury had been more or less able to

pick and choose between private bankers. Now a certain dependency began
to reemerge.

Austria made peace with the French at Campo Formio in 1797, but
gained little economic respite; in 1799 a new war erupted. The presses went
to work again to pay for it. Public confidence in the currency soon disappeared. The Bankzettel soon reached a circulation of 200 million, ceased
altogether to be convertible into silver at home, and was quoted abroad at
a discount [*agio*] of 115% and more. Peace came in 1801, but was followed
by a great political transformation in Germany that cost Austria dearly; and
in 1805 the Kaiser yet again went to war. The results were not only the
military disasters of Ulm and Austerlitz, the punitive Peace of Pressburg
[Bratislava], and a new reorganization of Germany, but the raising of the
amount of paper currency in circulation to almost 450 millions (naturally
not covered) which was quoted abroad at 175. After yet another war against
Napoleon in 1809 Vienna had to pay the French an indemnity of 85 millions
in hard cash, and to raise the amount of paper currency in circulation to
846 millions, quoted abroad at 296 (later up to 469). In 1811 the government
in effect declared itself bankrupt by reducing the currency to one-fifth of
its value.[21] This was followed by a new war and a new horrendous inflation
spurred by excessive printing of paper money. Only after 1815 was a relative stabilization achieved through the establishment of a National Bank
of issue, which according to its statutes was independent of the regime.[22]

Austria's financial catastrophe in the Napoleonic era, especially the
bankruptcy of 1811, destroyed the savings of much of the lesser middle
class, of the guildsmen and the new civil servants at Vienna, but had an
opposite effect on the emergent upper bourgeoisie of wealthy Christians
and Jews. This is not to suggest that the rich ran no risks and suffered no
losses. It is rather that their risks were, like Oppenheimer's, ultimately very
profitable. In the long run, because they were indispensable to the regime,
these people could recoup their losses and then look back on what had
happened with pride of caste. Just as important in our context, moreover,
is the fact that a caste did emerge. Before the wars the Jewish bankers in
Vienna were considered and treated as a group apart. By 1815 such Jewish
houses as Arnstein and Eskeles were considered indistinguishable from
the great Swiss Protestant houses (Fries, Parish, Steiner) or from the Greek
(Sina) because all were equally indispensable to the regime.[23] In this respect
also the regime sensibly pushed integration with acts of policy. Perceiving
at the end of the wars that his dependence on the Vienna banking community was great, Franz called in a great bankhouse from outside to act
as counterweight. He selected his new ally, Salomon Rothschild, with perfect blindness towards religion; and though he refused to modify the Tolerance rules for Rothschild's convenience, he cemented the whole
Rothschild family's attachment to Vienna by pressing them all into the
"second nobility," first ennobling them, then making them all barons.[24]

V

In matters of ideology also the Jews and Christians of the Vienna upper bourgeoisie had a profoundly integrating experience in the Franciscan era. The story begins in March 1797, when after years of indecisive fighting in northern Italy, the French revolutionary armies scored a breakthrough. Led by Napoleon, they penetrated into the Austrian Tyrol and into Carinthia. By 7 April they were high in the Alps at Leoben in Styria, three short days' march from Vienna itself. Hereupon the Austrian regime, caught off guard, its armies wearied and in disarray, appealed to the Viennese to show their patriotism by volunteering to defend their homes.[25] This was the first time the Habsburgs on their own territory sought to use against the French Revolution the sort of democratic nationalist war cries that the Revolution had developed in its own defense.

Vienna's behavior in April 1797 has often struck historians as disappointing. The populace responded above all to government propaganda, according to which the French armies were a thuggish mob like that which had applauded the guillotining of Marie Antoinette. There was a panic, and everyone tried to flee. Later on certainly patriotic volunteers did flock out onto the open *Glacis* surrounding the walls of the inner city and paraded in front of the Kaiser before marching off into the lovely springtime mountains. The multitudes did thrill to the then newly published *"Gott erhalte Franz den Kaiser"*; and the town's upper bourgeoisie (and especially the Jews) footed the bill.[26] In this demonstration by the citizens of Germany's largest city, however, there was nothing remotely resembling the great eruptions of popular feeling that had frequently occurred in Paris since 1789.

In the following years events led to the spread of a more convincing popular patriotism in the Austrian lands. In 1803–04, after the first great reorganization of Germany and Napoleon's self-elevation to imperial rank, Franz declared himself "Emperor of Austria", taking on a national title for the first time. Austria was now not just the leader of a German national resistance to the French, but of a continental resistance. In Vienna hearts thrilled with *Kaisertreue*, and the population went eagerly along with the inclinations of the government. After the ignominious defeat of Prussia in 1806–07, nationally minded intellectuals from literally all over Europe (though especially from Germany) flocked to Vienna and contributed to that odd chemistry that induced poor, timid Franz to raise the banners of nationalism once again and in 1809 to provoke another disastrous though very popular war.

Yet a definitional problem hindered the Viennese in those years from developing the sort of modern secular nationalism then nascent in other parts of Europe. One may dramatize the matter as follows. The Parisians could without effort be nationalistically French, because the inhabitants of France on the whole spoke French. Correspondingly, the people of Cologne, Frankfurt, or Hamburg could then (had they been so inclined) have been patriotically German because all around them were German speakers, although there was no single German state. But for the Viennese to be nationalistic in the same way would have required them right from the start to confront the baffling political and ethnic complexity of central Europe. It was all very well to have at Vienna a German national theatre and for the respectable classes to follow Sonnenfels into speaking a proper German, or even to boast that Vienna was Germany's largest town. But to become "just German" would have meant even then for the Viennese to abandon the dialects which most of them spoke, and also the manifold tongues of the crownland populations. Much easier to declare warm allegiance to the Habsburgs (as even most of the *Reichsdeutscher* intellectuals then did), to be cool in one's patriotism, and to leave ambiguous the exact linguistic character of the all-embracing state one desired in the future to build.

As for the Habsburg regime itself, popular nationalism was almost by definition dangerous to it, and this not just because it stood for autocracy and despotism. The regime and the Kaiser personally had recent memory of how strong throughout the Empire the "national" Crownland Estates still were. In 1790 when Joseph II died, Leopold II had sought to calm the rebellious provinces by inviting all the provincial Estates to submit complaints. Virtually every one of them had responded with unwelcome vigor. The regime had at that time been able to steer between them, setting different Estates against each other. But the danger was clear in 1797: any appeal to popular nationalism in the Danubian lands might stir up again these separatist institutions of the pre-Habsburg medieval past.

Given the discomfort of the Austrian public and of the regime alike with modern nationalism, a word about the cultural development of Vienna in this period is relevant.[27] In the 1780s, when the Viennese populace had been free to write and publish political pamphlets (which it did in outrageous numbers and in bombastic form), it had expressed regrets for the Hanswürst, the old theatre in the local dialect whose drunken gaiety Josef von Sonnenfels and Joseph II had driven away. Even then little theatres had begun to spring up in cellars and awkward old buildings of the new suburbs where barely-disguised revivals of the forbidden comedy could be performed—a sort of "off-Broadway." When Kaiser Franz came to the throne he had stopped the flow of pamphlets and bad poetry, but had allowed these new theatres to survive as an outlet for what was apparently a very great popular thirst for self-expression. The three greatest of the nineteenth-century Viennese popular theatres, those of the Leopoldstadt, the Josefstadt, and the Theater an der Wien, all originated in the 1780s, and they expanded in the 1790s and after with police consent.

One reason for this theatrical renaissance of the Franciscan era was the Kaiser's personal predilection for the stage. When he was in Vienna, he is said to have attended the theatre virtually every evening; and in striking contrast to his brotherly French-speaking kings at Berlin and Saint Petersburg, he understood and spoke the dialect of his people.[28] But the other reason was the Kaiser's recognition (and that of his police) that through popular theatre, Revolution could be controlled and watched. It is in the very nature of the theatre that it *seems* free, but is not; that it *seems* real, but is manipulated; that it engages the emotions of the audience and channels them. It can be documented that long before 1797 the Viennese police encouraged the coarse, the gay, and the sentimental on the Vienna stage so as to inhibit serious political thinking.[29] As the Austrian "national" crisis began in the later 1790s, a dynamic tension emerged between the more formalistic and state-supported German-language—and German na-tionalist—*Hoftheater* and the ever more grandiose privately-run local-dialect theatres of the suburbs. The groundwork for the great age of the Viennese theatre, the age of Grillparzer, Raimund, and Nestroy, was laid during those years when the Napoleonic enemy was at the gate and the appeals to popular nationalism were being made. It was as if even then the gov-ernment wished to distract the middle classes of its greatest city from the dangerous national question by giving them something else to do. And these classes were only too happy to oblige.

Nor was this the only "distraction" the regime sponsored. Even in the late middle ages Vienna had been fanatical about music. Since the sixteenth century the court, with its Italian and Spanish connections, had patronized the popular craving and had made the city a musical capital of sorts for northern Europe. Leopold I had been a talented musician in his own right; and in the eighteenth century the great magnates of Austria had heavily subsidized musical endeavor. In the decades before 1800, Vienna became the scene of a musical revolution. Although Mozart died in poverty there in 1791, shortly after the first production of "The Magic Flute," Beethoven arrived in 1792. By the turn of the century, while Haydn was composing and presenting the great works of his old age—the "Creation" in 1798, the "Four Seasons" in 1801—Beethoven composed the symphonies of his youth: the First in 1800, the Second and Third in 1803, the Fourth in 1807, the Fifth in 1809.

As a literary historian has put it, because music has "narrower pos-sibilities of direct statement" than literary genres of self expression, it could be regarded as a harmless distraction from those other genres.[30] No sur-prise, therefore, that here also the Franciscan police regime showed re-markable tact. Indeed, the more the regime applied censorship and police methods to quiet those other genres (political literature and belles letters) during the 1790s and early 1800s, the more its support was available to music, and the broader the middle-class public allowed into the concert halls.

Then came the defeat of 1809, the rise of Metternich, Franz's decision to accommodate the French, and the financial bankruptcy of 1811. In a matter of months Austrian nationalism became both politically inconvenient because it was anti-French, and dangerous because at a moment of financial bankruptcy it acknowledged the rights of the Estates. In 1810–11 Vienna repressed the national theme and assumed the nationally neutral stance it would maintain for half a century to come: Legitimacy, Conservatism, Religion became the slogans of the day; nationalism became taboo.

As if to dull the shock of the change, which was very great, Franz's government doubled its support of the popular distractions which it had been cultivating right along. In music as in the theatre it was evident that the government preferred the sentimental, cloying tones of early Romanticism and of the waltz to the heroics of the late classic years. But it is a matter of record that to facilitate its new policies it tolerated and encouraged heroic tones too. Beethoven could and did create and produce the most "expressive" of his symphonies, the Seventh and the Ninth, during the years of the worst political reaction after 1809. And the tactic was effective. In the wake of the government's encouragement of Vienna's musical and theatrical traditions, the political behavior of that premier city's middle class consolidated on a level that struck outsiders as aggressively light-hearted, transcendently gay, not politically serious.[31] Franz Schubert now appeared upon the musical scene (1814), as did Josef Lanner (1813) and Johann Strauss (1819). Grillparzer started writing for the theatres (1817) amidst a whole galaxy of fresh young poets and dramatists. The people who could afford to do so waltzed and drank wine in the ballrooms; those who could not, danced in the street. The city whose bourgeoisie had surged so happily into politics in 1781, and which had expressed its *Kaisertreue* so bombastically in 1805 and 1809, intoxicated itself now with music and the stage.

It is useful here to point to a certain symmetry between the Franciscan retreat from nationalism in 1810 and the initial "self"-denying decisions reached by the Jews in Europe towards the end of the eighteenth century. Franz by no means abandoned the task launched by his grandmother, Maria Theresia, of building a modern Austrian state; but he decided in doing so to eschew the roots characteristic of a modern nation. Admittedly the definition of a modern Austrian "self" would have been difficult, but he decided not to try. Systematically preventing such a "self" from emerging, he gave no competition to those democratic currents of modern nationalism then stirring the ethnic groups under his rule. Was not this very like what the Jews had decided to do? At the very least it was a sort of "self"-abnegation that, through its negation of all positive national currents in the empire, gave them great opportunities.

One may judge how great from the experience of the famous Fanny Arnstein, who came to Austria as a young bride in 1776. At that time rigid social rules governed the social life of the city's upper strata. Leading gentlemen of the realm attended her salon, male visitors from abroad likewise;

but despite her enlightened ideas and lavish entertaining, ladies of high society did not visit her, nor at first did the Christian ladies of the "second nobility."[32] But then things changed.

Fanny Arnstein traveled back to Berlin fairly frequently in those early decades. This is not surprising. Her father was the leading Prussian banker, her family exceptionally prominent. In Berlin she encountered exciting people, for the ladies with whom she had grown up—the Mendelssohn daughters, her own Itzig sisters, Rahel Levin—were then playing a critical historical role by bringing together at their salons the modern-minded and innovative intellectuals from all over Germany, the heroes of the nationalistic generation then emerging: the Humbolts, the Schlegels, Schleiermacher and Schelling, Novalis, Tieck, Gentz, and even the young Börne—the inventors of the fascinating passionate and romantic German nationalism of later years. As a result, when the great Austrian turn to patriotism began in the late 1790s, it was Arnstein who pioneered the new ideas in the Austrian capital, and this made her fashionable.[33]

Further, after the great "turn" in Prussia's fate during 1806–07, many of Fanny Arnstein's anti-French nationalistic Berlin friends and acquaintances fled to Vienna, and naturally appeared at her salon. She herself participated passionately in the preparations for the war of 1809. She and her husband even took a personal interest in the fate of the Tyrol, and allowed its conspirator-patriot, Andreas Hofer, to organize from their house a rebellion against the French. All this brought them concrete social rewards. During those patriotic years the style of Viennese society changed, became more "bourgeois," less dominated by the aristocratic ladies of the court. Step by step the barriers within the "second nobility" broke down. From the early years of the century on the Christian ladies, notably the patriotic Carolina Pichler, began to receive the wealthier Jewish ladies of the town.[34] And one may generalize that Austria's experiment with nationalism in the Napoleonic period facilitated such integration throughout the "second nobility."

It was particularly the new cultural emphases in Austria's ideological development, however, that opened doors for the bourgeois Viennese Jews. Cultural activity required money, then as now; and then as now the older, aristocratic patrons were willing to grant new people a modicum of social courtesy in exchange for the opening of new money coffers. Even in the late 1770s, when Fanny Arnstein opened her salon, other members of the upper bourgeoisie—the Heniksteins, Sonnenfelses, Bienenfelds, and Wetzlars—were well known for their house-concerts and the financial emoluments they extended to leading musicians.[35] By the time of Napoleon's defeat of Prussia Fanny Arnstein was regularly giving balls and concerts at her house. Then in 1811–13, when the regime allowed Vienna's national passions to find outlet literally only through music and the theatre, she took a lead in founding a *Gesellschaft der Musikfreunde* [Society of the Friends of Music] which rapidly became one of the prime institutions of

Vienna's musical life. It was then that the new cultural development most dramatically affected the upper bourgeoisie. In her work at this musical institution, Fanny Arnstein, a Jew, was able to meet and associate with ladies of the higher aristocracy, princesses and countesses whose husbands and sons she had known for years, but who had hitherto always shut her out.

After the great turn away from nationalism in Austrian policy in 1810 Fanny Arnstein had reason (as did many others in Vienna) to feel indignant with the new course, and decided (unlike most others) to say so. She was a woman of 52 by then; she had developed (as salon ladies often do in their later years) a tendency to be outspoken, sharp. She decided not to waft with the winds but to speak her mind against the compromise with Napoleon and to castigate those responsible for the Austrian defeats. She kept up with her Prussian and now increasingly German-nationalist friends, many of whom remained at Vienna until 1813. Her daughter formed an intellectual liaison with Theodor Körner, the fiery young German poet who in 1813 found the patriotic death he craved at the battle of Leipzig. All this brought Fanny herself a severe rebuke from the police. Even loyal Nathan Arnstein was briefly arrested in this period after a police raid on a private gambling house.

Yet despite her "Prussianism" and explicit alienation from the Vienna regime after 1810, Franz I's new "nationally neutral" policy facilitated Fanny Arnstein's assimilation, and this is the most extraordinary result of the ideological development of Franciscan Vienna. The reason was in part fortuitous. Among the Prussians who fled Napoleon into the Austrian dominions after the defeat of 1806–07 were a number of intellectuals of generally conservative bent who were attracted by the Catholicism of the Habsburgs. Notable among these were the philosopher and romantic critic, Friedrich Schlegel, and his wife, Dorothea, the daughter of Moses Mendelssohn.[36] Together they had just recently converted from Protestantism into the Catholic Church, and in Vienna they very early became a focus for passionate neo-Catholic and proselytizer Catholic sentiment. In 1808 their circle was joined by a famous Slovak-born preacher and confessor, Clemens Maria Hofbauer, a leader of the monastic Redemptorist Order who for a decade had been helping the Prussians Germanize Warsaw but had been expelled from there by Napoleon.[37]

The "Hofbauer circle," as it was known, throve at Vienna after 1809. The Schlegels had a good deal of political influence because of their literary eminence; and Hofbauer himself made contacts in lofty places, because he vented anti-Josephian ideas that pleased high-placed Catholics who burningly resented Joseph II's nationalization of the Austrian Catholic Church. The new circle proved attractive at other, lower levels of society also. Its saintly preacher seemed the very opposite of the cool enlightened rationalism and "spider-like" scheming of Count Metternich, the architect of the state's new course. To follow Hofbauer was for some people a way to express resistance to the regime. Perhaps it was for this reason above all that many young Jews heard the call, and converted.

Through the Hofbauer circle whole networks of intricate relationships began to bind the Jews of the upper bourgeoisie to leading Christian circles. Fanny Arnstein now, through her friend Dorothea, gained much broader access to Vienna high society—an access symptomized by her successful introduction of the Christmas tree at Vienna in 1814.[38] But it was not only this fortuitous factor that led to Fanny Arnstein's final triumphs. A time was approaching when leading Jews would participate in Catholic religious processions in Vienna without causing surprise, and when the brother of the secretary of the newly-founded Jewish religious congregation could be a leading preacher at Saint Stephen's Cathedral. Because Kaiser Franz had turned against nationalism, even the Judeophobia which would shortly re-erupt in the *Reich* failed to erupt in the Austrian lands.[39] Under the impact of Austria's decision to eschew nationalist roots, a genuine neutrality to the Jewish question had developed at Vienna.[40]

In 1814–15, Fanny Arnstein's house became one of the principal places of relaxation for the international peacemakers at the "Congress that never met." She was particularly hospitable to the statesmen of Prussia, and many Austrian historians have been annoyed that after her decades-long residence at Vienna, she thus made her house a center of "foreign" activity.[41] For different reasons her behavior has annoyed Jewish historians. They cannot understand why, if she had so much energy to devote to Prussian interests, she "neglected" the final emancipation of the German Jews.[42] In our context, however, the real significance of Fanny Arnstein's performance at the Vienna Congress is its illustration of how the ideological evolution of Napoleonic Austria had facilitated the integration of Jews into Vienna's upper bourgeoisie. Before the wars, before 1792, the bourgeoisie had played quite literally no social role in Vienna. The high court aristocracy had then been the whole thing. In 1815 the leadership of Viennese society had passed not just to a wealthy member of the upper bourgeoisie, but to a lady who was still a Jew, and a Prussophile to boot.

These were fluid times, of course. Later on the ladies of the imperial aristocracy retreated from the "second nobility" contacts. By 1830 Vienna's "first society" had hermetically sealed itself off again from the *misera plebs* of the upper bourgeoisie, and would remain so until 1918.[43] But by then the damage had been done: a part-Jewish, part-Christian "second nobility" had achieved a life of its own based on the integrative experience of 1797–1815.

VI

Often enough historians rank the post-1790 Austrian turn against "Revolution" and "Progress" as an unhealthy development, a dark page of European history that boded ill for all the continent's peoples, especially for those of the center and the east. Yet in this chapter we have seen how coincident with that turn, at the very center of Austria, a small Jewish-Christian "neutral society" crytalized, compounding and enlarging the footholds earlier afforded modernizing Jews by the work of Maria Theresia and Joseph II. Even though only a few wealthy Jews were involved, was not this advantageous from the Jewish point of view? Was not this a positive step towards the broad modernization of the Jewish people under Habsburg rule?

Nor is this the whole of it. In the annals of modern assimilation the norm has been for a "visitor" people to cleave to a well-defined "host," for one identity simply to give way to another. In the Austrian Empire at the start of the nineteenth century, because of Franz I's decisions, a different enterprise was undertaken. Coincident with the Jewish bourgeois efforts to assimilate, the "host" decided not to build up its own identity, but instead to build it down; not to overwhelm the "visitor" with clouds of positive nationalism, but in effect to ease the transition by making few demands on the visitor's old identity. Was not this advantageous to the mass of Habsburg Jewry?

It seems fair to judge that because of this parallelism between Austrians and Jews, a conscious historical experiment was undertaken by the Vienna Jewish elite in the Arnsteins' day. It is important to distinguish here between the perspective of historians and that of contemporaries—between what we can see and what they could. Nathan Arnstein and his wife were not modern sociologists! Nonetheless, contemporaries knew perfectly well that the Franciscan regime was specifically abstemious in matters of developing its own nationhood; and if the Arnsteins as individuals happened to be advocates of a German national course, and against Metternich, they and everyone in their circle ardently favored Austrian "neutralism" in so far as it affected Jews. By collaborating with Austria, they expected to gain. Theirs was a bourgeois experiment, of course. There were no Jewish masses in Vienna then, and the Arnsteins did not press for the betterment of those masses. But in those days of limited modern education, the bourgeoisie swung weight, and was much more "representative" of the masses than later on. And the experiment at Vienna certainly paid off for the happy few.

FIVE

Bohemian Breakthrough

I

In 1833 Baron Rothschild rented a huge estate at Witkowitz in Austrian Silesia from the Archbishop of Olmütz. (Because of the legal restrictions on Jews, he couldn't yet buy it.) Not only did this involve him in the development of an iron works there as a mainstay of his wealth; it also brought him into contact with Franz Xavier Riepl, a young engineer who had recognized the possibilities of developing Silesian coal and iron production if rail transport were on hand. The contact led to a most characteristic phenomenon of the Metternich Era: the building of Austria's railroads.[1] In the 1820s the Greek banker Sina had financed a horse-drawn line from Budweis [Budějovice] in southern Bohemia to Linz on the Danube, but it was Rothschild who introduced steam when in 1835–36 he started construction of the *Kaiser Ferdinand Northern Railroad Stock Company* or *Nordbahn* from Vienna to Silesia. The first stretch of track was opened in 1837. By 1839 Rothschild had linked Vienna to Brno, the textile center of the empire. In the 1840s, the state itself began to build lines. By 1848 the capital was linked with Prague, Bratislava, and the Prussian railroad system in Silesia. Austria by then was only slightly behind France in railroad mileage and stood in the forefront of European rail construction.

Not only railroads: the start of the industrial revolution characterized this politically reactionary era in Austria. One may best sense its modernizer dynamism from tycoon careers such as Alexander Schoeller's. Born in 1805 at Düren in the Rhineland into an old Protestant patrician family of that city, Schoeller came to Brno in 1823 in response to massive dislocations in his family's wool-weaving business.[2] First, the incorporation of Düren into Napoleon's empire brought the firm a huge new reservoir of customers in northern Italy; then the fall of Napoleon, the Prussianization of the Rhineland, the cutting off of northern Italy from Germany by Austria's prohibitive tariffs, and the reentry of cheap British textiles onto the continent all threatened the firm with ruin. At the Congress of Aachen in 1818, therefore, Schoeller's uncles obtained from Franz I a permit to establish a branch of their firm at Austria's woolen-weaving capital, so that they could keep on provisioning their old Italian clientèle.

Schoeller was resented by the guildsmen weavers who dominated

Brno, but with his imperial privilege he escaped their rules. He made the most of the Greater Austrian markets, and within ten years he could afford to leave the factory in Brno to his subordinates. He himself now moved to Vienna as a Grosshändler. Within a second decade he had become one of the major Austrian importers of cloth-dyes, and had made his woolens factory independent of the Düren firm. He then got as deeply involved as did the Viennese Jewish Grosshändler in the export of Hungarian wool and Italian silk. By 1840 he was also dealing in barrel staves and other lumber products from Hungary, was going into banking, and had gotten into real estate in Vienna. Then in 1843 he turned back to manufacturing and set up first a brass factory, then (with his friend Hermann Krupp of Essen) a metalworks at Berndorf in Lower Austria where he manufactured cutlery and eventually guns. By 1848 Schoeller was deep also in the refining of sugar beets in Moravia and Hungary and was managing an already huge industrial empire.

The industrial revolution did not come with as much éclat to the Habsburg Empire as it did in western Europe. There was no true boom-time between 1815 and 1848. In fact there were periods of deep depression at the start and end of the era. There were years of bad harvests in between. The cholera ravished the population in the 1830s. The weight of serfdom remained (and brought on a great peasant revolt in 1846 in Galicia). In the 1840s the factories of industrial Bohemia were strike-plagued, foreshadowing the revolutionary outburst of 1848. Nonetheless, surely and steadily industrialization did begin, transforming the Styrian, Moravian, Lower Austrian, and north Bohemian towns in particular, everywhere producing a new entrepreneurial bourgeois social element and challenging the guildsman of the past. And all this was done with the participation of the state. Indeed, the new industrialists were eager to be protected from excess of competition: in 1833–34 many of them did their share in obtaining Austria's self-exclusion from the German *Zollverein*.[3]

How did this aspect of the repressive Franciscan era affect Habsburg Jewry? Did Jews other than Rothschild significantly contribute to the Empire's industrial growth? Did they become industrialists? Was the new industrial bourgeoisie of the Austrian provinces as accommodating to them as the "second nobility" of the capital? What of the rest of Austrian provincial society? These are the essential questions of this chapter. To obtain answers we will focus on developments in just one rather "advanced" region, the Bohemian Crown lands, the old core-land of Habsburg Jewry.

II

For the essence of the story, one must go back to where we left the Bohemian Jews in an earlier chapter: to the epoch of Ezekiel Landau, the seemingly latitudinarian Oberrabbiner of Prague. We can start with a key event.[4] When in the fall of 1781 Rabbi Landau heard about Kaiser Joseph's

new Bohemian Judenpatent, he decided, despite the Kaiser's explicit can-
cellation of many old Jewish self-governmental rights, to give the new laws
public welcome. What is more, together with Joachim Popper, the Primator
of the Bohemian Rural Jews, and Löbl Duschenes, Primator of the Prague
Jews, he actively collaborated in the fateful project of establishing a Jewish
German-language modern school at Prague. And so he continued through
the decade. Even in 1788, when Joseph decided to require military service
of the Bohemian Jews, Landau and the primators cooperated, though this
was a matter of high alarm for practicing Jews. They obtained the government's agreement that normally Jewish recruits would be employed only
in the commissary service, where their religious requirements could most
easily be met. Then Landau himself appeared at the induction center to
bless the first 25 Austrian-Jewish military inductees. One may not deduce
from this record that Landau accepted all Enlightenment. From the early
1780s he assumed an increasingly conservative stance against the Haskalah
of Berlin Jewry, refusing his approval, for example, to Mendelssohn's translation of the Pentateuch. In all probability he endorsed Joseph II's program
largely out of traditional Jewish deference to acts of the State. Yet because
of his endorsements, Bohemian Jewry's embrace of modern education was
remarkably whole-hearted.

The Jewish German-language *Normalschule* at Prague accepted both
boys and girls and early on was visited by as many as 215 boys and 63
girls in one year. Altogether some 17,800 children attended between 1790
and 1831, about 424 a year.[5] Under governmental pressure many other
Jewish communities set up schools; and throughout the Bohemian Lands
the state encouraged Jews to attend Christian elementary schools instead
of going to the *Hederim* of the past. As early as the 1790s there were enough
graduates of the new schools to provide the government with the Jewish
teachers needed for a network of Jewish schools in Galicia. However ill-
trained and clumsy these graduates were in the east, they were sure evidence of how change was affecting the Jews of the Bohemian Lands. And
meanwhile the sheer cosmopolitanism of Rabbi Landau's Prague encouraged the emergence of an enlightened Jewish intelligentsia there. By the
1790s a group of young enlightened Prague Jews were carrying on great
literary debates with the Mendelssohnians at Berlin. One historian has
perceived them as verging on an enlightened sort of Jewish secular nationalism, for they were critical of the Berlin Jews as too anti-traditionalist.
Despite their modernism they evidently felt obligations to the great mass
of Jewish people.[6]

Did modernism go unopposed at Prague after 1781? One may ask
because Prague had hitherto been a major center of Ashkenazic Jewish
learning, and at other such centers a reaction against the Enlightenment
unfolded after 1781. The answer is that opposition did appear, but late and
in weak form.

In the spring of 1790, for example, the rabbis of Prague were provoked by a petition that Primator Popper had addressed to the throne requesting the promulgation of a new Bohemian Judenpatent. The old patent, issued by Joseph II on 15 October 1781, had been the first such decree the Kaiser had penned, and (reflecting his early hesitancy) had left intact the limitation that Karl VI had imposed on Jewish marriages, a restriction infinitely burdensome to every Bohemian Jew. After 1781, morever, Joseph had issued piecemeal a great deal of supplementary legislation affecting the Jews, for example the edict subjecting them to military service and a regulation giving them the right to acquire real estate. There was a real need for codification of all this and for its confirmation by the new ruler, who was systematically trying to put his realm in order; and, as Popper pointed out, there was a simple method by which the confusion could be dispelled. Joseph had issued in 1789 a Judenpatent for Galicia which made no provision for marriage control and which incorporated a good deal of the piecemeal legislation. Why should not Leopold simply extend this Galician patent to the Bohemian Lands?[7]

Just three days after Popper submitted his petition, a group of seven Prague Jews, who were in Vienna for market purposes, submitted a counter-petition opposing the extension of the Galician patent to Bohemia on the ground that it would confirm the subjection of the Jews there to military service, which these businessmen abhorred. A few days later in Prague itself another group, led by Rabbi Samuel Landau, the Oberrabbiner's second son, drew up yet a third petition, requesting this time a general repeal of Joseph's negation of the force of Talmudic Law, and also the return of Jewish marriages from civil to rabbinical courts. This was handed to the Kaiser on 24 May with 34 signatures, and was followed by a fourth petition detailing this same group's objections to Jewish military service. Hereupon Popper came back with an elaboration of his own document, signed by 68 leading Prague Jews.

All this Jewish petitioning and counter-petitioning in 1790 at Prague surely attests a welling discontent there with the Enlightenment. But the most interesting aspect of it is the absence of any clear petitioner categories. Evidently after almost a decade of sniping at "modernism," rabbinical conservatism was only just then beginning to result in separate "orthodox" and "reform" groups there.[8]

Shortly after the petitioning episode, a series of changes occurred that might have led to a great strengthening of Jewish conservatism in the Bohemian capital. The first was Austria's change in regime. In 1792 when Kaiser Franz II mounted the throne, Rabbi Landau and the primators petitioned once again for a new statute to replace the Patent of 1781, which Leopold had never gotten around to revising. Franz hesitated. A new Patent did not appear until 1797, and characteristically of the reign it retained virtually all the noxious regulations of the old one. The hopes of the Prague reformers remained thus unfulfilled.[9] Meanwhile in 1793 and 1795 respectively Rabbi Landau and Primator Popper died. Their departure seemed to leave two conservative rabbis, Eleazar Flekeles and Samuel Landau, in charge. Third, the oppressive new police regime affected the more modern minded, and a wave of conversions began that could only undermine the Jewish reformers. One of the first to convert, for example, was Karl Joel, who was the apple of the Prague reformers' eye because in 1790 he had forced the Prague University to give him a degree in law, breaking thus a major barrier against Jewish modern education. Joel abandoned his faith at Vienna in 1797.[10] Conversions occurred at the turn of the century in enlightened Berlin too. There, indeed, David Friedländer, one of the civic leaders of the community and self-proclaimed intellectual heir of Moses Mendelssohn, seriously considered precipitating a mass defection from Judaism in hopes of facilitating Prussian social acceptance of the Jews.

Conversion out of Judaism was a much rarer offense to Jewry in those days than it is now. To conservatives, it seemed tantamount to death. Consequently one might well enough understand if, in the face of such behavior by prominent modernist Jews late in the eighteenth century, faithful Jews had rallied to a stricter observance. Yet such a resurgence of conservatism did not just then capture the Jewish community at Prague for several reasons, of which one was surely a surprising and distractive eruption of Frankism.

During the years after his expulsion from Brno in 1786 Jakob Frank had increasingly stressed the religious aspect—the cabalistic rites and authoritarian discipline—of his sect and spoke more and more about the approaching end of the world.[11] Upon his death his children, left on their own and perhaps bewildered by the responsibilities of leadership, became specific about when the fatal moment predicted by their father would occur. They began to circulate a *roter Zettel*. Today we might call it a "Red Book" like Mao Tse Tung's: it indicated that the coincidence of the Christian year 1800 with the Jewish year 5560, which had cabalistic significance, would bring the critical turning point in the history of the Jews.

Ezekiel Landau had suspected the presence of a Frankist following in his city in the early 1790s, and had interrogated a number of leading Jews about it. They swore to him they were not heretics, and perhaps at that moment there actually were rather few Prague Frankists. There is no doubt, however, that those few were prominent. Such names as Wehle, Mauthner, Hönig, Bondi, and Zerkowitz, the cream of late-eighteenth-century Jewish Prague, can be associated with the sect. During the 1790s moreover world events lent spectacular justification to the Frankish prognosis, and the Prague membership multiplied. The French Revolution swept aside the entrenched institutions of western Europe, and made it seem as if a new world actually could be constructed. In 1798–99 Napoleon appeared in Egypt and Palestine. Frankist propaganda (and perhaps specifically Bohemian Frankist propaganda) began to claim that this was a preparation for the Jewish return to the Promised Land. Excitement began to spread. Finally, just before the Jewish New Year in 1800, the Prague Frankists made themselves known and called upon all Jews to prepare for the imminent Final Day.

For a century and more Sabbatianism had been anathema in the learned Jewish circles of central Europe. The discovery of the horrible infection in Prague caused consternation among the conservative rabbis. When the Frankists revealed themselves, rabbis Samuel Landau and Flekeles, not content with fulmination and the issuance of a ban, intervened personally to drive the Frankists from the synagogues and ritual baths. They encouraged demonstrations in the streets and came close to violence. Hereupon the Austrian police intervened and it was the two rabbis, not their enemies, who spent some days in a Christian prison.

This was one reason why Jewish conservatism failed at this time to capture the Prague community. Another, no doubt, was that the Austrian government, for all its own conservatism, was still vigorously strengthening its own sinews, and had no interest in restoring administrative autonomy to the Jews. What is more, to the distress of traditionalist Jews, the government pressed the cause of modern Jewish education. In Prague after 1810, for example, it installed two outstandingly "enlightened" Jewish intellectuals as teachers in the *Normalschule*: Peter Beer and Herz Homberg. Naturally there can be no question here of Kaiser Franz supporting Liberalism. To Beer personally the appointment to the Prague school in 1811 no doubt seemed redeeming. Because of his liberal views, he had been in village exile for over a decade, teaching at his home town in rural Bohemia. To Homberg, however, Prague was a major come-down. As we will see in a later chapter, he began his career in Galicia. After 1807 the Kaiser decided he was too modern-minded to be tolerated either there or in Vienna and sent him to Prague by way of banishment. Moreover there was certainly no freedom in their teaching. Like all other schools in Austria in the Franciscan era, the Jewish schools were subject to strict oversight by Vienna. Kaiser Franz did not intend to free Beer and Homberg in Prague to spread some poison of new ideas; he intended to compel their participation on a prosaic day-to-day level in the education of the Jewish masses.[12]

From a traditionalist Jewish perspective, however, the Kaiser's purpose could not have gone more wrong. Both men were authoritarian personalities, men of extensive teaching experience and very pronounced modern views. Moreover, they were not teaching the richer Jewish children, who tended to visit the Christian schools or private tutors, but rather the poor and the middling ones who still lived in the Jewish quarter. Since both were elderly when they arrived in Prague, perhaps they left a good deal of work to assistants and subordinates. But both stayed around for a considerable time. Beer lived until 1838, Homberg until 1841. Both were active as reformers not just of the schools, but of the ritual in the Prague synagogues; and they contributed their energies to the emergence of a Society for the Improvement of the Ritual among like-minded Prague Jews.[13] All in all, precisely because of their shackles, they constituted a bridge of sorts between the enlightened and the poor. As long as they were there, kept at their posts by the regime despite rabbinical objections, the pillars of Jewish Tradition would be undermined. And to extrapolate, the regime's support of the German-Jewish schooling outside Prague, in rural Bohemia, and in small-town Moravia had a similar subversive effect.

It is difficult to identify specific results of this sort of govermental intervention into the affairs of Jewish Bohemia, but there are some convenient rough measures of the changes that occurred. One has to do with Prague's Jewish schools. In Ezekiel Landau's day, as noted earlier, Prague's Jewish schools had been a Mecca for eastern Jewish scholars. By mid-nineteenth century these schools were in desuetude, and the Hungarian students were flocking to the new conservative *yeshivot* at Bratislava instead.[14] A second measure has to do with S. J. L. Rapoport, a famed scholar from Galicia who became rabbi at Prague in 1840 and dominated the city's Jewry until his death in 1867. In Galicia Rapoport was considered a radical reformer, a Jew so enlightened that he was hounded into exile by the Orthodox. In Prague, however, he was seen as a conservative, a pillar of Jewish probity who would not relax his ties with tradition. The intellectual atmosphere in the city's Jewry was now deeply divided from the Jewry in the east.[15]

In this connection we may point to a decisive demographic fact that affected the whole of Habsburg Jewish history in mid-century.[16] Immediately after the ending of the *Familiantengesetz* residence restrictions in 1848–49 and the abolition of the Prague ghetto in 1853, the Jewish population of both Bohemia and Moravia showed extraordinary mobility. Jewish desertion of the countryside was especially conspicuous. By the 1860s and 1870s, many small Jewish communities in the rural southwest of Bohemia were largely deserted, whereas the industrial regions of the northern border towns where Jews had never been allowed before now found themselves the home of a considerable Jewish population. Moreover, a root cause of the rapid growth of Vienna Jewry after 1848 seems to have been immigration by Jews from rural Bohemia and Moravia.[17] In all the places where the Bohemian and Moravian Jewish population immigrated after 1848, the immigrants were perceived not as tradition-bound country-folk but as mobilized and adaptable recruits to modern urban society. Such a massive demographic transformation of Bohemian Jewry is hard to explain save in terms of a widespread and effective impact of the Josephian school system during the Franciscan era.[18]

III

With this general developmental pattern in mind, let us turn to the main subject of this chapter: the extent to which Jewry participated in the industrial revolution in the Bohemian Crownlands, and the extent to which it affected them. What of the earliest period?

Bohemia and Moravia had even in the eighteenth century been the industrial heartland of the Habsburg realm, this in part because of the natural wealth of these provinces, in part because of their favorable position vis à vis the West.[19] And a single statistic suggests clearly why they became even more so in the early nineteenth century as the Theresian and Josephian reforms loosened the feudal regime: in these lands about 1800, there was only one noble for every 832 commoners, an exceedingly low ratio for eastern Europe. In Austria's Alpine lands, in contrast, the ratio was one noble to every 320 commoners; in Galicia it was 1:68, and in Hungary, the gentry paradise, it was 1:20.[20] Because of the eviction of the Protestant nobility from Bohemia in the 1620s, there was late in the eighteenth century no gentry class in these crownlands, as there was to the east—and this had a practical consequence. It meant that there was no one to fight tooth and claw for every inch of land, for every ancient privilege, no one to insist that the peasantry remain enserfed and illiterate on the land. Feudalism in Bohemia had lain for two centuries with German-speaking magnates and the Counter-Reformational Church. The new enlightened state proved its ability to handle these powers even in Maria Theresia's time, and under Joseph II it limited serfdom here far more effectively than anywhere in the East. From 1790 on, as a result, there existed a part-free labor force in these lands, and the gates for industrial development were open.

For Jews it was nonetheless inordinately difficult to participate in industrial enterprise. The case history of Samuel Kolin of Prossnitz [Postějov] in Moravia tells clearly enough why.[21] Kolin was a cloth-trader who came to that small-town Jewish settlement from Bohemia in 1752 in order to marry. Moravia was the textile manufacturing center of the Habsburg realm. Though Jews were barred from the larger cities, much of the retail trade in textiles was in their hands; yet Kolin found the industry almost impenetrable. Manufacturing and sales alike were tightly controlled and regulated by the Christian townsmen and their guilds. Guild regulation, the expense of new machinery, and the weakness of the domestic market had proved and would prove over and again insuperable obstacles even for Christian entrepreneurs, not to speak of Jews despite much encouragement from the government. Kolin tried to make his living by buying woolen cloth from wealthy importers, and then selling it by the piece to peddlers who would evade the sales monopoly of Christian shopkeepers by hawking the goods in the countryside from door to door. But in 1758 Maria Theresia sought to help domestic textile manufacturers by forbidding Jews to peddle imports; and in 1764 she placed a ban on textile imports. By the time she relaxed the bans in 1774, the whole class of Jews who had lived on the woolens import trade was close to ruin, saved only by smuggling, which was made profitable by the paucity and poor quality of the domestic products. Kolin himself went bankrupt a first time in 1779, and a second time in 1789 after Joseph II reimposed the ban on foreign products and placed dozens of other regulations on his trade.

Such was the fate in the eighteenth century of the lesser Jews of Bohemia and Moravia. In general they were condemned to eke out a living by trading goods or dealing in money, forced by the residence restrictions to spend much of their lives traveling. Even after Joseph commanded that they go into manufacturing, they were far too exposed both to every whim of a regulationist government and to the mean-minded complaints of Christian neighbors to do so. Those among them who managed to escape the general misery were rare. An astonishing continuity characterizes the professional profile of Bohemian and Moravian Jewry throughout the nineteenth century. Commerce remained overwhelmingly dominant (though much less so than in Germany, where Jews were not permitted to engage in *Handwerk*).[22] Important changes took place in the organization of Jewish commerce about 1800, especially in tobacco trading. The establishment under a Jew, Israel Hönig, of the State Tobacco Monopoly in 1788 led to a notable bureaucratization of trade relationships among Bohemian Land village Jews.[23] Yet it seems notable that Simon Laemmel, the greatest banker among the Bohemian Jews in the first half of the nineteenth century, was a figure not much changed from the Joachim Poppers of the late eighteenth.[24]

Under Joseph II and after, when modern manufacturing actually began in Austria, some Jews in the Bohemian Crownlands began to get involved. One was the son of Samuel Kolin, who bore the German name Veith Ehrenstamm. In the middle 1780s this son responded to the disaster of his father's ruin by shifting from the *Schnittwarenhandel* [piece-ware trade] of his forebears into contracting with the army for provisions needed in Joseph II's second Turkish war. It is not clear from the record why he did especially well, for he differed from the great military provisioners of the past in that he did not inherit his credit relationships. He was a self-made man. But as the Napoleonic wars drew on, he worked his way up from the bottom to become one of the most important Austrian contractors. He seems to have dealt eventually in most anything the treasury could ask: in salt and tobacco, wine, grain, horses and carts for transport, food for the soldiers, liqueurs and shiny brasses for the officers. But his speciality was uniforms. By 1805–06 he was in some sort of partnership with Simon Laemmel, the leading Jewish banker of Prague mentioned above, and evidently enjoyed a near monopoly on providing uniforms for the army. It was preparatory for this that in 1801 Ehrenstamm took the very modern step of purchasing a woolen cloth factory at Prossnitz from a Christian manufacturer. Thenceforth he was involved not only in the purchasing of cloth but also in its production and in the sewing together of the uniforms themselves. By the end of the wars he was immensely rich. He owned a whole collection of industrial establishments and was able to entertain the neighborhood nobility in flamboyant style at his Prossnitz house. His business even managed to survive (though not for long) the postwar depression which ruined many other Moravia manufacturers.

Though Ehrenstamm's case proves Moravian Jews could get into industry, there were few in that crownland who followed his example. The Tolerance Patent of 1781 had explicitly opened manufacturing to the Jews. Despite all the regulation, despite even the need for considerable capital and the perils of the trade, opportunities were available. Even the Judeophobic literature of the time sometimes advised Jews to go into industry on the ground that only they had the zeal, the cleverness, the persistence, and the money sense needed for success.[25] Yet as one student of the problem has observed, the Jews in Moravia just did not seem interested in industry.[26] There were even wealthy Jewish businessmen of Moravia who won wealth and influence enough during the Napoleonic period to buy permission to live in Brno, the center of the woolens industry; the Gomperzes and Auspitzes come to mind in this connection. Yet until the 1840s they remained aloof from industry.

One reason for this was assuredly the fanatical opposition of the Christian guildsmen of the region, who controlled manufacturing. And it seems well also to recall the distinctive cultural situation of the Moravian Jews. Here, as noted elsewhere, the Jews were not spread out in villages as in Bohemia, nor were they concentrated in one huge city as in Prague. Even in the early nineteenth century only one or two exceptionally rich families were allowed to live in Brno, Moravia's only significant city, where, as we have seen, they could encounter the likes of Jakob Frank. Most were forced to live in tight small-town communities, and were consequently singularly exposed to the conformity normal in such places. In addition the province had the unusually strong autonomous Jewish self-government system mentioned earlier. The powers of the Moravian *Landesoberrabbiner* had been consolidated far more over the centuries than had those of the Prague chief rabbi. They were formidable even after the Josephian legislation abolished the force of Jewish civic law. In Veith Ehrenstamm's time, moreover, from 1789 until 1829 the Moravian Oberrabbiner was Mordekai Ben Abraham Banet, one of the foremost neo-conservative defenders of Jewish-tradition in central Europe, a famous Talmudist Banet high-handedly kept his flock in order. He fulminated against those who fled to Vienna, growled even at those who spent too much time studying Christian learning. Moravian Jewry's failure to change profession and to go into manufacturing may attest to the strength of such cultural factors as well as the economic factors and hostility of the entrenched Christian bourgeois world to Jews.[27]

In Bohemia there was a much greater Jewish response to Joseph II's pressure to go into manufacturing. Here the start of industrialization centered not on woolens production, as in Moravia, but on cotton.[28] For decades before 1800 Christian businessmen had been observing the miracles of the cotton industry in England. In the 1770s the Austrian Government had made cotton-manufacturing a free trade, exempt from the guild regulations that continued to dominate the older woolens industry. Christian manufacturers, most notably the former serf Johann Josef Leitenberger

(1730–1803) and his son Franz (17??–1825), had in 1799 imported the first English Watter-frames and mule-jennies to Austria; and in the Napoleonic period (especially after 1806 when British manufactures were on the whole cut out from the continent), these Austrian entrepreneurs drew on Balkan cotton to make the production of cotton cloth one of the Empire's leading industries.

The Christian cotton industrialists, however, operated primarily in the towns of northern Bohemia, near the Saxon frontier. In Prague it was above all Jews who made this new industry grow. Another case history will illustrate the phenomenon. Moses Porges was born in 1781 into a humble Jewish family that produced rosewater in the Prague ghetto; his brother Juda (later called Leopold) was born in 1784.[29] When they first went into business shortly before 1800, Moses dealt in linen goods, Juda spirits, and they wholly lacked capital. Yet by 1808 they had opened a small calico and chintz printing shop in a dark cellar in the unsanitary old center of Prague. Textile-printing was more important than it now sounds. Until the decisive spread of mechanical spinning in the 1830s and 1840s, most of the actual spinning and weaving of textiles took place on a piecework basis in cottages. The dyeing and printing were the parts of textile production most suited to the factory, and they became the locus of modern innovations in the industry as a whole. The Porgeses were innovators. By 1819 their establishment was quite large. In 1830 they opened the first great mechanical cotton printery at the Prague industrial suburb, Smíchow, a plant so splendid that the Kaiser visited it in 1833. By 1835 they were employing 569 workers; by 1843, 700. Their factory was then the third largest in Bohemia and they had other plants as well.

The first known Jewish cotton printing plant at Prague was established in the Karlín [Karolinenthal] suburb in the 1790s by a Koppelmann Porges. Whether he was related to Moses and Juda is unknown, but by 1820 his plant also was among the largest in the crownland. Meanwhile in 1802 Aaron Beer Pribram and Moses Jerusalem, wealthy Grosshändler, had entered the industry, as had Meir Dormitzer, the wealthy descendent of a famous early-eighteenth-century Jewish scholar; so also members of the Epstein and Mauthner families, and of the Taussig, Bunzl, Brandeis, Wehle, Lederer, Lippmann and Schick families, all of them eminent in Prague. A convenient statistic reveals that by 1807 Bohemia had 58 linen, cotton, and calico "factories" of which 15 (all recently established and near Prague) were Jewish owned.[30]

It seems legitimate to attribute this vigorous expression of Jewish modernism at Prague, along with the others mentioned earlier, in part to the city's latitudinarian rabbinical leadership. But it is useful to reflect also on the record of Frankism, for late in the eighteenth century the members of the sect in another city, Warsaw, did similar things. They turned from their earlier aspiration for ennoblement and became leaders of the economic modernization of the city—and of Poland.[31] So pronounced was their

group coherence (maintained by significant endogamy) and their dominance in the "bourgeois" professions of the city (that is, law, education,
and manufacturing) that they can be held up as a fine example of how a
"religious ethic" leads to modern capitalism. Given the strength of Frankism in Prague about 1800, this record is more than suggestive, especially
since it is known that Moses and Juda Porges were the sons of a Frankist,
and that they themselves visited the Frankist court at Offenbach in the
final years of the eighteenth century just when another Porges was establishing the first Jewish cotton-printing establishment in Prague.

The Prague Frankists did not follow exactly the same path as those of
Warsaw. These people had not converted out of Judaism as had the Warsaw
Frankists. After the fiasco of 1800 they did nurture a memory of their earlier
religious deviation, and may have for a time practiced endogamy, but in
general they could and did reabsorb into the mainstream of Prague Jewry.
By the end of the nineteenth century their descendants were so averse to
the group's tradition that they tried to destroy whatever documents remained of what had happened, to root out Frankism even as a memory.[32]
Nonetheless circumstance indicates that at the beginnings of the Jewish
involvement in Prague's industrial growth, Frankism, with its loosening
attitude towards Jewish Tradition, played a role.

I V

The entry of Jews into industry in the Bohemian lands, and especially their
entry into the Prague cotton industry, is important to any assessment of
their record here under Metternich, for it had social consequences. The
Prague cotton industry was the "take-off sector" of sorts of the industrial
revolution in Bohemia during the Vormärz. By 1835 there were 117 cotton-
processing establishments in the crownland, of which 15 of the largest were
in Prague and owned by Jews. The industry by now produced annually
1,400,000 pieces of cloth (at lengths of 30–50 ells), of which 800,000 lengths
were produced in Prague.[33] Not unnaturally, therefore, here as in Vienna,
the leaders of this industry were able to enter the ranks of the imperial
bourgeoisie and to win a considerable acceptance.[34] By the 1840s the Porges
brothers and their partner Moses Jerusalem had been ennobled by the
Kaiser and were among the leaders of Prague's new bourgeois society. No
less socially prominent were the Dormitzers, Epsteins, Mauthners, and
Wehles. Some rich Jews, for example Moritz Zdekauer, had felt it requisite
to leave Judaism in order to attain their new social position; but this was
patently not demanded of them by the Prague upper bourgeoisie (or by
people like Schoeller elsewhere in the Bohemian Lands), for the very leader
of Prague's industrial bourgeoisie through forty years was Leopold von
Laemmel, the son of the great Napoleonic era banker, Simon Laemmel,
who had been ennobled in 1821. The Laemmels did not convert.[35] Even
in Brno, it may be mentioned, the Jewish banker, Philip Gomperz, won a

considerable acceptance in upper bourgeois circles during the Franciscan period, though most of his co-religionaries were barred by law from residence in the city.[36]

In this period, moreover, there occurred a massive shift in relationships between Vienna and Prague that contributed to the acceptance of Jews in bourgeois society. Above all there was a demographic change. In 1790 Prague, with 73,000 civilian inhabitants, was still a considerable town even against Vienna's 200,000. But whereas by 1850 Vienna had doubled to 400,000, Prague in 1820 had only 81,000 inhabitants, and in 1850, 115,599.[37] This demographic lag was compounded by the increase in political centralism, characteristic of the regime, and by an expansion of Vienna's financial power. In effect, the more the industrial revolution intruded into the Empire, the more the Vienna bankers—the capitalists—gained leverage in provincial affairs. The decline of Prague relative to the capital did not become final until after 1848; but for practical purposes even in the *Vormärz* Bohemia's capital was in international perspective no more than a provincial Austrian town. On the level of the new upper bourgeoisie one may see the new relationship especially clearly. Starting with Simon Laemmel and Philip Gomperz in Napoleon's time, virtually all the great Bohemian trading and banking firms opened offices in Vienna. In the 1840s the Prague manufacturers followed suit, first opening factory outlets, then building new factories in the capital suburbs. Few of them moved finally away from Prague; but in general sufficient duality of foothold developed so as to ensure that the new social values of upper bourgeois Vienna prevailed also in upper bourgeois Prague.[38]

The bourgeois successes of the Prague Jewish industrialists had noxious effects for the whole of Bohemian Jewry, because they awoke jealousies, and above all those of the city's workers. In Bohemia, as further west in Europe, the industrial revolution produced a whole new stratum of workers within the social system.[39] There is small mystery why by the early 1840s this stratum was showing its discontents. All over Europe during the early industrial revolution, working conditions were awful, and the Bohemian lands were no exception. Wages were pathetically low. Fifteen- and fourteen-hour workdays were the norm; the work-week comprised six or more days. Worker health and relaxation were of little matter to the factory-owners, whose prime concern was maximal profit, whose rule was exploitation. With the advent of mechanization in the thirties, moreover, employers began to oust adult workers in favor of children, who were cheaper, and as a result unemployment developed.[40] In the forties such new machines as the perrotin in the cotton-printing industry put whole classes of workers out of jobs. The year 1843 witnessed a large-scale strike at Brno.

The following year, 1844, was one of labor unrest all over Germany, and saw major troubles affect Bohemia. The spark, so far as one can determine from the surviving records, was a worker uprising in Prussian Silesia in early June—the uprising that inspired Gerhard Hauptmann's "Die Weber." In mid-June, despite the sealed frontier, labor trouble erupted in Prague. Later in the month and in July it spread to the northern textile regions. Everywhere, as in Silesia, the workers seemed interested above all in destroying machines. In Prague, the workers expressed a hatred not just of machines, but also of Jews.

In 1844 the authorities called out troops in defense of property. The strikes were all suppressed. But the Judeophobia lasted on. In the late forties, as bad harvest followed bad harvest all over Europe, strikes and attacks on Jewish grain-dealers ceased to be unusual at all in central Bohemia. There was an "objective" explanation: there was near famine in the land, and the grain commerce was in Jewish hands. When the burgher revolution broke out in March 1848, the danger of renewed labor trouble was immediately in everyone's mind. One of the explicit purposes of the new "national guard" in the capital was to exert control over the "proletariat," and indeed the workers soon began to demonstrate. In the first days of May, urged on by a flood of anti-Jewish pamphlet literature, large-scale Judeophobic riots affected Prague starting with attacks on the Jewish-owned factories. Later on, especially in June when the Prague workers formed the backbone of the so-called "Whitsun" uprising occasioned by the Slavic Congress, the Judeophobic motif abated. Periodically during the summer and fall, however, as the imperial army took command first in Bohemia and then in other lands, new anti-Jewish disturbances occurred.[41]

A main reason for the Prague worker Judeophobia of this period was a singularly direct relation between bad work conditions and Jews. In Prague the strikes began in 1844, because the Porges brothers introduced the perrotin at their factory in Smíchow, and then arbitrarily lowered wages. And the disturbances affected primarily the city's Jewish-dominated cotton-printing industry. There was also an ideological motif, however.

Let us pose the matter as follows. Although by then a worker class of sorts was clearly in formation in Bohemia, socialism as a modern ideological movement borne by the worker class was equally clearly not present. Even the proletariat in western Europe, far more developed and experienced than in Bohemia, conspicuously lacked what Marxists call "consciousness." Particularly in 1844, workers all over central Europe almost simultaneously went on strike or destroyed machines. The governing classes immediately deduced that there was an international organized conspiracy of some sort or "Communism" behind it all; yet in fact neither the courts of the time nor a century of diligent historical research has brought any such conspiratorial organization to light. It was the impact of hard times on a community of wretchedness created by similar industrialist exploitation that produced the common types of worker protest simultaneously in so many different places. "Communism" didn't yet exist, although the strike waves demonstrated that the workers needed something like it.[42]

May one not guess that this need for "Communism," that is, for ideology and organization, explains in some part the Judeophobia of the Bohemian workers in the 1840s? The people knew very well they wanted something, yet had no name for it; they knew perfectly that the machine was their enemy, but had no general explanation why. Because of the Austrian police regime, they had no contact with the early socialists of the west. In the resultant ideological void it was entirely natural that these workers should have grasped hold of the exceptional feature of the Prague industrial complex—its Jewishness—and given voice to their bitterness in traditional religious terms. Their Jew-hatred was the ideological "presocialism" of the nascent and naive Prague working class.

Nor was this all! The Prague workers were not just proletarians, but people of a specific ethnic and linguistic background. They were Czechs, members of the linguistic nation that comprised the greater part of the inarticulate lower stratum of Bohemian society. In this role also they now began to express themselves in Judeophobic terms.

It was in the post-1815 period that the Czechs began their national revival.[43] For the two centuries since the expulsion of their national nobility, this nation had been effectively inarticulate. Then in the final decades of the eighteenth century a narrow stratum of intellectuals emerged, the product as much of the Catholic Enlightenment as of Joseph II's secular schools. These went to work at the business of engineering a national "rebirth," and achieved remarkable success. By the 1840s the Czechs could boast an increasingly vigorous petite bourgeoisie as well as its now aging intellectuals, and in Prague the people of the new industrial suburbs audibly spoke Czech. In 1848 the Czechs as a nation began to play a political role in Austria. This was a major historical event in the sense that the Czechs were virtually the first "non-historic" nation of the world to successfully imitate the nation-states of the European west. For all such reasons Czech historians tend to argue that, despite the "Reaction," the Franciscan era was a golden age that afforded their nation an apolitical time in which to grow.[44]

In their day the Czechs were subject to much mockery. The nation-revivers, at first only a few intellectuals, had quite literally to invent a modern culture before they could lead the reeducation of their people. They had to write a dictionary as their first task, and there were anomalies in their work that made many educated Germans laugh.[45] It seemed comic that a Germanic national festival on the Wartburg had inspired the Slovak poet Jan Kollár to write romantically nationalistic sonnets in his native dialect about the beauties of a goddess, "Slava," and her alleged "daughters." Could one take him seriously? Another poet, Václav Hanka, discovered "medieval Czech" epics so opportunely in 1817 that from the start one suspected (correctly) he had forged them so as to put his national culture on a par with that of the Germans. Later on one laughed when the historian František Palacký started publishing in German his Czechophile history of Bohemia. The mockers missed the point entirely, of course. These derivative aspects of the Czech Renaissance symptomized not Czech incompetence but the titanic task that the Czech intellectuals had taken on. They were looking for a way to reverse the whole trend of central European history. Since German models were readily available, they used them. Why not?

Much the same may be said of the German impression prior to 1848 that the Czech intellectuals were politically insignificant tools of the Bohemian aristocracy and of the Catholic Church whose protection they sought. These landed magnates and the Church were, of course, the great beneficiaries of the seventeenth-century expropriation of the Czech-speaking Hussites—they were the "murderers" of the medieval Czech nation. They were also the masters of the enserfed Czech peasantry. That the Czech nation-revivers worked with them and accepted their patronage could hardly strike outsiders as evidence of Czech modernism, liberal principles, or political acumen. Yet one can understand today why the Czechs sought such links. The magnates and the Church had power. Moreover, the magnates were "Bohemian" in their political affiliation, supranational *Landespatrioten* because their rights and privileges were incorporated in the Estates constitution of the Bohemian Lands. So also the religious orders were above German nationality, devoted to a Latin type of Catholicism that adulated the specifically Bohemian (and Czech) Saint, Jan Nepomuk. The Czech patriots could not then openly claim all of Bohemia for themselves: they were far too weak, the Germans far too strong. In any case the regime permitted no political life, it banned all experiments at formulating political claims. By accepting the "Bohemianism" of the magnates and the Church, and encouraging a cult of Bohemian antiquities and the Bohemian past, the Czechs could articulate indirectly the political tendency that was implicit in their cause.

All in all the apparent missteps of the Czech national revival, like its apparent "silliness," are explicable in terms of the immense difficulty of what was undertaken; and this is true also of the phenomenon that interests us here: the Jew-hatred of the Czech revival in the 1840s. By then, as noted earlier, the fruits of the Czech intelligentsia's work were visible. As a nation, a self-conscious population, the Czechs were "growing up." Where earlier there had been only a few intellectuals, by the 1840s there was an articulate cohort of several thousand.[46] The vast majority among the Czech speakers, the peasantry, still lacked any modern consciousness of ethnicity, but in the towns and especially in Prague an artisan class was proliferating, as was the worker element we have been discussing; and here consciousness was taking root more rapidly than the intellectuals could handle. The problem was that even among the literary intellectuals and aristocrats, it was taboo in Metternich's day to say much about politics. It was even more strongly forbidden to formulate political goals for mass consumption. It was no more possible in the Czech newspapers that appeared in the forties than in the archeological and linguistic periodicals of the thirties to say that the Czechs had a "right" to their homeland, that the political past should be mirrored in a political future, that Czech-speaking artisans and Czech-speaking workers had a "right" to defy their German employers and German economic competition. Mass slogans were needed, but none was allowed.[47]

Hence in part the Judeophobia of 1844 and after.[48] We have observed how among the Prague factory workers the need for some sort of social consciousness led, in the absence of "Communism" in the 1840s, to expressions of overt hatred for the Jews who owned the Prague factories. We may construe that in the absence and indeed practical impossibility of any explicit Czech national political ideology, a comparable need for some sort of national consciousness had the same result. An aristocrat-led, Church-supported "Bohemianism" may have satisfied dictionary-writing intellectuals, but for Czech-speaking workers sweating in the factories of German-speaking Jews, "Bohemianism" offered no satisfaction. Judeophobia was a clearer way out. It was no accident that in these years a younger-generation, plebian Czech publicist, Karel Havlíček, could sense the advantage of refusing to print in a patriotic Czech journal the poems of the "Bohemianist," Siegmund Kapper, born a Jew. The Czech cultural leaders were organizing songfests, social events, and cultural rallies, founding ladies' journals, issuing historical manifestoes—anything to get through to a long-silent public that was clearly ready to move. But because of the police they could not mention the social issues about which the public really wanted to hear. Hence their resort to Jew-hatred, particularly during the most panicky moments of the revolution of 1848.[49]

The Czech nation-revivers were not the parents of modern anti-Semitism. Its parentage lay with late-eighteenth-century Frenchmen and with the German ideologists who early in the 1800s conceived philosophically that someone labelled a Jew could by definition not be a German.[50] But to the Czechs probably goes the credit for first discovering that Judeophobia, in modern secular garb, could substitute as an arouser of the masses for the hard thinking that modern ideology should involve. And this was no more pleasant news for the newly modernized Jews of Prague than was the Jew-hatred of the worker class.

V

Bohemian Jewry's achievements during the reign of Kaiser Franz were considerable, as one may see by looking back briefly on the base problem we observed at the start of this book. Then in the seventeenth century Jews in Bohemia were hermetically sealed apart, locked into abject poverty in part by Christian law, in part also by their own "medieval" institutions. Could this national "backwardness" be broken down? Were the very large numbers of Ashkenazic Jews ever to be able to emerge into the modern world? To these questions, only preliminary answers had been provided by the success of Jewish modernization in the tiny west European communities of the seventeenth and eighteenth centuries. As late as 1800 one could still only guess that comparable success might be achieved in the east. But at the end of the Franciscan and Metternichean era, Bohemian Jewry as a whole had been "mobilized" by a new type of education. Modernization, it could be stated now authoritatively, was possible on a large scale among Jews.

All the more should one stress that the picture that has emerged in this chapter is not as rosy as that of the Franciscan era's Viennese Jews. At Prague, the major seat of Bohemian Jewry, a vanguard group of modernizer Jews, the cotton manufacturers, had certainly leapt out of the narrow past, and had achieved both affluence and a certain degree of acceptance in Christian Austria. Like the Viennese, they had become bourgeois. But no illusion of a neutral society could reassure them here in their break with the past. Before the world these people had become the lightning rod of new types of Jew-hatred in both the emerging working class and the Czech national revival.

SIX

A Judeophile Revolution

I

1848 puzzles historians. Marxists believe that the year witnessed a single phenomenon: an all-European revolution led by a new class, the bourgeoisie, which was in some places consolidating its power against more progressive forces, in other places seizing power from the holdout forces of the feudal past. Non-Marxists disagree. They stress the diversity of what happened. At Paris and Vienna they perceive outbursts of urban class war; in Italy and Hungary, national wars of "liberation"; elsewhere in central and southeastern Europe, "revolutions of the intellectuals." In some places, they stress, nothing happened at all. These phenomena, they say, had little in common save their coincidence in time. Even in discussing the results of the revolutions historians radically disagree. Some claim that at least for the peasants of central Europe this was a victorious year, because everywhere legal serfdom was finally legislated away. Yet a recent historian of Hungary has argued that the peasant emancipation, in so far as it had any direct effects, was a step backwards economically.[1] And though one has long been accustomed to seeing 1848 as the year of the central European Jewish emancipation, a recent conference on the subject questioned whether the revolution had any independent practical effect at all for most Jews.[2]

Particularly in Austria, confusion reigns about the meaning of 1848, though its citizens regard that year as the culmination of the whole first half of the nineteenth century. Metternich fell, they say, though Metternich returned from his March exile to Vienna within a couple of years. The nations spoke, they say, although one after the other in 1848 and 1849 the Czechs and Germans, the Italians and Magyars, the Croats, Serbs, Rumanians, Slovaks, and Poles, having spoken against one another, were repressed. The age of constitutions began, they say, which is true literally because Habsburg subjects came under the protection of Piedmontese, German, and Hungarian constitutions in 1848, and tried to produce their own; but which is false in the sense that the new Kaiser, Franz Joseph, usurped power from all the democratic constitutionalists by issuing a constitution of his own in 1849, and then withdrew even that in 1851. All told, Austrians treat 1848 like a caesura in their history, a jolt far greater than the others we have discussed: the annexation of new peoples to the Empire in 1772, the Josephian revolution from above in the 1780s, the Franciscan decision to eschew national roots after 1792, and the industrial revolution. But how to define the event is unclear.

To simplify matters, we will limit the following discussion to the meaning of 1848 for just one Jewish community, that of Vienna. What the revolution meant for the great masses of Habsburg Jewry will appear later. And why Vienna? That community was especially important for contemporary Jews, because by 1848 it contained the leading Jewish community of the entire Empire; and it is important for our story, because the revolution there was the culminating episode in the Jewish bourgeois experiment at collaborating with Metternich.

II

Let us start with some demographic facts which lead to perception of an anomaly. During the pre-March decades the population of the capital swelled enormously. The 260,000 civilians of 1820 grew to more than 400,000 by 1848. The increment consisted above all of thousands upon thousands of villagers, ex-serfs, or small-townspeople, mainly from the German-speaking Catholic provinces of today's Austria (though there were some Czechs from Moravia and southern Bohemia, and more would come as the railroads advanced).[3] These people found work in the great variety of service and construction enterprises which characterized the Habsburg "Residence City," and increasingly in the many factories of the neighborhood.

One might well anticipate finding that these immigrant worker elements in Vienna society were anti-Jewish, for at home in the Alplands the Germans among them were notoriously Judeophobic, even though those provinces had for centuries been void of Jews. This is not to say that German peasants always hate Jews, but rather that a pre-capitalist mentality then prevailed among them. As a recent scholar has put it, they did not plan rationally, keep accounts, or think in terms of improvements, and they were suspicious of those who did. They shared a vernacular laden with anti-Jewish imagery, and their religiosity had informed them for centuries that the Jews were the "killers of Christ."[4] So also the Czech peasant immigrants to Vienna; and these could also have harbored Czech national anti-Jewish attitudes such as were then current in Prague.[5] And in Vienna there was an objective factor, just as in Prague in the 1840s, that could have stirred outbursts of worker Jew-hatred. In the 1840s Jews had begun to figure here as industrialists. Indeed, precisely the same families who dominated the cotton-printing industry in Prague—the Epsteins, Dormitzers, Porgeses, Pribrams, Jerusalems, and Mauthners—had now set up factories and factory outlets in the Vienna suburbs, and were acting towards the workers exactly as in Prague. These Jewish textile manufacturers were not very numerous: among 600 "weavers" listed in the Vienna business directory for 1846, there were only 6 Jews; among 72 cotton manufacturers, there were 11 Jews; among 120 sheetcloth manufacturers, there were 2 Jews; among 172 ribbon manufacturers, 3 Jews. But in the years before 1848 they were in the lead of a fast-growing new sector of the Viennese economy, a boom sector in the midst of a depression, and as in Bohemia there were solid reasons why the workers should have resented them: they introduced the new machines.[6]

For such reasons alone, an outbreak of Judeophobia was no remote possibility in 1848 in Vienna; yet when the revolution came no such explosion occurred. In the March days when Vienna cast off its bonds there were disorders: on 13 and 14 March the workers of the industrial suburbs burnt factories, and some of the worst devastated were owned by Jews and seemingly were attacked as such. There seemed to be something as elemental here as in the bread-riots at Paris in 1789, and it was anti-Jewish.[7] Yet then the storm passed. When over Easter the guildsman classes of nearby Bratislava and other Hungarian towns instigated riots against the Jews, there was no answering outburst at Vienna. When early in May Prague exploded, likewise! Periodically, there were waves of journalistic diatribe against the Jews at Vienna; yet though the mood of lower-class Vienna grew more and more pugnacious over the summer, the workers made no further attack on the Vienna Jews.[8]

The anomaly of Vienna's lack of Judeophobia seems the greater because of further circumstances which could have set the city against its Jews. One may recall, for example, that the German-speaking guildsman stratum here was not a bit unlike the one at Bratislava where there was extensive guildsman anti-Jewish rioting. Indeed, the Austrian capital differed in this respect from the other growing metropolises of the period in Germany. Though all alike were growing because new mechanized factory industries and improved transportation afforded jobs to the excess population of the land, at Vienna the old, demographically very large guild-dominated "petite bourgeoisie" remained intact and disproportionately significant. So did the old concentration in the city's economy on home-produced textile production and on the manufacture in small shops of luxuries: of fans and umbrellas, ribbons, laces and braid, gloves, purses and leatherware, furniture and metal decorations, candles and playing cards. The turn to machine production threatened all this, but did not essentially change it. Indeed, because of the somewhat slower development of railroads around Vienna than around Berlin, and because the Habsburg state did not abolish the legal power of the guilds in the eighteenth century, new types of industry developed more slowly in Vienna than in the Prussian capital.[9]

The Vienna petite bourgeoisie was by no means thriving in 1848. To the contrary, it had fallen increasingly into economic straits in the pre-March period. The guildsmen even had to face a challenge from the new factories, because these set out to satisfy the very market for luxuries that the *Handwerker* had supplied in the past. Saved by the guild system, yet challenged as in western Europe by the forces of modern efficiency, the guildspeople as a class were smothering slowly.[10] All the more reason why they might have been filled by 1848 with resentments, rational or irrational; and since in the past this stratum of Vienna society had been articulate in its Jew-hatred, since also in the future it would be fertile ground for anti-Semitism, one wonders why in 1848 it did not lend its forces to the worker attacks on the Jews.

There were other "objective" stimuli for Jew-hatred in Vienna on the eve of 1848, apart from the Jewish-owned factories. One could note, for example, that if the city's general population had grown recently, its Jewish population had grown more. As late as 1820, we have seen in an earlier chapter, there were only some 130 legally tolerated Jewish families in Vienna, and a legitimate Jewish population of only about 1,500. By 1848 this population had exploded. There were now 200 tolerated families, and the actual population was between 4,500 (as many as at Bratislava) and 10,000 (more than in Prague): the exact figure is unknown.

One may argue that the mere presence of Jews is not a guarantee of pogroms, especially if the Jews are not conspicuous. The Jews in Vienna did live primarily in the downtown parts of the old inner city, and across the Danube-arm in the Leopoldstadt; there was thus a ghetto of sorts here to act as a lightning rod for Judeophobic sentiments, just as in both Bratislava and Prague. But lots of other people lived in those same quarters, and the Jews had never been compelled to reside there; they had been allowed to live where they could afford to. Generally speaking Vienna was a city of mixed ethnic settlement. Further, though the capital was a colorful city, where peasants, soldiers, and visitors usually still wore distinctive garb, the Vienna Jews were increasingly not distinctively dressed. A few Turkish Jews remained, still wearing their ancient costumes; and there was now a number of orthodox Jews in Vienna, immigrants from Hungary or Galicia, who wore long beards and caftans. But the Jewish poor were still rigorously barred. Vienna Jewry was middle class and wore modern clothes.[11]

Nonetheless, any study of the professional make-up of Vienna Jewry will confirm the presence of tinder for anti-Jewish social resentments.[12] In the lists of "tolerated" Vienna Jews in the 1830s and 1840s, for example, there appeared increasingly large contingents of textile traders. The explanation of the increment is simple enough. Textile trading had always played a role in Vienna's economy, but before Napoleon not a dominant one. In the past Moravia had been the woolens manufacturing and trading center for the Danube valley.[13] With the increases in modern production of the 1830s and 1840s, however, and especially with the advent of the railway, the capital became the textile emporium of the entire Danube valley. This change led to a major influx of Jews, for in the past, as we have seen,

Jewish traders had lived in Moravia off the textile commerce. Further, in Bohemia Jews were now playing a decisive role in the new cotton industry; and at Bratislava they dominated both the legal and illegal (smuggling) trade of textiles into Hungary. So important was the textile trade to the Danubian Jews that when the center moved to Vienna, large numbers of traders who could not afford to buy "tolerance" took to commuting weekly from Bratislava, the Burgenland towns, and southern Moravia.

This change by itself need not have inflamed the feelings of the older Viennese commercial classes against the Jews, but combined with another development it clearly sufficed to do so. As it happened, the ateliers and workshops of the Vienna petite bourgeoisie were scattered in regions known as "suburbs" which lay between today's Ringstrasse surrounding the inner city and an outer "line," today's *Gürtel*. In the period before 1848, when the inner city was still walled, both communications and transport between the ateliers and the downtown area were difficult. This difficulty set the stage for a change during the 1830s and 1840s in the marketing of Vienna's artisan production. In effect the ever more numerous provincial and foreign buyers were unwilling to take the time to wander around the suburbs. The manufacturers were correspondingly loath to spend time and money trying to market their wares downtown. The newly arriving Jewish textile traders of the city were willing to do both, and consequently their downtown firms rapidly became the main sales outlets for Viennese luxury manufactures of all sorts. Jews became the middleman exploiters of the economically declining guildsman class.

Nor was this the whole of the new economic basis for anti-Jewish resentment in Vienna. The second most prominent professional group among the tolerated Jews at Vienna in the 1840s dealt in natural produce, and most notably grain. In one respect this was nothing new. For generations Jews had been involved remotely in the food-provisioning of Vienna. Especially in Hungary they had long been the buyers at the estates of the gentry and aristocracy, and had arranged the carting of grain and produce to the capital. Prior to 1815, however, grain provisioning for Vienna had been handled by the authorities. Since then, grain dealing had increasingly been given over to private dealers. A Fruit and Grain Exchange had opened, albeit informally, on the curb near the Stock Exchange. And as a contemporary observer has quipped: "the grain-dealers were almost exclusively Jews"—he could think of few exceptions, most of them Italians or Greeks.[14] Jews were thus now in some degree controllers of the food market for the populace of Vienna. In Bohemia, as we have seen, it was precisely such Jewish participation in the supply of food that fanned traditional anti-Jewish sentiments in the hungry 1840s.

Such changes seem in retrospect the more potent because during the Metternich period there had been shifts also in the proportion of Jews in the financial institutions of downtown Vienna—increments visible to all who could count. In the Vienna Grosshändler Gremium in 1797, for example, only 12 out of 77 firms had been Jewish, about 15%. By 1823 the proportion was 33%; in 1846, 45%. Comparably on the large governing committee of the National Bank, founded in 1817, the proportion of Jews in 1823 was 19%, by 1836 the proportion was 41%.[15] As it happens a peculiar relation bound the petite bourgeoisie of Vienna to the city's financial institutions, albeit most particularly to the Stock Exchange. At the turn of the century the State, engulfed by the expenses of the revolutionary wars, had sought to save itself *inter aliae* by tolerating an extraordinarily broad public involvement in the then-new Exchange. The times, as we have seen, had been wild, investment by "little people" had gone amazingly far, and then came the state bankruptcy of 1811. It ruined the Viennese "little man," and even forty years later 1811 ranked in "his" mind as the catastrophe to end all catastrophes.[16] At that time, it would seem, Jews had not been so prominent on the Exchange as to let the catastrophe feed anti-Jewish stereotypes in Vienna in the minds of the artisan class. But since then a new factor could have combined with the growing Jewish financial presence in Vienna to do so. The entire petite bourgeoisie was more indigent. Credit had become a matter of enormous import for these people. On their ability to obtain funding increasingly hung their choice between proletarianization and survival. And the credit-givers were now increasingly Jews.

One more conspicuous objective factor that might well have inspired anti-Jewish sentiment in pre-revolutionary Vienna was the presence of the house of Rothschild. Long ago, in 1816, the Vienna Government had induced Salomon Rothschild, a member of that prominent international banking clan, to settle in Vienna. By 1822, when Kaiser Franz baronized the five brothers Rothschild, their house was known as Metternich's bankhouse, and provided the financial underpinnings for the "Reaction" all over Europe. The stereotypic "cosmopolitan" reputation of the house was the greater because von Rothschild lived in Vienna as a "foreigner." He refused to accept Austrian citizenship, because that would have involved subjection to the humiliations of the "tolerance" system. He persisted in his alien status even after 1843, when he was made an honorary burger of Vienna, and thus became the first unbaptized Jew to acquire full Austrian civic rights. Yet everyone knew that periodically he was consulted by the rulers of Austria about matters of great domestic and international import. Effectively he was even the "representative" of the Austrian Jews at Court: his *Prokurator*, or chief business associate, Leopold von Wertheimstein, was by the 1840s the dominant figure in the *Vertretung* of the Vienna Jews.[17]

Amidst such circumstances, might not Vienna—and Austria as a whole—logically have become rather Judeophobic in the decades after 1816? Elsewhere in Europe even poets like Börne considered Rothschild identical with the Vienna regime, and drew logical conclusions about Vienna Jewry.[18] If there was one common theme that held all the revolutions of 1848 together, it was surely hatred of Metternich. Even the chancellor himself sensed the connection: early in 1848 as unrest spread from the

Italian principalities and the Vienna *Börse* panicked, he summoned Salomon Rothschild to the Ballhausplatz and told him bluntly: "If the Devil takes me, he'll take you too. I at least am looking Hell straight in the face. You're sleeping instead, not fighting. Your Fate is sealed."[19]

And yet though Metternich fell, in general for another thirty years after 1848 Rothschild and the Vienna Jews were free of popular assault. In October 1848, when an angry mob invaded Rothschild's house in its attack on the nearby state armory at Vienna, it did not loot.[20]

It is difficult enough to try to explain historical phenomena when they are positive: no historian would presume to offer a "definitive" explanation of such a negative one as the absence of active mass Jew-hatred during the Vienna revolution of 1848. Doubtless observable factors helped. In particular one may wonder whether the Franciscan Government's long repression of popular nationalism did not have an impact. Censorship failed to prevent outbursts of Judeophobia in Prague or the provincial Hungarian towns, but at Vienna, the center of the upper bourgeois "neutral society" it may have affected mass opinion. One may speculate correspondingly about the ideological Liberalism of pre-revolutionary central Europe, for throughout the Germanies one of Liberalism's major political demands was then Jewish emancipation. How the essentially middle-class attitudes of Liberalism may have been transmitted to the lesser bourgeoisie, much less the still peasant-minded labor classes, is open to debate. Study has shown that laborers are quite competent to work out their own political ideas, and that the "leakage down" of middle class ideas did not always happen.[21] But given the importance of opinion-making journalism in the Vienna revolution, perhaps a certain leakage did then occur.

Very important in the dulling of popular Judeophobia in the Vienna revolution was surely also the significant presence of Jewish intellectuals in the capital, and their prominence in the revolutionary actions. The only class of Jews who could settle more or less freely in the capital before the revolution were intellectuals, and above all writers and medical students.[22] Their presence indeed constituted the feature distinguishing the Vienna Jewish community from many others in the Habsburg Empire; and at every stage in the revolution they were conspicuous. Jewish students were among the first martyrs of the March Days, and their public funeral was one of the first great revolutionary triumphal marches. The first tribunes of the revolution were Jews, as were the leaders of the defensive Student Guard. In May when a Committee of Public Safety was set up, its chairman was Adolf Fischhof, a Jew, and for a time during the summer, after the Kaiser's flight, he was de facto Austrian head of state.[23] Later on as the radical trend of the revolution grew pronounced, its leaders were Karl Tausenau, Avram Chajzes, and Hermann Jellinek. Amidst such circumstances it is not surprising that mass anti-Jewish feeling remained within bounds. And finally it is worth mentioning a most peculiar quirk of Viennese history. In the lead of Vienna's Catholic reform movement in 1848 stood a small group of highly political convert Jews. This movement was the forerunner of the anti-Semite Christian Socialism of the 1890s. Presumably the presence of these men dulled Vienna's Catholic anti-Semitism during the revolution.[24]

Whatever the explanation, the surprising absence of popular Judeophobia in revolutionary Vienna had serious effects throughout Austria, and even elsewhere, in the sense that it lulled Jewish fears. For a moment just after the March and April riots in 1848 a Jewish "Away to America" emigration movement blossomed more or less simultaneously at Vienna, in Hungary, in Bohemia. For a moment Habsburg Jewish terror was very sharp indeed, and fed the fears inspired by anti-Jewish riots just then in Alsace and in southwestern Germany.[25] But then the tide of Jewish opinion turned. Matters remained perilously disagreeable at Pécs, Košice, Bratislava, and Prague, but because there was calm at Vienna, Jewish opinion began to deprecate the riots as "isolated incidents"; and this view became the myth of 1848. Nor was just Habsburg Jewry affected as a result. What happened at Vienna—rather what did not happen—confirmed Jewish illusions all over Europe; and the consequences would underlie the entire great European Jewish drama of the century to come. One may well construe how different things would have been had Vienna proved as anti-Jewish in 1848 as in 1895–96. Then no European Jew could have looked back on the upper bourgeois "neutralism" of the *Vormärz* and found it typical; no one could have learned to hail 1848 as evidence of some Austrian or all-European readiness to accept the Jews. Jew-hatred would have been recognized early on as the persistent danger it later proved to be.[26]

III

The events at Vienna in 1848 were important for central European Jewry not only because of this weighty negative factor, but also because they encouraged the crystalization of a certain tradition—indeed, of a behavioral style. One may observe this most clearly by studying Vienna Jewry's contribution to the legal emancipation of the Jews.[27] As noted earlier, historians argue whether the abolition of the old legal restrictions is pinned down too closely to the revolutionary year. This is because in some Habsburg crownlands there had been movement in this direction earlier. In Hungary the Diet of 1840 had voided many laws limiting Jewish residence and trade. In Prague during the 1840s individual Jews had been permitted to settle outside the ghetto, and the *Familiantengesetz* had been challenged. In Vienna the enforcement of the "tolerance" system had grown notably lax. The revolution simply extended these earlier initiatives. Furthermore, even during 1848 the emancipation was complex. In crownland after crownland, for example, the provisional authorities who came to power in March deferred full emancipation of the Jews until duly elected constitutional assemblies could take action. In Hungary the deferral was especially disappointing, because in all other respects the existing National Assembly at Bratislava had claimed competence to make new national laws. And even after 1848, as we will see, there were tergiversations regarding the emancipation, particularly in Galicia, where Jewish legal rights to own land and to settle in other crownlands remained nebulous until 1868.

The revolution did change things radically. From the March Days onward the ghetto at Prague and *Toleranz* at Vienna ceased alike to be enforced, and even in Galicia the Jews could act as if they were free of legal restraint. In October the elected all-Austrian Parliament, just before it fled the capital for Kremsier in Moravia, voted to abolish the remaining special taxes on Jews. During the winter that same Parliament wrote a full emancipation into its new all-Austrian constitution. When in March 1849 Franz Joseph negated the Kremsier document by issuing a constitution of his own, he immediately reassured the Jews by telling those of Vienna that the equalization of all citizens, regardless of religion, remained the law. Then in Hungary in July 1849 the revolutionary Parliament, as its final act, likewise emancipated the Jews.

Nowhere in the Empire after this was the old discriminatory system put wholly back together again in practice. The impact of the 1848 Jewish emancipation was very diverse, but nonetheless epochal. And to come to the point, much of it was, as is clear from the above, fought out at Vienna, and it was fought out in a peculiar way.

The story begins with a considerable change that had affected the city's Jewry mid-way through the Franciscan era.[28] Until 1792 Vienna Jewry had lacked even the corporate status needed to maintain a cemetery and hospital. In that year, essentially to manage such sanitary institutions, the regime established a three-man Jewish *Vertretung* or "Representation." Years later, in 1812, Franz went a step further. Having recognized the virtue of "religion" for all his subjects, he decided to allow the Vertretung to purchase a building in downtown Vienna for religious community purposes. It took another fifteen years then for the Vertretung (led by two memorable personalities, M. L. Biedermann and Isak Löw Hofmann, later von Hofmannsthal),[29] to arrange for the construction of a synagogue. They had to wrestle first with Franz's distrust of Hebrew, which was unintelligible to his police, and later with his fear that the attractions of a modern Jewish religious service might tempt his Catholic subjects to convert. But in 1826 they did manage to open a large modern Jewish "Temple" staffed by a brilliant preacher, I. N. Mannheimer, and a famous chorister, Salomon Sulzer. It remained forbidden to call the "Vienna Temple" a "synagogue," the "Jewry of Vienna" a "religious community," or the "Vienna preacher" a "rabbi." But the capital was now equipped with a clearly organized Jewry, and a highly indigenized one, for the Temple was among the sights of the town.[30]

As it happened, the Vienna Temple rite, though "improved," was not so modern as to offend the provincial rabbis. It was, therefore, widely imitated in the Habsburg provinces and this marked the start of Vienna's leadership among all Habsburg Jewry. The leadership was fortified in tne middle 1830s when, as noted earlier, agents of S. M. Rothschild pushed aside the original members of the Vertretung. By 1845 the members apart from the aging von Hofmannsthal were Leopold von Wertheimstein, Rothschild's Prokurator, Josef Wertheimer and Bernhard Wertheim, both of them von Wertheimstein cousins, and Heinrich Sichrowsky, the *Nordbahn* secretary general. The implication of special economic and political influence was visible to all.[31] And indeed the Vertretung did begin to take steps of an all-Austrian character. It furthered petitions regarding the emancipation of the Jews to the government, for example. Josef Wertheimer organized a *Verein* for the furthering of artisanry among the Empire's Jews (in other words to change the Jewish professional mold), one of a number of such national societies organized in Europe in the 1840s. In 1842 Wertheimer published (abroad) the basic Habsburg-Jewish publicist work of the *Vormärz*, a book-length tract identifying the modernization of Austria with the emancipation of its Jews.[32]

The curious thing about the Vienna Vertretung, however, was its avoidance of political activism and its delight in the development, through individual members of the community, of connection networks which it could manipulate. As an organization, it was highly secretive, autocratic, un-democratic, and wholly subservient to the police. Neither modern nor bureaucratic, it functioned through personalized relationships rather like those of the Jewish Hoffaktoren of the past, although the contacts were now social and literary, not just economic. And it had a wonderful touch for what today we would call "public relations." In this way in particular it was very "Viennese."

To emphasize this point it is worth looking at the network that revolved around Heinrich Sichrowsky, who just after 1815 had been a founding member of a society named *Ludlamshöhle* [Ludlam's Cave]. The story of Ludlam seems now singularly silly. It began with poetizing and drinking. After ten years existence it lost in 1826 one of its members to the jails of Saint Petersburg, where the authorities were investigating the "Decembrist" revolt. When the Austrian police minister, Count Sedlnitzky, followed up this "clue," he found that the Ludlam slogan was *"Schwarz ist rot und rot ist schwarz,"* and indeed that its tableware was red and black, the colors of Anarchism. He immediately banned further meetings and arrested the leaders (including Sichrowsky), who finally explained that the slogan derived not from some anti-Habsburg plot, but from the skin-tints of a leading member, a cigar-smoking, red-faced, aging and bibulous Saxon actor named Karl Schwarz—*Rauchmar der Zigarringer, der rote Mohr* [Smokemore the Cigar-killer, the Red Moor], as he was known within the group.[33]

The *Ludlam* society was important nonetheless because virtually all the leading Vienna literary figures of the day participated, from Grillparzer to Castelli, Zedlitz, and Saphir, and also many budding businessmen and bureaucrats; because it was the first and most admired of many such so-cieties around which the Vienna demi-monde of the *Biedermeier* period organized; and because within it Jews and Christians were equal.[34] Sich-rowsky, one of the most active members, acquired through it all sorts of personal contacts which served him well in Vienna later on when he was organizing the Norbahn for Rothschild, and when he became a Jewish Temple dignitary. And he served these organizations well with his deeply "Viennese" connections.

Sichrowsky was not the only Vienna Jewish leader to have such a network of contacts. Even staid Leopold von Wertheimstein had one be-cause in his middle age, in 1843, he married Josephine, the young but exceedingly well-educated eldest daughter of Philip Gomperz, the wealthy Grosshändler of Brno. In the following years she maintained a salon in their apartment in downtown Vienna that was as brilliant as Fanny Arnstein's had once been, because she attracted the liberals of the pre-revolutionary years.[35] She not only kept her husband awake, but enabled him through her friends to obtain much useful political information.

The most interesting and significant of these networks attached to Ludwig August Frankl, a poet and trained doctor whom the *Vertretung* hired as its secretary in 1838.[36] Frankl was an archetype Austrian romanticist. A child of rural Bohemia (where he was born in 1810), his melodic stanzas dwelt lovingly on the central European past without insistence that every-thing beautiful was German, everything ugly Slavic, or vice versa. With equal sadness he sang of the medieval glories of highland Bohemia, of the Alps, and of the wide-open spaces of frontier Hungary. This was fare that made Biedermeier Austria feel close to the new romantic nationalism cur-rents of the west—closer to an identity—yet it did not alarm the censor. Frankl was generous with his affections, embracing even the dynasty: in 1832 he published his early ballads, chronologically arranged, under the title *Habsburglied* [Song of the Habsburgs]. The book made him the literary sensation of the day, a velveteen boy of the 1830s, an Austrian Wordsworth, as it were, if not quite a Byron. His success contrasted with the fate of other sensitive youths in Vienna at that time, most of whom starved if they had no money or got corrupted if they had income.

Even before his employment by the Jewish community Vertretung, Frankl was notable for his social connections. He managed to win favor both with Anton Bauerle, the corrupt but powerful theatre critic, and with Bauernfeld, Lenau, and Anastasius Grün [Count Anton Auersperg], the purest and most honest cultural figures of the time. Though a student of anatomy he became an accepted figure of the "Silver Coffeehouse," the meeting place of Vienna's literary elite. Baron Hormayr, the famed patriot of 1809–12, virtually adopted him, as did Baron Hammer-Purgstall, a noted orientalist whose wife (a Hönig von Henikstein) kept one of the most dis-tinguished "second society" salons. So later on did Carolina Pichler, the daughter of a famous reformer *Hofrat* of Maria Theresia's day, a poetess in her own right, the doyenne of the Viennese demi-monde. It was he indeed who brought both Bauernfeld and Lenau to her drawing room, thus constructing the bridge of continuity between the generations of Austrian poetry.[37] He was at the center also of a group of young Bohemian intellectuals who wrote both in Czech and in German—of the pan-Austrians Moritz Hartmann, Alfred Meissner, Siegfried Kapper, who produced the nearest thing to a "Habsburg literature" that ever emerged. Frankl's *Sagen aus dem Morgenlande* [Lays of the East], his *Christophoro Colombo*, and his *Don Juan of Austria* are hardly read today. But some quality in his verse and personality lent him singular appeal in the deeply fissured society of his time.[38]

As secretary and for thirty years archivist of the Jewish community, Frankl became a living bond, as it were, between it and Vienna's literary world. His role was the greater in the 1840s, because precisely coincident with his new job, the regime gave him permission to function as editor of a newspaper. Later, in 1842, he was the first confessional Jew in Austria given permission to own as well as to run a paper. His *Sonntagsblätter für heimathliche Interessen* [roughly "Our Town on Sunday"] was ostensibly a weekly parlor-culture journal for the "second society." But during the 1840s it was the liveliest domestically published organ of Austrian political thought. It was tame compared to the *Grenzboten* [Frontier Messenger], the outspoken oppositional paper published at Leipzig by Ignaz Kuranda, another Bohemian Jew. But it was available, and it could be read in public in Metternich's Vienna, whereas the *Grenzboten* could not.[39]

As 1848 approached, Frankl helped the Vienna Jewish community leadership expand its public relations system. In 1839 the Kaiser allowed the establishment of a Niederösterreichische Gewerbeverein [Lower Austrian Manufacturing Association] into which modern-minded Vienna flocked. Frankl was a leading member. In 1840 came the hour for an association of writers, artists and actors named Concordia. Grillparzer, Lenau, Holtei, Castelli, Carl Carl and Nestroy were all leading members, as was Frankl. In 1841 came permission for a Juridisch-Politische Leseverein [Reading Society for Law and Politics] which attracted the cream of the professional and bureaucratic intelligentsia and which turned out to be the organization center of the 1848 revolution. Frankl was a founding member.[40] By a peculiarity of history the medical school at the Vienna University was both the only college open to Jews before the 1840s and the only one during the 1840s where freedom of speech was more or less allowed. As a result, Jewish medical students figured disproportionately large in the student fraternities which organized the demonstrations of March 1848. Frankl, a veteran of the medical school, turned out in 1848 to be personally linked to two medical students who became the greatest democratic leaders of the revolution, Adolf Fischhof and Josef Goldmark.[41]

When the revolutionary toll clanged in 1848, these elaborate, essentially cultural connection-systems served the Vienna Jewish *Kultusgemeinde* in extraordinarily good stead. Right at the start, for example, Frankl turned out to be one of the tollers of the bell! At 38 he was a bit older than most students. Because of his connections, however, he was able to parade on 13 March with the Viennese student "revolutionaries," they accepted him into their "Legion," and to the thrill of the occasion he composed a famous ode.

> Lo, who be these so proud in bearing?
> The bayonets flash, the flags fly free,
> They come with silver trumpets blaring,
> The University.
> . . . .
> Our tongues wake with the lark to singing;
> O! hear their dithyrambic glee!
> Heart calls, and heart sends answers ringing,
> All hail, the University.[42]

One hundred and eight poems were published in the first censorless days of the revolution at Vienna, and from the record some observers have judged that Vienna was inhabited largely by "larks"! Frankl's poem became especially popular. Within a few months it had appeared in half a million copies. Twenty-seven composers put it to music within the year. It became in effect the *Marseillaise* of the Vienna revolution.[43]

Clearly enough this poem was no clever political instrument manipulatively conceived in the *Seitenstettegasse* Temple to obtain the legal emancipation of the Jews. It was a sign at best that an individual member of the Kultusgemeinde staff was on the spot and free enough to have the time to write such ditties. The poem did, however, smoothly steer the Austrian revolutionary mind in peculiar directions, towards the egalitarianism of the youthful intellectuals, away from the persecution of the Jews which characterized the revolution in other Habsburg towns. And herewith one of the Kultusgemeinde's cultural networks became a transmitter as well as a molder of society's enthusiasms.

Frankl was not the only member of the Kultusgemeinde staff to rise thus to the occasion. In the wake of the March Days, the Vienna city government organized a public funeral for the victims. Since Jews had been among the martyrs, Preacher Mannheimer appeared at the ceremonies in full liturgical regalia, hoping to spark a reflection among the living of the egalitarianism among the dead. He succeeded. Spurred by the moment, the leaders of Christian Vienna, including a Catholic priest, acknowledged a rabbi as their equal and the Jews as their fellow men.[44]

Before and during the funeral many Vienna Jews had feared to call for emancipation lest such calls provoke further anti-Jewish riots. Others wondered whether it was wise to call for a Jewish emancipation separate from the emancipation of everyone else. But now the Vertretung took courage and let Sichrowsky and Frankl petition the government for immediate emancipation of the Jews. The cause took hold. By April enthusiasm for emancipation had become universal in the Vienna Jewish community, all doubts and scruples having been set aside.[45] By June the Vienna Jewish Vertretung was so far swept along by the revolution that its employee, Preacher Mannheimer, felt free to run (from a Galician constituency) for the all-Austrian Parliament which was to write a new imperial constitution. Frankl, the community secretary, was Mannheimer's alter ego in the electoral campaign, and later his principal assistant in the legislative work of the Reichstag.[46] Meanwhile, as noted earlier, Frankl's friend Adolf Fischhof had become the single most conspicuous leader in the Vienna revolution. Fischhof was a man of unexpected intellectual depth and charisma whose democratic ideals would far outlive the revolution. Frankl's *Sonntagsblätter* became his ideological mouthpiece.

Vienna Jewry as a whole strongly affected the political emancipation of the Habsburg Jews. In August, for example, in deference to the newly-elected All-Austrian Parliament, Fischhof resigned from his chairmanship of the Committee of Public Safety, thus effectively immobilizing it as a counterforce—as a possible Jacobin Club or Petrograd Soviet of the Vienna Revolution. This move, which has struck modern historians as the turning point in 1848 at Vienna, has never been explained. It seems reasonable to guess that it reflected Fischhof's own feeling, and that of his friends, that the Parliament rather than the Committee could better formalize the emancipation of society (including the Jews) towards which they aspired.[47] Later on, when the Reichstag met, Preacher Mannheimer, as one of its officers, pressed hard and effectively to have it emancipate the Jews. Such moves did not, however, reflect regular and organized Jewish Vertretung pressure to obtain political results. The wealthy bankers and priggish assimilee gentlemen who constituted the Vertretung exerted virtually no control. Through the summer of 1848 Baron Rothschild trembled in the suburbs, a bundle of paranoid nerves, and in the fall he ran away.[48] Fischhof and Mannheimer were their own masters when they pressed for the emancipation, just as Frankl was in his revolutionary poetizing. They succeeded not because they represented some power bloc, but because as well-connected, modernist members of the Jewish community, they acted in the most "Viennese" manner of which they were capable. Their assimilation, not their organization, won the day; and this was well known, which is the point. To everybody's knowledge the Jewish emancipation of 1848 was achieved at Vienna because leading figures of the Jewish community were indigenized.

This development had deep consequences above all for the Vienna Jews. For them a local behavioral style now became altogether irresistible. Before 1848 the Vienna Jews adopted a "Viennese" style of behavior because they had to. They revelled in silliness, thronged to music and the theatre, affected noble manners, involved themselves in the *Kitsch* of the

Biedermeier "second society," because they were aliens before the law, because they were only tolerated within the city walls, and were thus subject to all sorts of psychological pressure to conform. After 1848 the Jews of Vienna indigenized themselves because it was a "Jewish" thing to do. They now ardently threw themselves into the world of Kitsch for better or worse out of gratitude, because they wanted to. The "Viennese" style had won them their prize.

Yet one may note in passing also that this development, like the non-appearance of Judeophobia, had its significant impact on the history of all European Jewry. What if this had not happened? What if in Germany's premier city in 1848 either the emancipation had not come about at all, or it had come about through the confrontational leadership of the old-fashioned Rothschild element in the Vertretung? It is enough to ask such questions in order to see answers. In either case European Jewish history would for a considerable time after mid-century have been much more like Russian Jewish history than it actually was. More realism, perhaps, but more brutality also, and far, far less rapid an escape by the Jewish masses from the past! The success of "assimilation" at Vienna in 1848 greatly facilitated the whole of European Jewry's advance into modernity.

I V

Vienna's 1848 affected Jewry's history in central Europe significantly also in a third way, and this is the frightening part of the story. Let us observe it by tracing the career of an intellectual, Hermann Jellinek, who was not from the Rothschild milieu.[49]

Jellinek was born in 1823 at Ungarisch Brod [Uherský Brod] in Moravia, the youngest of three brothers whose early lives were dominated by the contradiction of the time: on the one hand by poverty and by Jewish Tradition, on the other hand by a family passion for education and intimations of modernity. In the 1840s all three brothers proceeded to the great center of German Liberalism, the university at Leipzig. The elder, Adolf, a latter day rabbi of Vienna, used his time at Leipzig to learn German Protestant preaching methods. He became a modernized religious Jew. The second brother trod "secular" paths, and learned enough modern science to build the Budapest tramway system and to become without conversion a Hungarian noble. He became a typical Jewish member of the Habsburg upper bourgeoisie. Hermann, however, went one step further, and became an intellectually articulate areligious questioner of that bourgeoisie. He studied philosophy at Leipzig, discovering the most radical currents of German social and political thought, the extraordinarily cerebral world of Bruno Bauer, Ludwig Feuerbach, and Karl Marx. Conceiving that Religion was oppressive to the Spirit, he broke with Judaism altogether. Sensing that the existing state system might be a prison, he declared against existing secular authority. And since there was no strong Austrian national community because of Austria's rejection of national roots, Jellinek accepted international values, and judged that the Habsburg regime, his own government, might be especially bad.

Early in 1848 young Jellinek moved to Vienna, arriving there shortly before the March Days, aged 25, facile with his pen, and filled with elevating ideas. He soon found like minds because, for all the censorship, Vienna was a major educational center, abounding with intellectuals.[50] Jellinek fell in above all with Karl Tausenau, a Jew born in Prague in 1808, who had already organized before March a circle of worker-reformers, an orator who would hold the attention of the masses throughout the year because he had mastered the Viennese dialect and peppered his speeches with phrases from the Vienna stage. Jellinek also met Ernst Violand, a lawyer, later the sociologist of the revolution; Anton Füster, a worker-district priest; Anton Becher, a lawyer and music critic; Baron von Stifft, a well-known agricultural economist; Sigmund Engländer, a journalist; Ludwig Eckhardt and Anton Schütte, professional radicals; Johann Berger, the great Liberal parliamentarian of the future; Avram Chajzes, a Galician Jewish journalist and opera lover who abhorred the fat and rich—the list is long. In April these men founded a *Verein der Volksfreunde* [Union of the Friends of the People]. Endlessly talking, endlessly imaginative, open to modern social ideas, they sought to steer the great World.

At the start of the revolution Jellinek was already a radical. Still willing enough to work as a journalist for Ernst von Schwarzer, the Trieste economist who became Minister of Public Works in the revolutionary regime, he was certainly a violent critic of the old regime. For him it was not important (as it was for L. A. Frankl) that in the early days the workers attacked Jewish firms. It was important that the workers had rebelled and that the regime had given in. For Jellinek and his friends, Frankl's poetic appeal for student unity was something less than the pure voice of the masses; it was more a middle-class call for order, and perhaps a bit deceptive. The petitions for Jewish emancipation seemed in their perspective plutocratic in origin, divisive in intent, and addressed to a corrupt authority. These men wanted the revolution not stabilized, but pushed on, and precisely for this reason in those early months of the revolution, they were isolated.

The raw fact was that after the long Metternichean censorship the Viennese "masses" lacked, as one expresses it today, "consciousness." Like the Bohemian workers of 1844, the Viennese knew well enough that they wanted to revolt, and wanted relief from the new machines, but they were politically naive and sentimental, attracted by cloying middle-class slogans.[51] During the spring Jellinek and his friends gained so small a following that they factionalized, adumbrating the embattled radical intellectuals of later east European revolutions. Chajzes and Tausenau went at each other's throats. Jellinek himself soon found he could not work with Schwarzer. These young cosmopolitans were so sensitive to a distant future that the present got in their way.

By August and September, however, the pretty world of L. A. Frankl had cracked, and the Viennese radicals came into their own. In Prague in June, Windischgrätz had suppressed the revolution. Marshal Radetzky was defeating it in Italy. No one (save possibly Frankl) in Vienna had much sympathy with the Czechs and Italians. But everyone, bourgeoisie and proletarian masses alike, recognized that through the army the old dragon was striking back, that danger threatened the revolution. Meanwhile at home also clouds gathered. The return of the Kaiser to Vienna, the meeting of the Parliament, and the decision to emancipate the serfs awoke popular enthusiasm and satiated the revolutionary thirst of the middle classes, richer and poorer alike. But signs that "Property" was gutting the Revolution angered the worker population. Workers could sense well enough the ever increasing reluctance of the bourgeois National Guard to protect their interests. As the treachery of the army and the "ingratitude" of the nationalities came into view, the Vienna "masses" became socially conscious. And now the Volksfreunden reassembled. Under Tausenau's lead, they won the ear of a broad public. Hermann Jellinek's own paper *Der Radikale* now reflected the mainstream of revolutionary opinion as sensitively as Frankl's "University" had done so in the spring. In September there were new riots. As more and more conservative-minded people left the city, Vienna became in all Germany the most active center of political radicalism.[52] After 6 October "Democracy" ruled the streets of the capital, and Jellinek was among its heroes.

On 23 October the army under Prince Windischgrätz attacked, and in a week-long assault mercilessly put the rebel city down. Officially about 400 defenders and 200 attackers were killed; about 750 defenders and 800 attackers were wounded.[53] Several of the outstanding radical leaders, including Tausenau and Chajzes, managed to slip away and lived on in exile. But young Hermann Jellinek was caught and shot, a symbol ironically of the boastful bourgeois Liberalism which he and the army alike had rejected.

Hence the third and most contradictory impact of 1848 on Habsburg Jewry. First the revolution created illusions about the environment, making one think that further modernization here was safe. Second, it gave Vienna Jews in particular all sorts of optimism about how more assimilation would lead to more emancipation. Then, third, it destroyed the confidence and pride of the bourgeoisie into which Jewry was merging. The Habsburg middle class splintered catastrophically in this revolution. If the Jews won, the bourgeoisie lost; and as a result the signals guiding further Jewish action were bewildering indeed.

V

In three chapters now we have studied how Habsburg Jewry fared in Franz I's long reign. Beyond question, despite the political "Reaction," the Jewish experience was less than altogether grim. In the early part of the reign circumstance made possible at Vienna the successful merger of a narrow but significant segment of Jewish society with the capital's then newly forming Christian upper bourgeoisie. In subsequent decades this new "neutral" social stratum expanded to include provincial elites, especially those of the Bohemian Lands; and meanwhile the work of the Enlightenment lent to an overall mobilization of the Bohemian Jews. After Franz died, leaving a too-rigid heritage to his legitimate son, the leadership of Vienna Jewry organized, and in the explosion of 1848 managed to extract the legal emancipation of Habsburg Jewry from the flames.

These advances on the path of modernization are the more interesting in retrospect, because we can observe what a singular experiment was taking place. Often in the history of modernization it is supposed that a "visitor" element will absorb into its "host," taking on a new positive identity in place of its old one. Yet here things were different. Franz I made a decision early on to pursue the construction of a modern Austrian state while deliberately not laying the nationalist roots for it that characterized state construction elsewhere in Europe at that time. This decision in no small degree resembled the current Jewish national tendency to deny in the interests of modernization the positive manifestations of Jewish national identity. Host and visitor alike here were thus in the Vormärz pursuing parallel policies of "self"-denial; and we can see now that the experiment bore fair fruit. Jewish modernization seems to have been singularly easy in the face of Austrian abstention from conformist demands.

But let us note also the limitations to the experiment and indeed to the entire development examined in these chapters. At each stage there were negative as well as positive aspects to what happened. At Vienna throughout the period the "neutralism" of society was dependent on sharp political repression, including an especially tyrannous legal discrimination against economically deprived Jews. In Bohemia the emergence of a Jewish industrial bourgeoisie roused a new sort of active Judeophobia in significant sectors of the Bohemian population. These are blemishes not easily disregarded. And in addition one should bear in mind the limitations of our story in these chapters. In effect they have touched only on the western Habsburg Jews, and the richer ones at that. Galicia and Hungary have not entered the story at all, although the vast majority of all Habsburg Jewry lived in those lands.

Further, there was a catastrophe at the end of the experiment. In 1848–49, at a moment when many of the initial tasks seemed accomplished, the Jewish bourgeoisie suddenly came face to face with a contradiction. On the whole, the revolution swept away the legal chains of the past. This meant that as Jews seeking to be modern citizens of the Austrian state, the bourgeois Jews had won. Yet coincidentally this revolution, middle-class as it was, shattered and was repressed. Did this failure not mean that as modern citizens the bourgeois Jews had lost?[54]

In effect 1848–49 saddled the modernist elite of Habsburg Jewry with the fearful burden which would overshadow their whole later history. Hitherto, to become bourgeois in the Habsburg Lands offered them a way out; henceforth, it would weigh them down. Hitherto, to become bourgeois here seemed an escape from the enormous problems of being a Jew in a repressive Christian world. Henceforth, it meant to compound their own, Jewish, problems with the immense and growing problems of the already failing Habsburg middle class.

PART III

Facing the Challenge, 1850–1875

SEVEN

Galician Deadlock

I

The reign of Franz Joseph, the new young Kaiser of 1848, began most inauspiciously. By the time of his accession the imperial army had by force put down the revolutions at Prague, Vienna, and Lwow, and was on the way towards repressing revolutionary Italy. But the whole Empire was disrupted by the revolutionary crisis, and in Hungary, the largest Habsburg dominion, the generals found themselves fighting a losing war. Early in 1849 they decided to invite military help from the Russian Tsar. Hungary was ravaged by the time of her collapse in August 1849; and meanwhile the imperial treasury had survived only by exploiting the supposedly independent National Bank and by issuing vast quantities of paper currency. Since Salomon Rothschild had fled Vienna, the regime did not even enjoy the international credit which his presence had assured it for a generation past.[1]

At the start Franz Joseph had some brilliant and modern-minded advisors. His first prime minister was Prince Felix Schwarzenberg, who aspired to restore Austria's political primacy in central Europe and might have done so had he not died in 1852. The first trade minister was the economist Karl Ludwig Bruck, whose dream it was to underpin Schwarzenberg's state with a vast customs union binding Austria to Germany under the banner of free trade. But the Kaiser listened also to backward-looking people: to his mother, to his confessor, to Metternich (who returned to the *Renngasse* in 1851), to various generals. As a result he grew used to relying on force, and on the first day of 1852 he withdrew the very constitution that he himself had issued in the spring of 1849. Meanwhile the state's financial problems persisted. In 1853–54 Finance Minister Andreas Baumgartner almost achieved stabilization of the currency by persuading Rothschild (who was in Paris) to help float a state loan, and then by imposing a forced domestic loan on the Austrian provinces. But most of the money disappeared because of the government's policy of armed neutrality during the Crimean War (which entailed an expensive military occupation of the Rumanian Principalities). At the end of Franz Joseph's "decade of absolutism," as it is called, he was caught off-guard by military defeat in Italy and a new financial debacle. With indecorous haste he had to issue a series of new constitutions. The instability of his state persisted until 1867, when after a lost war in Germany he made a formal compromise with the nobility of Hungary, converting his Empire into the Austro-Hungarian "Dual Monarchy," which, with a different constitution on either side of the Leitha, it would remain until 1918.

Yet there were constructive forces at work behind this tale of misfortune. Serfdom had finally been ended in 1848. The execution of the new laws freeing the peasantry took several years; and the benefits to agriculture may not have been as dynamic as was once thought. Still, politically and socially, the reform made an enormous difference. In the years just after 1849, moreover, the government introduced administrative reforms which favored modern economic activity. An efficient postal service came into being, for example; a network of chambers of commerce was set up; the internal customs frontier around Hungary was abolished; local administration was vastly improved; the first steps were taken towards freeing manufacturing from the guilds. Such factors were responsible for a fairly rapid recovery of the private sector of the economy. And then came the state's sale of railroads to private enterprise.

This particular innovation lent itself to a flashy capitalism that characterized the whole era both in the Habsburg lands and in neighboring Germany. As noted earlier, railroad construction had begun in the Empire in the 1830s under the private aegis of Baron Rothschild.[2] In the 1840s, however, though Rothschild kept his Nordbahn, the bulk of the new mileage was built by the state, which indeed drew up after 1850 vast systematic plans for further construction. In 1854, because of the perilous condition of the treasury, the government decided to raise money by divesting itself of the state railroad lines; and at precisely that moment a constellation of events in western Europe favored the sale.

A banking revolution was underway. In 1853 and 1854 the brothers Emile and Isaac Pereire, French financiers, had established a new type of bank in Paris, a joint stock investment company called the Crédit Mobilier.[3] By its very nature this bank was a challenge to the old-fashioned private bank houses (and most specifically to Rothschild) that until then had dominated the continent. By its very nature also it required new investments. All over Europe, therefore, during 1853 and 1854, the Pereires were aggressively seeking allies. In Vienna they found some in the Greek banker, Baron Sina, and in the old Arnstein and Eskeles bankhouse, whose chiefs apparently relished the idea of outdoing Rothschild whom they had long resented.[4] During 1854 these Viennese houses agreed to support the Pereires in two enterprises: first, in the establishment of a private railroad company that could purchase the Austrian State's railway holdings; second, in the establishment at Vienna of a branch of the Crédit Mobilier that could supply credit to new Austrian industries.

During 1855 the Pereires succeeded in the first of these enterprises, but failed in the second. In December 1854, Baumgartner, in one of his last acts as finance minister, agreed to sell to the Pereire-Sina group a number of state-owned railroads (the line from Brno to Prague, and a half-built line from Budapest toward Belgrade) and various concessions in Hungary, including coal mines and much real estate. To manage these properties, Sina set up a new, wholly private holding company paradoxically entitled "Österreichische Staatseisenbahngesellschaft" or *STEG* [Austrian State Railroads]. This new company promptly purchased Sina's own railroad holdings in Hungary; they were linked to Vienna, thus gaining a seemingly enormous head start towards binding the Balkans and the Ottoman East to western Europe's railroad system. This was too much for the Rothschilds (no longer led at Vienna by old Salomon, who died at Paris in mid-1855, but by his son Anselm).[5] They had hitherto resisted involvement in the new type of banking institution typified by the Crédit Mobilier; but in March 1855, after Karl Bruck became Austrian finance minister and took under consideration the Pereire group's proposal for an Austrian Crédit Mobilier, Anselm Rothschild embraced the new bank model. With extraordinary acumen he persuaded some of Austria's greatest aristocrats, longtime clients of his firm, to back a new-type credit institution of his own, which would have the enormous basic capital of 30 million florins and which in addition would not be under French control. The Austrian government, after years in the financial wilderness, could not have been happier and promptly approved the establishment of this *Creditanstalt für Handel und Gewerbe* [Credit Institute for Trade and Industry], which to the present day remains Austria's largest private bank.

It was a measure of Bruck's genius as minister that he did not come down entirely on Rothschild's side, but encouraged the Pereire-Sina group to strive onwards in its efforts to expand the central Europe railroad network. All through 1855 the Pereires and the Rothschilds competed vigorously to purchase the remaining state-owned railroad lines and the concessions for projected new ones. First the Paris Rothschild House, through gigantic expenditure, captured the Lombard-Venetian lines (1855). Then the Vienna Rothschild House obtained the concession to build a western rail line from Vienna to central Germany, and finally (late in 1858) the two together won the *Südbahn* concession to Trieste. But the key struggle was in 1855 over the railroad to the Balkans whose concession was already almost in Pereire's hands. For purposes of the battle, Baron Sina now organized a consortium of Magyar aristocrats (the Zichys, the Apponyis, the Károlyis, and others who had long been his clients), a clear parallel to the Rothschild tactic of mobilizing the Austrian aristocrats. An *Orientbahn* across Hungary to the Balkans was projected, and a *Theissbahn* into eastern Hungary. The stocks of all these companies became the center of speculation on the Vienna Börse [Stock Exchange]. At that point Baron Sina died, and far away in Paris the Pereires began to suffer reverses which foreshadowed their ultimate defeat.

Meanwhile the battle had raised the question of railroads in Galicia.[6]

In 1851 the state had bought a short privately-constructed line from Prussian Silesia to Cracow, and had extended it eastwards a third of the way
to Lwow, the crownland capital. But work had then stagnated. In 1856–
57 there was no concrete prospect of construction beyond Przemysl, still
a hundred kilometers short of Lwow; and it was now projected to sell the
concession to the Nordbahn which, because of Rothschild's struggle with
the Crédit Mobilier, seemed little inclined to actually build a remote new
line. Hereupon a construction consortium appeared in Galicia itself. Named
after the Archduke Carl-Ludwig, its general secretary was a Bruck associate,
the convert-Jew, Johann Herz, and it had prestigious directors—a Prince
Sapieha, a Prince Poniński, a Prince Jablonowski, counts Borkowski, Dzie-
duszynski, Krasinski, Stadnicki, and Wodzicki; an assemblage quite as glittering as the ones Baron Rothschild had gathered in Bohemia for the
Creditanstalt and Baron Sina had gathered in Hungary for the railroads
there. The company's mission was to build the line from Przemysl to Lwow,
and thence northwards to the Russian frontier. Funding was initially hard
to find: in 1857 western Europe was abruptly overtaken by financial depression. But by 1859 financing had been found, and inside two years the whole
distance to Lwow was built. The extensions to Brody and to Tarnopol were
delayed until 1869; those to the Russian frontier were not complete until
1872. But meanwhile another company decorated with Galician aristocrats
appeared on the scene, a Lwow-Czernowitz Railroad Company organized
by the Viennese Jewish entrepreneur, Victor Ofenheim. It was one of the
more speculative and corrupt enterprises of a notoriously speculative era,
and its real objectives were profits available in Rumania. But to get them
the Lwow-Czernowitz railroad had to be constructed, and with British
capital Ofenheim built it between 1864 and 1867. Now even eastern Galicia
was linked with the western world.[7]

Under the impact of the railroad construction, the whole private sector
of Austria's economy began to flourish. The war of 1859 interrupted progress, but the constitutional reforms of 1860 and 1861 again raised entrepreneurial ambitions. By the time of the political *Ausgleich* of 1867, the
country was embarked on a *volkswirtschaftlicher Aufschwung* [upswing in the
people's economy], as it was called, or *Gründerzeit* [Era of Entrepreneurs].
The industrialism which had begun in the Metternich decades now spread
apace. Companies were founded, factories built; Austria entered the modern world economy perhaps not with the vigor of the Germanies, but
nonetheless with a resounding bang which left no crownland unaffected.

Without more ado, let us pose the questions of this and the following
chapters. Did the economic and political opportunities of the 1850s and
1860s challenge Habsburg Jewry to break further out of its past? If not,
why not? If so, how? In discussing the Jewish responses (for we may note
at once that there were several such responses) we will cast our net much
more broadly than in the preceding section of this book, in which we largely
ignored the masses of Jews in the eastern Habsburg provinces and con-

centrated on those in Vienna and Prague. We will first study what happened in Galicia, the *vagina Judeorum* of late-nineteenth-century parlance; then we will look at what happened in Hungary, which acquired an increasingly large Jewish population. Finally we will turn back to Vienna to perceive that major changes took place there also in the absolutist period. All in all we will paint a picture of increasing diversity. But by mentioning at the outset the railroad entrepreneurs, most of them resident in the capital, we have pointed already to a basic unifying feature of central European Jewish history in the whole later nineteenth century: an appalling contrast between the wealthy Jewish leading stratum in the west of the Empire, and the multitudinous poor in the east.

II

When Austria annexed Galicia in 1772, it acquired a Jewry with major problems. For two reasons it is now relevant to focus on these. First, as hinted earlier, they had not disappeared. Despite the countervailing forces discussed in an earlier chapter, Galicia and its Jewry remained "backward" during the Vormärz. We should know why. Second, even the new opportunities of the 1850s and 1860s failed to shake the province and its Jewry out of lethargy. In theory the new challenge should have changed things at last, but it did not. Again, why?

One can best start with education. In Bohemia, as we have seen, a new type of education was a critical factor during the Vormärz enabling Jewry to modernize. Specifically, it was the schools set up under Joseph II that untied the knots of the past. In Galicia also Joseph founded schools for the Jews, and more even than in the Bohemian lands where many Jewish children were expected to go to the network of Christian schools. In Galicia even the Christian school network was under-developed in Joseph's day. Within two decades the imperial authorities had set up some hundred elementary German-language schools for the Jews and two middle schools (at Brody, the richest trading center, and at Lwow, the capital) together with one more advanced "seminary." They imported teachers from the west, especially from Bohemia.[8] Yet in Galicia the Josephian educational reform failed, and this is the primary fact that affects all considerations of how Galician Jewry responded to challenges and opportunities in the nineteenth century.

Why this failure? The main reason was that in 1806, for reasons to be detailed below, the Austrian government withdrew its support from the schools. But other factors lent to the real disaster—to the overall collapse of the school system then, and its failure ever to revive. Above all, it may be noted that the task undertaken was exceedingly big: success was problematic at the conception of the system. There were some 200,000 Jews counted in Galicia in Joseph's time and some 250,000 by 1800, double the number in the Bohemian Lands. As noted elsewhere the numbers actually present were probably much higher than those counted. This was a population overwhelmed by poverty which had never encountered non-Jewish learning, or observed (as had the Jews of Prague) a modern non-Jewish world. If the school system collapsed after only two decades of existence, this was surely in part because the schools were expected to do too much.

Beyond this, as noted earlier, the Galician Jews differed in point of separatism from the Jewries of the western Habsburg Lands. Their *kehillas*, or Jewish local councils, inherited the prestige of the now withered but once strong and imposing central Jewish councils in old Poland. The Austrian regime, as its first administrative step in the 1770s, reinforced the autonomous Jewish institutions by establishing an all-Galician Jewish General Directory through which to rule. Even after abolishing this institution and with it the communal courts in the mid-1780s, the Austrians never really managed to intervene their authority between the *kehilla* elders and the mass of the Jews in Galicia as effectively as they had further west. Given this insulation of the Jewish population, one can construe that rabbinical opposition to secular schooling may have been hard to evade. And there was such opposition. By 1806 the school system had many rabbinical foes.[9]

This is not to say that the Galician rabbinate from the start abhorred the schools. As in Ezekiel Landau's Prague, so in Galicia, the rabbinical authorities were in the early period deferential to the state. For example, Aryeh Lev Bernstein, the conservative Theresian "Grand Rabbi of Galicia," willingly acted over several years as a state agent. The latter-day division between "Orthodox" and "reformers" did not at the start exist. But rabbinical opinion in Galicia was probably much more rigidly against innovation than in the west; and under the influence of various provocations, it soon became actively hostile to the schools.

What provocations? Above all, the Austrians in no way sought to make themselves beloved of the Jews here. Even under Maria Theresia the *Gubernium* officials viewed the Polish Jews as a plague, useful to the state only as a source of profit. By the middle 1770s they had imposed special taxes and prohibitions on Jewish marriages, placed an exorbitant tax on kosher meat, and ordered the expulsion of "beggar Jews," a category which in the Polish Lands included very many people. When Joseph came to the throne, he found it advisable to bar Jews from one of their principal forms of occupation in this crownland, the rental and management of village taverns. Some 100,000 Jews are said to have been threatened by this decree, which fortunately was enforced with the mildness of corruption. The Kaiser also went about commanding all sorts of changes in Jewish life: he wanted to bar old-style Jewish clothes, demanded that all Jews adopt civic names, introduced military service, tried clumsily to get Jews out of their old professions by settling them on farms, and of course barred Hebrew in public documents and contracts. Then after his death the Franciscan government not only brought into question the rights Joseph had granted the Jews (for example the right to own real estate, granted in the general Galician "Ju-denpatent" of 1789), but introduced new burdensome taxes (most noto-riously a candle tax designed to extort money from all Jews who observed the Sabbath). Since the authorities proved in no way loath to use the school employees as collectors of these hateful fees, it is no wonder that Jewish opinion turned against the schools.

The greatest by far of the provocations was the mission of a famous Jewish reformer, Herz Homberg, whom we have seen elsewhere ending his career after 1815 at Prague. Homberg was born in Bohemia about 1749.[10] At age 10 he was already a rabbinical student at the school of Ezekiel Landau. Subsequently he moved to Berlin where he studied philosophy, became indeed one of Moses Mendelssohn's leading disciples, and passed from Talmudism to extremes of enlightenment. In 1781 he went to Trieste to set up a modern school for the Jews there in the spirit of Joseph II's legislation. He was effective, which is probably why in 1787 the Kaiser sent him to Lwow as superintendent of the freshly established Galician Jewish school network. From the moment of his arrival Homberg encountered resentment because he wore a wig and culottes. The Galician Jews had rarely encountered a Jew in such costume, and he could hardly even find lodging in Jewish houses, though the Austrian authorities insisted he live only there. But Homberg also suffered from his own elitist zeal. Steeped in the "refined" Jewish Enlightenment of Berlin and Trieste, he approached Galicia in a schoolmasterly spirit, and took vengeance on those who greeted him with disdain. He acted as if he were on a cleansing mission, and in the pursuit of his educational goals did not hesitate to use or to let himself be used by the police. He herded the Jewish children into his institutions. On the one hand, the government deliberately used him (a notably willing tool) to further increase the taxation of the Jews; and on the other, to cap his difficulties, it placed Galician Jewry once again in free communication with the great Jewish cultural currents of eastern Poland. At the third partition in 1795, Austria received a large hunk of central Poland (thence-forth known as "West Galicia") with a huge Jewish population amongst whom the Hasidic movement was entrenched. Amidst such circumstances, it is no wonder that the schools became unpopular.

In the end Vienna showed Homberg gross ingratitude. In 1806 he circulated a pamphlet against the *Sanhedrin*, or Jewish National Council, which Napoleon was convoking in an effort to reconcile Jewish and French civic law. This pamphlet persuaded Kaiser Franz and the police, perversely, that Homberg might be a French spy.[11] Abruptly they recalled him from Galicia, and in a fit of conservatism abolished "his" schools! At this point Napoleon himself entered the Polish scene, smashing Prussia and estab-lishing a rudimentary new Polish state. The wars sent streams of refugees into Austrian Poland. In 1809 Austria lost "West Galicia" to Napoleon's Grand Duchy of Warsaw. Amidst such upheavals it is not surprising that Austria did little about refounding Galicia's Jewish schools; and Homberg had made his "Enlightenment" so much a focus of Galician Jewish exe-cration that there was no Jewish effort to preserve the school system.

When order was restored after 1813, the basic tools of Jewish mod-ernization had to be founded anew in Galicia.[12] Some of the most brilliant figures of the east European Jewish enlightenment put themselves to the task: Josef Perl, a wine merchant of Tarnopol, Nachman Krochmal, an intellectual at Brody, S. J. L. Rapoport, son of a tax-farmer of Lwow. With their leadership, clusters of enlightened Jewish merchants (*Maskilim* as they were called) founded German-language schools at Tarnopol (1813), at Brody (1815), at Cracow (1830), and at Lwow (1844). But relative to the overall Jewish population, these second-wave Galician German-language Jewish schools had few students; these enlightened intellectuals had few followers; and meanwhile conditions grew basically unfavorable to the spread of modern education among the Jews.

In the first place there was an adverse demographic trend. Galician Jewry had approached the quarter million mark in 1800. By 1840 it num-bered some 300,000; by 1857, 450,000; and these figures reflect the situation after enormous emigration (to be discussed later) to Hungary.[13] Three-quarters of this ever more vast population was crowded into the remote eastern half of Galicia, much of it into smallish cities or villages. 75% to 80% of it was dependent in some degree on "trade," in this province where there was very little to be gained from trade.[14] Perhaps already large num-bers of *Luftmenschen* were among them—people who were said to live off air because they had no means of sustenance. These realities of Jewish existence in Galicia did not encourage the spread of modern education.

In addition, leading members of the Galician rabbinate now opposed any and every sort of deculturation among the Jews. Rabbi Jakob Ornstein of Lwow, for example, was more reactionary than his contemporary Mor-dekai Banet of Nikolsburg, and left a rigidly anti-modernist educational heritage. There were others like him, masterly Talmudists all, but obscur-antist vis-à-vis western knowledge. Further the rabbinate in general was composed of men who wholly lacked experience with enlightened school-ing, whose training had been left largely to chance, who knew nothing but the Talmud. One may hardly deprecate the proven efficacy of their Tal-mudism as a vehicle for religious self-expression and group defense. But no less may one duck the "fanaticism" and sheer ignorance of modern science that were here at a premium among the Jews. Until late in the century, because of the condition of the rabbinate, most Jewish children grew up in Galicia literate (and decidedly more literate than the peasantry), but knowledgeable only of the Talmud and both inured and opposed to "Reason" from the western world.

Finally, Hasidism was on the ascent in Vormärz Galicia, and offered many Jews an alternative which in Jewish cultural terms was as attractive as the Haskalah. It is difficult to date the spread of the movement, which of course originated in the eighteenth century close to Galicia in Podolia.

It may have become widespread here only during the Napoleonic up-heaval.[15] But after 1815 it throve especially among the poorer village Jews. It was then that Shalom Rokeach, the founder of a major dynasty, settled at Belz; Zwi Hirsch Eichenstein at Zhydachov; and Hayyim Ben Leibusch Halberstamm at Nowy Sącz [Zanz]. Other *zadikim* appeared at Ropczyce, Zolochev, Buchach, Stretyn, Zbaraz; and in 1839 Galician Hasidism received a great boost when Israel Friedmann, the Rebbe of Ruzhyn near Kiev, the spiritual heir to the great Dov Ber of Mezheritz, fled Russian persecution to Sadgora in the Bukowina. By mid-century Hasidism was becoming a major factor in Galician Jewish society. No doubt the new sobering trends within Hasidism made it here, as in Lithuania, more Talmudic and thus more respectable than in its nigh-ecstatic early days. It was no longer just a rural Jewish movement, though the zadikim often continued to hold their courts in country towns. Now the urban Jews also were attracted. Even richer Jews in Brody and Lwow paid allegiance to visionary rabbis who in principle rejected the Enlightenment. And Hasidism brought into being a new type of Jewish community organization, whose great virtues were its absolute imperviousness to the administrative assault of the modern secular state and its indifference to modern schooling.

The cause of Jewish education became the more difficult in these years, finally, because the Galician reformers violently scorned the Hasidim. In the oldest of the "enlighteners," Josef Perl, this was not surprising. He gave his life to the school he founded in Tarnopol, and was by no means utterly dismissive of Jewish tradition. But he was a radical "improver" of the Jews and inherited some of Herz Homberg's zeal and arrogance. In 1838 he denounced the Hasidim to the government, appealing for their expulsion from the Habsburg Lands.[16] But Krochmal also shared such attitudes. Krochmal, the greatest intellect among the Galician Jewish "enlighteners" of the Vormärz, a man much more "national" in his ideas than Perl and Homberg, saw the Hasidim as "rabble," poor and dirty. And S. J. L. Rapoport, the latter day Grand Rabbi of Prague, was so abrasive in his relations with the Hasidim of Tarnopol that in 1840 he fled Galicia, fearing for his life.

The development of Lwow Jewry is the clearest symptom of how the Jewish educational debacle affected Galician Jewry's ability to take advantage of the mid-century opportunities mentioned earlier in this chapter.[17] This was a very large Jewish community, numbering 30,000 persons in mid-century. The wealthy here did not live off international trade, as at Brody, the other great Jewish community in Galicia, but off money-lending and tax-farming. Perhaps for this reason the Judeophobia of the Christian community was unusually strong, and the Maskilim were more than elsewhere intent on appearing as "cultured" as the Mendelssohnian reformed Jews of Germany itself and as those of Vienna, in order to "fit in" to the Christian world. Most of the poor, on the other hand, were either traditionalist admirers of Rabbi Ornstein or Hasidim. By 1839, when Ornstein died, the Maskilim were filled with resentment and impatience, blaming both the Jew-hatred of the Christian population and the poverty of the Jews on the "fanaticism" of the deceased and of the Hasidim. In the interests of "intelligence" and "progress" they now organized the equivalent of a coup d'état. They encouraging the Austrian *Statthalter* governor to install new, more radically modern-minded community leaders chosen from among themselves; and then they sought to employ an "enlightened" rabbi. In 1843 they called to Lwow, from Hohenems in the Vorarlberg, a young scholar educated in Bohemia named Abraham Kohn.[18]

Over the next few years Kohn did what he could for the modernization of Lwow's Jewry: he presided over the completion of a modern synagogue, opened a German-language Jewish school, and launched a campaign for the abolition of the obnoxious meat and candle taxes that oppressed all Galician Jewry. He encountered vociferous resistance, however, from the majority of the congregation both over his German-language preaching and his proposals about ritual reform. Worse, it turned out that the Hasidim had allies among the wealthy, some of whom were the collectors of the hated taxes and who resented Kohn's assault on their income.[19] Further, the "progressive" elders themselves soon factionalized: some were offended by Kohn's preaching during the famine year (1847) against ostentatious Jewish wealth; others felt he was reforming too slowly. Even before the revolution erupted in 1848, releasing a torrent of polemic from all sides, the unfortunate rabbi was beleaguered, subject to stonings and insults on the street.

Kohn chose to be active in revolutionary politics. He was not averse to the younger "intelligence" among the Lwow Jews managing to evict the "plutocratic" leadership installed in 1839, and to embark on radical reforms. But that coup led to his undoing during the revolutionary months that followed. Because of the reforms, the Lwow Hasidim directed ever-greater violence against the rabbi. If the wealthy tax-collectors did not inspire the assault, they at least tolerated it. In August 1848 poison entered Rabbi Kohn's food, with the result that he died.[20]

Three years after Kohn's murder, in 1851, Mayer Kallir, a wealthy Jew who was president of the then-new Brody Chamber of Commerce, sent a proposal to the government that expressed the sheer desperation that enlightened Jews then felt in Galicia. He suggested "solving" the Jewish question through "peasantization" of the Jews; in other words, through renewal of Joseph II's project for encouraging Jews to go into farming. That project had not succeeded in the past, Kallir admitted, but it was worth trying again because, as he saw it, Jewish resistance to educational reform was almost absolute. He noted that despite all the efforts since 1781 to introduce German language schools for the Galician Jews, there were still only two or three rabbis in the whole crownland who could be counted upon to encourage Jewish children to attend them. The improvement of the Jewish condition, he said, could only be achieved through firm action by the Vienna bureaucracy aimed at changing the Jewish professional mold.[21]

Today one tends to look with nostalgia upon the traditionalism of east European Jewry at that time. One tends to acknowledge that tradition was humane and familiar, that it allowed for individual dignity, that it preserved what today one calls Jewish "national" or "popular" culture. Still, one may recognize that because of the all-encompassing character of that culture in the first half of the nineteenth century, it became not easier but ever more difficult for Jews in Galicia to change.

III

In the western Habsburg crownlands, as we have seen elsewhere, the Vormärz witnessed a slow economic upswing and a good deal of social change in Christian society, and this helped the modernization of the Jews. Was this not true of Galicia also? The answers are mostly negative, and this for one major reason.[22] At once the cause and the principal symptom of Galicia's "backwardness" was the nigh universal involvement of Galicia's Christian population in primitive agriculture. As late as 1910, sixty years after the serf-emancipation, 60.1% of all the Poles in Galicia were still engaged in agriculture, 92% of the Ruthenians.[23] As late as the mid-nineteenth-century Lwow had only some 60,000 inhabitants, Cracow (until 1846 an independent, self-governing city-state) about 40,000, and Brody, the most active and prosperous town in this kingdom, only 25,000. Everyone else was out on the land: in 1774 about 2.6 million people, by 1850 some 4.5 million. Joseph's decrees were even less able to change this situation than they were to alter the life of the Galician Jews; and the Napoleonic upheaval and Franciscan "calm" alike were just as perverse in their effects on the Christian world as on the Jews.

In Galicia even the *szlachta* [gentry] was poor, though here as in Bohemia there were a few extraordinarily wealthy magnates and prelates ruling over a feudal world. The reason for the poverty was first the ruination brought on all Poles by the partitions. For decades after the great "deluge" began in 1648, Poland was the scene of intermittent wars, and more came just before and during the final partitions of the state. Second, what one might call the "natural" trade of Galicia's estates had been broken off since 1772. Prussian and Russian tariff policies had blocked the transport of the Carpathian forest products and the grain from the Galicia down the San and the Vistula to the shipping centers along the Baltic, whence they could be sent to the hungry west. By 1800 the noble estates throughout the old Commonwealth were burdened with debt and remained so in mid-century and even later on. And then, third, in the early nineteenth century, as noted elsewhere, there was one noblemen in Galicia to every 68 commoners, a ratio unparallelled in the western Habsburg Lands.[24] The nobility was here inherited from the old Polish-Lithuanian Commonwealth, the "gentry paradise," and its size meant that there were too many gentry mouths to feed.

Commerce there was in Vormärz Galicia. The dearth of locally-manufactured goods made for a constant demand for imports. Lwow was the main distribution center for Austrian goods. Brody (until 1879) and Cracow (until 1846) were free international markets, exempt from the customs regime. But to balance these centers, one may recall that a prohibitive Austrian import tariff inhibited the old east-west through-trade from Russia to the German lands.

During the Vormärz some improvements came. As noted earlier, a short railroad linking Cracow to Prussian Silesia opened in 1847, but there were still only rutted roads eastwards to the main centers of population.[25] In mid-century conditions in the rural areas of Galicia remained primitive. One traveler recounts:

> In Makow [near Cracow] in the mountain foothills we attended a weekly market. We saw wagons there made out of oak trunks—just slices of wood without spokes—and also evidence of a true exchange economy where on one side potatoes and onions, on the other iron nails served as money.[26]

And this "kingdom" possessed none of the industry, old or new, that by then gave Bohemia her modern allure. A crude statistical index suggests the degree of this industrial lapse. In all Galicia in 1851 there were some 20 steam-run machines with a total of 251 horsepower. Even in Hungary, another "backward" part of the Empire, there were then 107 such machines with a total of 1515 horsepower; in the Austrian Alpine provinces there were 40 with 770.5 horsepower; in Lower Austria (in other words, Vienna) 130 with 1717 horsepower; in the Bohemian Lands, 498 with 7050 horsepower.[27] Compared to western Europe or even Bohemia in the nineteenth century, Galicia was a roadless, cold, foothills region leading nowhere. If Galicia's Jews were poor and multitudinous, its Christians were more so.

Was there no escape? In Bohemia and in Vienna in the early nineteenth century the enlightened Jews allied themselves politically and socially with the rising new class of the period, the German-speaking Christian bourgeoisie. In Galicia such an alliance was impractical in part because there was minimal bourgeoisie, but more important because most of it (despite Austrian encouragement of middle-class German immigration) was Jewish. At the most active commercial center of the east, Brody, characteristically, some 80% of the entire population was Jewish! Yet here there existed an alternative basis for a political alliance—the Polish noble "nation". The Polish nobles may have been poor, but until the completion of the peasant emancipation in 1848 they were the exclusive owners of the land in Galicia, they had political leadership, and even had some political power. In the "Kingdom of Galicia and Lodomeria" Franz I allowed the consolidation of a Diet [*Sejm, Landtag*] after 1815. Only the nobles of Galicia had the right to elect its members. In practice, it was to a considerable extent a mere tool of the royal governor. The nobles possessed no strong institutions of local administration. They could place no effective brake on the imperial bureaucrats who actually ruled the province and exacted taxes and military recruits as they wished. Compared to the peasants and the tiny non-Jewish "middle stratum" of society, however, the szlachta was a significant political force, a worthwhile ally in any effort to escape the Jewish impasse.

It was for such reason that in 1848 Rabbi Kohn at Lwow, though he was a German speaker, took steps that won him a place in the Polish national pantheon.[28] In the early days of the revolution he joined with the Crownland Polish leadership in its first petition to Count Stadion, the governor, for constitutional and adminstrative reforms. He then encouraged a friend, Meyer Rachmiel Mieses, to accept nomination to the Galician Diet and then (when the authorities postponed the proposed meeting of the Diet) to join a Polish National Council.[29] Whether Kohn favored a linguistic Polonization of Galicia's Jews is not clear. He spoke out also in those last months of his life for the Ukrainians, and his first allegiance (and Mieses' allegiance also) was to the Austrian *Statthalter*. But thanks to Kohn it can be argued that a political alliance between the reform Jews of Galicia and the Polish nobility actually got underway in 1848.[30]

Even Kohn's Haskalah contemporaries knew, however, that a Polish-Jewish alliance had limits. Above all, they could observe that the patriotic movement among the Poles had a depressing record.[31] It was not a movement parallel to the national rebirths in other crownlands, which began with language revival, then gradually expanded to advocate economic reform, and finally, as Austria's regime grew feeble, took on a politically Liberal complexion. In Poland high politics came first, socio-economic issues last. In 1815 a residual of the articulate and violently fratricidal political parties of old Poland still survived. Even in Galicia, the patriarchal Potocki, Czartoryski, and Sapieha families had great estates and (at Cracow) palaces. As long as they were present there was neither room nor need for forward-looking national politics. The Polish dream remained the restoration of the old state, notoriously unfriendly to the Jews, not the formation of a new one. In 1830–32 the situation changed a little. Political Poland made a final gamble: it launched a revolutionary war against the Tsar and lost. During this great outburst, national economic and cultural revival did appear as principal planks in the Polish movement. But after the failure of the great rising, these were of little avail. A grief-stricken Mickiewicz might now represent Poland as the martyred "Christ" of Europe. A Lelewel might delve into the country's history in order to explain her lamentable present. Poets and novelists—alongside the great aristocrats and the emigrant revolutionaries—become principal spokesmen of the "nation." Yet these intellectuals patently could not by themselves produce concrete economic reforms and a social reconstruction; nor could they change szlachta opinion.

In Galicia in 1846 another Polish nationalist rising further undermined the credibility of the szlachta. Planned as a glorious rising of the "intelligent" Poles against the wickedness of the Metternich regime, this rising ended, to the tacit applause of the Austrian bureaucracy, as a *Jacquerie*-like massacre of Polish nobles by Polish peasants.[32] This exhibition of militant romanticism revealed the Polish nobility to be socially isolated in its own country and at the mercy of the Austrians. Then in 1848 the democratization of society brought other demographic realities to light. During the revolution the Orthodox Christian peasant people of eastern Galicia began to voice themselves politically as Ruthenes, or Russians, or Ukrainians; and from the censuses of the time it is known that they comprised 50% of Galicia's population.[33]

For such reasons enlightened Jewry in Galicia was anything but united in 1848 on a Polonophile platform. In fact at Brody, where the Ukrainian presence was more evident than at Lwow, the reform Jews not only stuck loyally to the German language but also advocated a Viennese political allegiance. They possessed a certain political clout here: because so much of the Brody population was Jewish, the community could dispose of Brody's vote in the all-Empire election, and had it so desired, it could have sent a Pole to the new Vienna parliament. Instead, led by the youngest and most reform-minded among them, the Brody Jews invited that apostle of German-language eloquence, Preacher Mannheimer of Vienna, to be their Reichstag representative. They gave the Poles a slap in the face.[34]

Nor was this the only division that emerged among the Galician Jews in 1848 over the choice of political allies. At Cracow, the ancient capital of Poland and the only part of the old Commonwealth which had retained independence after the partitions of the late eighteenth and early nineteenth centuries, Orthodox Jews made overtures to the Poles. One reason was that demographic realities did not always figure so largely in Jewish calculations then as in the minds of the Lwow and Brody reformers (or as they do in historians' minds today). To ordinary Jews it was simply important then with whom they did their business; and at Cracow the answer was fairly simple. For centuries the szlachta had owned the land, and the Jews had dealt with the owners of estates. More than anywhere else in eastern Europe, in Poland the Jews had carved out a standard position for themselves within the feudal world. On many estates the *arenda* or actual manager had been a Jew. In the villages owned by the nobility, the tavernkeeper and shop-owner and collector of debts had been a Jew. And since most of the Galician Jews were Orthodox, from this long-standing economic relationship it was but a short step to an Orthodox Jewish political support for the Poles.

There was also a complex political situation behind the Jewish Polonophilia of Cracow. As at Brody and Lwow, there were German-speaking Maskilim here. Since 1830 they had been able to establish a German-language Jewish school and then to expand it. But because the administrative language of the city was until 1846 Polish, the Maskilim were of necessity Polish speakers too, and many favored the Polish political cause. In addition, during the period of Cracow's independence, large numbers of very orthodox Jews from Russian Poland had immigrated to the Jewish suburb, Kazimierz. In 1832 when the community had to select a new rabbi, the successful candidate, a wealthy man named Ber Meisels, was opposed by an Hasidic "counter-rabbi"; and that gentleman took it upon himself to deny, in the name of Jewry, Meisels' rabbinical existence. As a result, a good portion of Cracow Jewry behaved in the 1840s as if the chief rabbi was not there; and faced with that sort of opposition, Meisels had both to appear staidly orthodox in point of ritual and prayer, and yet to maintain a political stance stronger than that of the Enlightened.[35]

Ber Meisels had assumed a pro-Polish stance even during the rising of 1846. In the revolutionary springtime of 1848, German speaker though he was, he showed the same affections. Early in April, he made himself a member of the Galician delegation to Vienna, and drew considerable attention because in point of patriotism he proved more Polish than many leading Poles.[36] Later on, in May, a polemic broke out in the central European Jewish press when the Jews of Posen [Poznán], a city then in Prussia, proposed that all of old Poland's Jews should now become Germans. With Meisels' blessing, the Jews of the Cracow region replied with testimonials to the glories of Polish, as opposed to German, culture and to the "historic alliance" between the Jews and the Poles.[37]

The more Meisels spoke out in favor of the Polish cause, the more the modernists in Galician Jewry had reason to feel wary. For them, Meisels seemed the harbinger of an Orthodox Jewish coalition with the Christian Right. And then events confirmed that a Polish alliance was for reformer Jews a bad idea. In mid-July 1848, the Austrian authorities showed their might at Brody, making the entire Jewish community there keenly aware of what one might call "German reality." The army needed recruits: when the Jewish elders refused to produce a suitable number of young Jews, the authorities simply surrounded the city and in a midnight raid extracted 300 "volunteers."[38] In a western crownland, the active Liberal press of the day might have invoked such a horror story to persuade the Jews to abandon German with all due speed. At Brody, however, right next to the Russian frontier, the Jews quickly recognized that no Pole, no Ukrainian could help them. It followed from the outrage that only the German-speaking Vienna regime was strong! And that was only the first of the army's interventions in Galicia. In November 1848 it found occasion, in the interests of public order, to bombard Lwow.[39]

In mid-nineteenth century, in sum, one could argue that the Polish nobility was an indigenous force which offered Galicia a prospect of breaking the bonds of "backwardness." But nothing was clear; and among the Jews the question of political allies in the Christian camp was already subject to the split between the followers of Orthodoxy and the Haskalah.

I V

To suggest that Galicia and its Jewry derived no benefit from the opportunities of the 1850s and 1860s would be unfair. The absolutist government of 1849–60 brought in administrative reforms here as elsewhere. Gradually then changes did begin. New banks appeared. New industries slowly blossomed. Eventually the railroads did get through. But it was characteristic of Galicia's development that the age of modernism dawned with a natural catastrophe. It began at Brody just after the great raid of July 1848. In the summer heat the cholera attacked the city. By October there were 2,500 dead, ten percent of the population, four-fifths of them Jews; and during the following year a terrible fire ravaged the town. Its free trading status was not yet abolished—that happened in 1879. But 1848–49 put Brody on the way to losing its prosperity.[40] Meanwhile disease spread in other parts of Galicia, specifically typhus, and a potato famine occurred. In 1855 the cholera returned. Over the half decade the population of Galicia is believed to have fallen by 400,000 and more.[41] Though war wasted other Habsburg crownlands in the years 1848 and 1849, nowhere else was there a catastrophe on the scale of the one in this most needy province.

For Galician Jews, there were other such tribulations just after 1848. In most parts of the Habsburg Empire, as seen elsewhere, the emancipation of the Jews was for practical purposes more or less final by 1849. The state then ceased to enforce the residence restrictions on Bohemian and Moravian Jews, and the "tolerance" system at Vienna. Everywhere else the special taxes on Jews lapsed. In Galicia, however, even in 1848–49 the state administration proved much more rigorous in sticking to old regulations than elsewhere. By 1852, when Franz Joseph retracted his own "dictated" constitution, the Austrian bureaucracy in Galicia was enforcing anti-Jewish laws that everyone had imagined abolished. In October 1853, thereupon, Vienna decreed the "provisional" reinstatement of the pre-1848 laws restricting Jewish rights to own real estate. This created havoc especially in Galicia. Here since Joseph II's time the szlachta had sought to escape its debts by mortgaging or selling estates. The abolition both of feudalism and of the restrictions on Jews in 1848 had encouraged a large-scale Jewish acquisition of land. Now all that had to be reversed.[42]

Just a few years later there was an equally unkind blow from another quarter. At the moment absolutism collapsed in 1859, one might have expected a reversion in Galicia, as in other Habsburg lands, to the heady atmosphere of societal solidarity that had characterized the spring of 1848. During that thrilling moment, Poles and Jews had embraced in the streets of Brody and Lwow as well as at Cracow. Galicia had been notable then for a general dearth of the Judeophobia that erupted in Bohemia and Hungary.[43] One might have hoped now for more of the same. In 1859 and 1860, however, the Poles did not embrace the Jews. Instead, a startling wave of overt Jew-hatred swept the Polish political world. In 1861, as a result, when the Galician Diet assembled, when the fire of crownland freedom was hot because of Vienna's debility, and when four Jews appeared to claim seats, the Polish deputies proved themselves wholly unwilling to grant civic equality to the Jews. They hesitated even to approve the freedom for Jews to reside in all towns. Later on in 1863, during the new great Polish revolutionary rising in the Tsar's Congress Kingdom, Poles and Jews were for a time reunited in Galicia. But ill impressions had been made, and they were preserved when, in the end, it was not the Galician Diet that initiated the legal emancipation of the Galician Jews but the Reichsrath in Vienna. The Galician Diet only ratified, with a reluctant majority vote, the new Cisleithian Basic Law.[44]

In the face of these blows the modernization of Galician Jewry proceeded slowly. To cite just one index, in 1851 there were 260 Jewish students in Galicia's Christian gymnasia (to which they had been admitted in 1848), 6.1% of all the students there. By 1867 there were 556 students, 8% of the total; in 1869 there were 620, 8.2%. Meanwhile in small but rising numbers Jews were entering the other Galician schools, the *Realschulen*, the universities.[45] The Jewish students were small indeed in numbers relative to the 575,000 Jews in the Crownland in 1869. Eventually, accumulation paid off. The Galician Jewish intelligentsia was beginning to turn into an educated middle class. The problem was not, however, that no change came, but that it came at a painfully slow pace relative to the progress in other crownlands further west.

What is more, political splits survived among the Jews of Galicia and did so in a fashion that made ever more difficult that modernization of Jewry which did occur. We will discuss this at greater length in a later chapter, but can mention here an early disaster resulting from the reform Jews' fear of the Orthodox. Even in the revolution, we have seen, this led to compulsive submission to the central imperial political power at German Vienna. By the 1860s, there were strong reasons for modifying such compliance; and these increased in 1867 when Franz Joseph made a compromise with the nobility in Hungary, allowing them constitutional home rule in the largest of his inherited lands. Now there was a very clear danger he would grant a comparable autonomy to the Polish nobility of Galicia, and by 1871 he proceeded to do exactly that. Yet the enlightened Jews of Galicia stayed strictly on their Germanophile course. One may admit that the Polish show of Jew-hatred in 1859 lent a distinct justice to their choice, but the main factor was the belief that German Liberalism alone had the strength to beat back the fundamentalist rabbis. Only in western Galicia, around Cracow, did a Polonizer movement remain strong among Jewish reformers in the 1860s. The passion of reformer allegiance to Germanism grew so

strong that in 1869 a specifically anti-Polish Jewish political union appeared,
the Shomer Israel. In 1873, when as we will see an Orthodox Cracow rabbi
got elected to the Austrian Reichsrath on a Polonophile platform, the
Shomer Israel cooperated with the Ruthenians in the election to the Crownland Diet, thus placing the enlightened Jews of Galicia in organized confrontation with the noble "nation" which was in control of the land.[46] Not
until the middle 1870s was the difficulty—essentially a matter of Jewish
communal sectarianism—gradually smoothed out. By that time the Poles
were on the way to perceiving the political combination through which
they would actually rule until the end of the Monarchy: a pragmatic bond
with the anti-modernist Orthodox elements among the Jews.

V

Galician Jewry fell into a deadlock in the middle of the nineteenth century.
This largest body of Habsburg Jews was overwhelmed by the "backwardness" of Galicia itself, ill-equipped with the basic tools of modernization
(schools), deeply split ideologically, and multiplying at a rapid pace. Its
problems grew greater rather than smaller with time. The economic opportunities of Greater Austria in the 1850s and 1860s in no way afforded
it an escape.

Whether in broad historical perspective, or in the narrow understanding of contemporaries, this was a bitter truth for Habsburg Jewry as it faced
the coming of industrialism in the decades after 1848. It was all very well
for Viennese Jewry to congratulate itself on its enlightenment then, and
on its success at winning emancipation in the mid-century revolution; all
very well also for Bohemian Jewry then to contemplate the increasing embourgeoisement even of the village Jews. The situation of Galician Jewry
countered these western Austrian Jewish accomplishments. The more the
democratization of society occurred now, the more society developed a
social conscience, the more would the poverty and need of the eastern
Habsburg Jews endanger the prosperity of the rest.

EIGHT

Hungarian Success

I

1848 led not only to a twenty-year political crisis in central Europe, backed by rather speedy economic growth; it also launched a crisis in each of the nationality groups which had expressed themselves during the revolution. In Germany, to cite an obvious example, the revolution shook the old organization of society, and led to a widespread breakdown of the con-census that had enabled aristocracy, *Bürgertum*, proletariat, and peasantry to live together. Though the violent social disorders of the revolutionary year did not last, a sense of uncertainty did, and the goal of political uni-fication lived on. After twenty years Bismarck's Prussia brought it about. Comparable crises affected the Magyars and the Poles, nations that had been held together in the past by rigid feudal structures. The revolutionary explosions of mid-century sprang those structures asunder, forcing the old ruling classes to experiment and to seek out new social allies until stability was restored in the later 1860s.

Mention of these crises recalls the vast differences between the Jews and the other European peoples. In point of organization, for example, all the others sought to construct greater and more elaborate "secular" political frameworks for their national life. The Jews did the opposite: it was pre-cisely in this period that they sought to demolish the final remnants of their old nation, to cast aside any last sign that they were more than a "religious group."

Yet on one level it did appear throughout central Europe in those decades that Jews and Christians were all experiencing a single crisis. In France one heard much before 1848 about the alleged immorality and soul-lessness of Guizot and of Louis Philippe's bourgeoisie. After the revolution, the same bitter taunt was flung at the entrepreneurial Second Empire. In the Germanies such complaints attached to the *"Gründer,"* the ruthlessly aggressive capitalists who wholly changed the economic and social land-scape even before Bismarck's wars. In the Habsburg Empire in the 1860s the "Volkswirtschaftlicher Aufschwung" was referred to simply as *"die Kor-ruption."* And among the Jews there were sighs that somehow the old spirit of the people was gone, that there had taken place a moral degeneration, that religious indifference had taken over.

One may also observe that the Jews, just like the Christian nations, did in this period have an institutional crisis, albeit the institutions were very different.[1] In the Habsburg Lands the old Jewish *kehillas* had lost most of their legal power in the 1780s, when Joseph II cancelled the force of Jewish civic law. But until 1848 the sheer weight of the Franciscan regime had in most localities enabled kehilla authorities to carry on much as before. Then the revolutions shattered them.

In the past, for example, Jewish taxpayers, kept in place by the state, had paid the community officials and subsidized the necessary institutions of Jewish life: the synagogues and schools, the ritual baths and slaughter-houses, the hospitals, the burial houses, and the cemeteries. The emancipation now removed the residential restrictions. Consequently, the taxpayers in smaller localities (especially in Bohemia and Moravia) began to move away, leaving the communities penniless. In the larger cities, on the other hand, many community members used the emancipation as an excuse to stop paying community taxes altogether, even though immigration was causing community expenses to shoot upwards. Particularly in Vienna, at Brno and Olomouc in Moravia, and at Pest in Hungary, the sudden arrival of literally thousands of provincial Jews put an unprecedented strain on the community facilities. Overcrowding and deterioration came fast, yet there were no funds for new construction and repairs.

The disappearance of the Franciscan state also raised political questions within the Jewish communities. Even in the past the governance of the Jewish kehillas had in theory been "democratic." Every Jewish male had been supposed to pay taxes and to participate in the election of community elders, although in practice many were unable (because of poverty) to sustain this role, and power lay with the rich. Now, in 1848, the new ideologies of the outer world reinforced the old egalitarianism and generated pressure for new, more democratically produced leadership. These pressures were the greater because control now made a difference. In the past all Jews, rich or poor, had been in general agreement about what it meant to be a Jew. Now there were increasingly unbridgeable divergences of view. Sometimes, as in Galicia, "democracy" might imply greater traditionalism and the rejection of reform; sometimes, as in Prague, it might imply the reverse: more reform, less tradition; but everywhere it meant now that Jews of one tendency might be forcibly subjected to the followers of another.

With the return of civic order in 1849 and 1850 the emergency in Habsburg Jewish communal life passed. Franz Joseph's absolutism put an end to any sort of local politics. His rejection of constitutionalism restored the need for some sort of Jewish common action. Yet just as among the Christian nations, tension and uncertainty remained. The new freedom of movement alone kept a "communal crisis" of sorts boiling on the practical level, as did the absence of any law regulating the communities. How could people be persuaded to pay new or higher taxes? Who was going to govern the communities, and in what style? In addition there were basic questions unanswered. How was Judaism to function as "just" an emancipated religion? What were to be the relations between Jewish authority and state authority? Were Jews still to be subject to any laws of their own? If so, which ones? These questions were not unlike the great ones which kept central European Christian society in tension in the post-revolutionary era. In one way or another they remained open and unanswered until after the Austro-Hungarian constitutional arrangements of 1867–68, when new laws finally regulated the status of the emancipated Jewish religion.

All this is very relevant to the topic of this chapter: Hungarian Jewry's response to the post-revolutionary time of troubles, and the economic challenge. Nowhere else was the crisis in the Christian nations so pronounced as in the vast kingdom where these Jews lived; and nowhere else did the Jewish communal crisis produce so much surface change among the Jews.

II

Before turning to the crisis itself, let us note some differences even in the early development of Hungarian Jewry from what we have seen in Galicia, and first of all the demographic difference. As noted earlier, there had not been many Jews left in Hungary at the end of the Turkish occupation of Hungary in 1699. Most of them were at Bratislava and at other places on aristocratic domains along Hungary's western frontier. After 1726, when Karl VI imposed his marriage restrictions on Bohemian and Moravian Jewry, an immigration began that brought the Hungarian Jewish population to some 83,000 by 1787 (most of whom were still gathered along the frontiers with Austria). This was almost as many as in the Bohemian Crownlands, though nowhere near yet as many as in Galicia.[2]

After 1781, a massive new immigration of Jews into Hungary began from the Polish north. The Hungarian Jewish population leapt from 83,000 in 1787 to about 130,000 in 1805. By 1825 the total seems to have been about 190,000; by 1840, 242,000; by 1857, 407,800; by 1869, 542,200; by 1880, when the Galician immigration slowed down, 624,700. These increases of 40% and 50% every twenty years in the Franciscan period endowed Hungary as early as 1848 with a Jewish population almost as large as that in Galicia. By 1910, we may note here in advance, the total Jewish population of Hungary was 910,000. This was almost double what it had been in 1868, and exceeded the Jewish population then in Galicia, that former greatest reservoir of Jews in the Habsburg Empire.

This demographic difference between Hungarian and Galician Jewry was accompanied by differences between community institutions. In neither kingdom at the start of the nineteenth century was there any longer an all-national Jewish organization, but in both a regime of kehillas governed the Jews. In Galicia, however, the old hierarchy of Jewish councils had just recently been destroyed, its memory was strong, and the local communal organizations were hoary with age and prestige. In Hungary it was centuries since there had been an effective central Jewish organization (though in 1711 Kaiser Karl VI had appointed the Hoffaktor, Simson Wertheimer, titular "Grand Rabbi of all Hungary");[3] and most of the local Hungarian *kehillot* were new. "Privileged" Jewish communities had no doubt existed from the time of the reconquest from the Turks in western Hungary near the Austrian frontier at Bratislava, in the "seven communities" of today's Burgenland, and also at Pest, Óbuda, and Buda, the three cities which later united to form Budapest.[4] New kehillas were formed ad hoc in Hungary as the Jewish population grew; and this meant that the immigrant Galician Jews, who wandered into the villages of today's Slovakia, were "mobilized" (as we would say today) far more than they had been at home. When Arminius Vámbéry, a famous Jewish explorer and orientalist, an intellectual titan of late-nineteenth-century Europe, was born in 1832 in today's southern Slovakia, his birth was not recorded because there was no Jewish community in his village.[5] Though very poor, his family was "free" in a sense they had never been in Galicia, and his career suggests the heights to which such "freedom" could lead.

Another early distinction of Hungarian Jewry regarded the character of the "Orthodox," who were far less rigid here than in Galicia.[6] It had not always been so. In the eighteenth century, in Hungary as in Galicia and in rural Bohemia, the rabbinate was unsystematically trained, provincial, "fanatical." Early in the nineteenth century, moreover, just when the immigration from the north began, the older Jewish communities in western Hungary began to look away from the Enlightenment and sought conservative Talmudists to be their rabbis. Exactly what precipitated this trend is not clear. Presumably these communities were alarmed by the revolutionary work of the Berlin reformers, some of whose followers had appeared in their midst. Perhaps they were influenced by the conservative Judaism propagated after 1789 at Nikolsburg by rabbi Banet (who was Hungarian-born, and had been rabbi for a community near Bratislava before he moved to Moravia). It was in this way that Moses Sofer (Szofer, Schreiber) was called first in 1798 to Mattersdorf [Nagymarton], one of the "seven communities" next to the Austrian frontier, then in 1806 to Bratislava.

Born of an old rabbinical family in Frankfurt am Main in 1762, Sofer was rigidly against the application of rationalism in matters religious, and he was especially against change in Jewish life, tolerating no departure whatsoever from the *Shulchan Aruch* (the sixteenth-century codification of the Jewish ritual law).[7] Because Sofer possessed immense learning and magnificent teaching abilities, he managed to stir a wave of eastern Jewish scholarly reaction against the Enlightenment. He attracted very great numbers of students. His yeshiva replaced the older schools at Prague and (after Banet's death in 1829) the one at Nikolsburg as the intellectual center of Jewish orthodoxy in all central Europe. Some scholars estimate that Sofer's school was the largest Talmudic academy to emerge since Baby-

lonian days. When he died in 1839, he was succeeded by his equally traditionalist son.

There were major differences, however, between this center of Jewish
conservatism in Hungary and the rabbinical reaction against Herz Homberg's mission in Galicia. The Hungarian conservatives accepted the need
for higher educational standards, for example, provided the rabbis defined
the standards. The Galician rabbis did not. Even more importantly, the
Orthodox yeshivot dominated by Rabbi Sofer admitted there was a need
for Jews to learn German and to be at least aware of the outside world. In
Galicia, as we have seen, the Hasidim kept this window closed.

In Hungary Hasidism also experienced a different development from
that in Galicia. Hasidic Jews were present even in the eighteenth century
in Hungary. In 1808 Rabbi Moses Teitelbaum established one of the greatest
dynasties in eastern Europe at Sátoraljaújhely in northeastern Hungary.
By the 1840s a prominent zadik was settled at Munkács. But Hasidism never
acquired either numbers or influence here comparable to that enjoyed north
of the Carpathians. And the most famous Hungarian Hasidic dynasty appeared at Szatmár [Satu Mare] only much later, in the 1890s.[8]

Not only were the Orthodox milder in Hungary before 1848, and the
Hasidim weaker; also modernism was more firmly rooted.[9] Joseph II did
not need to set up a broad network of German-language Jewish schools
here, because he could count on the activity of the emigrants from Jewish
Bohemia and Moravia, some of whom (but by no means all) were as modern-minded as the prosperous Jewish merchants of Vienna and Prague.
Many of the thirty-odd schools he did set up were abandoned after his
death, but the fallback was nowhere near as total as in Galicia.[10] Furthermore, Joseph was more tactful here in his choice of the Jewish intellectuals
he sent out in support of his reforms. One, for example, was that Peter
Beer whom we encountered in his old age at Prague. Born in rural Bohemia
about 1758, the son of a sub-contractor in the tobacco-farming business,
Beer studied Talmud at the yeshivot in Prague and Bratislava but then in
his twenties broke with tradition. Early in the 1780s he studied modern
subjects at the University of Vienna. Josef von Sonnenfels is said to have
been his protector and patron. In 1785 he went to Mattersdorf as master
in a new Jewish German-language school there and pioneered educational
modernism among the west Hungarian Jews. In 1796 he published a history
of the Jews which became very popular among the enlightened all over
central Europe, because it blatantly omitted all episodes which might suggest that the Jewish religion was dissimilar from a "rationalized" Chris-
tanity. The omission was characteristic of Beer's attitude towards the
"national" and Talmudic traditions in Jewish education. Yet Beer was no
Herz Homberg, who deliberately provoked the hatred of traditionalist circles, and in any case the Viennese regime came to recognize him as a
"problem" and early on recalled him.[11]

A less ardent but more consequential Jewish reformer in Hungary was

Aaron Chorin, born in Moravia in 1762, educated at Mattersdorf and Prague yeshivot. Chorin went as rabbi to Arad in eastern Hungary in 1789, and at the time seems to have been far less of a radical than Beer. Nonetheless, out there on the great middle Danubian plain, physically and spiritually far removed from the centers of Jewish traditionalism, his views changed. By the turn of the century he had become involved in scholarly quarrels with other rabbis, not least of all Mordekai Banet at Nikolsburg in Moravia. From 1805 onwards Chorin became a pioneer reformer of Jewish observance. He advocated German-language preaching and modification of the sabbath ritual. Eventually he even came to favor organ music in the synagogue. But he was never a man of violence, as Homberg was, or a radical secularizer like Josef Perl. He introduced the idea of reform slowly, skillfully, and so far as he could manage it without confrontation with the bearers of Jewish tradition.[12]

As a result of such teaching there came into being in Hungary by the 1820s and 1830s a stratum of "enlightened" Jews who were decidedly stronger than the Galician Maskilim. Bratislava and the "seven communities" even contained "nice" Germanized Jewish Biedermeier households whose heads commuted to Vienna every week.[13] Pest and several of the so-called *mezővárosok* [prairie towns] of southern and eastern Hungary gave refuge to some highly activist reformer rabbis who would have been at home anywhere in Germany.

One should not exaggerate these early differences between Hungarian and Galician Jewry. To balance the picture one may mention that in all Hungary as late as 1850 there were only 50 modern Jewish schools.[14] Eight of these were in one locality, Pest. Most of them offered only one or two years of elementary education. Many were recent foundations. A demographer of the 1840s estimated that only one in ten Hungarian Jews had received a German-language elementary education.[15] No matter that this was the highest "educated" proportion of any ethnic group in all Hungary; it meant that upwards of 350,000 of the 400,000 Hungarian Jews had not received a modern education and still carried on as in the past on the basis of their Talmudic knowledge and their Yiddish jargon alone. The schooling situation here was not as acute as in mid-century Galicia, but there was no effective instrument for the "melting" of traditionalism among nigh half a million Jews!

After mid-century, however, some truly key differences emerged. One of these derived from a relative unity of Hungarian Jewry. In Galicia the divisions within Jewry were such that there was no striving for organizational unity during the early nineteenth century, much less later on. In Hungary the reverse was true. As the Jewish population grew during the 1820s and 1830s and the possibilities of a legal emancipation emerged, the idea of a central, "all-Hungarian" council grew strong. Sometimes it was reformers who took the initiative, sometimes conservatives. At no point prior to the 1860s did the Hungarian rabbinate give general backing to the conferences convoked to discuss this subject. All the projects put forward were in some degree designed to push a sectarian political point. Regardless, the Jews of Hungary were talking to each other in mid-century in a way those of Galicia were not.[16]

By a curious indirect path, this led to a beneficial result. When the revolution came in 1848, Hungarian Jewry (as shall be seen in greater detail below) was able to speak credibly through a single delegation; it was not unified, but gave a certain appearance of being so. Consequently, when the revolution collapsed in the summer of 1849, just after the Magyar Parliament had emancipated the Jews, Hungarian Jewry received a unitary punishment. The Austrian authorities exacted, by way of retribution for allegedly rebellious Jewish behavior, a huge unitary fine. Negotiations during 1850–51 led, thereupon, to an important compromise. The Jews agreed to the immediate payment of the money, but obtained in exchange first a reduction of the sum, and second a promise that it would be devoted to schools—that it would parallel a school fund established much earlier in Moravia. With the backing of the Vienna Ministry of Religion and Education, plans were drawn up and implemented for a departure from old Jewish ways as thorough-going as had occurred in Bohemia and Moravia under Metternich.[17]

In Galicia during the Jewish communal crisis after 1848 the state provided little funding for Jewish schools, and the Jewish parties exhausted themselves in internecine struggle. In Hungary, however, the state's initiative pushed both "moderns" and "conservatives" competitively onto fresh paths. Whereas in 1850 there had only been 50 modern Jewish schools all told in Hungary, by the end of the absolutist decade there were over 300. These were no longer just one-year elementary schools, but began with three years and went up to the gymnasium level. By 1860 the *Heders*, where Jewish children studied nothing but the Talmud, were fading. Rabbis who knew nothing but the Talmud were by then in Hungary on their way out. By then reformer Jews and the Orthodox were battling about a project for replacing the old yeshivot of Bratislava altogether with a modern rabbi-training seminary. All the new schools, of course, initially taught German. But they were adaptable. After 1860, once a more accommodating regime emerged in Vienna, the Hungarian Jewish schools began to offer Magyar; and they were the real instrument which in the following generation lent to a massive Magyarization—and modernization—of the Hungarian Jews.[18]

III

In Galicia, as we have seen, the "backwardness" of the Christian environment had an important retarding effect on the modernization of the Jews. To some extent this was true also of Hungary, where indeed until 1800 the environment was very similar.[19] The feudal enserfment of the great majority of the population and the primitive condition of agriculture here meant that in 1910, sixty years after the serf emancipation, the agricultural sector of the population was still 62% and the proportion that lived in the countryside was still 79%.[20] In Hungary about 1800 there were a few small cities in the north and in Transylvania. In the west the proximity of burgeoning Vienna gave a promise of future commerce that was lacking in contemporary Galicia. Hungary's through-trade with the Balkans may have been more active than Galicia's trade with the Ukraine. But whereas Galicia retained a fairly large number of stagnant lesser cities, the ancient towns of central and southern Hungary had been ravaged by the Turkish wars and had few pretensions to urban status. And it is well to remember that Hungary was territorially three times as large as Galicia. All told, the magnitude of the modernization task was in some ways greater here than in the north.

During the Vormärz, however, improvements came to Hungary at a swifter pace than to Galicia. Because of the demanding market nearby at Vienna, for example, grain could be exported in ever-greater quantities. Because of Vienna, also, a crosstrade in tobacco and cotton from the Balkans throve. By the mid-nineteenth century Vienna was feeding off Serbian pigs, herded across Hungary. By 1848 Pest-Buda had regular steamship connections with the west. Bratislava had a railroad link to Vienna, and the line to Pest had been started (and would be completed by 1850). Hungary by then had her first joint-stock company bank, a savings bank, and even, as we have seen elsewhere, a few steam-run machines, the slender beginnings of her later industrial strength.

The greatest early-nineteenth-century factor that pushed Hungary ahead of Galicia, however, was political, and stemmed from a difference between the two nobilities. The aristocrats and ecclesiastical princes were similar in the two kingdoms, of course, and in both possessed feudal estates so huge that anywhere else in Europe they could have passed as independent rulers. But in Hungary the gentry class, the *nemesség*, was more numerous and politically significant by far than the Galician szlachta. In the 1840s, as noted earlier, there was one noble in Hungary for every 20 commoners, whereas in Galicia, the next most "ennobled" region of Europe, the ratio was one *szlachtić* to 68 commoners.[21] Some of the *nemesség* was impoverished, creating a problem of excessive privileged mouths; but its sheer numbers gave it strengths in the democratizing nineteenth-century world that other European nobilities lacked. The French nobility, under one per cent of the population, could not claim in the nineteenth century to be a modern nation, much less a "people." The Hungarian nobility could, and did.

Further, the Hungarian nobility possessed unique institutions. In Hungary an estates constitution had developed in unusually pronounced form during the later Middle Ages. It had survived the Turkish invasions of the sixteenth and seventeenth centuries, had been reconfirmed by the eighteenth-century Habsburgs, and had endured even against the assaults of Joseph II. Right up until 1848 Hungary's aristocrats and gentry had a national Diet and a network of county assemblies which far exceeded in point of independence and administrative power the Galician szlachta organizations. With these legitimate institutions the nemesség in the eighteenth century could and did sustain home rule, avoid new taxation, and fend off the enlightened bureaucratic Habsburg administrators who overwhelmed the Poles of Galicia. Vienna from the 1740s onward had sought to compensate the difficulty of taxation by collecting a special tariff on Hungarian exports to (and through) the Austrian lands. But even this tariff had in certain ways strengthened the Hungarian nobility. To public knowledge it had built up Austrian markets; it had correspondingly discouraged Hungarian manufactures; and for both reasons it had an important psychological effect.[22] Whereas in the west of the Empire Vienna's economic policies very frequently appeared to be "progressive," in Hungary because of the tariff barrier Vienna had the appearance of standing against a modern economic course. The Hungarian nobility stood for "progress," that is, the destruction of limits on trade; Vienna stood for the old regime.

In the first half of the nineteenth century the Hungarian nobility managed to increase even further its defenses against the throne.[23] When Franz II (I in Hungary) ascended the Hungarian throne in 1792, he found the nobility there violently reacting against Joseph II's attack on privilege; they were on the brink of rebellion. Initially he temporized about this insubordination (the claims of the nobility were after all "legitimate") and he concentrated on repressing social rebellion among Rumanian peasants in Transylvania, and the "revolutionary" conspiracies of Jacobin intellectuals. But as the requirements of Franz's purse escalated during the following war-filled years, and as the noble-dominated Diet grew ever less willing to vote new taxes, tensions between the throne and the "nation" grew until in 1811, when the Diet protested the royal bankruptcy, the King dissolved the Diet and for 14 years undertook to rule by decree. Starting in 1817 he even sought to eliminate noble assemblies in the Hungarian counties as overseers of the local royal administrators. Not until the fall of 1825 did he finally give in and convoke a Diet to give him taxes and army recruits in legal fashion.

Not only did he give in! The consequence of the show of royal absolutism was the crystalization of a new type of opposition inside Hungary. An enlightened noble intelligentsia had even in Joseph II's day launched a revival of Magyar as a literary language. In the face of Franz's autocratic behavior the nobility accepted the intelligentsia's initiative, and grafted onto its old legalistic political platform the modern notion that Hungary should be governed no longer in Latin, as in the past, or in German, as Joseph II had suggested, but in Magyar. After 1815 Count István Szechényi, the head of one of Hungary's most wealthy aristocratic families, lent his prestige to a further expansion of the national platform to include modern economic reforms. By the 1830s and 1840s, when the Vienna regime in its decrepitude began to convoke the Diet regularly, a fairly large number of younger men from the propertied "middle nobility" (as economic historians call it) were advocating a nationalist program that involved overall constitutional modernization, the abolition of feudalism, and broad economic modernization along western lines. In 1840 reform ideas were so popular in the nobility that the Diet could force the throne to accept the Magyar language as the exclusive language of government in all the Lands of Saint Stephen's Crown.

Exactly at this time a political coalition of sorts flowered between the Hungarian ruling class and the Jews, and contributed directly to the differentiation of Hungarian from Galician Jewry. The coalition was rooted in an old, typically east European relationship between Jews and noble landowners. In the late seventeenth and eighteenth centuries, for example, members of the Hungarian upper nobility frequently took Jews under their wing. It was the Pálffys who made it possible for the Jews to settle at Bratislava early in the eighteenth century by permitting them to live on a family estate next to the city walls. Comparably the Zichys allowed the Jews to settle at Óbuda; the Eszterházys introduced them into the "seven communities." We have seen comparable relationships in Moravia, Bohemia, and all the Polish Lands.[24]

The late eighteenth century witnessed a significant enlargement of the relationship. Prior to 1780, one may generalize, Hungary was insulated from west European economic developments. In those days most noble estates were self-managed, wandering Greeks from the Balkans handled what trade there was, and there were few Jews.[25] But in the later years of Maria Theresia's reign, at a time when large numbers of Jews were appearing in Hungary, the Vienna government decided to exclude "foreigners" (that is, Greeks) from the Empire's domestic commerce. Consequently all over Hungary in those decades Jews took over from the Greeks the functions of peddlers and traders. Thereupon in Joseph's day, and especially in the Napoleonic period, the economic needs of Vienna and the west exploded into Hungary, greatly stimulating export agriculture, pulling even medium-sized estates for the first time into a money economy, and attuning the owners of estates to slothful living and the use of manufactured goods. The new business opportunities in Hungary figured importantly then in the fortune-building of the Vienna Jews—of the Hofmanns, Biedermanns, Todescos, Liebenbergs, Leidesdorfers and others. All over Hungary Jews became the main middlemen between noble estate owners and the western markets; and a few began to step into a new business, that of managing estates for nobles who either wished to live away from home or who did not want to be bothered.

This sort of economic interdependence between Jews and nobles was parallel to the *arenda* system long practiced in Poland, but there was a difference. In Poland the Jewish agricultural exporters and peddlers were as poor as the rest; there was no nearby Vienna to make them rich. In

Hungary the reverse was true. Here Vienna was next door; the western markets were accessible; and given the peaceful times, improvements could be introduced, and were. Consequently the interdependence of the Jews and the nobility in Hungary lent a substantial enrichment to both.

Initially there seemed little to incline the Jews to the further step of forming a political alliance with the nobility. Not only were the Jews wholly excluded from Hungarian politics; also both the conservatives and the modernizers among them were engaged in Germanizing the Jewish population. They were in no way different in this respect from enlightened Jews elsewhere in central Europe. The Hungarian nobility, on the other hand, was seeking with equal zeal to stem Germanization and to extend the use of the Magyar tongue. Only one factor really led to a further coming together of Jews and nobles now: on both sides, the modernizers were in the minority. For all their activism, for all their creative ideas, the Jewish modernizers seemed to have as little real prospect of determining the course of Hungarian Jewry as did the Ferenc Deáks and Lajos Kossuths who were trying to capture the entire Hungarian Diet for reform.[26]

Signs of what was coming appeared shortly before the Diet of 1839–40, the great "Reform Diet" that would pass the law making Magyar the official language of the kingdom. By then emancipation of the Jews figured among the leading planks in the political platform of German Liberalism. The Magyar reformers, led by Baron Jozsef Eötvös, decided therefore that such a plank would be ideologically suitable in Hungary also, and in addition might enhance their case in a land where much of the population was comprised of minorities who spoke no Magyar. They designed for the Diet a law proposal emancipating the Hungarian Jews, which the gentry-dominated Lower House of the Diet then proceeded to pass. The magnate-dominated Upper House blocked the final passage of the law, refusing to do more than remove residence restrictions on the Jews. Further, at the next Diet (1843–44) even the Lower House proved rather anti-Jewish. But the noble reformers nonetheless raised considerable enthusiasm in Jewish circles.

Meanwhile on Eötvös's prompting, Moritz Bloch, a young Jewish linguist (who later on called himself Mór Ballagi), not only campaigned to induce Jews to speak Magyar but translated the Torah into that tongue.[27] The Diet's attempt at emancipation encouraged Bloch's cause. Not only gratitude prompted a Jewish response, however. At repeated conferences in these years between reformer and orthodox rabbis, it became clear that without outside help orthodox strength would continue to block any general reform of Judaism in Hungary. The modernist rabbis felt increasing frustration at the slow pace of things, and by the middle 1840s several of them took up the Magyarization cry. It was now that Löw Schwab, a rabbi at Pest, and his son-in-law, Leopold Löw, rabbi at Pápa, and even the aged Aaron Chorin began to advocate Jewish preaching in the Magyar language instead of in German.

By 1848 frustration was very high on both sides.[28] In 1844 Eötvös and

Deák had had to advise their Jewish friends that total Magyarization of Jewish life might be necessary before the emancipation could be passed, and that in addition immigration had to be stopped, orthodoxy eliminated! More than one prominent modernizer Jew had responded to this news with cultural despair, by converting.[29] And then when the Diet reopened in the fall of 1847, it began to seem to the noble reformers also that reform would never come. Conservatism still seemed to hold overwhelming political strength in Vienna, in the Hungarian House of Lords, and even in the provincial gentry assemblies. The revolution thus found reformer Jews and nobles alike ready for radical steps.

The news that there had been a revolution in Paris not only scared Kaiser Ferdinand on 4 April into granting Hungary an autonomous Magyar-language government and the right to redraw her constitution and to liberate her serfs. It also, as noted elsewhere, provoked the German-speaking burghers of many Hungarian towns into attacking Jews.[30] At this point the Jewish reformers went into action. German-speaking though most of them were, they moved very largely into active support of the Magyar cause, hoping that Liberalism in power would bring them emancipation and defense against the Judeophobes. Kossuth and his friends had long felt that a major reform of Judaism was needed before political emancipation could be passed. Now in Pest, the president of the Jewish congregation dramatically converted, suggesting that the whole Jewish flock might thus win favor on the Magyar side. Though he had few imitators, many other Jewish reformers proposed "sanitizing" the rituals of Judaism. At Pest during the summer one group actually set up a new congregation with its sabbath on Sunday.[31]

The outspokenly conservative rabbis of Bratislava were horrified by these excesses, and advised caution and non-participation in the revolution. But because of the German-led pogroms, many traditional Jews also joined the Magyars. In the months that followed, Jewish support—particularly Jewish economic support, but also the contribution of young men to the army and a lot of propagandistic help—was of very great importance to the new Magyar government as it struggled to consolidate its position. The Magyars did not respond immediately with a legal emancipation of the Jews. The government was worried by Judeophobic tendencies not just among German burghers but in the gentry itself. But among the reformer leaders, gratitude to the Jews was widespread and lasting.

The joint Magyar-noble and Jewish reform enterprises did not succeed in 1848–49. Even in the opening months the noble defenders of "Hungarian liberty" found themselves at odds with the ethnic nationalities inhabiting the country's periphery, especially with the Croats. By fall, Hungary was at war with her Austrian King. In the summer of 1849 an embattled Magyar National Assembly finally voted for the emancipation of the Jews, but it had meanwhile declared the Habsburgs deposed, enabling Franz Joseph to obtain help from the Tsar. It then dispersed in defeat. The price of the

Magyar-Jewish reform coalition in 1848–49 turned out to be bloody punishment for some; ignominy and exile for Kossuth and his friends; and the
earlier-mentioned immense retributive tax on the Jews. This defeat did not
favor continuation of the recently forged political alliance.

It may be stressed, moreover, that during the 1850s in Hungary, as in
Galicia, all the normal indices that in the past had prompted Jewish political
choices suggested allegiance to Vienna.[32] Especially in economic matters
the "absolutist years" were as we have seen a period of considerable innovation for Hungary. Vienna now brought in railroads with a vengeance.
All sorts of new-style capitalistic enterprises now came to Hungary from
Vienna. Vienna carried through the serf-emancipation and in 1853 abolished Maria Theresia's internal customs frontier. The Jewish benefit from
these changes was manifest. Not only were the pioneer railroad financiers,
Rothschild and Pereire, both Jews: the new capitalism both in Vienna and
in Hungary was conspicuously open to Jews;[33] and the Viennese bureaucrats who now governed Hungary (Alexander Bach's "huszars," as they
were called) introduced the new Jewish schooling system along with other
administrative reforms. As we will observe below, the enlightened Jews
of western Hungary showed their full understanding of the political au-
guries in central Europe by actually migrating to Vienna. For several years
the Magyar noble cause seemed dead.

Then, however, came the political turn-about of the 1860s.[34] In a few
short, astounding years Franz Joseph not only allowed the rebel Magyar
nobles to reestablish themselves, but in 1867 gave them political power to
an extent he never gave political power to the szlachta in Galicia, or to any
other social group within his Empire. This turn-about caught both the
Magyar reformers and the Jews of Hungary in many ways unprepared.
The former no doubt had the old network of noble assemblies in the rural
counties, but they had no central bureaucratic apparatus of their own, and
their finances were famously weak. The enlightened nobles were, moreover, a small minority even of Magyar society; yet they were saddled now,
in the railroad age, with the task of governing a vast country whose population, thirty million strong, did not even have a Magyar majority. The
Jews, on the other hand, were isolated. They were increasingly moved into
towns in the absolutist years, becoming modern and middle class. There
were 17,618 Jews in Pest-Buda about 1850; 44,890 in 1869. Because of their
new property and status they were more reliant than ever before on whatever political regime happened to be around.

These were the factors that cemented the alliance between the Magyar-
speaking nobility and the reformer Jews with which we are concerned. It
was symbolized by the formal re-emancipation of the Jews by the Hungarian Parliament at the end of 1867, and by the Jewish acceptance of the
Magyar tongue in their schools. The alliance, quite as much as the schools
themselves, made possible the great differentiation of Hungarian from Galician Jewry during the ensuing fifty years.

IV

One more factor completed this differentiation: an overall popularity of the Magyar cause among Hungarian Jews far below the elite level, that spilled over into the modernization movement in ways quite unparallelled in Galicia. One may best trace its emergence by observing some changes in Hungarian Orthodox Jewish concerns during the mid-century communal crisis.

Until the 1840s the Hungarian Jewish conservatives firmly eschewed any sort of "secular" politics. As was conventional throughout pre-Enlightenment Jewry, they were willing to cooperate with the authorities of a Christian state—that was a necessity of life in the Diaspora. But to take sides in Christian politics, or to allow Christian interference in Jewish communal affairs—that was quite a different thing. In Hungary in the Vormärz the conservative Jews characteristically resisted any sort of state-backed all-Hungarian Jewish organization that might have placed authority in non-rabbinical hands.[35] During the early months of 1848 they counseled neutrality and caution. They saw their objectives in the defense of Jewish tradition, and generally found the modern world irrelevant. But then in the fifties, the rabbis of Bratislava changed policy. They had been led since 1839 by the great *Chatam* Sofer's sons, Abraham and Simon, and Abraham's son, Bernat. For the first time they decided to get involved.

Why the change is nowhere clear. Perhaps the prolonged war of 1848–49 shook the rabbis: it had left little room for political quietism in Hungary. Perhaps the pogroms in the towns of the west and north scared them. Perhaps they were encouraged by the absolutist regime's conservative—indeed, clerical—propaganda. Perhaps they were worried by the danger they perceived in the modern schools that Vienna was introducing. We know only that their political involvement began in a context that suggested the effects of the communal crisis. Between 1850 and 1869 the Jewish population rose in virtually every county in Hungary save three that lay on the Austrian frontier: Nyitra, where it fell, and Sopron and Moson, where it remained stable. It also fell in the city of Bratislava. Meanwhile, thirty miles away from Bratislava, at Vienna the Jewish population skyrocketed from under 10,000 to 40,230 in those same years, with some 43% of the immigrants coming from Hungary.[36] These two decades witnessed right under the noses of the Bratislava rabbis a sudden flight of Jews from traditional communities into the great modern world. Their own flock was disappearing.

Amidst these circumstances in the 1850s a businessman named Ignaz Deutsch, born at Bratislava in 1808 and trained in the 1820s under Moses Sofer for the rabbinate, began appealing to the the Vienna Government to help him keep the Jewish immigrants in the capital free of reformer hands.[37] We will discuss Deutsch's campaign in a later chapter. Here it is relevant simply to underline his ties with Bratislava and to mention that by the end of the decade, claiming to act in the name of conservative Jewry all over the Empire, he was talking to the Vienna Ministry of Religions and Education about the possible signing of a Concordat between the state and the "Jewish Church" (that is, the rabbinate). In theory this would have parallelled the Concordat Franz Joseph signed with the Vatican in 1855 (which destroyed the statist controls Joseph II had placed on the Austrian Catholic Church). In practice, it would have placed state-backed organizational power over all Hungarian Jews in the hands of the Bratislava rabbis.[38] The proposal was important, because it terrified the "Neologs" (as the "modernists" were called by then in Hungary) at Vienna and Pest alike, and spurred them into political activities of their own. And meanwhile Bratislava itself emanated signals that alarmed the Neologs. In 1859 Rabbi Abraham Samuel Sofer, who had banned all secular studies, including reportedly the reading of newspapers, at his yeshiva, induced the Vienna authorities briefly to make that school Hungary's rabbi seminary.[39] And in 1860 Rabbi Simon accepted a call to be rabbi at Cracow, and there promptly embarked on a campaign to politicize Galician Orthodoxy. It would culminate in his election to the Austrian Reichsrath in 1879.[40]

These various Orthodox Jewish initiatives in 1859–60 were probably little coordinated, but they show that the Orthodox were becoming sensitive to the mobilization of Jewish masses—and that the Orthodox were fighting back with modern tools. More advanced fighting followed, because the modernist Jews, driven by fear, responded in kind. After 1860, the "Neologs" aggressively sought to ingratiate the Magyar nobles, advancing onto an anti-German path that contrasted with the German-speaking character of most of Hungary's Jews. Characteristically, the Pest Jewish congregation, given a chance in 1861 to name a new board of elders, elected a Magyar-speaking board headed by an entirely westernized ophthalmologist, Dr. Ignac Hirschler.[41] The new leaders at no time went to the modernist extremes of liturgical reform proposed by the Pest "reform congregation" during the revolution of 1848, but they were sufficiently zealous to scare even the moderate Rabbi Benjamin Meisel of Pest in 1863 into denouncing them to the Austrian authorities, who still ruled in Pest-Buda, for "irreligious" practices.[42] The resulting deposition of Hirschler greatly embittered the Neologs, but inspired the traditionalists to new heights of political activity. In 1864 and in 1865, when the Magyar case again seemed dark, considerable groups of conservative rabbis met in such agitation that they anathematized even the practice of non-Yiddish preaching.[43] In 1866–67, therefore, when the political tables turned in Hungary and the time came for closing the Jewish communal crisis, the Orthodox were as exposed to the hostility of the Magyars as were the reformer Jews of Galicia to the Poles.

There was only one way out of the confrontation. The Orthodox now had to appease the new regime by joining the Neologs in feigned or real enthusiasm for the Magyar language.[44] Though they actually spoke Yiddish or German, they had to open their flocks to the possibility of language change. This, of course, greatly encouraged the Jewish mass enthusiasm for Magyar that we are attempting to explain, and other developments soon vastly increased the exposure. In the late fall of 1867, after the compromise with Austria, not only did the Hungarian Parliament give civic equality to all the country's citizens, regardless of religious adherence, confirming thus the emancipation of 1849; also, the Hungarian Minister of Religious and Education Affairs, Baron Eötvös, indicated to the Jews that he would be pleased to hear how they wished to organize themselves.[45] Dr. Hirschler and his friends had by now been restored to the leadership of the Pest congregation, the largest in Hungary. They volunteered to organize a Jewish Congress to decide the matter, and proposed that since only legal questions were involved, the Congress be elected in accordance with the classic Liberal principle of separating "church" from "state." Rabbis would not be eligible. Eötvös, a passionate Liberal and long-time advocate of the emancipation, concurred. Both he and Hirschler seem honestly to have wanted to avoid burdening the Congress with the Talmudic "religious" disputes which were wracking Hungarian Jewry, but their distinction did not fit well with Judaism. Rabbinical Hungary with some justice responded that the Hirschler plan was a Neolog conspiracy for sneaky political gains.

The Minister compromised. Rabbis were elected to the Congress which met late in 1868. But the damage had been done. Filled with suspicion, the Orthodox withdrew from the Congress shortly after it began; and the Hungarian authorities found to their dismay that there was not just one Jewish Faith, but two. Worse, by 1870–71 they found they had to give legal recognition to three entirely separate Jewish religious organizations, because it turned out that many Jews wanted to have nothing to do with either the Neologs or the Orthodox, but to remain faithful to the *status quo ante*. The communal crisis of 1848 ended in Hungary with the formal shattering of the traditional unity among the Jews into three parts.[46]

This result even further exposed the mass of Hungarian Jewry to modern inputs—and modern enthusiasms. On the one hand, once again the Jewish school system was "improved." The 250 new schools of the past twenty years had been, in the main, community elementary schools of three-plus years. The Orthodox did not especially approve of them, but through the community leaderships they often had a good deal to say about curriculum. After the split a good many of these schools were expanded and made more "secular" and Magyar. Many others were liquidated, in part because the Orthodox felt no need for them, in part because many reform communities felt it would be easier (and cheaper) to send their children to Christian schools. By the 1880s, therefore, Hungary's Jewish children were very much more exposed to modern and Magyar nationalist influences than before 1868, and the Orthodox had a very much lesser hold on Jewish education.[47]

In addition, Orthodoxy's moral hold was deeply undermined. Until 1868, because Jewry was unitary in Hungary as thorughout Europe, modernization had usually been morally repulsive to any given Jewish individual moving into a city or otherwise departing from his traditional congregation. Usually he had had consciously and deliberately to abandon or to dilute his ritual obligations in order to become modern. People did this, but it was morally wrong, as was underlined constantly by the old-ritual synagogues to which all confessional Jews had to belong. In Hungary after 1868, however, such moral bonds virtually disappeared. Because of the split, provincial and orthodox Hungarian Jews coming to the capital could disguise their choices. On the one hand they had been taught even in the orthodox communities at home that Magyar was all right. On the other hand, in Budapest such a Jew could enter a Neolog community, which was no doubt different from what he was used to, but which was recognized by the state as just legitimately Jewish. There, all of a sudden, all the forces of bourgeois conformity told him it was perfectly all right to be a Sabbath Jew. Modernization thus became morally palatable. The two- and three-level division within Hungarian Jewry acted as a Magyar-speaking production line of sorts for the remodeling of Jews.

V

Hungarian Jewry was an extraordinary pendant to the deadlocked Jewry of Galicia after the middle of the nineteenth century. Though initially these two eastern segments of Habsburg Jewry were remarkably similar, although indeed Galician immigrants comprised a large part of Hungarian Jewry, the twenty years between 1848 and 1868 witnessed a major differentiation between them. First the Jewish school system in Hungary underwent an expansion and elaboration unparallelled in Galicia. Next, Hungarian Jewry's reformers hooked their fortunes to a noble class significantly more successful than the Galician szlachta. Third, the Jewish communal crisis ended here with Orthodoxy having to encourage language change, while abandoning the hold on Jewish education and the moral power over individual Jews that gave it such weight in the Polish lands. These factors led to the rather rapid modernization of Hungarian Jewry while Galician Jewry stood still.

From the point of view of Habsburg Jewry as a whole the sweep of events in Hungary was surely beneficial. But one may recognize also a flaw; the very essence of the "Hungarian solution" was a "second acculturation"—a new language choice, away not just from the Yiddish and Hebrew of the Jewish past, but from the German of the central European Jewish Enlightenment. May one not say that Habsburg Jewry's success in Hungary in this sense prepared the ground for its destruction?

NINE

Vienna Confused

I

About 1870 Europe ended its mid-century crisis with a sweeping territorial settlement that recalled the post-Napoleonic peace-making of 1815. Italy, Germany, and Rumania found themselves united; Russia was driven back; France was cut down. The Powers even consecrated their new state order with a great international Congress in 1878, and negating the reactionary 1815 Vienna Congress, there launched a revolutionary process of reshaping the rest of the world to European specifications.

Just like the 1815 settlement, that of 1870 had a social aspect. 1815 had paeanized aristocratic "conservatism," while excluding middle-class Liberalism from the governments on the continent. The new settlement made bourgeois Liberalism nigh ubiquitous from the Atlantic to the Russian frontier, but fulminated against urban Socialism. Whether brutally as in 1871 at Paris, or with bribes such as the universal suffrage of Bismarck's Reich, the new Europe made itself capitalist with a vengeance at home before reaching out to conquer and partition the world. And then it celebrated its new shape. Whereas in 1815 the aristocrats had "danced," as it is said, now the bourgeoisie staged great international industrial fairs, crowned "national" emperors, and launched monumental construction projects for its capital cities.

Austria was uniquely humiliated by this new settlement. Solferino was as personal a defeat for Franz Joseph's countrymen as for himself. So was Königgrätz. So was the unification of Germany around Prussia. So, despite the coming of constitutionalism, was the *Ausgleich* with Hungary. Even Russia came out better from the settlement: by 1870 Alexander II's grandiose sequence of modernizer reforms had expunged the (not very serious) military defeat in the Crimean War. France also escaped more cleanly than Austria. France experienced military catastrophe in 1870–71, but her defeat brought back a democratic type of government that many Frenchmen considered natural and national.

Yet at the dawn of Europe's progress into world conquest in 1866–71 Austria rejoiced as ostentatiously as did the other nations of the continent. This was a peculiarity of Habsburg history in this period. Symptomatically, the defeat of 1859 coincided with the first constructions on the Ringstrasse around the old city of Vienna and the start of a popular enthusiasm for public theatrics there that would culminate in Hans Makart's medieval pageant on the Kaiser's silver wedding anniversary in 1879. The defeat of 1866 precipitated the elaborate coronation at Budapest in 1867. The Austrian exclusion from Germany fanned a fantastic popular indulgence of gambling on the Vienna Stock Exchange. In 1873 an international industrial exhibition at Vienna would have been all Europe's key celebration of the new era, had the Stock Market not just then collapsed and had the cholera not come.

These paradoxical celebrations in defeat form the backdrop for Habsburg Jewry's third major response to the economic upswing of the post-1848 period: the response at Vienna. It is, therefore, relevant here to explore the social character of the Austrian celebrations, and to do this let us first define them negatively. These were not spontaneous rejoicings from depth of Austrian society. All too evidently, the peasant masses of the countryside were quite uninvolved in what happened on the Ring in the capital city, much less in the antics on the Stock Exchange. These were urban celebrations. Further, since Budapest was not united as a municipality until 1873, nor suitably decorated with imperial monuments until the 1890s, the locus of the celebrations was mainly Vienna; and even here not all of society was involved. The Austrian celebrations of the period were above all Viennese middle-class phenomena.

This said, however, one should take note also of a peculiar framing of what happened. At Vienna there was considerable room for the transmission of what we will call "enthusiasm" between the middle class participants in the celebrations and people lower down the social ladder. The Ringstrasse began, for example, as an urban development project.[1] In 1848 the territory of Vienna had housed perhaps 410,000 people. Two decades later the population was up to over 607,000 (875,000, if one calculates for the present-day territory of the city). Two thirds of this population (about 400,000 persons in 1869) were "workers" of one sort or another, a vast mass of people whose source of income was to say the least tenuous, whose living conditions were plain awful. The original *Stadterweiterung* project was intended to relieve the housing shortage for these masses. That idea, of course, soon fell into oblivion, and the splendid new buildings were designed increasingly for the rich. Yet even so there was a legend of social purpose for the masses. Further, after 1860 no one in Vienna who passed from the lower class suburbs into the city center could fail to observe what was happening on the Ring. Even if the poor were stopped from actually living here, the broad new avenue on the former *Glacis* was a permanent theatre for their entertainment. And in this connection one may recall another demographic factor. A great part of Vienna's increasing population was immigrant. Whereas in 1840, 37.5% of the population had been born outside Vienna, in 1870 the corresponding figure was 50%, and by 1890 it would reach a peak of 65.5% of the population.[2] Insofar as migration makes people sensitive to novelty, alters their ways, exposes them to modernity, surely the Vienna population as a whole was singularly susceptible to new sights in the city during that period. It may further be recalled that 14% of the new Vienna population comprised "servants," lower-class people whose occupation specifically exposed them to the goings-on among the rich. Amidst these circumstances, one may premise a certain mass involvement in the celebrations on the Ring in the form of admiration—gawking.

The Stock Exchange boom of the late 1860s enjoyed another but not dissimilar kind of mass audience. In all probability the number of people who were actually involved in the speculation at the Exchange was rather small—a few thousands who had money to spare and invest. There is evidence, further, that a considerable section even of the Vienna middle class could not participate: this was the city's petite bourgeois and artisan stratum, which as noted elsewhere had for decades been in decline. Between 1848 and 1880, for example, the proportion of Vienna artisans in the "five-florin" lowest tax category went up 60%. Between 1848 and 1880 also whole categories of once prosperous local manufacture disappeared, wiped out by the new mechanized factories in the outer suburbs. All the old crafts had been forced to reorganize themselves by the abolition of the guilds in 1859. A new type of house-industrial piece-production system took over in all the clothing trades, helping the new factory owners, ruining the old independent producers. The growth of larger retail sale outlets likewise cut into the profits of small producers who had once sold for themselves. The list goes on. The suffocating downward pressure on the once self-sufficient Viennese "little man" is unmistakable, and one may hardly see all these people avidly flocking to the Börse to invest their millions.

Yet precisely because the former guildsmen were in such economic straits, may one not construe that they were singularly sensitive to rays of economic hope? And this particular Stock Exchange boom offered just that. Its peculiarity was first of all the involvement of the "yellow" press, then a new feature of European urban life. In popular newspapers, which were allowed ever wider room for expansion under the new Liberal legislation of the 1860s, the opportunities for enrichment through stock speculation were brought daily to the entire literate class of Vienna society, a class which by then included many artisans. Who in the lower middle class knew that stockbrokers could buy space in the papers for fraudulent optimistic "news" about various stocks, and thus manipulate stock values? For the barely literate, what was written was surely "true"; and a whole new class of Stock Exchange "jobbers" emerged at Vienna in the 1860s who circulated literally from door to door in the city in search of investors, repeating the fraudulent "truth" in persuasive fashion. One may say, therefore, that though most Viennese could not themselves share in the enrichment opportunities, a great many could and probably did share in the enthusiasm. Just like the gawkers on the Ring, the lower middle class thus abetted with supportive admiration a "craze" among the more affluent of their peers.[3]

And such support was important, because the very essence of the celebrations at Vienna was enthusiasm, and first of all a rush to be fashionable. In all Europe's capitals at that time freshly wealthy middle classes were striving to be seen and were building new ostentatious houses close to the aristocracy, but nowhere else was the aristocracy so generally closed to newcomers as in Vienna, and nowhere else, accordingly, were the opportunities for middle class social climbing so alluring as on the Vienna Ringstrasse. Not in Mayfair, not on the Avenue de l'Opéra, not in Berlin's Westend was there such a theatre for nouveau riche display. And at Vienna there were significant enticements for the "second society" to increase such strutting in the 1860s and 1870s. Most notably, the Kaiser was ever more lavish in distributing not just honors and medals of every sort but new noble titles. He made 57 businessmen nobles between 1860 and 1866 in Austria, 22 in 1867 alone (plus 6 businessman barons and 127 other category rank-changes). Between 1867 and 1870 alone he issued 398 Austrian ennoblements, and this does not include a massive distribution in Hungary. Then he issued as many regularly every three or four years until 1884. No other monarch in Europe seems to have been so generous.[4] No wonder the Vienna bourgeoisie responded with enthusiasm!

The lure of fashion was significant even in encouraging speculative enthusiasm on the Stock Exchange. As noted earlier, the Austrian capitalist enterprises of the 1850s—the Creditanstalt and the great railroads—all recruited members of the higher aristocracy for their governing boards. By implication, investment and participation might bring social mixing; and during the 1860s and 1870s it became almost *de rigeur* for a new company floating its stock at the Vienna Exchange to present such an aristocratic facade. Pallavicini, Bourgouin, Salm-Reifferscheidt, Zichy, Kinsky, Sapieha were among the illustrious old names that figured in the directorships of the day. Even Habsburgs participated: Friedrich Schey, the vice-president of the Stock Exchange, was banker for the richest of them, the Arch-Duke Albrecht.[5]

Alongside fashionability, there was a distinctly Viennese type of enthusiasm in the celebrations of the 1860s, especially again the Ringstrasse craze. The Ring was laid out not just for promenading, but for theatrical purposes—for processions and parades. It was lined not just with balconied private palaces for the rich, but with theatres and concert halls where the whole of middle-class society could show off; and at the old Kärntner Tor, the focus of it all was the new Opera. The most eminent artists were employed to enhance the imaginative aspect of the new edifices: the Rennaissance-style architects, Van der Nüll, and Siccard von Siccardsburg and the painter von Schwindt in the 1860s; the gothicist and classicist Ferstel, Hansen and Hasenauer in the 1870s. The newspapers brought home the theatrical squabbles of these prima donnas with each other (and with their patrons) to the public, raising high passions in the style of movie stars today, all told making for a revival of the city's historic absorption with public spectacles.

Coincidentally, cultural revolutions both in the theatre and the music worlds of Vienna encouraged a renewal of cultural sublimation in the literate populace. The change in the theatres began during the 1850s, while political activity was barred, and constituted a sublimation of politics exactly parallel to the one in Kaiser Franz's era. Heinrich Laube, the Burgtheater director, had then cast aside the classicist style of the Vormärz, and opened his stage to the nationalist and social themes of the new era. The private theatres had compulsively followed his initiative.[6] In the 1860s there was a great leap in music, the second in a century. Bruckner arrived at Vienna in 1861; Brahms became conductor at the Singakademie in 1862. Richard Wagner had first appeared at Vienna in the forties. His operas were sung there from 1857 on to loud applause from his fans and tooth-gnashing by the critics. By 1863–64 he was so pleased by his reception that he took up residence in the Penzing suburb, composing much of *Die Meistersinger* there. And whereas in the first Viennese musical revolution, fifty years earlier, there had been minimal press participation, this time a war amongst the critics was so intense that it won enshrinement in Wagner's masterpiece itself.[7]

One may understand in this context why there was such a burst of enthusiasm, a "craze" of sorts, for the Vienna Ringstrasse after 1860. Middle-class fashionability, encouraged from above by the throne, fanned by the press, meshed neatly with the city's cultural traditions in the face of a real cultural revolution. Of course there was a strong "theatrical" motif in the Stock Exchange bubble too. The speculators purveyed a notion of enrichment overnight that does not find much support in real life, but which is often supported on the stage. And to this one may add a psychological factor which encouraged middle-class leadership enthusiasm.

For the politically minded middle-class Austrians, the celebrations at Vienna in the 1860s and 1870s were a distraction from more serious things. In part this means that these people (especially the "Josephian" state employees among them) desired, consciously or unconsciously, to soothe the national humiliations, to assuage their pain over the lost wars. In part also, however, it recalls that they faced difficulties. As thoughtful members of the middle classes, they were being asked now abruptly to share power in a complex world that the Habsburgs themselves could no longer handle. During the revolution of 1848 and afterwards they, the spokesmen of Austrian Liberalism, had fulminated against the autocracy and demanded a constitution, an elective parliament, the administrative legalism of a *Rechtsstaat*, the separation of church and state, a balanced state budget, a successful foreign policy, an army that cost less but which won wars, freedom for the press, resolution of the nationality problems, protection of a free economy, better public education, and the modernization of the nation's physical infrastructure as well. Now that power was to an extent in their hands, the execution of all these demands proved difficult. The solutions were the more elusive because the Kaiser kept changing the constitution, and further, he refused to let the parliament control his army and foreign policy; he regularly favored noble-class over bourgeois interests; and he was more even-handed by far in the intractable nationality question than the bigotedly patriotic middle-class Germans of the Reichsrath. Amongst these circumstances political Liberals not infrequently found it desirable to run away from realities, on the one hand by following doctrinaire principles to the dead and bitter end, on the other by luring their followers into the delights of the Ring and the morass of the Stock Exchange. The Viennese escapism of the Napoleonic era thus gained new life.[8]

To define in greater depth the sociological character of the Ringstrasse celebrations and the speculative bravura at the Vienna Stock Exchange is not possible here. Suffice it to conclude that the celebrations at Vienna in this period were highly complex middle class vogues, sustained over a considerable period of time. This is really what matters here, as we turn to the Vienna Jewish community's response to the modernization challenge of the post-1848 era.

I I

Let us look first at some demographic trends.[9] Before 1848, as we have seen elsewhere, there were probably about 6,000–7,000 Jews regularly present in Vienna, although only some 1,800 were legally registered there. Within one or two years after that year's relaxation of restrictions, there were probably at least 10,000. In 1869 the first reliable modern census recorded 52,350 Jews in the province of Lower Austria and 40,926 inside the city limits. By then Vienna had more Jews than Moravia. A decade later, in 1880, with the city's overall growth rate approaching its maximum, there were 95,058 Jews in Lower Austria (up 81.5% in ten years) and 72,538 inside Vienna (up 80%). The Vienna region now had more Jews than did Bohemia or Budapest.

This rapidly enlarging Vienna Jewry centered on a highly modernized elite. A recent study of census materials from 1857 indicates that about 20% of the 6,217 Jews then legally present in Vienna (1,243 individuals) were born there.[10] By the 1869 census the proportion of Vienna-born members of the Jewish population was down to 3.5% (1,399 out of over 40,000 persons). But the 1869 material reveals in addition that a remarkably stable number of Vienna's Jews were rich: about 6% (some 2,400 persons) lived off property and income. Some were very wealthy indeed, occupying palaces and apartments with as many as 30 rooms.

These established people were clearly enough the heirs of the pre-1848 "tolerated" Jews, the relatives and "household members" of the 200-odd Jewish Grosshändler who had managed to live in Vienna because they could show great wealth. It has been said that the "tolerees" were a frequently changing, constantly varying group because the lists naming them vary.[11] Nothing could be further from the truth. Some of the leading families ceased to be listed as Jews because they converted (thus Dobruschka, Eskeles, Kaan, Borkenstein, Ofenheimer, Leidersdorf, Liebenberg). But they didn't move away. The survival of many other families in the charmed and cultured city was masked when sons-in-law took over the family firms. Landauer survived through Schey; Baruch through von Hofmannsthal; Kuh through Sichrowsky; Oesterreicher through Weikersheim; Baumgarten and Poppe through Boschan; Levinger through Lieben; Selkes through Löwenthal. But the principal "toleree" families were on the lists virtually from start to finish: Wertheim, Arnstein, Hönig, Liebmann, Todesco, Brandeis, Biedermann, Kohn, Eppinger, Lehman, Neustadl, Schlesinger, Trebitsch, Zappert. As seen elsewhere, moreover, the actual leadership of the Vienna Jewish community, the narrow *Vertretung*, was even more stable and unchanging over the years than the community as a whole. All in all the former "tolerees" were a cohesive elite who behaved in conspicuous ways that invited imitation. Hardly distinguishable from the Christian "second society" with whom they mingled, they displayed their luxury and cosmopolitan culture, and put a premium on modern education. They were German-speakers who looked down on Yiddish. They were relaxed in their ritual observance of Judaism, and open to modern ideas.

At the other extreme in Viennese Jewish society, there was now some poverty. By 1869 some 1,133 families, 16% of all the Jewish families in the city, had no independent residence but rented a room. 390 of these families squeezed in more than one family to a room. In addition 2,585 of the families who did have separate apartments (29.6% of the total number of families) rented out rooms to pay the rent. In both 1857 and 1869 the overwhelming majority of the Vienna Jews lived in the relatively poor second administrative district, the Leopoldstadt. Although there was also a wealthy section of the Leopoldstadt, these data imply that a good 45% of the Jewish population was living in severely restricted economic circumstances, a figure perhaps not as impressive as the two-thirds of the Christian population that was poor, but impressive enough. Yet one can tell from both the 1857 and the 1869 materials also that the poverty and crowding did not necessarily mean Jewish indifference to the standards of the rich, or to the modernization possibilities of the big city. In both years there was a striking excess in the Jewish community of males over females. To some extent this reflected the considerable numbers of Jewish students who were now coming from all over the Empire to study at the Vienna schools, especially at the university: in 1869 there were 3,684 such students, 13.75% of the community. But the surplus also suggests that a large number of provincial Jewish males had come to Vienna without their families because they were ambitious to make their way up in the world.[12]

Who now were the immigrants? Were they people apt to reject the modernism of the city and its Jewish elite? Both in 1857 and 1869 a large contingent came from Hungary.[13] In 1857 the Hungarians made up about

25% of the 6,217 registered; in 1869 they comprised 43.5% (17,395 persons) of the 40,230 present. Beyond doubt some of these people were far from starvation. In 1857 four-fifths of the "Hungarian" Jews at Vienna came from Bratislava. One may presume they were the "commuters" of the pre-March era—people who had come to the capital on business during the week, and then retired to Bratislava or Eisenstadt across the Hungarian frontier for the sabbath. Since both Bratislava and Eisenstadt were centers of Jewish Orthodoxy, there is a presumption of orthodoxy among the im-migrants. All the more is this true of the much more numerous "Hungari-an" Jews who had congregated in Vienna by 1869. These could hardly have all come from Bratislava, which had only about 4,500 Jews in its city limits in 1848 and about the same number in 1869. It follows that the immigrants to Vienna were probably rural Jews from today's Slovakia, and this implies that they were thoroughly observant. They even went on record as such: in the 1850s a congregation of them (the so-called "German" Jews) that was archly conservative appeared in Vienna and demanded a traditional synagogue of its own.[14]

At the time, during the period of political absolutism, there was no way of telling that these "Hungarian" Jews were anything but strongly traditional. Yet today one can guess that their nigh spontaneous mass flight to Vienna after 1848 might signify a certain weakening of rabbinical power. As observed in the preceding chapter, this is probably what the rabbis feared at the time. And indeed, in 1868 when the Vienna community lead-ership for the first time was able to count the members of the city's Or-thodox prayer-houses, it discovered only 1,764 members, 501 of them sufficiently rich to pay community taxes (and thus vote). Since in 1870 there were 1,626 taxpayers all told in the city, this meant that the Orthodox were about one-third of the voters, very considerably less than the 54% of the community then comprised by "Hungarian" and Galician Jewish immi-grants.[15] At Vienna in the period of mass migration, the Orthodox Jews who might have delayed the process of embourgeoisement were not strong.

In 1857, 4% of the Vienna Jews were from Bohemia, 15% from the small Jewish population of Moravia and Silesia. In 1869, 14% (5,617 persons) were from Bohemia, 20.6% (8,251 persons) from Moravia and Silesia. The Bohemian contingent would hardly have challenged the culture and edu-cational aspirations of the "toleree" elite. Particularly at the start it com-prised a number of wealthy Prague Jews who were fleeing Czech Judeophobia; and as we have seen elsewhere, even the Bohemian village Jews had been well infected by modern attitudes long before 1848.[16] At first one might guess that the Moravian Jews were different, for as at Bratislava the rabbinate there had been strongly traditional all through the Vormärz. Yet here also the Josephian educational reforms had done their work of loosening the hold of Orthodoxy. In no other part of Habsburg Jewry was there such a pronounced flow from old small-town ghettos into modern cities in the decades after 1848.[17]

Prior to 1848 very few Galician Jews had found their way to Vienna.[18] Late in the eighteenth century their migration to the capital had been banned, and they were "represented" there by a small number of privileged "Sensals" who took wares for sale on consignment from the great firms of Cracow, Lwow, and Brody. By the middle 1840s, because of "leakage" of immigrants into the city, the "Polish Jews" in Vienna were numerous enough to organize a prayerhouse of their own with a ritual more traditional than Preacher Mannheimer's. Yet until the 1860s the bars against immigration remained high. In 1857 the Galician-Bukowinian contingent among Vienna's Jews was only about 10% of the total (about 600 people); in 1869, 11.8% (4,747 individuals) of the much larger total. It seems probable, moreover, that the bulk of these early Galician immigrants were from the western, more enlightened part of Galicia, not Hasidim from the east.

In many respects, especially at the start, the Galicians in the Austrian capital did as other Jewish immigrants: they entered the modern world. In the memoir literature one encounters case after case in which Jews of Galician ancestry integrated into the Vienna bourgeoisie.[19] A recent student of the problem has discovered that during forty years, from 1870 through 1910, 51% of all marriages at Vienna of Galician Jews involved partners who were not Galician-born. In so far as provincial endogamy seems to have been the norm among Galicians, one may sense here that the Vienna "melting pot" was working.[20]

Later on no doubt the picture changed. After the Ausgleich, Galician Jewish migration to Vienna was opened. By 1880 the Galician proportion of Vienna Jewry was up to 18% (17,110 persons). This represented a very great increase over a single decade, and presumably included poorer east Galician Jews of the sort who after 1880 emigrated overseas. The researcher just mentioned came away impressed that by 1900 the general assimilation of Viennese Jewry into Christian society was slacking off. Viennese Jewry was remaining "Jewish" in its modern locus. Vienna Jewry had become a class society, deeply fissured by the differences between rich and poor, renegades and faithful, Orthodox and reformed. The Galicians were then an unassimilated "bottom class."

It seems clear, nonetheless, that until the Galicians began to migrate in large numbers during the late 1860s, and perhaps even later, Vienna Jewry was overwhelmingly not a stratifying class community, but an upward-funneling, mobile, and integrative one. Most of the Jews here were immigrants, impressionable like the immigrant Christians. The tiny core of elegant "tolerees," entirely different from anything the immigrants knew, set the tone and aspirations for the whole community. The immigrants then through imitation became "Viennese."[21]

In the context of the middle-class celebrations of the time, all this integrative character of Vienna Jewry seems significant. It suggests that the Jews could have played a role in channeling the enthusiasms of the day from above to down below within the middle class, and then, in the form of supportive emulation, back up again. It is worth recalling in this connection that the Jews were an ever more important element in the Vienna middle class, and especially in its leadership, the "second society." Even back in Fanny Arnstein's day, as we have seen, "neutral" attitudes towards Jews had prevailed, with the result that Christians had accepted in many ways a Jewish lead. By mid-century Jews were dominant in much of Vienna's commercial life. In 1848 the Jewish Vertretung's system of personal connections had enabled Vienna Jewry to ride the waves of so vast a social upheaval as the revolution—indeed, to act sometimes as the voice of society. In the 1860s not only were the neutral society, the commercial dominance, the personal connections still intact and thriving, but in addition Jews were entering the "Christian professions": law, education, government. Does it not follow that what the Jews as a group did could easily reinforce, even exaggerate, what the middle class as a whole was doing?

III

To probe this hypothesis, let us look now at the organized core of Vienna Jewry, the old Vertretung of pre-revolutionary days. Let us inquire whether it provided the immigrants with a sober, as it were "just Jewish," leadership, or something else.

In the spring of 1849 the Vertretung underwent a transformation. Franz Joseph then acknowledged officially for the first time that a Jewish religious community existed at Vienna. His act led the old leadership to reorganize. It held elections for a Community Advisory Council. It began to call itself a *Kultusgemeinde Vorstand* [Praesidium of the Religious Community]. It tried to write a community statute acceptable to the civic authorities, and otherwise set about filling functions that had been denied the old Vertretung.[22] In these activities a personage encountered earlier, Heinrich Sichrowsky, the Nordbahn secretary general, was the leading activist. He was a prime mover of the new statute. He solicited funds for the poor. Soon it was he who perceived the need for a new synagogue, found a suitable location for it, contacted architects, and so forth. When the time came in 1855 to employ a new preacher to first supplement and then succeed the aging Mannheimer, it was Sichrowsky who did much of the searching and the interviewing. By tracing a culminating episode in his career, one may gain a first concrete insight into what kind of leadership the Vorstand gave.

In 1854–56 Heinrich Sichrowsky was involved in a negotiation with the Vienna city authorities over the possibility of setting up a Jewish *Volksschule* or grade school such as had existed at Trieste and Prague since Joseph II's time.[23] During the Vormärz, as we have seen, such schools had been a major instrument for spreading the Enlightenment throughout Habsburg Jewry. The Jews of Vienna had not established one in the 1780s primarily because they had been so few in number then and had so completely lacked official recognition. When in June 1854 the Vienna city authorities suggested that the community set up such a school, the leadership was receptive to the idea. The only problem seemed to be money.[24] But early in 1855, Sichrowsky and his colleagues heard about some new activities of the Vienna agent of the Bratislava rabbis, Ignaz Deutsch, who was mentioned in the previous chapter.[25]

Even before 1848, Deutsch had emerged as spokesman for the immigrant Hungarians known as "German Jews." Just after 1848 he had tried to separate them from the main Vienna community; and in September 1850 he had used business connections with high-placed aristocrats to obtain an audience with the Kaiser. It turned out that Deutsch presented himself to the sovereign as the offical representative of the "real" [rechtgläubige] Jews throughout the Empire; and worse, that he had contrasted his alleged "following" with the allegedly "impious and revolutionary" Neologs in the capital. A clerical party was on the ascent at court. It knew little enough about what "piety" might mean within Austrian Jewry, and was impressed by any show of "religiosity." It let him know it was willing to be convinced.[26] Hereupon Deutsch created one scandal after another. In 1853, for example, when the decree suspending Jewish landholding was issued and the Maskilim all over the Empire were trembling for their property and well-being, Deutsch responded with enthusiasm. He told the government that the decree was a measure that might halt an "unhealthy" polarization of wealth and poverty among the Jews and inhibit the "greediness" that was sucking village Jews away from their traditional life into the modern cities! Next in 1855–56 Deutsch made a fuss when L. A. Frankl received a commission to visit Jerusalem and to set up a school there for poor Jews. It turned out that Deutsch was attempting to centralize in his own hands the collection in Austria of charitable funds destined for Palestine, and was seeking to persuade both the regime and west European Jewish charitable organizations that he had a special authority among the Palestinian Jews. His threat to the "nice" Jews in the Kultusgemeinde elite was the keener because the regime did not tell them what exactly he was doing—they had to guess—and because they did not know how strong or weak his immigrant following might be.

As soon as the Vorstand discovered Ignaz Deutsch's Palestinian ambitions in 1855, Sichrowsky changed stance in the negotiations about the Jewish Volksschule at Vienna. He began to express concern not just about the excessive financial burden which the Volksschule might entail: now he was deeply worried that Austria's Jews endanger their emancipation by allowing themselves to appear distinct from the rest of the Austrian population. Would not a separate school for Vienna's Jewish children do just this? he queried. In his eyes this type of school, which earlier had been a symbol of Enlightenment, had become an instrument for cutting the Jews out of society again.[27]

At the start of 1856 the regime began to talk of instituting not one but two Jewish schools in Vienna. Sichrowsky and his friends immediately perceived sinister intent. Now in a panic they began to devise cunctatory tactics whereby the regime could be tricked into delaying the whole project.[28] By September 1856, when the Volksschule came up for a vote in the community council, the old leaders were assuming it would be a tool whereby Ignaz Deutsch could gain control of the Jews in the city and perpetuate traditionalism among them. Sichrowsky now delivered an impassioned speech, making it seem as if all the principles he had stood for from start to finish of his career depended on rejection of the school. The laws were absolutely clear, he declaimed. Jewish children had a legal right to attend the existing Catholic schools. As the premier Jewish community in all Austria, therefore, the Vienna Jews had a high moral obligation to bring Christian and Jewish citizens as close to one another as possible, and to oppose any such innovation as a Jewish school.[29]

In resisting Ignaz Deutsch the Vorstand acted very negatively toward a project that deserved attention. One must note in extenuation the hard evidence that the regime really did have sinister motives in 1855–56. Its anti-Jewish measures were continuing. In August 1855 it signed a new Concordat with Rome, which undid Joseph II's subjection of the Church to the State. Enlightened Jews of the 1850s saw the Concordat as a return to the Middle Ages.[30] Finally it is important to repeat that the Vienna Vorstand did not itself know how much or what kind of support Ignaz Deutsch enjoyed within Jewry. There seemed a real danger that an anti-enlightenment majority might emerge and somehow gain control over the new institutions.[31] Sichrowsky and his colleagues became immobile, unwilling to move politically, paralysed. They simply did not provide the city's immigrant Jews with positive political leadership.

At precisely the same moment, however, they did provide a more than positive leadership in other modes. In 1855, as recounted earlier, old Salomon von Rothschild died, the Pereires made their assault on Austria, and Anselm von Rothschild responded by organizing the Creditanstalt. His two prokurators, Leopold von Wertheimstein and Moritz Goldschmidt, both of them Vorstand members, hereupon became his spokesmen in the greatest European business-world speculative enterprises of the epoch. Coincidentally, Sichrowsky, as secretary general of the Nordbahn Company, led the business world's response to the de-nationalization of the Austrian state railroads. The Jewish community elite, in a word, became very active in a "demonstrative" mode of leadership, just at the time it became paralysed in its conduct of Kultusgemeinde affairs.

This conjunction of political paralysis with active economic role modeling grew more pronounced in the later 1850s, as Ignaz Deutsch grew ever more outrageous. During the "Mortara affair" of 1858, when enlightened Jewry all over Europe was protesting in horror over the abduction from his parents in the Papal State of a secretly baptized Jewish child, Deutsch curried favor in the Austrian Government by declaring that the "hubbub" resulted from "Neolog manipulation" of the international anticlerical press. Starting in 1857, he presented petitions to the government requesting the negotiation of a concordat with his "real Jews" along the lines of that recently concluded with the Catholic Church. It was to be negotiated through him, naturally, and it was said that in reward he wanted to be made a privileged Hoffaktor comparable in status to the Samuel Oppenheimers and Simson Wertheimers of the past. In response, in 1858 Count Thun's Ministry of Religion and Education assigned Deutsch authority over a Talmud school attached to the new synagogue in the Leopoldstadt. It seemed thus to be openly encouraging him to organize a traditionalist Jewish community in Vienna, separate from the Neolog Jews. In that same year Deutsch sought to get money for his school from the Hungarian Jewish School Fund (which implied he could get rabbinical backing within Hungary); and he started a campaign, appealing to the traditionalist rabbis in Galicia, to win them also separate schools.[32]

An event in 1859 suggests how these developments affected the Vorstand. As Austrian absolutism tottered towards its downfall in March of that year, and as war-clouds gathered abroad, a distinguished group of Habsburg Jews decided to petition the government about ending the "provisional" legal status created by a decree of 1853. The petitioners came from all over. They included Leopold Laemmel from Prague, Elio Morpurgo from Trieste, Max Gomperz from Moravia, Friedrich Schey from Hungary, and the publicist Ignaz Kuranda from Vienna, as well as Josef Biedermann and Jakob Brandeis, both members of the Vienna Vorstand. All these men were notoriously modern Jews—no danger of traditionalism here. The petition was drawn up by Heinrich Jaques, whose mother was a Wertheimstein (it came from "within the Vorstand family," so to speak) and it reflected the same spirit of absolute submission to the laws of the state and denial of Jewish nationality that had infused a recent petition from the Vorstand itself. One could have anticipated Vorstand endorsement.[33]

In that august body, however, discussion of the petition began with von Wertheimstein, the chairman, casting doubt onto the credentials of the petitioners. Then gravely he reminded his colleagues that in recent years the Kaiser had communicated with the crownland Jews through the Vienna community. This suggested, he said, that it was the Viennese, not the crownland Jews, who should be initiating petitions to the throne. He went on to say that no "group" of petitioners could possess sufficient ontological substance to present a legal petition. To be legitimate, he indicated, a petition had to come from an officially recognized organization. His colleague, Goldschmidt, then chimed in that any appeal initiated outside legal channels might be perceived in "high circles" as propaganda, which he deemed counterproductive. Both men added that highly placed personalities had privately advised them to wait until the state itself took an initiative. With such stark immobility, they prevented Vorstand endorsement of the petition.[34]

Yet coincidentally in the demonstrative mode of leadership they were highly active, for the Kaiser signalled his shift to constitutionalism by casting favors to prominent Jews. In 1860 he ennobled Philip Schey of Guns in Hungary, and two Jewish bankers of Vienna, Jonas Königswarter and Simon Biedermann. Schey himself was just a rich provincial banker, but his nephew Friedrich was one of the flashiest railroad entrepreneurs, Stock-Exchange speculators, and cultural patrons of Vienna, and was also prominent in Jewish community affairs there. Königswarter was a member of the Vorstand inner circle, and later in the 1860s would be president of the Vienna community. Both ennoblements seemed to honor the social core of Vienna Jewry as a group—and there were no refusals in that distinguished forum to these overtures from outside.[35] Even more in 1861 did the Vienna community leaders accept honor. Franz Joseph invited Anselm von Rothschild to enter the Reichsrath House of Lords, and then ennobled Eduard and Moritz Todesco, millionaire brothers-in-law of Rothschild's Prokurator, Leopold, Edler von Wertheimstein. In 1862 the Kaiser then made Moritz Goldschmidt, the second Rothschild Prokurator, a *Ritter*. In 1863 he promoted von Wertheimstein from *Edler* to *Ritter*, and ennobled Friedrich Schey. In 1865 it was the turn of the Schnappers, Rothschild cousins from Frankfurt; in 1866 that of Leopold Epstein of the Kultusgemeinde and Heinrich Sichrowsky of the Nordbahn. Almost without exception the gentlemen in question were leaders of the Vienna Jewish Kultusgemeinde. And in these same years these same leaders (Rothschild and his two prokurators apart) reciprocated in demonstrative fashion by taking up the Kaiser's invitation to build the grand new avenue on the Vienna *Glacis*.[36] The Todescos (with their in-laws, the Gomperzes of Brno) build the palaces across the Kärntnerstrasse from the new Opera. Königswarter built on a nearby block across the Kärntnerring, and later on the Bellaria block. Schey put up his palace next to the Jockey Club, overlooking the Kaiser's own garden. Epstein built the palace between the future parliament and the museums. Thanks to this exchange of ostentatious compliments in the early 1860s, the Kultusgemeinde may be said to have led the society of Ringstrasse barons, which all Vienna imitated in the following years.

In 1860–61, as a new chapter opened in Austrian politics, Sichrowsky and von Wertheimstein gave way in the Vorstand to a new guard headed by the Liberal journalist-politician, Ignaz Kuranda and the merchant, Moritz Pollak (later "von Borkenau").[37] The new team set about cleaning house, and for a while it seemed as if the immobility of the old oligarchs might disappear. The Vienna community seemed about to provide thoroughly positive political leadership to Austria's Jews.[38] But soon the reformer initiatives bogged down. The trouble was first of all that the new leaders themselves were busy. Kuranda, for example, was a central Liberal Party figure in the Reichsrath. Both he and Pollak belonged to the new Vienna City Council. Together they assumed responsibility for a general reform of Austrian public education, and faced with all the great conflicts of the empire's political life, they had little time for Kultusgemeinde affairs. Most of their colleagues were comparably engaged in outside affairs, mainly on the Stock Exchange and in the business world. Meanwhile, the conservatives in the old Vorstand proved most reluctant to change. Moritz Goldschmidt, for example, the Vorstand's financial secretary, for some years flatly refused to allow the reformers to scrutinize the Kultusgemeinde accounts! Over and again he and Königswarter obstructed any change.[39] And for another decade there were periodic scandals by Ignaz Deutsch, or by conservative Hungarian rabbis, which so alarmed even the Vienna reformer Jews that all their great modern projects died. When finally in 1872 Kuranda succeeded Königswarter as president of the community, he immediately caved in under pressure and during eight years changed next to nothing.[40]

The Liberal-dominated Vienna Kultusgemeinde sustained a claim to "all-Empire" Jewish leadership in the 1860s and 1870s, first by organizing an *israelitische Allianz zu Wien*, a charitable organization on the lines of the Alliance Israélite at Paris; second, by coopting elegant Jews from the crownlands into its leadership. But in point of actually initiating reforms, it was as immobile as the oligarchs of the 1850s; and like the old oligarchs it set a behavioral model. Kuranda himself had been an arch-Liberal all his political life and had always boasted of his bourgeois virtue and simplicity. After Königgrätz in 1866, he had expressed his German middle-class despair by vowing to retire from politics altogether, throwing in the sponge. Yet he proved willing in 1867 to accept the highest decoration Franz Joseph had hitherto succeeded in bestowing upon a Jew: the Leopold Order, Second Class. This medal made him higher in rank than most barons.[41] A veritable eruption of coincident Kultusgemeinde baronizations highlighted the model: Schey and Todesco in 1869, Königswarter in 1870, Springer in 1872, all of them Vorstand members or former members. Königswarter summed up the fabulous atmosphere emanating from the top of the Jewish community at this time when an aristocratic fellow gambler on the Stock Exchange congratulated him with the words: "What wonderful times: nobody blinks when Jews become barons!" He replied: "And when counts become Jews!"[42]

Now to make our point: the Vorstand's record of leadership (the dearth of positive initiative combined with stress on the demonstrative, behavioral model) very much enhanced Vienna Jewry's potential for involvement in the great Austrian middle-class celebrations described at the start of this chapter. Given such leadership, the rapidly growing immigrant Jewish population was surely affected by enthusiasm for the Ring and the Stock Exchange. And what so many middle-class Jews did with enthusiasm could hardly have left the "neutral" Christian middle classes unaffected.

It will help nail this point down to recount what a Jewish community looked like, in point of organization, in late nineteenth-century central Europe. Generally it consisted of three parts: a leadership, an administrative apparatus, and affiliate organizations.[43] In command were a "president" and an executive council of five or six men, chosen for their considerable piety, great personal dignity, and seriousness. They met weekly or more often. They were supported by an elective consultive council (or councils) comprised of dignitaries, usually men of considerable wealth and public status, who had committee responsibilities for matters of finance, the synagogue, the school(s) and ritual buildings, the hospital and cemetery, but who convened far less frequently. Elections by taxpayer curias renewed a large portion of the leadership each year, but the voters seldom toppled the slate proposed by the Praesidium, and the leadership was thus fundamentally oligarchical.

In this first respect, in point of prestige and reputation, one may say that the communities were strong. They even possessed a little legal strength. Despite the great weakening of Jewish community power in the nineteenth century, all citizens were still bound by constitutional law to belong to religious communities, to pay a tax to them, and to accept religious education. And in point of social integration and propaganda instruments they were notably strong and effective. Each Jewish community was the center of a nexus of private social and charitable organizations, usually very active; and big-city Jewish communities usually possessed press organs: weekly newspapers, and monthly, quarterly, and annual literary and cultural instruments.

In their actual administration, on the other hand, the communities were notably weak. Apart from the rabbi(s) and the often poorly paid school-teachers and ritual attendants, there was minimal bureaucracy. The apparatus of Jewry in no way compared to the structures of the Catholic and Protestant churches, not to speak of the national and nationality political institutions that mushroomed in the later nineteenth century all over Europe.

This peculiar organizational shape clearly led to the sort of Jewish leadership in Vienna's middle-class fads that we have suggested. Recall the situation within the community. Down below, a stream of immigrant Jews from the provinces was at full flood in the 1860s: predominantly young males, people who probably had some modern German-language education, great ambitions, but little wealth. These people had just been transported from the mud of Moravian and Hungarian small-town life to the splendor—real splendor—of Vienna's new great avenues, and had little else to do but find their way up. Meanwhile, up above, a glittering new nobility of Stock Exchange speculators and palace-builders on the Ring was encouraging behavioral imitation, as movie stars do today. At a celebrated libel trial in 1868, for example, Paul Schiff, a Jewish community leader, convinced a jury that he was not a *"Piratenschiff auf der Börse"* and not a *"Strauchritter"*[Highwayrobber] by calling in his fellow Jewish-community leaders to testify under oath that the principal kinds of robbery and piracy then practiced on the Stock Exchange were quite all right because they were not specifically against the law. One by one, from von Königswarter to von Goldschmidt and von Schey, these Jewish leaders thus propagated the new Stock Exchange morality.[44]

One may even be specific, through an analogy with the Stock Exchange itself, about how the Kultusgemeinde may have contributed to the "crazes." The Exchange had been modernized in 1854 and in the 1860s *seemed* to be as modern a financial organization as Europe possessed. But actually its institutional structure was simply too archaic to handle the tidal wave of business that emerged during the boom. Today one can see that precisely in this contrast between reputation and actuality lay a disastrous weakness. The Exchange had all the mechanisms needed to *encourage* business excitement, but was grossly inadequate for *retarding* over-excitement.[45] May one not say the same of the Jewish Kultusgemeinde? Was it not a wonderful vehicle for stirring up a madness of crowds, while absolutely lacking the teeth to control the euphoria once it got out of hand? We have seen earlier that there were many clearly non-Jewish inputs to the Viennese "crazes" of the 1860s. But central to any calculation of their causes must surely figure the peculiar condition of the Jewish community at that time. Far more even than in 1848, certainly far more than in Fanny Arnstein's day, Jews had became the pace-setters of Viennese middle-class society during the *Ausgleich* period. When forces of conformity, like a whirlwind, swept the immigrant Jews into accepting pseudo-aristocratic social values, aesthetic escapism, and economic speculation as a way of life, the Christian world followed.

IV

In these terms there really was assimilation at Vienna in the 1860s. For a while a new great Jewish success seemed on hand. And then the pricking of the speculative bubble at the Stock Exchange in 1873 proved a greater trauma by far for the Jews of the capital than for the rest of society. This was the tragedy of Vienna Jewry's response to the great modernization challenge of the post-1848 era.

As a result of the "Black Friday" *Krach* of May 1873, a great cleavage opened in the Viennese middle class. Among the artisans and former guildspeople who had pinned their hopes on Stock Exchange miracles, it was said from the start that the disaster was a "Jewish betrayal" of the "Christian *Volk*." This led within the decade to the flowering of the new European anti-Semitism, most especially at Vienna, a development that left no Jew unscathed. For the Christian bourgeoisie no doubt the disaster was also great: the victims of the crash had no doubt that upper bourgeois Liberalism, alongside the Jews, had betrayed the little man. Free capitalism fell into disrepute with the lower middle class, and within the decade Liberalism had suffered political ruin. Austria's Christian bourgeoisie did not recover its unity until after 1945. But for the Christians, that was the extent of it. Though politically fragmented, they lived on. Not so the Jews.

Under the new pressure of Christian hatred, Viennese Jewry shattered. One sector, the leadership sector we have been observing, hardly changed at all (save that the rich converted out of Judaism apace). Its symbol was precisely an actor, Adolf von Sonnenthal, the hero of Laube's Burgtheater, the outstanding representative of what one called the "declamatory pathos" school of the German stage. As assistant manager of the Burgtheater and a prominent member of the Jewish community, Sonnenthal developed an association first with Makart and then with the other great organizer of upper bourgeois Christian celebrations, Princess Pauline Metternich. He was deeply involved in the great jubilee procession of 1879, when Makart paraded 10,000 costumed elegances around the Ringstrasse before an estimated 470,000 spectators. In the 1880s, it was Sonnenthal who organized Princess Metternich's charitable fiestas on the same avenue for the first of May. More than anyone else, Sonnenthal acted out how a whole class of Jewish Vienna strode through the late nineteenth century with heads still in the skies, imitating the Christian higher aristocracy as if 1873 had never happened.[46]

Some of the middle-class Viennese Jews tried to head in radically different directions after the 1873 crash.[47] Exemplary were Heinrich Friedjung and Victor Adler, offspring of Gründer, who sought in the 1880s to reform the old Austrian Liberal Party, deposing the oligarchical leaders of their father's generation and coining a fresh German-national political program. It was characteristic of the frustrating new age, however, that they failed in this effort because of lower-middle-class defection. And it was even more characteristic that they, like their fathers, then responded with dreams. Friedjung left politics to become an historian. Adler set about organizing a Social-Democratic Party for all Austrian workers, rejecting not only the financial corruption of his father but both Judaism and Liberalism as well. One of their Jewish colleagues, Gustav Mahler, sublimated his politics into music. One of their Christian colleagues, Georg von Schönerer, sublimated his by trying to reorganize German nationalism against the Jews. Meanwhile in the Jewish world Dr. Josef Bloch, a rabbi from Galicia, settled in a suburb of Vienna and sought to rally his co-religionists on a specifically Jewish neo-Liberal program. He spent much of the 1880s and 1890s in simultaneous battle against anti-Semites, the rich elders of the Kultusgemeinde, and the young assimilee reformers such as Friedjung and Adler; a quixotic yet terribly divisive figure. Later on, other Viennese Jews of this generation, Max Nordau and Theodor Herzl, made the capital the center of a second imaginative movement designed to save the Jews from anti-Semitism and assimilation alike, but actually dividing them. By the turn of the century, it was easy for Freud at Vienna to discover the anatomy of dreams. All he had to do was look around at the fantasy politics that had replaced the theatrical escapism of the Gründer.

V

It is difficult in nineteenth-century Jewish history to find turning points, moments before which all seemed well, after which or because of which the downfall began. This is because the Jews did not have state politics of their own. During the middle of the century, when most of the peoples of Europe were developing a national political spectrum, the Jews were building their own nation down, systematically trying to retreat into what seemed to be "just religious" political groups. Meanwhile, moreover, individual Jews entered all the Christian parties and only late in the century began to found fragile small political parties of their own.

Nonetheless, this and the two preceding chapters have brought to light a genuine turning point in the history of Habsburg Jewry during the twenty-year European political crisis after 1848. Prior to the revolution of 1848, Habsburg Jewry had lofty visible prospects for finding a place for itself among the peoples of central Europe. Tensions existed, the road would clearly not be easy, but there seemed strong reason for hope. In 1848 itself, moreover, emancipation occurred, although at the same moment Jewish success began to contrast with the failures of the Habsburg bourgeoisie amidst which the Jews were seeking to stand. But then in a short twenty years it appeared, first, that the great mass of Jewry in Galicia was not moving forward; second, that while in Hungary an effective formula for mobilization even of Galician Jews was found, the price was Jewish disunity—a Jewish break with the centralizing German language of the Enlightenment; and third, at Vienna, the logical leadership point for all Habsburg Jewry, the Jews were swept by the Christian disasters into escapism and splintered disarray.

One should not imagine that by 1875 Habsburg Jewry had reached its end. Over forty years were to elapse before Franz Joseph's empire collapsed, and, as we will see, those years were fruitful indeed for the Jews. But there can be no doubt about the structural changes. Whereas before 1850 the great project of Habsburg Jewish modernization had still seemed feasible, now after 1875 vast obstacles and contradictions had appeared. Nor can there be any doubt that the changes were important for the future of all European Jewry. As we have hinted repeatedly in earlier pages, Habsburg Jewry was a test case, lying as it did between westernized Jewry in Germany and the eastern one in Russia. Had this Jewry proved in the Ausgleich era that it could offer effective leadership, some third way between the optimistic symbiosis that throve in Germany and the sheer "backwardness" of Russian Jewry, all European Jewry might have fallen in behind. Instead this Jewry fragmented. One may understand why and sympathize. But one cannot blink the fact that a chance was lost.

PART IV

The Catastrophes,
1875–1918

TEN

Imperialism and Anti-Semitism

Trieste, the Bukowina, Bohemia

I

As Europe's might grew after 1878, she turned outward and devoured the world. The southern Americas, already ruled for a long time by indigenized Europeans, witnessed primarily economic penetration. But in Africa during the 1880s the Powers cut up the whole continental interior, claiming desert and jungle alike as their own. In Asia, after long skirmishing, Britain and Russia established a buffer state in the Afghan mountains, promising not to intervene in each other's ventures on more accessible Himalayan slopes. They then prepared a division of Persia. The French meanwhile conquered those regions of southeast Asia that the British and Dutch did not already rule. Then all the Powers assaulted China, some claiming coastal concessions like the earlier Portuguese and British treaty ports, the Russians claiming vast parts of Mongolia, the Manchu homeland, and Korea.

Toward 1900 the great imperial enterprise slowed down. For the French at Fashoda, the Italians at Adowa, the British in the Transvaal, the Germans at Agadir, the Russians at Tsu Shima, tangible limits appeared. In China in 1899, symbolically, the Europeans burnt the Empress's summer palace and looted Peking, but shirked the difficulty of taking onto their own shoulders the government of all the millions of Chinese. The limits were especially clear in 1908, when the Powers turned homeward again. Whereas in the last crisis to affect Europe herself, that of 1875–78, the stimuli had come from Balkan peasants rebelling against an "oriental" ruler, now the stimulus was the military defeat of Russia by "oriental" Japan, the consequent collapse of the most "oriental" of the European Powers, and the derivative revolution of the "Asiatic" Turks. Feebly, but certainly, the "East" was striking back, forcing Europe into an introspection of sorts. Nonetheless, the thirty years' conquest had been so great that the Europeans ducked the signs that it was over: in 1908, as in 1878, they once again libidinously grabbed other peoples' territory for themselves, as if they were still free.

For much of Europe the great imperialist adventure was a welcome distraction from the pressures of modernization. These thirty years witnessed on-going scientific and educational "progress" that transformed the very fabric of life. Coal replaced wood. Electricity replaced the candle. Indoor plumbing arrived. The automobile challenged the horse. The steamship made the sail obsolete. The telephone revolutionized communications. The very necessities of life, food and clothing alike, began to come from overseas. Metropolitan cities tolled the knell of the age-old agrarian village. And alongside "Progress," "Revolution" reappeared. Socialism, excluded from the European political settlement of the late 1860s, reorganized. In 1889 Marxists founded a Second International Working Man's Association. By the turn of the century it had "sections," or affiliates, in all the major European countries, even in parts of the Russian Empire, and it was showing an ability to absorb into a broad political front the fractious anarchist and nationalist social groups which had proliferated across Europe since the original revolution in France. When Russia exploded in 1905, Socialism was able to play as strong a role as Liberalism there. Pressure was felt now in every part of the continent for universal suffrage and massive social reform. To all this challenging domestic turmoil, the imperialist adventure overseas offered most of the European regimes no panacea, probably not even a compensating profit, but at least an on-going relief from the constant, condemnatory scrutiny of the new public's eye.

Not so Austria, although the pressures of modernization here were as dramatic as in every other continental state—witness Victor Adler's Austrian Social Democratic Party of 1889. Austria alone among the great European Powers indulged in no overseas enterprise in the 1880s and 1890s. Her sole "colony" was Bosnia, acquired at considerable expense in 1878–79. And Austria's strain was the worse in the new age, because here far more acutely than anywhere else in Europe social transformation led to nationalist, "anti-imperial" pressure from the middle classes that adumbrated the later anti-European revolution of the "third world." The attack was as many-sided as the Danubian nationalities were in number. On the one hand, the noble-dominated middle classes of the "historic" nations (Magyars, Poles, and to some extent Croats) insisted that the constitutional arrangements of 1867 be adhered to meticulously—indeed, that further federalization of state power should take place with as little regard for social issues as before. On the other hand, Czechs, an upwardly mobile, quintessentially bourgeois nation, pressed for sufficient expansion of the 1867 federal formulae to give themselves a share, and also for moderate democratization. Slovenes, Slovaks, and Ruthenes, still very "backward," intelligentsia-led peasant nations, lacking "history," sought radical changes in the "system," although basically, like the Czechs, they just wanted places in the sun. Italians, Rumanians, and Serbs, finally, developed a political Irredentism. They all had "brothers" who lived independently just beyond the Habsburg frontiers; and witnessing the weakness of the Austrian constitutional system, they began to talk of abandoning it altogether.

Beyond question, strong measures seemed necessary to those who wished to effect changes in Franz Joseph's realm, for the Kaiser was stubborn. Until 1900 he flatly refused, for example, to entrust the leadership of his government to non-aristocrats. Not until 1906–07 was he willing to accept a universal suffrage. Even then he was content to bargain the great reform away in Hungary, if only the Magyar nobility would "behave." Until the end he insisted on keeping foreign policy and the army as his private preserve. Yet the degree of nationality pressure led even in the 1890s to a political cannibalization of sorts in Austria-Hungary. The emergent national bourgeoisies, in their frustration, attacked not just the present form of the state but its integrity. In single-minded pursuit of particular interest, they lamed and devoured the imperial power that still protected them.

For the Habsburg Jews there was a specially bitter pill in this Austrian debacle. In 1878 "international Jewry" had managed to exert some clout at the great diplomatic congress at Berlin.[1] That minor Jewish initiative catalyzed an anti-Jewish crusade. Within the year a new political slogan, "anti-Semitism," revealed its potential in the then-new German Reich for focusing diverse anti-modern social resentments. Liberal inhibition had hitherto restrained upper- and lower-class victims of modernization alike from identifying any single cause of their discomfort. Now the new secular, racist definition of the word "Jew" enabled them to hit back at a considerable number of capitalists without having to attack money or capitalism per se, and to hit out at Jews without having to assault religion in general. This key made it possible to mobilize all the arsenal of past Jew-hatred against a modern demon. Bismarck's anti-Liberalism of 1880–81 fanned the attack. Then in 1881, after the assassination of Tsar Alexander II, Russian officialdom gave the new slogan international credibility by tolerating a great wave of pogroms in the Pale of Jewish Settlement. By 1882 the anti-Semites were widespread enough to stage an international congress of their own at Dresden.[2] The movement spread into Austria and Hungary. For several years a deputy at the Budapest parliament, Gyözö Istóczy, had been campaigning to stop Jewish immigration into Hungary. In the spring of 1882 a ritual murder charge was laid against a Jew at the village of Tisza-Eszlár, and the resultant trial led with Istóczy's help to vast agitation both by opponents and defenders of Jewry throughout the Danubian world.[3]

Within a few years of Tisza-Eszlár, the Magyar-run government at Budapest had seen to it that political anti-Semitism died for a generation in Hungary.[4] Perhaps in a less frustrated world, anti-Semitism might have flared up as transiently elsewhere in the Habsburg Lands too. But a key element in the Empire's middle-class society just now reached new peaks of frustration. The ethnic Germans had been barred as a group by Bismarck from participating with the western Germans in the unification of the modern German nation. Yet in their own country they, the victims, were being attacked by nation after nation among the east Europeans as if they were responsible for every transgression of the *Hofburg*, as if they were a ruling

Volk. And in their capital, as we have seen, the middle-class rich had abandoned the middle-class poor. Especially for these latter (artisans, lesser bureaucrats, or small-scale merchants as they might be), humiliation seemed piled upon humiliation, and in the resultant bitterness anti-Semitism took root.

The same summer of 1882 when Tisza-Eszlár captured the headlines in the European press, anti-Semitism cropped up in Vienna. The year had opened there with Stock-Exchange scandal that besmirched the conservative, Catholic, and pro-Slavic "Iron-Ring" government of Count Eduard Taaffe, which had displaced the Liberals in 1879. Not just the Liberals, it had appeared, but Taaffe also was deeply involved with the corruption and betrayal of the Christian petite bourgeoisie.[5] In the wake of the scandal a then still young German patriot, Georg von Schönerer, decided to veil with anti-Jewishness the anomalies of his program (which called on German-speaking Austrians to prefer a "just-German" Hohenzollern Kaiser and a "just-German" non-Austrian empire to what they already had). He recruited allies first in the student fraternities, then in the ruined-artisan suburbs, and during 1883 provoked them with golden-toned demagogy to ever rowdier demonstrations in the capital's just-recently Judeophile streets. In this atmosphere a new scandal broke when the government rejected an opportunity to nationalize Rothschild's Nordbahn railroad company. In 1884, when Schönerer led a campaign for nationalization against the will of "the Jews," even respectable sectors of the Vienna press were willing to lend him an ear. It took some years and a change of leadership before anti-Semitism conquered Vienna. But in 1895–96, conquer it did. And in 1897 the anti-Semite, Karl Lueger, forced the Kaiser to install him as the city's mayor, which office he held until his death in 1910.[6]

This was the special cross the Habsburg Jews had to bear in the era of Europe's imperialism. While the lesser Habsburg nationalities cannibalized the Habsburg state in their frustration, the leading nationality—the Germans– cannibalized the Jews. Whence the question of this and the following chapters: how did they take it? What were the responses of Habsburg Jewry to the Austrian misfortunes, which were thus doubly their own?

II

The Jewish community of Trieste gave a telling, if unique, response. To perceive it, however, one must interject here some background material about that community and about the Habsburgs' only major city on the sea.

Let us touch first, as so often before, on matters of demography. Trieste was throughout its history, as the following figures show, a relatively small commercial city. Trieste Jewry was of course considerably smaller. Jews had been present at Trieste probably throughout its history, but in 1700

PRINCIPAL HABSBURG CITIES. 1700–1910[7]

Year	Vienna	Budapest	Prague	Trieste	Cernauti
1700	123,500	12,200	c 38,000	5,000	—
1800	249,380	54,176	c 73,000	30,200	6,000
1857	—	143,289	200,722	c 60,000	26,345
1869	875,460	280,349	239,790	123,098	33,884
1880	1,147,260	370,767	314,442	144,844	45,600
1890	1,404,800	506,384	397,268	157,466	54,171
1900	1,742,720	733,358	514,345	178,672	69,619
1910	2,057,140	863,735	—	226,458	87,113

they numbered barely 100, in 1800 about 1,200, in 1848 something over 3,000, in 1869 4,421, in 1910 only 5,161.[8] They were moreover isolated. Culturally, they were Ashkenazim. Yet in the territories immediately inland from Trieste—the Alpine duchies that extended to Vienna and the other Ashkenazic settlements—there were until the 1890s virtually no Jews. To the west, on the other hand, the ancient and significant Jewish communities in the cities of Venetia and Lombardy were Sephardim.

Despite their small size, both Trieste and her Jewry from early on had very special legal and economic positions. Throughout her history the overweening fact of Triestine life has been rivalry with Venice, across the Adriatic. This rivalry explains why in 1386 the town accepted Habsburg rule, beginning a long history of extra-Italian involvement. It explains also why in 1719 Karl VI made Trieste a free port, increasing its distinctness even from the small County of Gorizia and Gradisca, with which he had inherited it; and why in one form or another the city remained privileged and administratively distinct right down until the end of the monarchy. The Jewish community followed a similar pattern. From 1696 until 1785 the community was forced to live in a ghetto, yet its members dominated Trieste's financial business; and in the interest of the port's prosperity, one Habsburg ruler after the other granted them exemptions from the run-of-the-mill anti-Jewish legislation.[9] From 1771 onwards Maria Theresia even allowed them to visit her then largely Jewless capital, Vienna, without paying a special tax or getting special permission. When Joseph II offered them "tolerance" in 1781–82, their privileges were already so extensive that they asked him in lieu of a new charter just to reconfirm the old ones. Emancipated by Napoleon, they remained so important economically after 1814 that Franz I did not re-enchain them. From 1814 until 1848 they remained the only Habsburg Jews who could own land, move freely, hold public office, and pay no special tax but one on marriage.[10]

Linguistically, Trieste in the distant past was ambivalent.[11] The language of her burghers in the eighteenth century was Italian, yes, but a bastard dialect Italian mixed with German, Greek, French, Armenian, and other tongues. The hinterland then, as in the twentieth century, was South Slavic. Further, though the communal authorities conducted business in Italian, they had nothing against corporate groups within the city which spoke other tongues. Only with the spread of modern education in the nineteenth century did the upper and middle classes Italianize themselves; and even then the marketplace retained its dialect, just as did the marketplace of Germanized nineteenth-century Vienna.[12] And in this environment the Jews for a long time abstained from language choice. For secular purposes they used Italian when called to do so, because that was a language of a segment of the population of their city and to some extent even of the Vienna Court. But in the synagogue that Maria Theresia allowed them after 1747, they used a German rite and the Hebrew language just as did all the other Jews of the north. At home they spoke a variant of Yiddish, allegedly grating to Italian and German ears alike.[13] And in 1781 when Joseph II indicated that the Jews of his realm should establish modern schools, the Trieste Jews sought advice not from anywhere in Italy about how to go about the new task, but from the Mendelssohn circle in Berlin.[14]

It should be mentioned here anew that in the eighteenth century when the question of Jewish modernization came up, German was not, like English or French, just a language of high culture in a restricted territory where most of the population spoke variants of it. German was then the language of high culture, commerce, and to some extent of government, in all those parts of central Europe where the local population was polyglot (thus from the Oder to the Bug, even in Russian Poland, and from the Baltic to the Ottoman frontier). Trieste was at the very edge of the German cultural empire, but from the start the Trieste Jewish community had a perfectly good reason to modernize (as did the Jews in other Habsburg-ruled cities) by speaking German.

Early on, however, came a first sign that they might not do so. It turned out that Kaiser Joseph, here as elsewhere in his dominions, wanted the new Jewish school taught exclusively in German. The Trieste community objected, claiming that Italian would be easier for them since many of them knew it already.[15] One may judge from the protest that on this side of the Alps in Joseph's time the mystique of German was a bit weaker than in the north. And then a major power-input affected Trieste Jewry's language choice. In 1790–91 the French National Assembly made all French citizens equal before the law, irrespective of religion. In the following years as France's revolutionary energies overflowed the Rhine and the Alps, carrying the destruction of the Jewish ghetto into Germany and Italy, it became licit for the emancipated peoples to speak German and Italian as well as French. And in 1797 when Napoleon, having destroyed the independence of Venice, appeared for the first time at Trieste, he brought "liberty" in the Italian language to its Jews. When the liberator reappeared in 1805–06, annexing the Venetian lands, the Jews of Trieste welcomed him almost unanimously and with ostentatious joy in the Italian tongue; and they did so again in 1809 when he annexed their city.[16]

The peculiarity of this "liberation," however, was that it directly countered the self-interest of both of Trieste and of its Jews. The French, with their continental blockade and their equal-handedness towards other Italian ports (including Venice), meant commercial disaster. Trieste had no trade left by 1813 when the French went away, none at all.[17] When the Austrians returned, therefore, the Triestini, Jewish and Christian alike, were by no means unhappy, and quite ready to make sacrifices in exchange for prosperity. And they found that Kaiser Franz was a benevolent master. He bridled the city, but he restored the free port, and in fact made Trieste a free city of the German Confederation.[18] During the Biedermeier period Trieste, with her Jews in the lead, throve. Morpurgos and Parentes, Levis and Hirschels, Vivantes and Daninos made her the insurance capital of the Mediterranean and central Europe, and the home of the great Austrian shipping company, the Lloyd. Meanwhile, since the Kaiser did exert some pressure on the Trieste business class to speak German, the Trieste Jews seemingly did not make a final language choice. Italian certainly retained widespread acceptance. Kaiser Franz even encouraged Italian as a language of preaching in the synagogues (so that his police could keep track of what was said).[19] But the community was then tiny and wholly dominated by men of wealth who, like the Sephardim of the latter day Balkans, learned well whatever tongue was required of them for the pursuit of their interests. And in the Jewish world Trieste then shone not as a center of modern Italian but as one of modern Hebraism. Trieste was the home town of S. L. Luzzatto, the founder of the famous Paduan Seminary, and of his cousin, the Hebrew poet Rachele Morpurgo.

Trieste Jewry did make the decisive choice for Italian (as against German) in mid-century, and this above all probably because of demographic changes. From a population of about 1,700 in 1800, it grew to 2,555 in 1842, and by 1848 was well on the way to its 4,421 of 1869. Especially during the 1840s the increment consisted of Italian Jews, fleeing persecution in the Papal lands.[20] Meanwhile, though many continued to live in the old ghetto quarter, others mingled with the general population; and the introduction of modern schooling led to a drastic democratization of the community. The old community elite was still very much in power, but particularly after the Austrian emancipation of all the Jews in Danubian Europe in 1848, it had to reorganize and could not ignore the by now increasingly explicit linguistic wishes of the congregation.

Other factors contributed to the choice. For one, Austrian political pressure proved soft. The language of government at Trieste remained German throughout the Vormärz and through the absolutist period after 1848. Correspondingly, the Vienna regime through all these decades encouraged the immigration to Trieste of numerous Germans (the most fa-

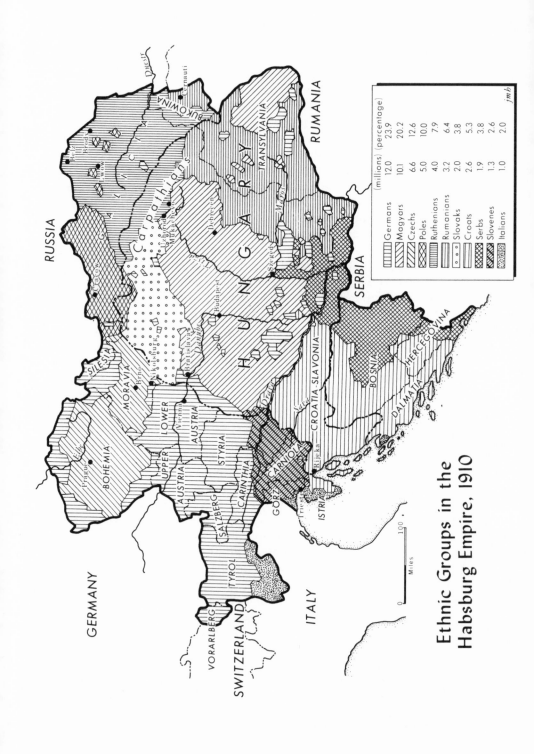

Ethnic Groups in the
Habsburg Empire, 1910

	(millions)	(percentage)
Germans	12.0	23.9
Magyars	10.1	20.2
Czechs	6.6	12.6
Poles	5.0	10.0
Ruthenians	4.0	7.9
Rumanians	3.2	6.4
Slovaks	2.0	3.8
Croats	2.6	5.3
Serbs	1.9	3.8
Slovenes	1.3	2.6
Italians	1.0	2.0

mous was Karl Bruck) and even of some German Jews, and it seemed intent on installing and maintaining German teachers in the Trieste schools. But anyone could observe that Italian also was respectable in Vienna's eyes, for right next door to Trieste was a vast expanse of Austrian territory in Venetia and Lombardy where the language of government was Italian, and where for all one could tell the rulers of Austria never dreamt of Germanizing the countryside. Even after 1848, when Austria punished her Italian subjects at Venice and Milan because of the great rebellion, Germanization did not come into question; and at Trieste in the absolutist years, Austria, in part because of Karl Bruck's eminence at Vienna, was especially indulgent to her Italian speakers.[21]

Meanwhile Italian became the language of ideological Liberalism south of the Alps, and it became commonplace at Trieste that the Italians were "oppressed freedom-fighters" against the German-speaking heart of the European "Reaction." When the Revolution came, the bourgeoisie of Trieste, Jewish and Christian alike, throbbed to the romantic melodies of the Italian national cause. Even the city fathers found themselves deeply moved by the overthrow of the Metternichian authority. Some of the youth actually joined the Italian rebellion. Twice there were attempts to evict the imperial officials from their offices, as had been done across the narrow sea at Venice. And even when an Italian fleet appeared off Trieste's shores, blocking its trade, ruining business, the city's Liberal middle classes bemoaned Austrian attempts to incorporate their city into a renewed German Reich, and decried threats of systematic Germanization. As in Napoleon's day, ideological trends tended now to obscure the immediacies of Trieste's economic self-interest.

Finally there were three political developments which affected Trieste Jewry's language choice. First, in the summer of 1848, at the peak moment of the Italian rebellion, the imperial authorities at Trieste sought to break the back of Liberalism there by organizing a mob attack on the Jews. This murky episode, the event of one long summer evening, had no follow up but seems to have had devastating effects on Jewish trust of the north.[22] Coincidentally, the Austrians tipped the linguistic scales by unsubtlely backing (or seeming to back) outbursts of South Slavic political activity in Trieste's hinterland, awakening the Trieste bourgeoisie to the possibility of a lower-class rebellion against them. Finally, Austria in the long run lost her struggle with the Italian rebels. The events of 1859 and 1866 and 1870 placed at Trieste's front step a new Liberal state as vigorously assertive of its nationalism as Habsburg Austria was deflated. By then, to judge from Trieste Jewry's confessional publications, their cultural allegiance lay exclusively in Italy.[23]

In view of this record it seems initially not surprising that in the age of European overseas imperialism, while anti-Semitism was conquering Vienna, Trieste Jews tended to the most extreme wing of Italian nationalist opinion in their home city. Felice Venezian, a scion of one of the greatest

Jewish commercial families, actually founded the Italian Irredentist movement there; and during the decades when Karl Lueger was mayor at Vienna, Venezian was Trieste's most vocal politician.[24] In some ways there
seems no great divergence between the earlier group decision to speak
Italian and the new one to actually try to join the Italian nation. Indeed,
such a step can seem initially a fitting response to the indecency of Habsburg German Jew-hatred.

The anomaly appears, however, when one recalls the constant factors
which logically bound both Triestine society as a whole and the city's Jews
to the Austrian camp. Above all, there was the economic prospect that
Triestine unity with Italy would bring the subordination to Venice which
actually occurred after 1918. So long as Trieste was Austrian, she remained
a principal sea-outlet for the entire Danubian world. Even if the times were
hard, as they seemed to be to many Trieste businessmen in the 1870s and
1880s, and even if Vienna did not press as hard as she might have to develop
foreign trade through Trieste, a long history told that the status quo out-
shone anything Trieste might expect if detached from the Alpine hinterland. Trieste's Jews remained in this period the city's commercial
leadership. For almost three-quarters of a century after 1850, for example,
the brothers Elio and Josef Morpurgo and their sons not only shared in the
Jewish community lead, but headed the city's principal shipping company,
its biggest bank, the Lloyd, the Assicurazione Generale [General Insurance
Company] and the Chamber of Commerce. This family also had personal
links to Empress Elizabeth and to the Rothschilds, and provided Trieste
with Reichsrath deputies.[25] Other Jewish families were not far behind; and
though they spoke Italian, these leading Jews had no illusion about where
their allegiance lay. In the 1890s, the moderately *Austriacante* Trieste politician, Pietro Kandler, whose father was Viennese and whose mother was
Italian, once confessed in public that if one were to cut him to pieces, one
would discover that despite his devotion to the Kaiser, he was entirely
"*veneto.*" To this Raffael Luzzatto, a Reichsrath deputy of Jewish Brahmin
extraction, replied that were one to cut *him* up, the pieces would be exclusively yellow and black.[26]

A number of important sociological factors explain how Triestine Jewry
could endure the terrifying identity stretch between self-interested loyalty
to the Kaiser and Irredentism to Italy, and why indeed it seemed almost
natural at the time. One such factor was certainly again the demographic
development of the community. In the forty years between the censuses
of 1869 and 1910, the religiously affiliated sector of Trieste Jewry drastically
shrank. Though the community on paper appeared to grow from 4,400 to
5,500, almost half of the 1910 Jewish population were not Austrian citizens.
Some of these "foreigners" may have been refugees from Crete, others
may have been Italians from across the border. Regardless, their presence
makes dramatically clear a religious disintegration that had affected the
community in the 1870s and 1880s. Discipline became so lax that until 1882

converts could be buried in the Jewish cemetery, and until 1888 uncircum-
cised children of mixed marriages could be registered as Jews. As a result
conversions and mixed marriages proliferated. In 1898, 15 out of the 61
marriages involving Jews at Trieste were mixed.[27] Amidst such circumstances one may understand that secularized middle-class Jews of the
younger generation may have felt special pressure to make manifest not
just their rejection of their fathers but also the intensity of their assimilee
feeling by becoming Irredentists. There was no strong organizational bond
to hold Trieste's Jews together.

To this one must add that the Trieste Jews were overwhelmingly middle class, if not always wealthy middle class, and as such were subject to
another sort of pressure. Even in 1851 a partial census had revealed that
Italians comprised only 34.45% of the population of the Küstenland, most
of the rest being either Slovene or Croatian. In subsequent censuses the
realities were veiled because the administrative rearrangements of the 1850s
isolated the city from its hinterland. In 1880, for example, Trieste boasted
a 73.76% Italian majority, and barely 20% Slavs. One discovered the reality
only when one searched out the figures for the adjoining Gorizia region
(36% Italian, 63% Slovene) and Istria (40% Italian, 58% Slovene and Croatian). The census deceived because it defined Trieste within very narrow
territorial limits. Yet after 1900 the Slavs began to flee their villages and to
urbanize, and even in Trieste itself the Italian percentage of the population
went down to 62%.[28] To an Italian-speaking middle class this was a challenge which might well have stimulated extremist nationalism.

If one may judge from the work of Italo Svevo, the greatest Jewish
writer to emerge from this milieu, the pressures of Trieste Jewry's identity
stretch in the age of imperialism were not so severe as to produce the rank
despair or the sense of slavery that affected other Habsburg Jewish writers
of the time. Svevo lived in a world of many tongues; he thought in German,
wrote in Italian. But he was master of his words, he made them move, not
they him.[29] Withall, the reality remains. In the age of imperialism Trieste's
Jewry had rushed to incompatible ideological extremes. Because of Christian Austria's misfortunes, it experienced a division of identities the more
traumatic because it was slow coming and long around. And these identities
were not even expressed in Jewish terms.

III

Very different but not less alarming was the development of a second small
but significant Jewish community not earlier discussed: the Jewry of the
Bukowina. Once again, demography affords the necessary prelude to discussion for this was quite a different Jewish community from that in Trieste.
In 1774–75 when the Austrians unceremoniously annexed this northern
part of the Ottoman vassal principality of Moldavia, there were perhaps
206 Jewish families in it, 986 heads, no more than in either tiny Trieste or

restricted Jewish Vienna at the time. By another count a decade later, there were 360 families, 2,131 souls, in an overall population of some 150,000. The Austrians hereupon joined the new territory to the Galician Gubernium, but despite the implicitly free immigration Jews still comprised only 3.12% of the total population in 1846 (11,581 out of 371,131). Then in 1848 Vienna separated the two provinces, making the Bukowina an autonomous duchy. Whether for this reason or because counting methods improved, the Jewish population steeply rose. By 1857, 29,187 Jews were counted, 6.5% of the population; in 1869, 47,000, 9.3%; in 1890, 82,717, 12.8%; in 1910, 102,919, 12.9%. Increasingly, moreover, this population was gravitating towards the capital city, Cernauti [Czernowitz, Chernovtsy]. Whereas in 1857 some 4,678 Jews comprised 21.7% of that then small town, by 1880 14,449 Jews were 31.7% of its poulation. In 1910, 28,613 Jews, a third of all the Jews in the Bukowina, comprised 32.1% of Cernauti's 87,000 people.[30]

In some ways the Bukowina in the early decades of Austrian rule was very like Galicia and the neighboring Russian lands. The population was probably sparser, but the same feudal conditions existed, the same general dearth of modern trade and industry, the same lack of roads and transportation, the same impoverished and unlettered "Ruthene" peasants. As we have seen, the railroad only came in 1870, even later than in Galicia. The major difference between the Bukowina and the neighboring lands was that the landlord population (and a major part of the peasantry) was Moldavian [Rumanian], not Polish. The Bukowina's Jewry was correspondingly very like that of Galicia or the Russian Pale, whence much of it came. In the first half of the century a tiny cohort of "enlightened" Maskilim had to battle with an overwhelming mass of "fanatical" tradition-minded rural Jews. Hasidism came later here than it did to Galicia, but it came more strongly. In 1840 the Ruzhyn Rebbe, Israel Friedmann, settled at Sadgora. A few years later, one of his sons-in-law, Menachem Mendel, a son of the famous Kosow Rebbe, established himself at Vizhnitsa and drew a large following to his court. Later still, one of Israel Friedmann's sons split with his father's heirs and set up a separate court at Bojan.[31] These three courts made the Bukowina one of the strongest Hasidic centers in the world.

After the separation from Galicia, however, a differentiation of Bukowina Jewry from Galician Jewry began. The province itself remained backward and abysmally poor, with an extraordinarily high illiteracy rate. But among the Jews, especially in Cernauti, an education movement caught on. As early as 1854 the Maskilim of the capital managed (with Austrian administrative support) to wrest control of the city's kehilla from the Orthodox. They immediately founded a modern school. By 1872 there were no less than 58 Bukowinan Jewish students enrolled in Austria's universities. When in the following year Vienna set up a university at Cernauti itself, the Jews flocked to it. By the end of the century an articulate educated class dominated the city's Jewry, German-speaking and modern in its outlook. This remarkable blossoming was in many ways similar to what happened at the principal Galician cities at the same time, notably at Lwow, which also had a university. The difference lay in the proportions. The Lwow Maskilim never formed more than tiny proportion of east Galician Jewry, which abhorred them. The Cernauti Maskilim were no less alien to the Jewish mass around them, but the latter was much much smaller.[32]

One more factor also affected the development of Bukowinan Jewry: the nationality situation. Whereas in Galicia, as we have seen, a very large Polish nobility endowed with a strong sense of nationality dominated the countryside, and the German-speaking middle class and state bureaucracy were relatively small, in the Bukowina the Moldavian nobility had a weak sense of identity and the German population grew proportionately more swiftly. The strength and authority of the Austrian state was here, therefore, never in doubt. The Rumanians did not gain special powers in the settlement of 1870, as the Magyar and Polish nobilities did; nor did they seek in the Reichsrath in the late nineteenth century to federalize the state. They were tamely loyal to the Kaiser. For enlightened Jews this meant that until the broadening of the suffrage late in the century, there was never any reason to think of a non-German cultural-political alliance. Then, moreover, other factors not only reinforced this preference, but placed the Jews in the role of political arbiter. The closely matched Rumanian and Ruthenian electorates (34% and 38% respectively in 1910) both looked to the German-speaking 20% of the population to further or protect their national interests; and within the German population, particularly in Cernauti, the Jews were the majority. As a result, Cernauti had Jewish mayors from 1905 until 1908, and from 1913 until the Russian occupation during the First World War. Although a Rumanian anti-Semite Party emerged just before the war, nowhere else in the Dual Monarchy were the Jews so free of that Christian plague as in the Bukowina; and nowhere else did such a broad spectrum of specifically Jewish political groupings flourish.

Nonetheless, here as at Trieste, Austria's misfortunes raised identity problems for the Jews, because the freedom of organization and the absence of fear revealed dilemmas. Whereas at Trieste until the First World War the Jewish identity stretch was between Christian parties, here it was between Jewish ones. Everyone was loyal to the Kaiser, but there was sharp dispute about what Jews should do under his aegis. Among the Hasidim, Bojan abhorred Sadgora for the Rebbe's material luxury; Sadgora detested Bojan back for the Rebbe's presumption. Though neither had the slightest interest in becoming politically active, both abhorred the Maskilim who betrayed Tradition and did become active. The Maskilim, in their turn, were divided amongst those who were content to participate in the bourgeois Christian parties and those who felt it useful to be more Jewish—to represent not just the rich Jews, but the "little man." Foremost among these last was Dr. Benno Straucher, an inimitable character who by denouncing assimilee Liberalism got himself elected to the Reichsrath in 1897 and to the leadership of the Cernauti Kultusgemeide in 1900. Retaining these offices (and others) he then turned his most intense fire for some years against the Hebraist ultramontanism of Zionism, insisting that Jews should build their future here, in central Europe, not far away, and that they should do so in the prevailing German tongue. In 1907 he shifted stance a little. After accepting a vaguely Zionist platform, he spent his last years in bitter personal struggle with those elements of Habsburg Jewry who felt one could only get through to the Jewish masses by using Yiddish.[33] Either in unison with Straucher's Jüdische Volkspartei of 1902 or against it, there flourished in pre-war Bukowina the whole array of Zionist, "autonomist," Hebraist and Yiddishist, religious Zionist, and Zionist-Socialist political opinion. In addition, agnostic Bukowina Jews were active in organizing Social-Democracy here, and it was in fact the Cernauti Jewish vote that sent George Grigorovici, the head of the Rumanian SDP, to the Reichsrath from 1907 until 1911.[34]

In sum, Austria's misfortune in the age of imperialism made it possible for the Jews in the Bukowina to look to Jewish nationalism. But the more they did so, the more they had painfully to recognize that there was no truth. For twentieth-century Jews in the Galut literally dozens of political alternatives were open. There was no straight and correct line.

IV

End-of-the-century Bohemia was very different from Trieste and the Bukowina, larger and more complex by far than either. Different also was its Jewry, which as seen elsewhere was older than Trieste's community, not to speak of the Bukowina's, yet which was between the two in point of westernization. Yet the story of Bohemian Jewry during the era of imperialism reveals more sensitively than either of the other cases recounted above a basic entrapment that affected all Habsburg Jews in those years.

The tale begins with the industrialization which transformed the Bohemian Crownlands in the early part of the century. As recounted earlier, the Prague Jewish exchange-houses and the rural Jewish credit networks were the financial backbone of the new industries. In Moravia, the textile center of the whole Empire, Jews were the distributors of the new products. And from 1800 to 1850 at Prague, Jews were the pioneers in the building of the cotton industry, the vanguard sector of the city's modernization. After mid-century the industrialization process proceeded at an increased pace. It was typical that Prague, which before 1848 had been a textile center, grew to be one of the machine-building centers of the entire Empire, so great was the industrial expansion. Ostrava, the seat of Baron Rothschild's Witkowitz estate, became the coal- and iron-mining center of the Empire. Plzen became the weapons center. Meanwhile, in the mountain foothills of Bohemia's periphery—in the latter day Sudetenland—the older local industries, glass, ceramics, and textiles, modernized and expanded, and a great new chemical industry developed. Coincidentally, steam-driven breweries sprang up in almost all the major Bohemian towns, and on the fertile plain of southern Moravia new, modern beet-distilleries made Austria a major world producer of sugar.

The fateful concomitant of this vital expansion, however, was an unsubtle shift of power, population, and economic influence away from Prague to Vienna. As the table earlier in this chapter reveals, Prague in mid-century was still larger than Budapest, and over a third the size of the Austrian capital. In 1900, despite escalating population figures for all three cities, Prague was only two-thirds the size of Budapest, and well under a third that of Vienna. In economics and politics Prague fought for a while, establishing a stock exchange of its own in the 1870s, insisting on the importance of its regional *Landtag* or parliament, and trying to retain control of local industries. But the great economic efflorescence was in a fundamental sense an all-Austrian affair. The more high-powered and dynamic capitalism became in the Bohemian Lands, the more important the great Vienna banks became in their development, and the more German-speaking Bohemian businessmen tended to centralize management at the political, communications, and international financial center that Vienna was.

The history of a single Jewish family, the Mauthners, suggests both the dynamic of this development and its shattering consequences for Bohemian Jewry. Originating at Smírice [Smiritz] on the upper Elbe near Hradec Králové [Königgrätz] in Czech-speaking northeastern Bohemia, this family began its career in brewing, but from the very start "business" carried its sons away both from their original profession and from their native land.[35] Even in the late eighteenth century, one branch of the family moved westward to Prague and another moved eastwards to Györ in Hungary. In the Prague ghetto, the Mauthners were among the first Jewish families to enter the cotton-printing industry (and were Frankists to boot),[36] but the first Mauthner to reach real eminence was named Ludwig and came from the Hungarian branch. He studied medicine and then, still young, converted and entered the army so as to practice. In 1850, after ennoblement as "Mautner von Mautstein," he became a German-speaking professor of medicine at the Vienna University.[37] The second eminent Mauthner was Adolf Ignaz, of the name. In the later 1830s he moved directly from the original family village to Schwechat, outside Vienna. In 1840 he took over a brewery, pioneered new chemical brewing methods, converted to Roman Catholicism, and became one of the greatest of Austrian brewers of beer. Eventually (in 1872), he too was ennobled, with the name "Mauthner von Markhof."[38]

Early in the absolutist period the Prague branch of the family, not to be outdone by the successes of these cousins, sent three sons, Max, Philip, and Ludwig to Vienna for their education. The eldest, Max (born 1837), converted about 1860 and became one of the Austrian capital's greatest entrepreneurs, a long-term president of the Lower Austrian Chamber of Commerce, a director of the Lower Austrian Discount Bank, of the Austrian Lloyd Shipping Company, of the Creditanstalt, and a dozen other leading firms, until he died just after his ennoblement in 1902.[39] Max's brother Philip, ennobled in 1887, was one of the few in the clan not to convert. This does not mean he was either a pious Jew or a good Bohemian, however. In religion almost agnostic, he became one of German Vienna's leading lawyers.[40] Brother Ludwig became, like his namesake and deceased cousin, a professor of medicine at Vienna. And then the provincial branch of the family produced a Gustav Mauthner, born 1847, who converted, entered the Creditanstalt, and in 1880 rose to its presidency (for which honor he too was ennobled). Eventually he became a great landowner near his home town, but as an historical figure he was as impeccably Viennese as they came.[41] Gustav's brother, Fritz Mauthner, the writer, was one of the few in the family who remained in Prague, and even he was notorious as a convert out of Judaism and as a passionate anti-Czech.[42] One may note in conclusion of this survey that the Hungarian branch of the family moved from Győr to Budapest in the 1870s and there contracted marriage connections with a family named Weiss, which had a meat-canning factory on the Csepel island south of Budapest. Through diligent use of the Vienna Mauthners' various connections in the war ministry, the Weisses were able to advance from meat-tins to cartridges, then to filling the cartridges with powder, and to handling a broad variety of other military supplies. After 1900 they were among the greatest munitions industrialists of central Europe, and controlled a banking empire that quite literally dominated Hungary's economy.[43] By the end of the century there was even a branch of the Mauthner family settled at Trieste.

High capitalism had an atomizing effect on Bohemian Jewry, which one may trace not only through such family histories but through the overall statistics. While the Jewish population of Vienna was skyrocketing in the late nineteenth century decades, that of the Bohemian Lands showed passive and eventually negative patterns.[44] There is plenty of evidence that there were also internal Jewish migrations which gave Prague, Brno, and other cities substantially larger Jewish populations at the end of the imperialist half century than at the start. Prague Jewry rose from some 7,706 domiciled persons in 1857 to 18,986 in 1900; Brno Jewry rose from 215

JEWISH POPULATION

	1869	1880	1890	1900	1910
Lower Austria	52,350	95,058	128,729	157,278	185,779
Bohemia	89,933	94,449	94,479	92,745	85,826
Moravia	42,899	44,175	45,324	44,225	41,158
Silesia	6,142	8,510	10,042	11,988	13,442

persons domiciled in 1857 to 8,328 in 1900.[45] It was the Bohemian and Moravian rural Jewries that lost out the most under the impact of the later nineteenth century economic "Austrianization." But the truism remains: the Empire's industrial flowering drastically weakened the one-time core community of Habsburg Jewry.

What is more, another kind of sweeping socio-economic development drastically changed the Jewish position in Bohemia's capital. This was the Czech national movement's challenge to the German *pays légitime* there, in which the Jews participated. As observed elsewhere, the Czech national movement was slow in organizing. Hardly had it gotten off the ground politically before 1848, but it was overtaken by the revolution and repressed. After that sad experience, however, the Czech intelligentsia leadership persevered in their educational work, encouraging the political consciousness of the Bohemian bottom social strata. When political life resumed in the 1860s they presented the world a much braver face. High on their program was the "Czechization" of Bohemia's public life and economy. As early as 1861 the Czechs were numerous enough in Prague to seize control of the city council, and to threaten German control of the Landtag.

Thirty years before the artisan-class seizure of Vienna, the Czechs in Prague thus challenged the Liberal upper bourgeoisie. Symbolically they chose early on to write the Prague street signs in Czech, to campaign for the construction of a Czech national theatre, and for a Czech role at the ancient Charles University. But they sought also to establish Czech credit institutions, industries, houses of commerce; and since by now the Czech-speaking artisans and small shop-keepers of the Vormärz were more prosperous than before, they soon had the "German" economy on the retreat. By the turn of the century the combination of political pressure and socially-motivated petite bourgeois enterprise had created a "second economy" in the Bohemian Lands run exclusively in Czech.

For the Jews this would have been a baffling and profoundly unsettling development even had the Czechs not, as noted elsewhere, evinced a strong Judeophobia. In Bohemia, just as elsewhere in central Europe, the Jews had tended before 1848 to Germanize; and they had entered the older and larger credit enterprises and industries of Prague and the crownland's Sudeten periphery—in other words, the above-mentioned "German economy." Who could feel secure while such a different economy was growing up beneath this one, challenging it, threatening it? And in addition, Czech Judeophobia did not evaporate after the suppression of 1848, but flickered on until well after 1900.[46]

The initial Jewish response was taken by the rich and enlightened Jewish community at Prague, which in mid-century to some extent spoke for the whole of Bohemian Jewry.[47] Observing in 1848 that the Czechs were Jew-hating at the moment, this elite turned massively to Germanism. In the 1860s the Prague Jewish leadership even went around the smaller synagogues of Prague making sure that Czech was not used (as was customary in rural Bohemian communities) to call Jews to worship. They kept the whole network of Bohemia's Jewish schools rigidly German, and tried harder than ever to become perfect Germans themselves.[48] For the wealthier Jews of the capital, this policy brought rich rewards. The Prague German upper bourgeoisie—which was increasingly isolated in these decades in a Czech city—saw well enough what the issues were, and embraced the Jewish vote. Prague and Cernauti were the two cities of the Habsburg Monarchy where the Jews were least plagued by German anti-Semitism in the Ausgleich years. At Prague the upper-bourgeois Germans made it easier for Jews to participate in political life and social festivities than did even the "second society" of Vienna.[49] In the Sudeten regions also the Germanizer policy seemed rewarding: here in the rapidly industrializing rural towns of Bohemia's periphery, right next to the Reich, Habsburg German bitterness over the exclusion of 1866 and frustration with modernity was as great as in suburban Vienna, and led in the 1880s to a vicious anti-Semitism of the new kind.[50] The Jews of the region felt that to speak German might disarm the foe, whereas to speak Czech might inflame him.

Yet Bohemian Jewry was never united on this policy. In rural southern Bohemia the very ancient Jewish communities resented Prague's efforts to speak for them; and here the Jews had always spoken Czech alongside *Mauscheldeutsch*, because that was the language of the countryside. As these rural Jews were flocking into the cities after mid-century, they still spoke Czech. They found themselves entering increasingly Czech-speaking cities. Why change? Why not appease the Czech anti-Semites, who were right here, rather than the Germans who were far away? These questions were the more telling because there were a number even of prominent Prague Jews who spoke Czech. For the Prague Jewish Brahmins, perhaps, it was acceptable amidst such circumstances to worship German as in the past. For the Jews of the countryside and for the immigrants to Prague, such a policy made no sense.[51] Gradually over the years after 1870 the Bohemian rural Jews began to report to the census that they spoke Czech, and at Prague a modest "Czech-Jewish" cultural and political movement emerged.[52]

In the last years of the century the language debate among the Bohemian Jews came to a head. There were moments in the late 1890s when everyone in Bohemia seemed against the Jews. Czech politicians were bitterly denouncing the Jewish schools in the countryside as the last bastion of Germanism; German bullies in the Sudetenland as in Vienna, and even sometimes in lower-class quarters of Prague, were screaming to the effect: *solltet alle aufgehängt werden, ihr keckigen, schmutzigen Saujuden.*[53] Things grew especially bad during 1897–98, when Prime Minister Count Badeni failed in his attempt to extend the use of Czech as a language of administration in Bohemia. The Czechs in their frustration attacked the Jews for maintaining German-language schools. Hereupon came a breakthrough.

In 1899 the Czech professor, T. G. Masaryk, ostentatiously took up the cause of a Jew charged in Bohemia with the Blood Libel.[54] Now abruptly in the census of 1900, which was heavily politicized, 55.2% of the Prague Jews declared to the census-takers that Czech was their *Umgangssprache*, a 10% change from ten years earlier.[55]

What had happened? Against the will and advice of their community leadership, some 4,000 Prague Jews, most of them presumably immigrants, had abruptly changed sides. Just as in the general economy a Czech sub-sector had pushed the German superstructure aside, so the Czech-speaking Jewish immigrants to Prague asserted themselves against the Brahmins. This division was in some ways reminiscent of Trieste Jewry's more or less simultaneous embrace of both "Veneto" and "Schwarz-Gelb" as the preferred color of their blood! But there was a disturbing difference: the Triestini did not divide amongst themselves so much as within themselves—they internalized the contradictions, refusing to be dragged in their daily lives one way or the other. The Bohemian Jews, on the other hand, sharply divided. There was no possibility here by 1900, for example, of Jewish society acting as an upward-funneling, mobility-creating middle class element, as Vienna Jewry had been twenty years earlier. Prague Jewry was as irremediably split, bottom against top, as was the Christian environment. The upper class Germanizers, perhaps, felt they had a synthesis; but they were far more alone than the Schwarz-Gelb Jews of Trieste.

During the decade before the war Bohemian and Moravian Jewry did experiment a little with the political alternatives we have seen represented in the Bukowina. Jewish nationalism found adherents among students at the Prague higher schools. A Jewish fraternity appeared there, first under the name Macabaea, later on as Bar Kochba. A Jewish Labor group was organized at Brno, the most industrialized city of the Dual Monarchy.[56] Yet Bohemia-Moravia lacked a major factor that gave life to Zionism in the Bukowina. The Jews here had virtually no contact any longer with the Jewry of the past. At home Tradition had withered under the impact of modern education. Until the war, there was virtually no Orthodox Jewish presence here. Symptomatically, the Bar Kochba Zionists discovered traditional Jewry through a Galician Yiddish theatre troupe which visited Prague in 1911. To find out about Hasidism, one of them, the poet Jiří Langer, village wandered to Belz in Galicia before the war. There were no Hasidim at home.[57] No variety of Jewish roots was available to the Bohemian Jews.

Turn-of-the-century Bohemian Jewry is the reputed source of Franz Kafka's expressions of human agony. Kafka's apparent slavery to words—the agony with which slowly, slowly he followed words first into aphoristic expression, later into stories and never-completed novels; his inability to decide; his failure to finish; his extraordinary sensitivity to double meanings—all this can be associated with the "in-betweenness" of the Jewish world in which he grew up. One may doubt certain aspects of some of the more deterministic assessments of Kafka: it is not certain, for example, that from the start his creative career was assertively Jewish—he seems rather to have discovered a Jewish identity when he was well along. Further, Bohemian Jewry's malady was perhaps less "in-betweenness" than prolonged "slipping and sliding" of the late nineteenth century. Once the Czechs gained power in 1918, the Jewish discomfort disappeared. But that Kafka's agony was native to his world, that seems beyond question. Bohemian Jewry's whole late-nineteenth-century experience was an agony of entrapment.

V

In this chapter we have examined three cases of Habsburg Jewish behavior during the era of European imperialism, when the Empire's nationality groups embarked on the process of cannibalism that would eventually bring the state down. None of these cases was central to Habsburg Jewry in that epoch. Trieste was a tiny, withering community on the Italian frontier. Bukowinan Jewry throve, but was equally far out on the Russian frontier. Bohemian Jewry had once been central, but was now shrunken, stagnant, extraordinarily isolated and divided. It would be difficult indeed to hold that these represent the "whole story" of Habsburg Jewry response to Austria's misfortunes. Further, all three cases were extreme: Trieste in its embrace of Irredentism; the Bukowina in its articulation of Zionist alternatives; Bohemia in its expression of pain. Nowhere else in the Empire did Jews respond in such specific fashions to their condition.

Yet from precisely this atypicality of Trieste, the Bukowina, and Bohemia, one may intimate the fate that all of Habsburg Jewry in different mixes came to suffer in these decades. Everywhere, to some extent, the polarity of Christian politics fell heavily on the Jews, casting a double burden upon their shoulders, someone else's as well as their own. Nowhere, moreover, was a clearly "correct" Jewish policy possible. All too often, indeed, what had seemed perfectly reasonable from a "Jewish" point of view in 1848 or 1858 was proven by a ground-swell change in 1900 to be the opposite. What earlier had seemed "Jewish virtue" could be construed by the end to be some sort of sin. And finally, in one degree or another everywhere after 1900, the Jews were in an "in between" situation socially, as bitter ethnic struggle ripped the Habsburg middle class to shreds.

ELEVEN

The Crisis

Galicia, Hungary, Vienna

I

In the final prewar years Europe's crisis came to center on the "Austrian Question." The Habsburg Empire had been the subject of international concern for a long time, universally hated under Metternich, generally mocked in the Ausgleich period. But Austria had not been the "sick man of Europe" about whose ability to survive one speculated until 1895–97, when not only the Reichsrath deputies but the German and Czech middle classes took to rioting over the details of a new language ordinance for Bohemia. The atomization of the Empire's middle class seemed now to herald the disintegration of the state.

Even after the crisis of the late 1890s the Vienna Government functioned tolerably in many respects, and resolved important political problems. In 1906, for example, Franz Joseph forced the Magyar "independence" forces to back down. In 1907 he gave Cisleithania its universal suffrage. In 1908 the government achieved a compromise solution to the nationality struggle in Moravia, in 1910 a second one in the Bukowina, early in 1914 a third in Galicia.[1] One can argue that under normal circumstances other compromises would have been worked out. And though Franz Ferdinand, the heir to the throne, was neither a Liberal nor an angel, he seemed vigorous and self-willed enough to force through major and perhaps salutory changes. Yet after 1897 pessimism about Austria was widespread. Inside the Empire one acknowledged that the government was too inept (witness the Friedjung scandal of 1909) and too venal (witness the Redl case of 1913). While admitting that the situation was desperate, one took nothing seriously any more. Outside, a new "hate Austria" movement sprang up among the intellectuals of Paris and London. And universally in Europe one observed how close the various Irredentist movements were coming to demanding the monarchy's truncation; how perilously the Balkan disturbances threatened to involve the Habsburg South Slavs; and how transparently Vienna's concern with prestige revealed its own worry about whether the state could survive.

What was the Jewish response to this crisis? Was Habsburg Jewry also on its last legs, or was it alive and kicking? This chapter will seek answers to such questions in the record of the Empire's three central Jewish communities: those of Galicia, Hungary, and Vienna.

II

In Galicia two new factors tinted the political crisis in the immediately prewar years; first, the national awakening of the Ruthenian (Ukrainian) nation; second, the revolutionary upheaval in Tsarist Russia.

As late as 1910, 91.7% of the Ruthenians in Galicia were still in the agricultural sector, as against only 61.7% of the Poles; the "backwardness" of the Ruthenian nation was still formidable. But whereas in 1880 the illiteracy rate among all Galicians over 6 years old was 77.1%, in 1910 it was 40.6%. And though among the Poles some 72% could read and write by 1910, among the Ruthenians the rate had crept up to 61%.[2] Further, new channels had developed to handle the discontents of this no longer voiceless people. The old, grass-roots outlet—mass emigration to America—in no way closed down,[3] but articulate political groups emerged also. Very few of them were as "pro-Russian" as the Poles liked to make out: the Uniate Church and a whole range of ancient Ukrainian resentments against Moscow saw to that. But almost all were anti-Polish, and as a result here, as at Trieste and in the Bohemian Lands, the democratization of society led to sharp new linguistic pressures on the by now German and Polish-speaking middle class.

Then, second, developments in Russia accelerated change in Galicia. Almost until 1900 the Polish nobility wholly dominated this crownland. They made it a pillar of conservative stability within the monarchy. Time after time their leaders became Austrian ministers and prime ministers. In the 1890s, however, the repression of politics in Russian Poland led to a radical expansion of the Galician Polish political spectrum. Galicia became the marshaling ground for all Poland's political groups. Suddenly alongside the old Conservatives there were a Polish Social-Democracy (1892), a Polish peasant party (1895), a Polish National Democracy (1895–1904). The violent revival of politics in Russia after 1902 then completed the political transformation. Even before the 1907 suffrage reform these and other more or less democratic political groups were pushing the old conservatives aside, and turning much more political attention to social and national issues. Indicatively, the Landtag in 1907 made the Polish language its exclusive tongue, completing the eviction of German and Ruthenian from the bureaucracy and universities. The Russian events of course mobilized the Ruthenes also. In 1907 the new language legislation, combined with the institution of universal suffrage in Austria, spurred the Ruthenes to counterattack, and made it possible just before the war for Vienna to arrange the political settlement mentioned above.

The Poles stood at 4 millions, 50% of the Galician population in 1910;

the Ruthenes stood at 3.2 millions, 42%.[4] This balance resembled the near parity of Rumanians and Ruthenes, which put the Jews in a commanding political situation in the Bukowina. But here there was no such profit to be extracted. In Galicia the Jews remained the whipping boy of the competing Christian nations. The reason was above all the on-going poverty of all concerned. Economic changes were slowly beginning to transform even Galicia; indeed, east of Lwow a major oil-extraction industry was emerging. But in the rural areas capitalism was still very weak and almost exclusively Jewish. As in the past, the Jews still seemed the envied and despised economic exploiters of the agrarian population. It did not help that a great part of their own society remained caught in the vicious circle of Orthodoxy, destitution, and lack of education, and shunned those opportunities for escape that were on hand.[5]

In addition, circumstance had worked against the Jews. In the 1860s and 1870s, as observed earlier, the enlightened Jews of Galicia had clung to the German language and to a Viennese political allegiance because they distrusted the flickering Jew-hatred of the Poles. Franz Joseph had then given the Poles political power. With small ado after that Jews of all religious orientations had made their peace with the Polish political leadership. Indeed, because the vast majority of the Galician Jews at census time now reported their language as Polish, the Poles were indebted to them for their statistical 58% of the crownland population. But there was a difference between this debt and the parallel debt of the Magyar nobility to the Jews in Hungary. There the Jews had given the Magyars substantial political and economic support on the road to power. The Galician Poles had gained power on their own. Consequently from the very start of the new political ferment in the late 1890s they allowed themselves the steam-cock of anti-Semitism. Though the old conservatives tended to be above such "vulgarity," the Church, particularly in its lower echelons, was not; nor were some of the new parties, for example Roman Dmowski's National Democracy. In 1898, peasant pogroms shook the westernmost corner of Galicia, its most solidly Polish part, and terrified the Jews.[6]

Meanwhile, as the Ruthenians "awoke" they too observed that in politics the Jews of Galicia stood on the wrong side, although in this case it was not the German but the Polish allegiance of the Jews which hurt. The observation confirmed strains of Jew-hatred that were deeply rooted in the Ukrainian past. The Galician Ruthenes did not in 1902 and 1905–06 take up the cudgels of the anti-Jewish pogromists then active in the Russian lands, but even so the disorders contributed to distrust and dislike between them and the Jews; the great wave of refugees from the Ukraine was evidence strong enough to convince all Galicia that Ruthenes hated Jews.

The primary Jewish response to the prewar crisis in Galicia was emigration. Of the 320,000 Jews who emigrated from Austria-Hungary to the United States between 1891 and the war, 85% were from Galicia. There was a step-up in the early years of the century, then a fall-off just before

1914, but the message was unmistakable: many Galician Jews wanted out. Meanwhile, attesting the same sentiment, the Galician-born share of the Jewish population of Vienna shot up. In 1880 it had been 18%; by 1910 it was 23%. The increment is the more significant because in the meantime many of the older Galician-born Viennese Jews died off—the 23% were substantially new immigrants; and whereas 18% of Vienna Jewry in 1880 comprised 13,180 individuals, 23% of the 1910 Jewish population comprised 30,325.[7] The net consequence of the flight was that between 1890 and 1900 Galician Jewry fell behind that of Hungary and ceased to be the largest reservoir of Habsburg Jews. By 1910 Galician Jewry was down even in Cisleithania from the three-quarters of the Jewish population it had formed in mid-century to two-thirds.

This popular movement among the Jews was by no means exclusively motivated by fear. Jews did not just go abroad, but also left the villages of Galicia for the cities, as evidenced by sharp rises in the Jewish populations of Lwow and Cracow. This was flight upwards as well as out. Correspondingly, although it was the Poles who were overtly anti-Semitic in this period in Galicia, the "Polish-speaking" percentage of Galician Jewry grew substantially between 1900 and 1910. The Jewish population was "awakening," just as were the Poles themselves and the Ruthenes, and was beginning to seek entrée into the modern European world.[8] As a function of this awakening, in Galicia as in the Bukowina, there appeared now a Jewish national movement based on the increasingly broad enlightened sector of the population.

As we have seen elsewhere, early in the 1880s a Galician-origin rabbi, Joseph Samuel Bloch, launched a prolonged attack on the young assimilee-Jewish intellectuals of Vienna, and even against the Vienna Kultusgemeinde establishment, for their inadequate defense of Jewish causes and Jewish identity. Coincidentally, he took up the cudgels against anti-Semitism. At a famous libel trial in 1882, Bloch compelled a Prague professor named Rohling to retract slanders that he had been propagating against the Talmud. Though Bloch's congregation was in a Vienna suburb, in 1883 he won election to the Reichsrath from a Galician constituency, remaining there until 1895. His political ideas were hardly Zionist (or even "proto-Zionist"): he insisted that Austrian Jews should become ideal Austrians, rising above the squabbles of the nationalities and proving themselves not a separatist nation but the pillar of the state. In a sense he was the ultimate "Habsburg Jew"! As such he was as annoying to the Zionists of Herzl's time as he was to the Polonophile assimilationists. But he was rigorously Jewish. He founded and was first president of the Österreichisch-Israelitische Union, one of the primary Austrian organizations for combating anti-Semitism. His Österreichische Wochenschrift was among the first and most lasting Jewish nationalist newspapers of the late Habsburg era. And until his death in 1923 he played an inspirational role similar to but rather greater than that of Benno Straucher in the Bukowina.[9]

Meanwhile in Galicia itself increasing numbers of educated Jews turned away from the radical assimilationism that had been common in the generation of 1848. Hibbat Zion, the "pre-Zionist Zionism" of the 1880s in southern Russia, does not seem to have acquired many followers here, but middle-class favor of consciously Jewish-Austrian policies did. A decade and more before Herzl founded his international political movement at Vienna, young intellectuals were organizing politically at Lwow and Cracow: the historian Wilhelm Feldmann and the journalist Alfred Nossig were good examples. Once Herzl's movement did emerge, it found its most fertile recruiting-ground within the Habsburg Empire to be Galicia.[10]

Despite the economic backwardness of Galicia, moreover, here as in the Russian lands, Jews got involved early on in Socialism. In 1892 a first Jewish Labor group appeared at Lwow, advocating recognition of Ruthenian and Yiddish as well as Polish. At the first convention of the Galician Social Democratic Party in the same year, Jews were present in sufficient numbers to bring programmatic recognition for the idea that the Jews might be a nation, albeit of course not one that had a right to a separate labor movement. The separate Jewish Labor group then withered until 1897, when Austrian Social Democracy as a whole reorganized on a federative basis. The Galician "section" thereupon became officially Polish, and shortly began to insist dogmatically that its members be "international" in the Polish language. In 1905 many of the Jewish members again split out, establishing a separate Jewish Social-Democratic Party modelled on the Jewish Bund in Tsarist Russia. It was this Party's appeal for recognition by Austrian Social Democracy that provoked Otto Bauer to write the famous tract on the nationality question that we mentioned in chapter one above. Bauer at once broadened Renner's earlier theoretical Marxist tolerance of nationalism, yet denied the desirability of recognizing Jewish Socialism; and his Party responded by denying the JSDP its sanction. Within a few years, however, the Galician section of the SDPÖ decided that opposition to the Yiddish speakers was hopeless. In 1911 it set up a new Jewish section, which then by subtle mergers absorbed the independent one.[11]

The story of Jewish Socialism in Galicia is the more complex because Poale Zionism [Labor Zionism] caught on there at the turn of the century, stimulated no doubt by the presence in Vienna at the time of the Russian Poale Zion's founder, Ber Borochov. In 1904, coincident with the emergence of the JSDP, a Galician Poalist Party was set up, and by 1906, thanks to the repressions of Poalism in Russia and its weakness in Germany, this party's press was serving as the central organ of world Poalism. Yet even Poalism was different in the Galician environment from elsewhere: it was far less doctrinaire than Borochov's Russian strain, more romantic, more apt to be involved in Galician issues. After the debacle of middle-class Jewish "autonomism" in 1911, some of the Poalists became the strongest advocates in Galicia of the autonomist idea.[12]

The most important form of Jewish nationalist expression in Galicia was precisely "autonomism": the advocacy of Jewish political and cultural autonomy in the Diaspora. The idea behind it developed late in the 1890s in the nationality theses of the Austrian Socialist Karl Renner, and it was adapted to Jewish purposes by the Vilno historian, Simon Dubnow.[13] In Russia it found root in the arena of Socialism, particularly in the Jewish Bund, but in Galicia it inspired a middle-class following. As early as 1902, some of its enthusiasts joined with Benno Straucher in Cernauti to establish a Jüdische Volkspartei. In 1905–06, in the wake of the Russian revolution and pogroms, a decided popular enthusiasm for Jewish issues swept Galician Jewry and inspired the autonomists there to take further action. In 1906, together with the Austrian Zionists, they held a conference at Cracow and sought to develop a unified political program. They also successfully ran three deputies for the Reichsrath in that year: two public figures from Lwow, the editor Adolf Stand and the lawyer Heinrich Gabel, and a Prague classical archeologist, Arthur Mahler.

In Vienna these three Jewish "autonomists," together with Straucher, formed a "Jewish Club" in the Reichsrath, ostentatiously rejecting the Polish one. Unfortunately, their personalities and programmatic vagueness militated against effectively unified activity. Straucher, for example, saw Yiddish as just "jargon," whereas the Galician deputies tended to recognize it as a "language." In 1908 the Galician section of the Volkspartei seceded; and in the census-taking of 1910 its leaders organized a write-in campaign, directly confronting both the Austrian law denying Yiddish Umgangsprache status and the myth that the Galician Jews were Polish-speakers. This was too much for the Poles. In the election of 1911, with vigorous help from the Galician authorities, Polonophile Jewish assimilationists managed to deny Stand and Mahler re-election.[14] The blossoming of political autonomism had one lasting effect. As a result of it, Galician Zionism in general became much less doctrinaire than the German and Russian movements, and much more involved in local politics.[15]

It is sometimes held that a "typical" Jewish mass political indifference led to the disappearance of the Galician Jewish Volkspartei from the Reichsrath in 1911—that once the immediate stimulus of pogroms and revolution across the frontier was gone, most Jews lost interest in politics. At least two other factors made a major difference, however. One was the large-scale principled quietism of the Orthodox. This quietism had not always been prevalent. In the 1860s and 1870s under the impact of the Hungarian Orthodox center at Bratislava, the great Hasidic Rebbes of Zanz [Nowy Sacz] in western Galicia and of Belz in the east had endorsed political involvement by their followings. They had been fearful then of "enlightened" Jewish efforts to impose a unified statute on Galician Jewry (in other words, to have the state force the Orthodox into compromises). Belz had even organized a political party of sorts: with his backing Rabbi Simon Schreiber of Cracow, a son of the Bratislava *Hatam* Sofer, sat from 1879 until his death in 1883 in the Austrian Reichsrath (as a member, characteristically, of the Polish Club).[16] But thereafter, with Belz in the lead, the Hasidim had relapsed into absolute political non-participation. Their "non-policy," based on religious understandings that are foreign to the twentieth century, acted as a dead weight most discouraging to politically minded modern Jews.[17]

Fear also deeply affected the Jewish response to the pre-war crisis in Galicia, more acutely even than in Bohemia, where the Jews only feared being disliked. Always in the background here lay Jewry's dread of po-groms. Hated by both the dominant Christian nations, the Jews of Galicia were less involved in Christian politics than elsewhere. Yet they could never afford to expose themselves fully in a Jewish cause, as did the Bu-kowina Jews. It was just too dangerous to risk the Christian anger of the Poles. Fear of this sort, not "typical" passivity, accounts for the fact that, though personally many many Galician Jews were enthusiastic for nation-alist causes, when it came to voting in 1911, they were very shy, and opted for the Poles.

Now to approach our point: was Galician Jewry at a complete dead end in the prewar years? Was Jewish society here as "sick" as Europeans sometimes then thought the Habsburg Empire? The evidence just mar-shaled makes an affirmative answer to such questions difficult. The anti-Semitism of the environment, the Jewish emigration, the flight from the *shtetl*, and the deadlock within Orthodoxy certainly suggest that the status quo was traumatic for most Jews. But was not the great problem—the modernization of a vast multitude of eastern Jews—being accomplished? So long as Greater Austria existed, Jews could after all get out of Galicia! They could go abroad, they could go to the cities! There was no frontier! Hundreds of thousands of one-time Galician Jews had taken advantage of this freedom in the century and a half of association with Austria. And even in Galicia itself, political and cultural opportunities that had been unheard of in 1772 were now available for Jews. And despite the atmo-sphere of fear, the blossoming of Zionism showed that there was Jewish hope in the future. In all these senses one seems bound to recognize that Galician Jewry, perhaps unlike the Austrian state, was very much alive before the war.

III

One may speak much more properly in Hungary than in Galicia about a prewar crownland "crisis" comparable to the international crisis focusing on Austria, and this not just because the vast unity of St. Stephen's King-dom made for a much more complex conjunction of political circumstances there. A crisis emerged because the narrowly centralized political system set up in 1867 had become obsolete.

That system derived from two conditions that had prevailed in the 1860s, but which had radically changed by 1900. The first was the relative indifference of the vast mass of the peasantry, whether Magyar-speaking (as in the center of the country), or nationality-affiliated (as in the entire long mountainous periphery), to politics. The constitution and laws established in 1867 had enthroned the Magyar-speaking *nemesség* both in the elected parliament at Budapest and in the local administrative organs in the counties. At and from the start the nationality intelligentsias had protested against this narrowness. But in 1870, 68.7% of the population over age six had been illiterate. In Transylvania the predominantly Rumanian population, and in Croatia the predominantly South Slav populations had had illiteracy rates of 83%.[18] The lower classes had generally been too "backward" in those days to mount an effective challenge to the system, and the nobles had been numerous enough to impose their will.

By 1900, in Hungary as in Galicia, demographic and educational factors had altered this passivity fundamentally. Just before the war the all-Hungarian average illiteracy rate was down to 33.3%. Even in Transylvania illiteracy stood now at only 49.5%. In Croatia it was down to only 47.4%. Among the Slovaks illiteracy now stood at 30.3%, among the Serbs, 40.2%. Meanwhile in the center of the country the metropolis of Budapest had developed with all its potential for luring the Magyar-speaking peasant off the farm. Budapest's growth rate was 36% in the decade of the 1880s, 46% in the decade of the 1890s—a rate unsurpassed among the other great cities of Europe. Though in 1910 the agrarian percentage of the Rumanian and Slavic population still averaged 80.2%, among the Magyars it was down to 55%. In 1910 the "industrial sector" of the Magyar population was up to 30.6%. Under such conditions, clearly enough, the parts of society excluded from the system were bound to become active. By the turn of the century ever more violent instruments of repression were being introduced to make sure that the electoral returns remained the same.[19]

The second condition which had shaped the system of 1867 was the economic self-sufficiency of the nobility. In those days, despite the end of serfdom, the nobles still owned the land and were always able to eat. Symptomatically, Austrian "absolutism" had not been able to starve the noble Magyars into submission, as it had the rebel masses in the cities. To counter this autonomy of the nobility, the political parties of the post-1867 period focused their attention on abstract constitutional questions. They formed around defense of and opposition to the constitutional link with Austria, because it was felt that the nobility would only come off its estates and submit to the government at Budapest if it were lured there with a crude, vague promise of national independence. One may doubt the actual validity of this expectation, but that was what people thought at the time; and that was why Kálmán Tisza, the "Magyar Bismarck," ruled the country for twenty years as if the relationship with Austria were still somehow open.

By 1900 the nobility's supposed ability to resist Budapest was manifestly no longer extant. It was well known that the nemesség was now sinking into poverty because of the incursion of capitalism, because of the ever greater spread of a money economy. Particularly the once prosperous "middle nobility" was losing its grip on the former bedrock of the economy, land. Far from coyly remaining distant from the urban world, the nobility was now ardently pressing for an ever greater and more lucrative monopoly of public office. The change was the more serious because the drive for office brought the nobility on the practical level into direct confrontation with the new urban middle classes which had developed under the Liberal banners of the Tisza era. Under Tisza, these classes had been the ally of the system, creating as it were enough new production to pay for themselves. But they aspired to meritocracy, fundamentally, and certainly not to the system of office-holding by birth which the old nemesség was demanding. All told, a new sort of politics was badly needed within the narrow Magyar-dominated *pays légitime*. The old polarization of issues (between national independence and the link with Vienna) simply plastered over with enthusiasm a menacing social cleavage within the ruling society.

In 1903 a confrontation between the King-Kaiser and Magyar nationalism over military questions brought the system to ground. First a new coalition began to take form that grouped the great majority of Magyar nationalist politicians for the first time in the "independence" camp. With wild oratory, these leaders made it sound as if a break with "Viennese tyranny" would resolve all of Hungary's problems. The nationalist hysteria was soon so great in Budapest that the coalition leaders could speak of introducing electoral reform, forgetting in their passion that an actual reform would destroy Magyar supremacy. In such fashion they lured even some of the nationality parties into their camp. Late in 1904 the elder Tisza's political machine (now run by his son, István Tisza) collapsed, and early in 1905 the oppositional "coalition" won an election. In June 1905 Franz Joseph, alarmed, threatened to introduce universal suffrage if the Magyars challenged the basic features of the Ausgleich. For some months in the fall and winter of 1905 (a period that happened to coincide with the revolution in Russia) Hungary was under martial law, and it seemed as if a fundamental change, whether universal suffrage and nationality dominance or virtual independence from Vienna, might be in the offing. Then in April 1906 the coalition's Magyar leaders bought their way out. Secretly they promised the King-Kaiser that they would not press their demands against him if he would place them in power. This he proceeded to do. For three years then empty bombast ruled in Budapest. The new government enlarged the number of offices that could be distributed to the nobility. Its Catholic members made some show of criticizing the impiety of "foreigners" (presumably Jews). But all the major political questions were postponed. Finally in 1910 the coalition collapsed, and young Tisza gained the opportunity to rebuild his party and to rule.

The end of the story is too complex for detailing here. Essentially, Tisza took over with an iron hand, but in his turn postponed the issues:

he produced neither an electoral reform which might have satisfied the nationalities and the Magyar lower classes nor a decision for or against meritocracy which might have appeased the middle classes or the "gentry." The war then postponed things forever. Important here is simply to note that the crisis in Hungary was deeply rooted and on-going after 1900, and far more than the crisis in Galicia invited a response by the Jews.

One may best broach what the response was by noting some evidence about the distribution of Orthodox and "Neologs" within Hungarian Jewry. On the eve of the war there was still no numerical count. The reason was clear in a Neolog report on the subject in 1911: of the 955,452 Jews then in Hungary, the Neologs were quite ready to grant that 400,000 (almost half) were Orthodox; they quibbled only about an additional 300,000 that the Orthodox claimed! Obviously they withdrew from precise counting lest the scope of the Orthodox majority become public knowledge. Even then, however, one had little doubt that a good portion of the 203,687 Jews in Budapest were reformed, at least in some degree. On the other hand, one suspected that the 87,360 Jews living north of the Danube, in latter-day Slovakia, and even more the 197,384 living in the northeast counties, might be Orthodox. The proof of these distributional suspicions came right after the war when the Neologs (now fearless) finally made a regular count. Of the 444,567 Jews remaining in "Trianon" Hungary, 292,155 (65.5%), a massive majority, were Neologs, 130,373 (29.2%) were Orthodox, and 22,373 (5.3%) were "status quo." Clearly the Neologs had had their major strength in the urban center of the country even before the war, whereas the Orthodox had been strong in the peripheral, nationality areas that were lost in 1918.[20]

These patterns make the more significant the first and foremost change which overtook all Hungarian Jewry in the Ausgleich years: its Magyarization. In 1880, 43% of the Jewish population still listed a non-Magyar "mother tongue." In most cases (all told, 35%) the preferred language was German, but 8% spoke Slavic or Rumanian. In 1910, 75.6% listed themselves as Magyar speakers, the Germans were 21.8%, and the speakers of the remaining nationality tongues were down to under 3% all together.[21] The abandonment of German took place above all in Budapest, where officially the use of that tongue almost disappeared. But the run on Slavic and Rumanian affected the Orthodox peripheral Jews, although in some remote counties of Transylvania and in the latter-day Carpatho-Ukraine Magyar suffered some reversals. These figures tell clearly that it was not only the Neologs of Budapest who Magyarized themselves. The Orthodox of the peripheral regions also, despite their antipathy for Neolog ways, opted decisively against the developing nationalities. Only Croatian showed a slight gain among Jews of Hungary in those decades.[22]

The official community of the Neologs at Budapest played, moreover, a peculiarly important role in fanning Magyarization even among middle-class Hungarian non-Jews; but to observe this one must look again at some demographic data. After the Austro-Hungarian Compromise, Budapest Jewry grew extremely rapidly, just as the capital city itself did. More than doubling from 44,890 to 103,317 persons in the 21 years between 1869 and 1890, it doubled again to 203,687 between 1890 and 1910. This growth brought the Jewish percentage of the Budapest population from 16.1% in 1869 to 23.1% in 1910.[23] It also brought the rate of influx up to that of Vienna in the 1860s. For present purposes, this is what is significant, for there were other resemblances to the Vienna 1860s too.

In and after mid-century, for example, the polarization between Jewish traditionalism and Jewish reform in Hungary led to a decided increase in the prominence and the institutional power of the Pest Neolog congregation. In the wake of the Hungarian Jewish Congress of 1868, the Hungarian state had felt bound to legally recognize three all-Hungarian Jewish groups—Orthodox, Neolog, and "Status-quo-ante"—as nation-wide organizations. Because the Pest Neolog congregation was larger and more wealthy than any other Neolog one, this recognition soon enabled it to speak for all the Neologs in Hungary. Further, it soon turned out that the Neologs had much better contacts in the government than the Orthodox did. They had within their ranks the very successful leaders of Hungarian capitalism. And because the Hungarian state legally acknowledged the disunity of the Jews, the Pest Neologs could make their own decisions without regard to the Orthodox. Their position was helped also because the Liberal state kept anti-Semitism at bay: there was no hostile outside pressure to inhibit the Neologs from outdoing the Orthodox. And the tides of the times worked for them. The more modern education spread among the nation's Jews, and the more the "little Jews" flocked to dynamic, capitalist, metropolitan Budapest, the more the Neolog community's enrollment grew. By 1900 they had as much prestige and more clout by far than Jewish Vienna had had in the 1860s.

In many ways, the Budapest Neolog Jewish leaders exercised their influence just as had the Vienna Kultusgemeinde. They were hesitant in direct political involvements, albeit nowhere near so immobile as Vienna had been in 1860. But they were active in creating social models. In the mid-1890s, for example, the Budapest Neologs acquired the same sort of social glitter that Vienna had earlier possessed: 23 out of the 29 Jewish new nobles created between 1887 and 1896 belonged to this congregation. The one-time congregational leader, Zsigmond Schossberger, became a baron in 1890. Meanwhile Ignac Hirschler, Károly Svab and Zsigmond Brody, all leaders of the Neolog community, won seats in the House of Lords. Soon after 1900 Zsigmond Kornfeld and Sándor Hatvany-Deutsch entered the Lords and were made barons.[24]

Given these circumstances, it seems significant that on the Budapest economic scene in 1900 there was excitement just like Vienna's in the 1860s. Here late in the 1890s, and again about 1905, there were movements forward that could qualify as great economic spurts. The latter one, the boom before the war, brought with it a mighty result that could hardly have been achieved without coordination at the center: the reversal of the historic pattern of Hungary's colonial subjection to foreign capital, and the assertion of Hungarian capital itself as an imperialist force.[25] One should be cautious before associating such economic achievements with the condition of the Jewish community at Pest. This was a rather different boom from that of Vienna's *Gründerzeit*. It was based far more on actual production increases in the factories of the capital city and of the provinces than on Stock Exchange speculation. The catastrophe at the end was not the pricking of a financial bubble, but the war and the bursting of a great political bubble represented by the Magyarizer State.

Nonetheless, the parallels are impressive. As in Vienna in the 1860s, now in Budapest there was a heavy overlap between the inner (and, one may note, increasingly narrow) leadership of the economy and the leadership of the Jewish community organization.[26] Then as now, the said leadership was addictively showing off: with its ennoblements and baronizations it was theatrically setting a behavioral model for people lower down, inviting imitation. Then as now there was an influx into the lower regions of the Jewish community. The influx to turn-of-the-century Neolog Budapest was no longer just a stream of indigent and ambitious unwedded males flowing from provincial traditionalism into the cosmopolitan big city, although there was a lot of that; now there was also a stream of wedded middle class females, eager to pass from the Orthodox world into the Neolog community because of social ambition. And the vigorous patriotic political activity of the Pest Neolog congregation provided a sterling vehicle for the transmission of mood from top to bottom and back.

One may perceive similar relationships between political and cultural phenomena and the condition of the Budapest Neolog congregation in 1900. Admittedly this whole question is blurred by the on-going Ringstrasse craze, which deeply affected the middle classes of both Habsburg capitals and made them seem deceptively similar.[27] But in Jewish Budapest patriotic enthusiasm reigned after 1900. Although the official leaders did not of course join the nationalist coalition (how could they? it was directed against the king, against authority), a great many individual members of the Pest Congregation did so. No doubt one could hear expressions of cultural despair in Budapest then, which reminded one of the Jewish self-hatred of Otto Weininger in Vienna. But it was being voiced not by Budapest Jews so much as by déclassé Magyars—Endre Ady, for example. And in sum the patriotic atmosphere sustained by the Neolog Jewish congregational leadership seems to have played a vital role in making credible the euphoric Magyar nationalism of the period. At Budapest even the younger-generation Jewish intellectuals, even the socialists among them, were as optimistic at the turn of the century as their enthusiastically philistine fathers. Oszkar Jászi, for example, was wholly confident in his book of 1912 that, if only the government would be fair, the Hungarian nationalities would flock to a Great-Magyar standard! And that younger generation centered on an individual close both to the Neolog religious community and to the country's economic citadel, Lajos Hatvany.[28]

In the last years before the war the Budapest Neolog Jews received a hint of the unpalatable realities of their behavior. When the coalition fell in 1910, they took up the advocacy of Jewish "autonomy." They had no use whatsoever, of course, for a Jewish "national" autonomy, but about 1908 they had perceived in a striving for formal "religious" autonomy a means for crushing the independence of Orthodoxy. The congregation turned out its full array of newly created barons and nobles to petition the government on this "religious" issue. The patriotism of Jewish Hungary was then such that there were practically no native Zionists to suggest that it might be better to have the Jews recognized not as an autonomous religious group but as a nationality like the rest. Though the Orthodox refused cooperation in the autonomy struggle, they did not oppose it, perhaps because their leader, Moses Freudiger, had like several Neolog eminences been ennobled in 1908. It was anticipated that autonomy might be granted as a reward for good behavior during the coalition years. Yet it failed, because the Tisza forces felt there might be complications if further concessions were made to the Jews.[29] This was a tiny indicator that the Christian Magyar "establishment" would not give unlimited support to the Neolog Jews.

The failure of the "autonomy" campaign did not interrupt Neolog support of the government, which support was rewarded in these years by a veritable flood of new Jewish ennoblements and other glitter. And meanwhile a "Jewish awareness" trend of sorts emerged at Budapest, not outside but inside the assimilationist framework. And this too supported the illusions. In the middle 1890s a then-young lawyer, Vilmos Vázsonyi, began to respond to precisely the same public demand as did Dr. Bloch in Vienna, Benno Straucher in the Bukowina, and the young "autonomists" in Galicia. Vázsonyi battled for the "little man" who was overlooked by the elegant elders of the official Jewish comunities. He began his career in 1894–95 by launching a campaign for the "reception" of the Jewish religion by the Hungarian state. The emancipation of 1867 had left the Catholic Church as the only such officially recognized cult. The Protestant sects were now trying to gain equality. Vázsonyi's agitation prompted the Neolog Jews to demand the same; and when the Parliament after a tremendous battle finally granted the prize, Vázsonyi gained much credit. Then he turned to the Budapest middle classes. He founded a "Democratic Party" in the inner city, was exceedingly active all his later life in urban politics, became in some degree Budapest's Karl Lueger, yet made no secret whatsoever of his own and his constituency's Jewishness.[30]

Vázsonyi, however, worked exclusively within the world of Magyar illusions. Characteristically, his second great battle was on the side of the patriotic Magyar coalition in 1904–06. Wholly ignoring the desirability to

the "little man" of a universal suffrage, and the presence within the
coalition of anti-Semite Catholic elements, this paladin of Jewish self-
awareness aroused Magyar passions as vigorously as any other Hungarian
politician in those rebellious years. He gained small reward, not even a
ministry, when the coalition gained power in 1906. He fought bravely on
regardless, now more and more against the evils of Socialism and against
the "cosmopolitan," sometimes anti-Capitalist young intellectuals of the
Budapest intelligentsia, but also against Tisza's political "corruption," and
most decidedly of all against Zionism. A warmer and more sympathetic
personality than either Dr. Bloch or Benno Straucher, his political choices
absolutely lacked the rapport with all-Empire and international Jewish interests which theirs did. As an historical figure he is incomprehensible save
in the bubble of Magyar national mythology.

This is not to say that there was no raised Jewish consciousness in the
country outside the Magyarization movement as the great political crisis
broke. In the 1880s in western Hungary, especially at Bratislava and various
Slovakian towns, "Hoveve Zion" apparently found some following. In 1897
seven Hungarians, including the Transylvanian lawyer József Ronai and
the Bratislava journalist Samuel Bettelheim, attended Herzl's First Zionist
Congress at Basel, and both officiated at the establishment of a Hungarian
Zionist League at Bratislava in 1902. A Jewish national movement thus did
emerge in Hungary, as in the Bukowina and Galicia. But suggestively, both
the leaders just mentioned shifted from the Magyar into the German tongue
when they entered Jewish nationalist politics. Further, when in 1908 Bettelheim founded an all-Hungarian Zionist journal at Budapest, he gave it
the German-language title, *Ungarländische jüdische Zeitung*! A Magyar Zionist paper had sprung up earlier, but the Zionists seemed to recognize
that their constituency stopped where Magyarization began. The limited
character of Hungarian Zionism before the war is evident also from the
fact that of all its branches, only the German-language Mizrachi movement
[Religious Zionism] really caught on. The Mizrachis even attracted the first
congress of the world Mizrachi movement to Bratislava in 1904; but no
effectively secular, Magyar-speaking Zionist movement throve in Hungary
before 1914.[31]

One may conclude this survey of Hungarian Jewry's response to the
pre-war crisis with the Socialist Jews and the new-generation Jewish intellectuals. Both groups were more conspicuous in politics than their opposite numbers in Galicia. In prewar Budapest, as we will see at a later
point, there were more Jewish industrial workers than in Vienna, a reflection perhaps of the more lower-stratum character of this community.
The Jewish Socialists include accordingly fewer middle-class refugees, more
lower-managerial types. They provided the Hungarian SDP with many
leaders, also with an internationally known hero (Leó Frankel, prominent
in the Paris Commune of 1871) and a pioneer in the formulation of a peasant
socialism of which much was heard in interwar Eastern Europe (Vilmos

Mezöfi).[32] The young radical intellectuals, on the other hand, were almost exclusively upper middle class, ranging from the Budapest-born sociologist Ervin Szabó to the above-mentioned province-born Jászi and plutocrat-born Lajos Hatvany. They are fascinating both for the brilliance of their own ideas and for the equally middle-class galaxy of latter-day internationally known "geniuses" amongst whom they grew up.[33] It is notable that the SDP and the young radicals alike were the only political groups in Hungary to escape the thrall of the national coalitionists in 1905–06. Yet for our purposes the most important point about both is that neither appealed to Jews as such. The SDPH showed none of the interest Galician Socialism did in the specifically Jewish masses. It was doctrinaire and ploddingly "internationalist" (which is one reason it fell in so easily with the Bolsheviks in 1919). Among the young Jewish intellectuals, most were specifically renegade; some, notably Jászi, tended to be anti-Jewish Jews;[34] and there were no Zionists as in Prague and Lwow.

Was Hungarian Jewry at a dead end in these years, comparable to the dead end some observers perceived for the Habsburg State? The answer seems far easier than it was for Galician Jewry. Overwhelmingly in the prewar years Hungarian Jewry, Neolog, Orthodox, and secularized alike, sublimated their Jewish problems and ambitions into the haze of Magyar nationalist politics. They committed themselves in this sense to the ideological illusions of the Christian world just as in the preceding chapter we saw the Trieste Jews commit themselves. But from a material point of view the commitment was not a bad bargain: very large numbers of Jews had very successfully modernized by collaborating with the Magyar nobility. And one can hardly say there was no life in Hungarian Jewry in 1914. There were perils on the horizon; and Hungarian Jewry was conspicuously not Zionist. But as a Jewish community of the Galut it was very much alive.

I V

Vienna, in contrast to Galicia and especially to Hungary, witnessed no local prewar political crisis apart from the general Austrian crisis. Given the violence of the nationalistic Viennese riots during the Badeni interlude, given the parliament's evident inability to function, and given the continued development of the city into a metropolis of 2,057,000 people, perhaps no political crisis was needed to make the era critical. The fact remains that the anti-Semite Christian Socialist, Karl Lueger, was without the slightest challenge mayor of the city from 1897 until his death in 1910; that the Marxist Vienna Social-Democrats, despite their abhorrence of Lueger's ideology, embraced his social reforms; and that even the universal suffrage of 1907, which suddenly gave the SDP 40% of the Vienna vote, did not interrupt the smooth accession of further Christian Socialists to the mayoralty when Lueger died: first Josef Neumayr, then Richard Weiskirchen. Vienna grew and changed enormously during the Lueger epoch, but the constant political agitation which had marked the deposition of Liberalism there in the 1880s and 1890s was a thing of the past.

For the Vienna Jews this absence of local crisis was veiled, indeed made irrelevant, by one awful reality: anti-Semitism had been welling up in their city since 1873, and since 1896 it had ruled. Whereas in 1849 the Jews had "won" and the Austrians had "lost," now the reverse held true. Vienna Jewry was in a sense embattled during the whole prewar period; and in historical perspective it is easy to say that it came up with immediate and impressive responses. First, the growth rate fell. Whereas until 1880 Vienna Jewry had grown faster than any other Jewry in the monarchy and had outstripped that of Budapest, by 1910, despite an increase of 57,000 in twenty years to 175,318, it was smaller by 25,000 than Budapest Jewry. If the Galician village Jews still flocked to Vienna, their opposite numbers in Hungary now chose a societal escape "upwards" nearer home.

Second, the Vienna Kultusgemeinde as an institution underwent a deflation. In the 1870s, as we have seen elsewhere, it had possessed immense vigor. As the prestigious acknowledged central organization of all Habsburg Jewry, it had been a major channel for the easy and spontaneous transmission of enthusiasms from top to bottom of Jewish society, and even of Christian middle class society, such as the Budapest Neolog Community had now become. Since then, however, the Viennese Jewish organization had faded. Its leaders, the knightly gallants on the Ringstrasse, had, for example, simply let slip their claims to be the national leadership. Jewish religious unity remained intact in the capital city, but the price was wholesale abandonment of control. By 1900 Prague, not Vienna, spoke for Jewish Bohemia; Brno for Jewish Moravia; Trieste for Jewish Trieste, and no Jewish communal organization at all spoke for Jewish Galicia. In Vienna, meanwhile, despite the official unity and the great wealth of the downtown synagogues, individual Jews practiced their religion more or less according to their choice—there was no unity in rite. And in the 1880s anti-Semitism had shattered the community's glittering crown. By 1900 most of the rich Viennese Jews were in hiding from publicity, refusing (as Rothschild had earlier) to hold community office. Many of the older and more prestigious families had converted; some were going so far as to change their names to obliterate the Jewish memory. The community was no longer in the slightest degree channeling enthusiasms from up above to down below and back, as in the *Gründer* years. On, the contrary it was doing everything in its power to negate anti-Semite charges of multi-level Jewish economic and social collaboration with other Jews.[35]

A contrast in the Vienna business world is suggestive of the new conditions. In 1870, virtually the entire leadership of the Stock Exchange had been visibly Jewish, and virtually all the great banks had been visibly led by Jews. Now the degree of Jewish participation in the business world was hidden by a vast array of straw men and by concerted efforts to avoid every appearance of Jewish control. At least one Jew was still in a position of formidable influence in virtually every bank; but in each one the power structure was different—no statistical generalization was possible.[36]

The social effect of the stagnation in the Vienna Jewish community is well known. Vienna Jewry resembled a peacock's tail in its rich variety, its partial but deep integration into the Christian world, and its ambivalence towards Jewishness. Rothschild was still there, very much a religious Jew, but living now with his accumulation of old European art works in a French palace on the Heugasse, culturally rather foreign to Jewish Vienna. Nearer to the Ringstrasse lived comparably rich Karl Wittgenstein in "second society" splendor, patronizing the modern art of the Secession, equally Jewish in point of blood and much more Viennese, but two generations divorced from the Jewish religion. In the Berggasse of the Ninth *Bezirk* lived Freud, a member of the Jewish religious community but deeply alienated from the whole of the city's Christian-Jewish academic middle class, resentfully exploring the psychological unknown. No less native to the "Jewish" Ninth Bezirk was Dr. Victor Adler, the head of the SDPÖ, a childhood convert out of Judaism whose myriad followers terrified the Jewish and Christian middle classes alike with their annual parades on the Ring and the Praterstrasse on the first of May. In the Leopoldstadt and the Brigittenau lived the recently immigrant Galician substratum of Viennese Jewry in great poverty, near the young Hitler, with no more promise of escape into riches than he had. At the Opera, wielding middle-class Vienna's favorite fetish, stood Mahler, a convert with passionate followers and foes alike throughout the city, regardless of religion. In the anti-Semite Josefstadt and Neubau were now settling the rising young Jewish professionals, the Stefan Zweigs, moving away from the perhaps overly Jewish Second and Ninth Bezirken in their eagerness to play with new ideas that were frowned on in Kultusgemeinde quarters, even with Zionism. Downtown at this old Christian city's business heart sat the official Jewish Community Vorstand, next to Mannheimer's temple. Far off in Floridsdorf beyond the Danube fulminated Dr. Bloch.

The contradictions within Vienna Jewry appear especially in the political activity of its embattled middle-class members after the turn of the century. Around 1900, several of them still sat in the City Council and the Reichsrath alike representing the old Liberal Party. Emil Furth from a prominent Bohemian Jewish family attempted to set up a new "democratic party" at Vienna for people who didn't care for the social program of Liberalism or for its Big Business connection.[37] Other middle-class people fell in with Straucher's "Jewish Club" in the Reichsrath of 1907, which had a "young Liberal" character. But early on, and very characteristically, these middle-class politicians caused the Vienna Jewish voters to run into bewildering dilemmas. Some of the staunchest "Liberals" in the political world were either apostates or Kultusgemeinde members who paid no attention to Jewish national issues—who rejected even the fight against anti-Semitism. In the great 1907 election this problem came up in the Leopoldstadt, where Julius Ofner, a wholly indifferent Jew renowned for his peerlessly Liberal credentials, opposed Jewish nationalist candidates; and in nearby Moravia, where the candidates for a "safe" Jewish seat were the peerlessly Liberal recent apostate, Josef Redlich, and a Christian Socialist.[38] What was a self-respecting middle-class Jew to do about such questionable Jews? The difficulty of deciding was the greater because everyone knew that the peers of these "nice" quasi-Jewish Liberals, the convert Jewish bureaucratic power-brokers Emil Steinbach and Rudolf Sieghart, were the forces who, by dealing discreetly with the Christian Socialists, kept the regime from collapse? Should one reward the renegade, or lose to the enemy?[39]

In socialism the dilemmas were just as complex and burdensome because here one had to deal with Marx's own ambivalence about Jews, and with Germany's ambivalence. In Vienna as throughout eastern Europe, Marxism and the Social Democratic Party were logical harbors for Jews who felt the bitterness of the oppressed; yet to accept Marx or to enter the Party was to predicate as one's ultimate foe a Capitalism which in this part of the world was dominantly Jewish. Marx himself had found no way out of this dilemma save not to talk about it. Victor Adler did little better; and, as we have seen, Otto Bauer, who most directly wrestled with the problem, came out with a strangled and inconsistent response.[40]

Vienna was the scene of political Zionism's birth. This must certainly be considered Vienna Jewry's third response (alongside the slowed growth rate and the deflation of the Kultusgemeinde) to the crisis of the Habsburg Empire around 1900. Theodor Herzl was born in Budapest (and was all his life a Magyar-speaker), but he moved to Vienna in 1878 before completing school, attended the university there, pursued a typically Viennese journalistic career there prior to his "discovery" of his Zionist idea in 1895 (the year Karl Lueger first stormed the Rathaus), and thence he organized the World Zionist Movement in 1896. Not only this: during the first eight years of World Zionism its international and Vienna leaderships were virtually identical, and its headquarters was Vienna.[41]

Yet here we encounter a problem. Beyond question modern political Zionism started in Vienna, and was founded by a notably Viennese Jew; but may one call it the product of Viennese Jewry? and may it rightly be labelled the general Viennese Jewish response to the embattlement of the Lueger era? No! The sad truth is that almost from the start official Vienna Jewry rejected Herzl's Zionism. Despite the founder's efforts at ingratiation, Rabbi Güdemann and the Ringstrasse leaders of the Kultusgemeinde were especially callous in their opposition to the new movement. Not until the eve of the war did they finally accommodate the nationalist idea. Herzl's own employer, that greatest of assimilee Jewish institutions in Vienna, the *Neue Freie Presse*, refused to mention Zionism in its columns, contributing thus in no small measure to the sense of rejection and exclusion that in 1904 brought on Herzl's death. Even Dr. Bloch was mightily disapproving in Herzl's lifetime. Though the number of Shekel payers was higher here than elsewhere in Austria outside Galicia, objectively it was conspicuously low. In sum, for a "native" resistance movement, Zionism was as remarkably unpopular in Vienna as elsewhere in the country of its birth![42]

A similar puzzle emerges from the history of Jewish autonomism in the capital, as one may tell from the career of Nathan Birnbaum, one of the heroes of that movement. As a young Galician-born journalist in the 1880s, Birnbaum found a ready market for the "Hoveve Zion" idea in the capital; he was able to raise funds for small-scale colonization in Palestine; he won subscribers for little journals devoted to Jewish subjects. In 1883 he was a founder of the Jewish nationalist fraternity, the Kadimah, at the Vienna University. By 1893 he had set up an Austrian *Zion Verband* to back colonization, was editing a journal entitled *"Selbstemanzipation,"* had coined the word "Zionism," and was talking (before Herzl did) of holding an international "Zionist" congress. In none of this was this pre-Herzlian Zionist vastly successful, but in all of it he clearly found the generally Jewish world of Vienna supportive. And it was from Vienna that he propagated his ideas with considerable success in Galicia.[43]

Yet despite this head start, late in the 1890s when Birnbaum took exception to the diplomatic priorities of Herzl's political Zionism and to its "personality cult," he found he had no deeper public backing than Herzl himself in Vienna. After Herzl's death in 1904, Birnbaum became one of the most articulate spokesmen for Jewish autonomism, lecturing about it far and wide; and the Viennese Jewish public responded ever less. In 1905 his colleague and fellow-autonomist, Leon Kellner, received an appointment at the Cernauti University and left Vienna. In 1907 Birnbaum followed, evidently convinced that only in the Jewish east of the empire, not in the capital, could his ideas find a suitable home.[44] When he returned to Vienna during the war, he was functioning as a philosopher-leader of the international Agudas Yisroel [Anti-Zionist Conservative Political Jewry]. No longer did he seek to depend on the Vienna Jews for his backing. No doubt this record had something to do with the nature of Birnbaum's ideas. In effect, for contemporary Austrian Jews, Yiddishist autonomism was as much a negation of the legal emancipation they enjoyed as was Herzl's movement. Still, Birnbaum's career does not bespeak any more ongoing enthusiasm in Jewish Vienna for Jewish causes than Herzl's does.

A recent sociological study of Vienna Jewry suggests the reality behind this seeming lack of Jewish enthusiasm.[45] Through intensive study of Jewish marriage, educational, residential, and organizational patterns in Franz Joseph's time, the author convincingly dispelled the idea that Vienna Jewry consisted on the one hand of unchanging, fear-filled religious Jews and on the other, of radically modernized, depressingly anti-Jewish intellectuals. The unchanging Orthodox Jews and the anti-Jewish intellectuals alike, she found, were peripheral to the city's Jewry, which was characterized by a new Jewish professional and cultural idiom. Observed en bloc, with its global characteristics emphasized, its individualism obscured, Vienna Jewry seemed a normally self-aware modern urban Jewry. No ancient kehillas, but a web of modern participatory social and charitable organizations held it together. No ghetto, but a variety of modern mixed neighborhoods formed its environment. It earned its living in a steadily changing spectrum of professions. Behind the facade of self-hatred and indifference lay the healthy, energetic variety of a specifically Jewish society of a new type.

V

This leads us to the answers to our question about whether Habsburg Jewry was so much at a dead end after 1900 as some observers felt the Habsburg Empire was. The answer is no! Habsburg Jewry responded to the crisis of the state with agony. Many Jews here underwent a traumatic stretch between irreconcilable extremes of political advocacy. This happened especially in places such as Trieste, where Jewry had little religious guidance. Elsewhere Jews were bewildered over the chaos of specifically Jewish political choices. This happened especially in the east, where the multitude of eastern Jewry was nearby—thus in the Bukowina and Galicia. Some Habsburg Jews beyond question felt a deep fear resulting from the Jews' in-betweenness in the east-German cultural world, where the challenge of rapidly self-educating linguistic minorities was never far away—thus especially in Bohemia and Galicia. But even in Galicia, where the economic condition of Jewry was perhaps worse than anywhere else, Jews could and were escaping from the worst of the past, they could and were changing, which means not that they were all single-mindedly destroying their old identity but that they were adapting it to the changing demands of the modern world.

In important parts of the Empire, moreover, most notably now at Budapest but also still in Vienna, Jews as a group were playing a massively important socio-political role in the middle class, determining the path of the whole Empire's society. And finally, especially in Vienna, Jews were living as modern people in the modern world. Some no doubt were still fleeing outward, as Birnbaum fled, or upward, as Herzl did. Others were falling into deep depression and self-hatred, as did Otto Weininger. But perhaps most indulged in cheerful sublimation into culture, a *Fortwursteln* such as was habitual among the Viennese. And the sheer diversity of all these responses showed that the community was alive, filled with potential for further modernization, in striking contrast to the Habsburg State.

TWELVE

The Collapse

Habsburg Jewry, Class by Class

I

In 1914 Austria started the war. In 1918 the war brought on Austria's end. On 28 July 1914 the Habsburg Government alleged that Serbia had inadequately atoned for the assassination of Archduke Franz Ferdinand, and opened hostilities. Within the week a well-known concatenation of events had converted this local conflict into a general European war. No quick military breakthroughs resolved the struggle. By early 1915 both the Central Powers and the Allies were negotiating with neutral powers for aid—and both were using Habsburg territories as bargaining chips, tolling the Empire's knell. In November 1916 Franz Joseph died, creating a long-awaited opportunity for revising his state's constitutional make-up. In conditions of war, his successor felt unable to use the opening to useful ends. Only in the face of an enemy military breakthrough into the Balkans on 16 October 1918 did Kaiser Karl finally promise a general re-making of the state along nationality lines. This was too late. The national middle classes were defecting, and in the great cities the populations were rising. On 28 October an independent regime emerged in Prague. On 29 October the core of a South Slavic regime appeared at Zagreb. On 30 October the German deputies at the Vienna Reichsrath responded to the outbreak of revolution with a declaration of union with the "German Republic." On 31 October, Hungary grasped for independence. On 3 November the Austro-Hungarian Military Command signed an armistice on the southern front. On 11 November, the day of the German armistice with the Allies on the western front, Kaiser Karl abdicated and Austria-Hungary ceased to exist.

What was the Habsburg Jewish response to this catastrophe? This is the ultimate question in the long history of Habsburg Jewry. One may hardly obtain clear answers if one considers Jewish behavior at the end of the war region by region, as if the new post-1918 states of eastern Europe were already extant. Habsburg Jewry still existed, after all, consciously, until destroyed. For such reason we will study the question of its response to the Habsburg catastrophe from an all-Empire point of view, class by class.[1]

II

Let us turn first to that remnant of the old national Jewish world, which held together under the admittedly vague label "Orthodoxy." This was not a class by the Marxist economic definition; but it comprised the masses of Jewry still in 1914 to such an extent, and was so universally referred to by contemporaries, that it cannot be ignored.

Where was Habsburg Jewish Orthodoxy strong? First, in Vienna, the capital. Over the decades, as we have seen, massive immigration originally from northern Hungary, more recently from Galicia, had lent sustenance here to a number of conservative prayer houses. Further, the hateful pressure of anti-Semitism had made the assimilee oligarchs who ruled the city's Jewry, despite their anti-Zionism, their snobbery, and the conversions from their midst, deeply anxious not to lose touch with the Jewish masses. There is little doubt that the Jewish Orthodoxy of Vienna lost in each generation to the modernism of the big city almost as many members as it gained from immigration, but at any given moment its conservative force was considerable.

In the Bohemian Lands, Orthodoxy was far weaker. Secularization and a net absence of immigration from or even of contact with the east had long since taken its toll of Jewish Tradition. Even outside Prague, in the Bohemian countryside and in Moravia, Orthodoxy was by 1914 a relative quality: the rabbis there were significantly more conservative than were the modernists in the big cities, but they were largely open to the ideas and teachings of the western world. So also in Budapest and in rural western and southern Hungary! Here the rabbis dominated an all-Hungarian Jewish "Orthodox" representational organization; they were better organized than elsewhere. But in practice they were sometimes not too different from the more conservative Neologs.

In northern and especially in northeastern Hungary, however, in what later became the Sub-Carpathian Ukraine, one encountered communities which by western Jewish standards had hardly changed since "medieval" times. At Szatmár, Sátoraljaújhely, and Munkács lived important Hasidic rabbis. Then across the mountain passes especially in eastern Galicia, but also in west Galicia and the villages of the Bukowina, the "medieval" and Hasidic kinds of Orthodox Jewry were wholly dominant. Here, as we have seen, it was only in the larger cities, at Lwow, Cernauti, and Cracow, that one found enlightened Jews. At Sadgora and Vizhnitsa in the Bukowina, at Chortkov, Przemysl, Zolochev, and Zhidachov in eastern Galicia, and above all at Belz reigned the great dynasties of zadikim.

What was the experience of the Orthodox Habsburg Jews in the war and the revolution that followed it? First came the call to the colors. In peacetime the K.u.K. Army made allowance for religious observance, but in time of war even that tolerant and ancient organization could do nothing but fight, if the Russians chose the sabbath for an attack. For traditionalist Jews, the conscription meant radical disruption of the regular course of Jewish ritual observance. Next, beginning in the first days of August 1914, six times great armies swept eastern Galicia before the fighting ended. Cernauti and Lwow both fell more than once to a foe, but it was the smaller towns, the *shtetls* where most of the Jews lived, that suffered from the shellings, the comings and goings of masses of soldiery, and the wanton destruction. Moreover, the Russian invaders had attitudes towards Jews. Right at the beginning of the great conflict the tsarist generals commanded that a broad territory on their side of the front be cleared of Jews, whom they considered "subversives." As they captured Galicia and the Bukowina and drove across the mountains into Hungary in the early fall of 1914, they allowed a comparable "purification" of the captured territories to take place, some of it by terror, some by pogroms, some of it by command.[2] As a result a great tidal wave of Jewish refugees overflowed into the western lands of the Empire, with the Hasidic rabbis of Belz and Sadgora in the lead. By some estimates there were 400,000 of them, half the Jewish population of Galicia. In western Cisleithania (the Alpine and Bohemian provinces), 173,000 of them were still homeless in 1917.[3] The record of the disaster is best dramatized by the nigh 20% overall fall of the religious-Jewish population of Galicia between the censuses of 1910 and 1921, and the effective halving of the east Galician small-town communities.[4]

After the invasions came a plague of anti-Semitism. Before the war Galicia had not been free of it, whether in the largely Polish landlord world or among the Polish and Ruthenian peasants. But Orthodox and assimilee Jews alike had then "pacted" politically in Galicia with the Poles, an arrangement that resulted, if not in love and friendship, at least in Polish forbearance from anti-Jewish political activism. Now, with the deterioration of economic conditions during the invasions, the pacts lapsed. The Christian population began to blame the Jews (who dominated Galicia's local commerce) for the shortages, the high prices, and every other sort of economic difficulty. In the latter years of the war, moreover, as hopes for political independence affected both Poles and Ukrainians, both accused the Jews of siding with the national foe. Whereupon in 1918 in a desperate bid for Jewish political support, the Ruthenian independence movement promised the Jews political autonomy in the state they hoped to found. The Jews remaining in the war zone responded by declaring their neutrality on the national question. The result was an eruption of violent Polish attacks on Jews. Poland was reborn in Galicia in 1918–19 to pogrom music.[5]

A similar development affected the area of Orthodox Jewish settlement on the Hungarian side of the Carpathians. Here the invaders came only once, so the physical destruction of the war was less; but the Jewish refugees were omnipresent throughout the war, and amidst all sections of the Christian population anti-Semite resentments rose as the economic hardship of the war grew worse. Before the war in Hungary the Jews had in general sided with the Magyars, and were regarded in the Slavic populated regions as anti-Slavic. In 1918–19, therefore, when "Czechoslovak" forces appeared in the northeast, there were anti-Jewish actions, not on the scale of the Galician pogroms but nonetheless most alarming. And they were followed in inner Hungary by the anti-Jewish outrages committed in 1919 by counter-revolutionaries intent on undoing the work of the Bolshevik regime of Béla Kun.[6]

As a general rule, thus, one may say that in Habsburg Jewry it was the Orthodox above all who were physically affected between 1914 and 1920 by the catastrophe of war. And in addition there was a radical legal development that affected them more than anyone else. After 1920, the frontiers closed. All through the eighteenth and nineteenth centuries, as seen in earlier chapters, the increasingly free right of Jews to migrate the length and breadth of Habsburg Europe had been a main instrument of their modernization. The Orthodox, of course, had not regarded modernization as undiluted weal! To the contrary, they had feared and avoided it as much as they could. By the end, however, even the Hasidic rabbis were using certain modern conveniences: the German language, for example, and the railroads which led to Bohemia spas. And very broadly the Orthodox acknowledged that for the Jewish poor of Galicia and the Ukraine, flight was a necessity, whether it be to America, Vienna, Budapest, or even to Polish towns. Until the war the open frontiers gave Galician Jewry its hope. After 1920 one could still flee elsewhere in Poland, if one were a Galician Orthodox Jew; but because of Poland's poverty, as everyone knew, that was no undiluted benefit; and the flight to the great cities of the west, which Habsburg rule had permitted, was as much a thing of the past as flight to America. In fact Prague, Vienna, and Budapest alike attempted vigorously at the end of the war to send their Galician refugees back "home."

How did the Orthodox respond? We may insert here first some evidence about the general eastern Jewish response, which is so massive that it clearly implies Orthodoxy's participation. It was observable, first, that the war refugees seemed reluctant to go home. Both before and after the collapse of the Monarchy, there were strong factors seeking to force their return. Even so, at Vienna where the overall population fell during the war, the Jewish population, apparently because of the refugees, rose from 8.6% in 1910 to 10.8% in 1923.[7] The Hasidic rabbi from Chortkov in East Galicia even settled permanently in Vienna, making the Orthodox community there stronger after the war than before.[8] In Budapest likewise the refugees stayed. Here the overall population rose at the end of the war, but the Jewish percentage rose too, from 23.1% in 1910 to 23.2% in 1920.[9] And in Galicia, where Jews did return, they returned above all to larger localities, no longer risking the isolation of the small town. The Belzer Rebbe delayed coming home until 1923.[10]

It is worth mentioning next some aspects of rabbinical behavior after the catastrophe which fit with legends about alleged Jewish behavior in other disasters, before and since. In Vienna it can be documented that Z. P. Chajes, the new Grand Rabbi of the city, turned out to have pronounced Zionist inclinations in 1918.[11] But in the east the Hasidic rabbis were consistent in rejecting political action of every sort. Indeed the Galician rabbinate proved outstanding in eastern Europe in this respect.[12] Their influence appeared, for example, in 1921–22 when the Polish authorities attempted to deter the Jews from entering an electoral bloc with the other national minorities of the new Poland. In former Congress Poland they were unsuccessful. There such a bloc emerged. But in former Galicia even the Zionists found it inexpedient, or just plain too dangerous, to take a stand with the Ukrainians against Poland, as it were. The rabbinate proved susceptible to supporting the Polish government; and the greatest single Hasidic voice, the Rabbi of Belz, refused to take any political position whatsoever.

In those years Galician Hasidism likewise rejected the political involvement represented by Agudas Yisroel, again in striking contrast to the Hasidim of Congress Poland. At Warsaw after the war the famous Rebbe of Ger accepted the proposition that Jewry must organize. While still opposing Zionism, he furthered the development of the originally German Agudas as the political organ of conservative Judaism in eastern Europe. In 1923 the Polish Agudas managed to achieve programmatic agreement with the Orthodox rabbis of Hungary. In former Congress Poland the Agudas became, alongside Zionism and assimilationism, the third great force in interwar Polish Jewish politics. Not so in former Galicia. There, not least of all because of opposition from the Rabbi of Belz, the Agudas failed. As late as the mid-1930s it hardly existed.[13] In Vienna, far away from Galicia, the Orthodox did join the Agudas, and so did the exiled Chortkower Rebbe there. But in Slovakia, just across the mountains from Galicia, though the Orthodox joined, they insisted throughout the interwar period on an extreme position of apoliticism within it. In the heavily Orthodox Sub-Carpathian Ruthenia, as in Galicia, the Agudas had scant following.[14]

But one should ask what such data mean. Do they imply that the tradition-minded Jewish masses remained passive in the face of disaster, that quietism was the Orthodox Jewish response in the once-Habsburg lands to the unparallelled aggressions of the war period? As it happens, data exist which undermine any such interpretation. The census figures of postwar Poland and Czechoslovakia provide hard evidence, for example, of a very active general Jewish response to the war in the east of the old Monarchy. In 1910 at the last Austrian census 96% of predominantly Orthodox, Yiddish-speaking Galician Jewry had, in the face of a census ban on Yiddish, declared Polish to be its "language of daily use." In 1921 in the first Polish census, only 31% of the Galician Jews claimed to be Polish. All the rest of the Jews by religion opted for "Jewish," German, or Ukrainian. The creation of the Polish state should have led to a 100% declaration of Polishness by the Galician Jews in the census of 1921, organized by that state. In fact the Poles, with all the instruments of state power to push their cause, had to accept a fall in their proportion of the Galician population since 1910 from 58.5% to 57.3%.[15] In Slovakia and Sub-Carpathian Ruthenia also, religiously defined Jews opted emphatically for a Yiddish as opposed to a Slavic speech in the first postwar censuses, and for "Jewish" as opposed to "Czechoslovak" nationality.[16] These expressions of Jewish opinion in these largely Orthodox regions were the more dramatic because the first post-war censuses in other regions revealed a sharp rise in the proportion of the Jewish population adhering to the newly dominant nationality—Czech in the Bohemian Lands, Rumanian in Transylvania.[17]

These data, like those about Hasid quietism, require careful assessment. Do they, as is often suggested, signify not just popular fear and resentment but also an outpouring of popular Jewish consciousness in the Orthodox masses? No doubt such an interpretation stands to reason. Both Zionism and Jewish national autonomism had caught on in the Empire's eastern regions before the war, even gathering some electoral strength. The tinder evidently existed there for an outburst of Jewish nationalism, and surely the war constituted an adequate spark to set it aflame. Furthermore, we know that in Galicia in 1918, as throughout the old Empire, Jewish national councils appeared; and here more than almost anywhere else Zionism was dominant in them.[18] Amidst these conditions there is no reason to think that the Orthodox masses of Galicia were not "infected."

Withall, let us recall the overall experience recounted in earlier chapters, whereby in Galicia Jewish Tradition, the ubiquitous strength of Talmudic education, the much-deplored weakness of modern schools, and deep poverty had shielded nigh-impermeably the eastern Jews of the Empire from pressures to change. Can it be expected that the war broke that shield absolutely? Better perhaps to accept a portrait of Galician Jewry that exists in certain literary works, for example, those of S. J. Agnon. Hereby the war devastated the traditionalist core of Jewry, but left it not clear about the future, not well defined in new, modern nationalist views. In this portrait the Orthodox were bewildered after the disaster, cognizant of the traditional significance of Zion to the Jews, but still unable to conceive of the Enlightened Herzlian "solution"; cognizant also of the traditional bar of Judaism to self-help in returning to the Jewish Home, yet able now because of the catastrophe to conceive that without self-help, the end of Jewry might be on hand.[19]

To sum up, the Orthodox bedrock of Habsburg Jewry more than any other section of Habsburg Jewry was hard hit by the war. The more radical the traditionalism of a locality, the more violent seemingly was the onslaught. At the end the Orthodox masses were for the first time "mobilized." But probably they were only half-"awake." They were now accessible to new, especially to Jewish nationalist, ideas. But they were not yet "modern," much less emancipated from poverty and the behavioral molds of the past.

III

Let us turn now to the stratum of Habsburg Jewry which one would logically study first, were one to follow the patterns of a class-by-class survey of some other national group within the old monarchy: to the lower economic classes. Let us first identify and roughly measure what these might be, then suggest their wartime experience, and finally assess their responses to the empire's collapse.

Habsburg statistics in general make no correlation between profession and income, and consequently provide an unclear picture of social classes. To identify the lowest stratum of Habsburg Jewry, one must look within it at professional groups; and we may conveniently start with the Habsburg Jewish agriculturalists, Jewish equivalents to the "peasants" of other nations. Surprisingly, given the well-known "Jewish professional mold," there were some. In the Austrian Lands in 1900, 1% of the agricultural population was Jewish; in Greater Hungary, 0.6% was Jewish. Numerically, in Cisleithania some 134,794 Jews were supported in the agricultural sector (*Berufszugehörige*); 57,004 actually engaged in agriculture (*Berufstätige*). Most of these were in Galicia (especially in the east of the province) and the Bukowina; and though there, as in Hungary, some of the Jewish "agriculturalists" were estate owners (indeed, large-estate owners!), there existed a considerable group of Jewish "peasants"—dwarf land-owners—also.[20]

These Jewish poor peasants were in part the product of deliberate colonization attempts dating back to Joseph II's time. Then, as may be recalled, one of the Physiocrats' projects for solving the "Jewish question" had been to convert them into "productive" occupation. Influenced by such dreams of transformation, Joseph, like the Russian Tsars of the early nineteenth century, had decreed not only the expulsion of Jews from "parasitic" professions, such as rural tavern keeping, but also the distribution of certain lands amongst Jews who would till them. Later on, numerous Jewish philanthropic groups had absorbed the Physiocratic ideal, and had launched similar agrarian projects. All told, however, such projects had not worked in the Habsburg Lands. In the 1850s, when the land was finally released from feudal tenure, there were only some 750 Galician properties in Jewish hands, less than in the 1820s; and this included properties owned by wealthy urban businessmen. The pattern here was quite different from that in the Russian-ruled Ukraine, where government efforts created the "Jewish peasantry." The Jewish agriculturalists in Austria were overwhelmingly a product of the free capitalism in the last decades of the nineteenth century, independent of the elite, free.[21]

It is important to note, however, that the Christian and Jewish elite continued to dream here all through the late nineteenth century of Jewish moral regeneration through agriculture. Gradually in the prewar years this initially Physiocratic attitude became integral to certain strains of central European Zionism also (as if the notion of acquiring land for Jews was not integral to Zionism altogether). Especially in Bohemia and Galicia, Zionist youth groups took over from German *völkisch* youth movements the notion of achieving moral health through communion with Nature. They by no means formed a political movement to create Jewish peasants, much less to protect those who existed in Galicia and the Bukowina. Their activity far more resembled the village-wandering cult of Russian *Narodnichestvo*, or of Tolstoy. But as a result the Habsburg Jewish pre-war scene featured not only Jewish "peasants" but also intellectuals who were attempting after a fashion to "represent" Jewish interest in the land, even though they had no connection whatsoever with the Jewish peasants themselves.[22]

In a class-by-class survey of a Christian "nation's" poor, one would turn, after identifying the "peasants," to the urban "proletariat." In looking for such a class among the Habsburg Jews, numbers once again spring to hand. According to the census of 1910, there were 30,581 active Jewish industrial workers ("Berufstätige" without "Berufsangehörige") in Galicia and the Bukowina, another 10,091 in Vienna, and 3,050 in the three industrially modern Bohemian crownlands. In Hungary at Budapest 21,537 Jews were counted in 1910 as "hired or day labor in industry." In the northeastern counties Jews comprised 19.1% of the active population engaged in "industry," and since there was little industry there, one may assume that these were mainly laborers.[23] Though the definition of "laborer" may not have been the same in Hungary as in Austria, some 65,000 Habsburg Jews seem thus to have been industrial workers, with rather more in the non-industrialized eastern regions than in the "modern" west.

As is obvious from these figures, however, the Habsburg Jewish "worker class" was not large, and by measuring it one clearly does not approach a definition of the poorer stratum of Habsburg Jewish society. This reality becomes the more pronounced when one learns that in prewar Vienna Jews comprised only 2.9% of all industrial workers; and that for every 100 male Jewish industrial workers at the city, there were 66 female industrial workers employed mainly in the textile industry, which played a big role there just as in other great modern cities of the time.[24] This statistic deprives one of the ideologically pleasing impression that the Jewish workers were a host of burly men, steeled in heavy machinery shops for violent class struggle. One finds also that in Galicia, though in industrial branch after industrial branch Jews were very important as workers, and though overall they were about 10% of the industrial work-force, paradoxically, the more modern the industry, the weaker their role. This was the case most conspicuously in Galicia's famed oil industry. So long as primitive methods of extraction dominated, and individuals could make a small-scale living, Jewish labor had prevailed here. But once modern methods of extraction were introduced in the 1890s, Jews disappeared from the fields. By the turn of the century there were only 698 Jews engaged in this industry in Galicia, alongside 10,000 Christians.[25] The Galician Jewish "workers" tended to work in printing establishments, match factories, textile branches where old-fashioned home manufacture still reigned, or in sweatshops (often owned by Jewish manufacturers) where paternal relations prevailed.

Once one gives up trying to find Jewish equivalents of the classes in Christian society, however, one discovers that in Jewish society there were lots and lots of penniless Jews who, as the Poale Zionists said before the war, somehow did not "proletarianize." These were in part what the census-takers described as "workers in commerce." In province after province, 50% and more of the Jewish population was engaged in "commerce": in Lower Austria 48%, in Bohemia 53%, in Galicia 52%, These figures stand in striking contrast to the proportions in the Christian population where (among Catholics) the commerce sector accounted in 1910 for 20.2% (Lower Austria), 6.2% (Galicia), or 5% (Dalmatia).[26] A good portion of the Jews in "commerce" were called "workers," "day labor," or "assisting family members": in Galicia there were 28,000 in the first two categories, 50,000 in the latter; in Vienna, 10,000 in the first. Overall in Cisleithania 15% of the Jews in commerce were "workers" and "day labor," 21.5% were "assisting family members."[27]

Furthermore, as many observers have pointed out, the overall 49.5% of the Jews in commerce who identified themselves as "independent" in Cisleithania in 1910 were rather more poor than rich.[28] In no other way can one explain, for example, why out of the 175,318 Jews living in Vienna in 1910, 40.5% lived in the two over-built and relatively insalubrious districts between the old inner city and the Danube, comprising 47.9% of the district populations. Over half of the Jews on charity in the city lived in just one of these districts, the Leopoldstadt. Observers found whole families of six and ten persons crammed into single rooms in the poor districts. Only by acknowledging that these people were impoverished Jewish traders from Galicia can one understand the statistics. The same goes for the fact that two-thirds of the city's Jews could not afford the very low annual religious tax.[29] Only by adding the "commerce" categories to the official "worker" categories can one justify this degree of poverty among the Habsburg Jews. Nor, in an east European context, was there anything unusual about these conditions. Across the frontier in the Russian parts of old Poland the sociological mix was comparable.[30]

For one reason, nonetheless, it remains useful to talk about "workers" when describing the very numerous lower strata of Jewish society: whereas before the war the political organization of the "commerce" Jews and Luftmensch Jews was hardly considered, there were sundry political efforts to organize the "workers." Just as deep in the mentality of Christian Europe

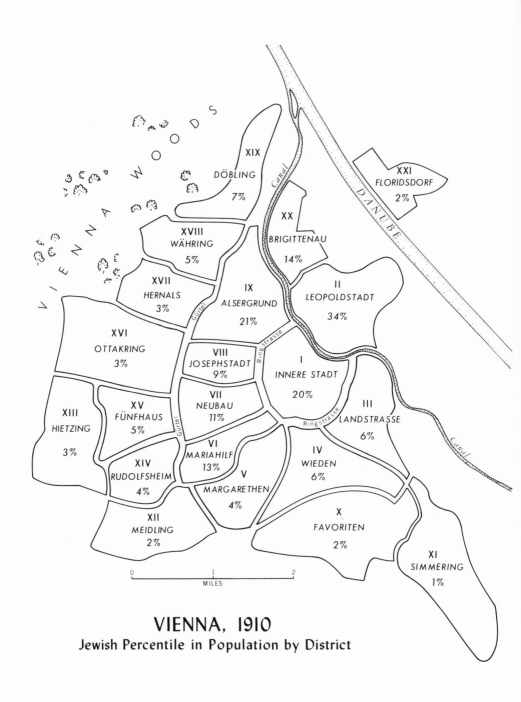

XIX
DÖBLING
7%

XXI
FLORIDSDORF
2%

XX
BRIGITTENAU
14%

XVIII
WÄHRING
5%

XVII
HERNALS
3%

IX
ALSERGRUND
21%

II
LEOPOLDSTADT
34%

XVI
OTTAKRING
3%

VIII
JOSEPHSTADT
9%

I
INNERE STADT
20%

XIII
HIETZING
3%

XV
FÜNFHAUS
5%

VII
NEUBAU
11%

III
LANDSTRASSE
6%

XIV
RUDOLFSHEIM
4%

VI
MARIAHILF
13%

IV
WIEDEN
6%

V
MARGARETHEN
4%

XII
MEIDLING
2%

X
FAVORITEN
2%

XI
SIMMERING
1%

VIENNA WOODS

Canal

DANUBE

Gürtel

Ringstrasse

Ringstrasse

Canal

0   1   2
MILES

VIENNA, 1910
Jewish Percentile in Population by District

as the notion of social health achieved through working the land was the notion of worker-led revolution. And just as Jewish philanthropy in the Habsburg lands and in the west had all through the nineteenth century seen virtue in "improving" the situation of the *Ostjuden* by getting them onto the land, so Jewish revolutionaries had sought to "improve" the Jewish workers.

Early on, as we have seen, some Jewish Socialist organizers in the Habsburg Empire had been inspired to approach workers who spoke mainly Yiddish in that language, not in German or Polish. They resembled the Jewish Bundists in the Russian Empire who also used Yiddish. All told, however, Yiddish-speaking Socialists had not achieved great success in the Habsburg lands. The "Jewish proletarians" were too few in number. The prejudice in the Labor Movement against Jews and Yiddish alike was too great. And there were just too many ideological alternatives available. By 1914 the organizers of a specifically Jewish Labor Movement were splintered and isolated, enjoying none of the tacit middle-class support that made the Russian Bund so potent. Meanwhile, the great bulk of the Jews in the Empire's Socialist Movement had proceeded in another political direction, for Jews no less alienating: that of orthodox Marxism. They were here in good company, and enjoyed very wide public support in this Empire where in 1907 universal suffrage had been established. But the condition of participation in the Marxist Movement was war against capitalist commerce, and denial of the significance of both religion and the modern nation. Austro-Marxism notoriously compromised on issues of Christian nationality, re-organizing itself after 1899 along linguistic lines. But, as seen elsewhere, the SPÖ found Jewish nationality to be one too much, and in 1908 rejected it. All told, the pre-war Austrian Socialist organizations were the first major effort to give the sociologically invisible Habsburg Jewish masses a political voice. But they involved a war against Jewish economic realities that was just as extreme as the Physiocratic one, and for Jews they involved an even more extreme ideological self-denial.[31]

What now was the wartime experience of the Habsburg Jewish lower stratum? In some respects it was identical to that of the Orthodox, for geographically the two groups overlapped. First there was massive disruption because of the conscription. Then there was invasion and Russian persecution, followed as the war wore on, especially in the north and east, by outbursts of anti-Semitism. Two peculiarities of the urban lower stratum experience stand out, however. The first derived from a general economic impoverishment that affected all the poorer strata of central European society during the war. In the cities food grew short. The amenities of life became prohibitively expensive or disappeared. The influx of penniless refugees crowded slums. Especially in the winters of 1917, 1918, and 1919, a dearth of heating materials developed, and health conditions deteriorated. For urban dwellers the wartime impoverishment was so great that it did not disappear after the fighting was over, but proved a permanent, as it were unbreakable chain. And it was reinforced in the early 1920s by the currency inflations, later on by the depression.[32]

The second special feature of the lower-stratum wartime experience was the revolution, which centered in 1918–19 in the great cities of the monarchy, and which in virtually all of them began with worker strikes and brought power for a time to regimes that claimed to act in the workers' name. This revolution had the initial impact, no doubt, of transforming the despair of being poor and helpless into hope. The psychological transformation may have been more important for Jews than for others, because so often Jews, or people friendly to them, were in the lead of the upheaval. At Vienna in November 1918, first Victor Adler, then Otto Bauer became Foreign Minister. In Budapest Oszkar Jászi appeared as Minister for Nationalities. In Prague T. G. Masaryk, who had defended the Jews a few years earlier from the blood libel, became president of a new republic.[33]

Subsequently, however, the revolution turned out to be a very mixed bag for the Jewish poor, and perhaps most notably for the workers among them. In the city of Vienna a Social-Democratic regime remained in power all through the 1920s. "Red Vienna" protected the Jews, and Austrian Social-Democracy became in the popular eye a "Jewish" Party. But the rest of the small new Austrian state became at an early date observably anti-Jewish, the new stomping-ground of the anti-Semitism that had ruled Vienna itself in the 1890s. With time gradually this rural Austria began to strangle the former imperial capital; and meanwhile it turned out that though Social Democracy might be friendlier to the Jews than other parties were, it was interested primarily and often dogmatically in "workers" who rejected all religious confessions.[34] In Hungary, meanwhile, in 1919 the revolution took a violent lurch to the left. The carving up of old Hungary by the victorious Allies, the success of Bolshevism in Russia, and worsening economic conditions within the country drove the Social Democrats to national radicalism, and to acceptance as a governing partner of an egregiously Jewish-tinted Communist Party. In mid-1919 the revolution collapsed, giving room to a nationally radical rightist regime that from the start cast much of the blame for the disaster on the Jews and took an active revenge. For lower-stratum Jews, Hungary in the 1920s was decidedly an unhealthy place.[35]

In Czechoslovakia the new regime of 1919 was both more stable and more democratic than those of Austria and Hungary. It was bourgeois capitalist in character, but throughout the interwar period acted as a bulwark of tolerance both for Jews and workers. The poor Jews there had little—save their chains—of which to complain. But as we have seen, in Poland this was not the case. Nor was it the case in Rumania, where especially in the Bukowina, both the Jews and the Socialists were from the start more or less actively persecuted.[36] All told, therefore, the imperial collapse brought large-scale disappointment to the poorer urban stratum of Habsburg Jewry, compounding the loss of territorial mobility that we observed when studying the Orthodox with a limitation on upward social mobility which had been so important a feature for the Jewish poor before 1914.

And what was the response? Just as in our consideration of the Orthodox, it is tempting to look at what leaders did for an answer, for some of these indulged in spectacular behavior. From a Jewish point of view, the most interesting were the "moral regenerationists"—the heirs to the Physiocratic and "village wanderer" traditions. During the war circumstances brought numbers of such intellectuals together at Vienna. From Prague came Martin Buber, the apostle within Zionism of a rediscovery of Judaism, and several prominent figures of the Bar Kochba Zionist youth group. From Galicia came large numbers of refugee youths, most often middle class by birth and well schooled, together with the elite of prewar Poale Zionism. From the east, evacuated early in the war from Turkey, came some members of and many witnesses of the Jewish colonist enterprises of the last pre-war decade—people knowledgeable about Russian Zionism, about the practical need in Palestine for Jews to go into agriculture, and about the Tolstoyan ideas of A. D. Gordon. In Vienna were gathered already the Jews of the pre-war cultural elite of the Empire. In the presence of the pitiable masses of Jewish refugees, Jewish consciousness rose; and by the end of the war the Galician youths in particular were swept by fervent Jewish communalism. Returning home when hostilities ended, these people cut their ties with the past and went out on the land, founding workcamps. In the early 1920s they were the core of the third "aliya" or "immigration" to Palestine, and the founders of the famed Hashomer Hazair organization—the root of the kibbutz movement of later times.[37]

In considering this manifestation of Jewish "peasantism" at the end of the war, however, one must have no illusion that it "represented" in any way the Habsburg Jewish "peasants." It was messianic for the Jewish nation. It stood for the regeneration of the Jewish people through work on the land, and it reflected paternalist attitudes like those in the original making of the east European Jewish peasantry. But it began quite specifically not with a vision of some uplifting quality in the Jewish farmer in Galicia. It was wholly elitist in spirit, intent on distant futuristic enterprise, willing for a while after the war to inspire the poor rural Jews of Galicia to dream, but hardly qualifiable as a rural Jewish response to the horrors of the war.

Much the same can be said of end-of-the-war activities of the group which most specifically sought to "represent" the Habsburg Jewish "workers": the Poale Zionists. Galicia before the war had been the stronghold of the Poalists. As just noted, much of the leadership fled early in the war to Vienna. There for a while they carried on propagandist activities, producing as it happens some of the most useful collections of information that have come down to us about Habsburg Jewry during the war. But significant elements in this very small political faction soon gravitated into leftist Marxism. In January 1918 they played a role in sparking the great workers' strike that shook the monarchy in that month. In the fall and winter of 1918–19, after the collapse of the state, some of them engaged in putschist activities at Vienna, and in 1920–21 they wholly abandoned Jewish organizational frameworks by entering the Austrian Communist Party.[38] In the Budapest revolution a small group of Poalists made a similarly abrupt voyage into supranational radicalism and were suppressed. In the Bohemian Lands Poalism at first fell in with the General Zionists within the framework of the Jewish National Council. But by 1920–21 they also had split out and abandoned their Jewish banners within the KPČS. In Galicia the Poalists were from the start too weakened by the war to act divergently from the general Zionists who dominated the national councils. They suffered in reputation here from association with the Russian Poale Zion and Bolshevism. Some of the leaders went over to the Polish Communist Party, and all told the Party played an insignificant interwar political role.[39]

One should once again be clear about the main point here. The Poale Zionists were in no way acting out the wishes of the Jewish "workers." No more than the Hashomer Hazair youths were they a "representative group." They were intellectuals, messianically inclined, and at the end they were hysterically capable of self-denial because they had no following, not because the Jewish masses stood behind them. Nonetheless, their failure was a portentious one for the Jewish poor. Since the Jewish Bund had never gained a foothold in the Habsburg Empire, and did not seriously take root in the Galician part of interwar Poland, Poale Zion's record of disintegration really means that the Habsburg Jewish lower stratum lost even its nominal political representation at the time of the collapse. Various other Zionist organizations sought to step into the breach, but for a considerable time in the 1920s there was effectively no political organ for the lower stratum onetime Habsburg Jews.

All the more isolated was the most famous group of Jewish "representatives" of the working class at the end of the war: the Bolsheviks of Jewish origin who sprang up at Munich, Vienna, and especially at Budapest. Some of these, like Gustav Landauer and Georg Lukács, were intellectuals who in their idiosyncrasy escape all sociological categorization. Others, like Béla Kun and even Otto Bauer (who never became a Bolshevik, but served in the Vienna revolution as a pole of radical opinion), swung left because as POWs they had got caught up in the passion of the Russian revolutionary upheaval. Some came from "good middle-class family" backgrounds; others emerged from the societal mass. Surprisingly many, one could discover, had enjoyed higher education. Most came to Bolshevism through the Social Democratic Party. Many were personally gifted with the talents that had made Jewish intellectuals prominent even in the Vienna revolution of 1848: a facile journalist's pen, a poetic orator's tongue, skill at making friends, organizational aptitude. Of all of them one may say that they acted as lubricants in the mechanism of central European Social Democracy, as conductors of enthusiasm from the revolutionary crowds upward through the Labor hierarchy, and back down again from the inspired leadership into the mass. They enlivened the revolutionary explosions of 1918–19 very much as the Jewish Kultusgemeinden of Vienna in the 1860s and of Budapest before the war had enlivened the middle-class "crazes" of their day. But of all these Jewish Bolsheviks one must premise also that they did not play their role as Jews, and that they specifically excluded themselves from any Jewish societal adventure. Their organizations were not the Kultusgemeinden, but the destroyers of the same.

The eruption of Jewish intellectual radicalism in central Europe at the end of the war raises major questions for the historian of Jewry. Were the people just discussed the successors of the Jewish messianists of earlier centuries—of the Shabbetai Zevis and Jakob Franks, actors whose heroism can best be understood in a Judaistic context? Or were they the advocates of individual moral rehabilitation, social revolution, and universal human improvement that they claimed to be, escapist geniuses who can best be understood in the context of turn-of-the-century Viennese intellectuality? Or, third, were they ultimately disgraceful specimens of a century of Jewish "self"-denial, the "self"-hating scions of "self"-rejectionist assimilee fathers, made doubly renegade by the "self"-denying record of the decadent Habsburg Reich? Though none of these questions can be answered clearly, all suggest at least a grain of truth; and together they drive historians to bewilderment about the contexts within which we write.[40] One thing cannot be said, however: the proliferation of Jewish radical groups cannot be characterized as the response of the poorer stratum of Jewish society in the Habsburg Empire to the collapse of the state. These groups acted not for the Jewish poor, but for an idealized "poor," and they often stood against the actual Jews.

What then was the poor Jewish stratum's response? One can stress first survival. Whereas the Galician *shtetl* inhabitants fled finally from their homes, the Jewish "peasants" remained extant as a class in postwar Poland; and the Jewish urban poor, of course, proliferated, swollen everywhere by the influx of refugees. Second, the Jewish poor, like the Orthodox, clearly participated in the general wave of Jewish self-assertiveness that affected all central Europe in the years of upheaval. In Vienna and Prague as at Brno, Bratislava, Cracow, Lwow, and Cernauti, and in some Hungarian provincial cities, Jewish national councils sprang up at the moment of the Empire's collapse. In Prague the Poale Zion even participated in the Council's work. There is no reason to think that poorer Jews were not supportive of these organs of the middle classes. At Vienna the worker quarters were strongholds of Jewish nationalist voting strength in the first postwar election. But then later on in Vienna, Bohemia, and Slovakia alike the poorer Jews seem to have turned to Social Democracy in their voting, away from specifically Jewish parties.[41] Here is evidence that just as the Orthodox

Jews of Galicia were awakened for the first time by the war, so the "worker" Jews were driven in many places to specifically class demands. Their "mobilization," begun before the war, was heightened.

Yet all told, it is difficult to identify any specific response to the war emerging from the lower-stratum Habsburg Jews. This seems the important point and requires explanation, and no doubt part of the answer is that, like the Orthodox, the lower-stratum Jews had been hit extraordinarily hard by the war and were suffering from exhaustion. These people were the butt of both Christian and Jewish society. They were knocked out. Surely it is also significant that, as we have seen, the lower-stratum Jews were sociologically not like the workers of Petrograd or the peasant rebels near Saratov, laborers living by their brawn. They were lower middle class, if one will, not keyed up by long experience of revolutionary activity. Hungry tailors, the heirs of Paris's artisanry, started the French revolution of 1789; but what place was there on the barricades at Vienna or Budapest in 1918 for an Orthodox Jewish cigarette trader, with his five starving children and breadless wife?

To complete an explanation of lower-stratum Jewish helplessness at the end of the war, one must observe that the Jewish labor movement in central Europe was tragically overshadowed at the end of the war by developments in Russia. The Jewish Mensheviks and the occasional Jewish Bolsheviks in Russia established the popular image of revolution for all central European Jewish revolutionaries a whole year before the central European revolution broke out. In the face of this precedent, it was extremely difficult for central European lower-stratum Jews to take any initiative on their own. Finally, one must return to the question of leadership. These people had to act at the end of the war in the wake of the bewildering intellectuals mentioned above. Which poor Jews in 1918–19 could have thought to resist such brilliant, and often inordinately doctrinaire, self-appointed "representatives" of the poor?

IV

Let us turn now to our final topic: the performance of the Habsburg Jewish upper stratum at the end of the war. In some ways the task is easy, because the basic data are well known. Historically this stratum began with the appearance of sometimes spectacularly rich Jewish money-men at the seats of Habsburg government in the seventeenth and eighteenth centuries; alongside them, a stratum of enlightened Jewish intellectuals and of Jewish renegades emerged. Steadily through the nineteenth century these three elements expanded, their numbers fed rapidly by the new schooling systems of the Empire, by the economic opportunities resulting from the industrial revolution, and by the development of the Danubian cities, until by 1900 one could speak of an all-Empire "middle class" with a strong Jewish contingent. The locus of Jewish affluence shifted significantly with time. Prague's community in particular became provincial, whereas Budapest's came even to challenge Vienna's. A marked professional shift also affected upper-stratum Jewry, as young men began to prefer intellectual and especially managerial jobs to the commerce of their fathers. In Vienna the percentage of Jews in the intellectual professions stayed the same between 1870 and 1910, though the Jewish population quadrupled in that period.[42] By 1910 in Hungary overall Jews comprised 43.3%, in Budapest 52.6% of all the "employees" in industry—that is, of all managers.[43] But as we have seen the major quality of the Jewish upper stratum came to be its sociological complexity and the degree to which it resembled the middle classes in the states of western Europe.[44] And this complexity was clearly expressed politically. Middle-class Jews could be found playing a strong role before the war in virtually the entire spectrum of non-Jewish political parties. Renegade (and not-so-renegade) Jews even played a role in the anti-Semite parties. In addition a full spectrum of Jewish political parties was emerging before the war, ranging from Vilmos Vázsonyi's forthrightly assimilationist "Democratic Party" in Budapest through the entire spectrum of Zionism and Jewish national autonomism.[45]

For present purposes, the most important fact regarding the pre-war Habsburg Jewish upper stratum regards language, for here reputation contradicts reality. According to its reputation, upper-class Habsburg Jewry was "Austrian" with a vengeance, meaning that it spoke German; that it identified with the Germans; that genealogically it was made up of the offspring of German-speaking Bohemian-Land Jews; and that just as German Jewry did, it looked down its noses at the Yiddish-speaking Jewry of the east and would not even marry them. In reality it was "Austrian," of course, but "Austrian" in the sense that it was linguistically as bastard as the other Austrians were. As we have seen elsewhere, a century of assimilation had led the Jews in each Habsburg land to adopt for some purposes at least the language of their locality, as well as German: Hungarian, Czech, Polish, Italian, as the case might be.

Do all the language figures cited in earlier chapters reflect a serious assimilation, or just acculturation brought on by political pressure? The truth seems to be that the second acculturation of the modern central European Jews had different seriousness in each region. In Hungary Christian observers often judged that the Jewish Magyarization was extremely superficial.[46] But even today one is hard put to find a Magyar Jew who denies its seriousness. In Bohemia likewise there is considerable evidence that the Jews turned to their second language, to Czech, seriously. Only in Galicia does it seem valid to charge that the Jewish second assimilation was predominantly politically inspired "acculturation." Quite unlike the German-language Jews of the Reich, these Austrian Jews were linguistically adaptable long before 1918 made adaptability de rigeur.

What now was the wartime experience of the upper-stratum Habsburg Jews? Much of the record needs little detailing. One cannot doubt, for example, that the well off suffered less in the course of the hostilities than did the Orthodox or the poor. Of the larger cities where the middle classes lived, only Lwow and Cernauti were in the war zone. Though the Russians did deport some respectable Jews from these centers to Siberia, for example Salo Weisselberger, the mayor of Cernauti, there is little evidence of systematic degradation of the rich; and note that Franz Joseph ennobled Weisselberger for his sufferings![47] One may argue that a higher proportion of Jewish officers died in the war than of Jewish enlisted men.[48] But this hardly rates alongside the sufferings of the impoverished Jews massacred or expelled from East Galicia.

By 1918–19 the popular exhaustion was universal in central Europe, and the influenza attacked all classes without discrimination. Then also the Jewish modern classes suffered diverse assaults. The loss of the war and the collapse of the state meant that the war bonds into which many middle-stratum people had placed their savings became worthless. The revolutions entailed a pointed attack on property—this especially in Budapest where the Bolsheviks ripped up stock certificates in the Stock Exchange building, confiscated art collections, and converted rich men's villas into nursing homes for the children of the poor. Thereafter the currency collapsed in Hungary and Austria and Poland; this hardly helped the middle classes. In Poland, Czechoslovakia, Rumania, and Yugoslavia, the landed estates of wealthy Jews were among the first to be confiscated in the postwar land reforms. And the anti-Semitism of the new world was directed no less at the rich and middle class Jews than at the poor. Indeed, in the eastern successor states (Hungary, Poland, and Rumania) the new anti-Semitism attacked above all the Jewish middle classes, who in fora of public education, as in the tilting grounds of commerce, came under strong pressure from upwardly- or downwardly-mobile elements in the "native" nations.[49] All in all, for the middle-class Habsburg Jews as for everyone else in central Europe in 1918, the astonishing economic stability of pre-war life, like the wonderful authority of *Gott, Kaiser, und Vater*, became features of "the world of yesterday."

One gains no impression that during and after the war iron chains tied down the modern elite of Habsburg Jewry, like the territorial and economic restrictions which then fell upon the poor. The pensioned Jewish widows of Vienna and Budapest and the middle-class orphans of Lwow and Cluj often lost all in the Habsburg catastrophe, and had to live out the interwar years penuriously. But one can hardly compare their plight with that of the Luftmenschen of Josef Roth's Szwaby, who now had no way either out or up. The record strongly suggests that the old elites, guided by the great Vienna banks and industrial concerns, found it possible with time to make do with the catastrophe, and that some people even made fortunes out of the economic realignments after 1918.[50]

A decisive geographical and economic change did now affect upper-stratum Habsburg Jewry, for politically the great cities in which these peo-

ple lived were very different after 1918 from before the war. Vienna, the
seat of the second-largest Jewish community of all central Europe, was
before 1914 a bastion whence Jews had been well able to look after Jewish
political interests. After the war it was a political backwater, the capital of
a state which did not want to exist. Budapest, the seat of the region's largest
Jewish community, had before the war been rapidly increasing its political
power and had been an El Dorado of sorts for Jews. Now it too became
the capital of a small, rather helpless state. Of all the cities of the former
Empire, only Prague enjoyed greater political influence after 1918 than
before. And here the Jews were small in number and divided. These are
schematic measures, but they suffice to show how drastically middle-class
Jewish political clout in central Europe was diminished by the events at
the end of the war.

Let us now ask: How did the well-off and modern stratum of central
European Jewry respond to the war and the collapse? One must point first
to fear. In all the big cities of the old monarchy, the collapse of public order
in 1918 launched a wave of conversions out of Judaism. Overwhelmingly
the very rich led the way, and one can hardly avoid concluding that after
the century of comfort and increasing security, panic had now broken forth
among the wealthy.[51] One may point secondly, of course, to a happier
fact: middle-class Jewry experienced something far more positive, a sort of
Jewish raised consciousness. As mentioned earlier, from one end of the
monarchy to the other, Jewish national councils sprang up, spontaneously
taking up the defense of Jews. In Vienna and Prague, Jewish National
political parties were formed. Everywhere such organizations called themselves Zionist, though as we will see there was confusion about what this
might mean; and everywhere their leaderships featured Dr. this or Dr.
that, who unmistakably stemmed from the middle class.[52]

One might be inclined next to suggest that a Habsburg nationalist
identity crisis affected the middle-class central European Jews. As evidence
one might recall not only such pillars of old Habsburg Austria as the converted Jews Josef Redlich, Rudolf Sieghart, or József Szterényi, but the
eternally loyal Jews in the old officer corps; the German-speaking Jewish
Brahmins of Prague and Cernauti; and Vilmos Vázsonyi, the Budapest
Jewish "democrat" of the 1890s. All were resolutely *Habsburgtreu* in 1918,
and all were cast into despair and bewilderment by the collapse of the state.
Or one might cite Stefan Zweig, who after the war wrote the far-too-often-
quoted sentimental *Die Welt von Gestern*; or Josef Roth, who wrote the
arguably masterful, but still too sentimental *Radetzkymarsch*; or Franz Werfel, whose *Barbara oder Die Frömmigkeit* is surely the best fictional chronicle
of Habsburg Austria's sweet rot.

Even within Zionism there was a clear pattern of middle-class Jewish
desire to save and abet the dying old Habsburg State. Before the war it
was from Cernauti that the "Jewish National Party" had emanated. In 1918,
likewise, the German-speaking middle-class Jews of that remote Habsburg

city sought salvation by organizing a Jewish Council in defense of the Empire. At Vienna all through the war, Jewish politicians made efforts to set up an all-national Jewish political representation, comparable to the Jewish Congress then being advocated by some Reichsdeutsch Jews. When the collapse came, the "Jewish National Council" at Vienna was all set to act as an umbrella organization for Jewish councils throughout the Habsburg realm.[53]

Yet the reality is that for each and every one of the regretful middle-class Habsburg Jewish bureaucrats and intellectuals just listed, there was a Karl Kraus who simply did not have much use for the monarchy at all, or an Otto Bauer who premised that the state needed fundamental readjustments to survive. This is not to speak of the younger-generation Jewish intellectuals, who (following their Christian-origin school-chums) did their bit with violence to strike down the old order in 1918–19. And in general one may recall that there was no former Habsburg Crownland in which, at the end of the war, the middle class Jews did not as a whole prove willing enough to cast aside German as their "national" language and accept for practical purposes the new language of state.

There were good reasons for this ready acceptance of the Habsburg collapse, of course. First there was hope. The war had been very depressing. The year of the collapse, with its hunger and disease, was worse. Sixty years earlier the old state may have emancipated the Jews, but now it seemed to stand for political failure and conservative reaction, whereas the newly emerging successor states stood one and all for bright and more democratic national futures; and at the beginning it was not clear how much some of them would turn anti-Jewish. For assimilees and Zionists, old and young alike in the Habsburg Jewish middle classes, the new states hinted at something better. Hope in those days was not to be despised. And to this one may add that even before the war the process of second acculturation had prepared the way in the Jewish middle classes for what happened in 1918. Middle-class "Austrianism" contained no barrier against changing that usually prime criterion of allegiance to a state, the use of the language of state; and because of this one may say that polylingual "Austrianism" even assisted the upper-stratum Habsburg Jewry in 1918, albeit differently in each former crownland, to avoid the crisis of identity that often comes to citizens with the collapse of a state.

Middle-class Jewry's final response to the new order was a dreadful division of Jewish forces, as one may see best in the framework of Zionism. At Vienna, as just noted, Zionism took a stand at first for the old state, then for the new one; and this one may judge was perfectly proper, given how much Vienna Jewry stood to lose and how much Zionism was a German-speaking movement. But at Prague, the parallel Zionist adhesion to the Czechoslovak state was much more problematic, particularly since German-speaking Zionists here usurped the lead even from the Czech-speaking assimilees in seeking a political compact between Bohemian Jewry and the new Czechoslovak government. The result was not only the final disintegration of any effort to keep old Habsburg Jewry alive—a net break with Viennese Zionism; but also a fresh local split. The Czech government was not averse to using Zionism as a tool for splitting the Bohemian German vote. All through the 1920s it favored the Zionists over the "Czecho-Jews," which policy made permanent the split within Prague Jewry, the weakest but now all-important bearer of central European Jewry's political clout.

And in Budapest, the revolutionary year, 1918–19, with its Bolshevism and anti-Jewish pogroms, so terrified the Hungarian Jews of all political complexions that they grasped for any stick and stone. In 1920 they proved willing to collaborate even with the "restorationist" Magyar regime of that year in exchange for protection. Thenceforth, just as before the war, the assimilationist Jews here repressed Zionism with all their energy. They fought even beyond the new narrow Hungarian frontiers to keep Magyar-speaking Jews from making any suggestion that Jews might be more than "just a religious group." Such efforts awoke a surprising welcome response in the new "old regime," which was led ultimately by "gentleman" upper class Magyars who considered anti-Semitism "vulgar." The result was that Budapest Jewry continued between the wars to occupy a place of some honor and importance within Hungarian urban society. It remained a lubricant in the passionately revisionist politics of the Magyar nation, and became thus an active force in undermining and eventually destroying the whole region's democracy. Because of Budapest Jewry's anti-Zionist, Magyar-patriotic stance, the middle-class Jews of Slovakia, Transylvania, and the Vojvodina continued to think of themselves as Magyars and to oppose the general settlement which, after the destruction of the old Reich, alone had the ability to protect the whole region's Jews from further change.

All in all, thus, the Jewish end-of-the-war middle-class awakening splintered the central European Jews far worse than they had been splintered before; and of course, the awakening by no means extinguished the old currents of Jewish assimilationism. All too soon in each of the new states, differently, assimilee Jews were participating in the whole new spectrum of non-Jewish political parties too.

V

Overall, what was the Habsburg Jewish response to the end of the Empire in 1918? We have found some traces of remarkable passivity, but above all patterns of consciousness-raising and active change.

The variations in Jewish behavior were great. Among the Orthodox, and particularly among the Hasidim of Galicia and the northeast of old Hungary, Habsburg tolerance had made possible the survival of an unparallelled other-worldly indifference to modern conditions. In addition the war was more stunningly savage in its impact on Orthodoxy than on any other sector of Jewish society, and the Peace of 1919 destroyed Jewry's freedom of movement outward and upward to the west. Yet even so, the Orthodox masses seem to have awakened politically as never before when the collapse came. Among the poor both in Galicia and in the Danubian capitals the story was similar, although here the self-styled leaders provided too activist rather than too quietist a model. Sheer exhaustion might have wholly excused Jewish mass passivity, especially in the cities, at the end of the struggle. Yet there were clear signs of heightened social conscious-ness: increased "modernity," first a trend toward Jewish political nation-alism, then one toward Socialism. Finally it is clear that the upper strata of Jewish society, individually and in each region of the former state, was anything but inactive at the end of the war. The problem was that these people were wholly fragmented by the peace settlement. The bases of their security melted. They lost access to the seats of political power that they had occupied before 1914. Even so, these classes were responsible for pro-ducing the large-scale Jewish nationalist outburst of 1919.

All in all, Habsburg Jewry displayed in its disintegration the same qualities of life and endurance that had characterized it throughout the two centuries of modernization reviewed in this book. The Empire died, but its Jews roared on, little dreaming of the fate that awaited them in their division only twenty years to come. And if they ended up in different states pitted against each other, compounding with their enthusiasm the political divisions imposed by the Peace, this was because of the complexity of the Christian world in which they dwelt.

THIRTEEN

Conclusions

Are there readers who still at the end of this book doubt the existence of a Habsburg Jewry between 1670 and 1918? Let them go back to the arguments of our introduction, and to the record of demographics released chapter by chapter above. Habsburg Jewry never had the clarity of identity of Anglo-Jewry or French Jewry in the nineteenth and early twentieth centuries. That we freely concede. But in the sharing of a vast though amorphous cultural-political experience, it was as much there as the Habsburg state itself.[1]

How to assess its story? This is the question with which we had best conclude the book. And it is tempting to respond frowningly, because our chronicle has been fraught with disappointments. In the late eighteenth century it seemed there was a chance in the Habsburg Empire, an opportunity unique in Europe, for substantial numbers of Jews, led by the integrated community at Prague, to modernize without the splits and alienation characteristic of the western Jewries. This opportunity did not disappear with the huge increment of eastern Jews that came to the empire after 1772, because coincidentally the Habsburg State intervened strongly in favor of the Jews. Even in the first half of the nineteenth century, both at Vienna and in the Bohemian Lands, developments seemed to support Jewish collaboration with the Habsburg State. In the Napoleonic decades, however, here as elsewhere in Europe, Jewish "self"-denial assumed significant proportions. In Bohemia before 1848 the Judeophobia of the past flickered up in new guise, an ill omen for the future. Then in 1848 itself there were widespread popular attacks on Jews in the Bohemian Lands and Hungary; and though in Vienna the revolution was Judeophile in spirit, a disturbing dichotomy appeared even there between the Jewish success at emancipation and the political failures of the "Christian" middle class.

After 1848 the tale turned grim. During the period of political absolutism and the decade of constitition-making that followed, Habsburg Jewry split. In Galicia Jewish modernization fell behind. In Hungary modernization leapt ahead, but the Jews began to abandon the German tongue of the Enlightenment. At Vienna, the Jewish community became a principal engine of the escapism which came to characterize the middle classes there. After the great crash of 1873, with its internal divisions proliferating, Habsburg Jewry was exposed to widespread outbursts of modern anti-Semitism.

Meanwhile, in locality after locality, the Jews assumed the full burden of the ideological splits in the Christian communities; and though toward 1900 forms of Jewish nationalism began to replace the "self"-denial of earlier decades, in place after place it turned out that there was no ideal nationalist solution for the Jews. Then came the decades-long decay of the state and its final collapse amidst a cataclysm of disasters that especially affected the Jews. The Habsburg Jews ended up "mobilized" even in Galicia, but exhausted by wars and revolutions, and massively divided amongst themselves—in fact pitted against each other in the new states of eastern Europe. This was surely no great success.

Yet in concluding our story, let us point to another way of looking at what happened. If "modernization"—a people's escape from the rigid "medieval" past—is seen as a prime measure of "success," and if moreover "modernization" is perceived as inescapable in these last two centuries— if, given the dynamics of the European Revolution, national pain and alienation are perceived as normal, not exceptional, experiences—then surely the story of the Habsburg Jews from 1670 to 1920 was a signal success. At Vienna, in the Bohemian Lands, and in Hungary alike large-scale modern Jewries had been created: communities that had effectively translated old Jewish values into a practical idiom fitted to twentieth-century conditions. Despite the depressing Austrian environment, these communities were thriving and vital up to the end. Further, even though Galician Jewry was never wholly integrated into the western Jewish world, literally millions of Galician Jews were able during the nineteenth century, because of the freedom of migration characteristic of the Habsburg monarchy, to escape the rigid frameworks and appalling poverty of the past. At the end Habsburg Jewry broke up into numerous barely connected parts, some of them conspicuously more modern than others. But overall an immense work had been accomplished since Joseph II's legislation in 1781, not to speak of the expulsion year, 1670, when our story began. No doubt such a positive evaluation of the Habsburg Jewish record is a matter of attitudes. But are not all historical assessments thus matters of attitude?

Too often the Habsburg Jewish record is condemned not just because of the disappointments listed above, but also because of latter day events. It is held, for example, that Jewish adhesion to the Habsburg upper bourgeoisie was a "mistake" because that class was the loser par excellence in the catastrophe of 1914–18. Or it is insisted that because of the record of Jewish assimilation in pre-1914 Hungary and Austria, the Jews in those states became isolated "middleman minorities," exposed to anti-Semitism, after 1918. Such arguments seem wholly false. They premise, first, that the Great War and the collapse of the Habsburg Empire were inevitable. Were they? The more one recognizes that the war and the Habsburg catastrophe were less than "inevitable," the less the Jewish "mistake"! So much for the first argument; and surely the second is patently untrue. In Old Hungary the Jews obtained their success because they were only one amongst several national groups, most of which the Magyars feared much more than Jews. There is no reason to think Magyar attitudes would have been altered if Old Hungary had remained intact. The Jews became isolated in interwar Hungary not because they had assimilated, but because Trianon removed the other nationalities from the field. Even in Austria it is clear that, because of the new frontiers, the Jewish position was very radically different between the wars from what it had been before the war. One cannot imagine the pre-war Austrian "provinces" ganging up against a "Red Jewish Vienna" as little rural Austria did between the wars. Before 1914 Vienna had for decades been "Black," not "Red"; the "provinces" were then universally true to the monarch who was notoriously friendly to the Jews; and the Jews were then not just in the capital, isolated, but spread out and integrated in many provincial towns and cities. An essentially optimistic assessment of the Jewish record in the old monarchy is in all these senses not an error.

One may perhaps best gain perspective on the Habsburg Jewish achievement by noting the comparative violence and upheaval that was needed on the way to the United States and Israel, and in Soviet Russia, to bring the Jews of those countries into a modern condition comparable to that of Habsburg Jewry before 1914. Despite the disappointments along the way, and despite the real catastrophe which overcame Habsburg Jewry twenty years after 1918, one may generalize that nowhere else in the world has the large-scale transformation of eastern Jewry taken place so relatively peacefully, indeed so relatively without major violence. Pain and grave disappointment there certainly was; but in the story we have told there was nothing comparable to the pogroms in Russia in 1881, or for that matter to the Holocaust.

This book has not only presented a case-study of Jewish modernization: it has also dealt with the history of the central European middle classes, in which the Jews played a great part, and with one of the great issues of modern social history—with assimilation. We have come upon clear-cut findings about both topics. It has turned out, first, that the central European Christian middle classes were debilitated by 1918, and unwilling to defend their own state. And second, assimilation affords an effective explanation of why Habsburg society as a whole had assimilated in the nineteenth century! It had undertaken the process of modernization without the compensation of asserting a national "self." As a whole it had been "self"-denying in much the same way as were the Jews. The Jew, Sonnenfels had described in the eighteenth century, was a bourgeois Austrian ideal, "Ein Mann ohne Vorurtheil"—a person who, through lack of prejudice against Reason, could understand and accept his lot. But it was a Christian Austrian of the twentieth century, Robert Musil, who saw the ideal as "Ein Mann ohne Eigenschaften"—a person without (implicitly debilitating) national or even bourgeois characteristics. Musil was not just reacting against the excesses of late-nineteenth-century central European nationalism; he was describing the positive fruit of Austria's modernization path.

Modernization in general entails a sharp reduction of one's ancient "differentness," and is always in this sense painful to a group's Ego. When as in the Habsburg societal case there simply was no new, modern set of symbols around which to reorganize, the Ego may well in compensation of the pain turn violently against its ancient "self," as many of the Habsburg nationalities did. If the Habsburg Jews were in some respects more "self"-effacing than other members of the Habsburg society, it was surely not only because they were more bourgeois—more middle class—than the others, but also because they bore a double burden. The problems of finding a modern "Jewish self" around which to rally were quite as baffling as those of finding a modern "Habsburg self"; and to have to seek them both together (as was the fate of the central European Jews) was a task fit to paralyze any modernizing nation.

This book has been finally about one of the great problems of modern Jewish history: the role of the Jews' behavior in the development of the world around them. More perhaps than expected, we have been able to define such a role. At major centers of the Habsburg Empire, first at Vienna and later at Budapest, for complex reasons, middle-class "crazes" or vogues were especially pronounced in the century and a quarter from 1800 to 1920, and drastically affected the development of society. At Vienna in the 1860s and 1870s middle-class enthusiasm, wholly artificial, indeed theatrical in its bases, enabled the state to transform itself from the absolutist unity of 1855 to the instituted disunity—the Dualism—of 1867–68. At Budapest at the turn of the century similarly ill-based enthusiasm made possible the perpetuation of Magyar hegemony in Greater Hungary. In both cases, our study suggests, Jewish participation in the middle class, and indeed the communal institution of the capital cities' Jews, greatly contributed to the popular delusion. Jewish enthusiasm was here in a very real sense the "leaven" of developments in the "Christian world." The Jews played a major role in what happened.

This need not mean, however, that in all historical situations there has been an identifiable Jewish behavior that has contributed to what happened. We have sought, for example, through study of the Jews during the catastrophic disintegration of the Habsburg state in 1918, to elucidate whether an allegedly quietist, unresisting Jewish approach to catastrophe contributed to the holocaust under Hitler—or whether what happened in the 1940s stemmed just from the circumstances of Hitler's assault.

Our answer is unequivocally the latter. In the Habsburg debacle, the Jews were divided in their response, and of course some of them for specific reasons were no doubt passive. But in the face of that very violent assault, the Jews were most remarkably active. In the face of the terrible swing of fate in 1918, they did not go to sleep, but awoke.

APPENDIX

The Jewish Population
of Vienna, 1780–1918

In Vienna from Joseph II's time until 1848 Jews could be legal residents only if they showed a certain amount of wealth and paid a "tolerance" tax. F. Pribram published the official lists of the "tolerees" in a massive document collection in 1918.[1] S. Husserl has published some slightly different official counts.[2]

TABLE I

| Year | number of families | | number of |
	Pribram	Husserl	individuals
1780		53	570
1787	61	66	
1789	72		656
1790		—	842
1793		102	
1799		—	1,431
1800		121	
1804	119		
1807	131		
1810		113	
1812	130		
1820		135	
1823	137		1,370
1827	126		1,256
1830		121	
1834	124		1,287
1840		152	
1847	197		1,800

There is debate about the actual Jewish population present in Vienna in the decades immediately before and after 1848, when considerable illegal immigration occurred. S. Husserl published official "estimates" that suggest a smooth upward curve, but two more recent scholars, Akos Löw[3] and Marsha Rozenblit,[4] have provided significantly lower estimates for the pre-1857 period, and a much sharper upward curve thereafter. Husserl's figures are supported by some contemporary police reports,[5] but many contemporaries support Löw and Rozenblit.[6]

TABLE II

date	Husserl	Löw	Rozenblit
1830	2536	1270	1270
1840	7136	1890	
1850	9675	4000	4000
1857	15,600		6217
1864	29,234		

After accurate censes began in 1869, the following figures were published:[7]

TABLE III

1869	40,230
1880	72,590
1890	118,495
1900	146,926
1910	182,700

In recent years Anson Rabinbach has stimulated considerable discussion by proposing first that there was a dramatically large Galician Jewish immigration to Vienna in the 1860s and 1870s, and then, second, that the birth of Zionism may be considered a "bourgeois" response to this demographic explosion.[8] Indeed, there does seem to have been a large influx of Galicians about 1870: between 1869 and 1880, a period of escalating population growth, the Galician percentage in the Vienna Jewish population rose from 11% to 18%.[9] But in my opinion, both Rabinbach and his critics[10] have been misled by their rejection of Husserl's figures for 1857–64. If one finds the Jewish population of the capital to have been fairly high in those earlier years, the Galician immigration just after 1868 seems less disturbing.

NOTES TO APPENDIX

1. Pribram, *Urkunden und Akten*, vol. I, pp. 586, 608–10, and vol. II, pp. 120–32, 175–78, 209–10, 419–20, 439–41, 462–63, 530–31.
2. S. Husserl, "Die israelitische Kultusgemeinde Wien" in *Ost und West* X (1910): 520.
3. Akos Löw, "Die soziale Zusammensetzung der Wiener Juden nach den Trauungs- und Geburtsmatrikeln, 1784–1848" (unpub. diss., Vienna, 1951), pp. 161–63.
4. Marsha Rozenblit, *The Jews of Vienna* (Albany: SUNY, 1983), pp. 16–17.
5. Sigmund Mayer, *Die Wiener Juden* (Vienna: Löwit, 1917); Rosenmann, "Ein vertraulicher Bericht" in *Die Wahrheit* XLII (1926), no. 23, pp. 2–4; *Wiener Kirchen Zeitung*, no. 6, 21 Jan. 1870; Hans Novogoratz, "Sebastian Brunner und der frühe Anti-Semitismus" (unpub. diss., Vienna, 1979), p. 93.

6. Siegfried Becher, *Statistische Übersicht der Bevölkerung der österreichischen Monarchie* (1841), p. 126; Josef Wertheimer, *Die Juden in Österreich* (1843); Heinrich Jacques, *Denkschrift über die Stellung der Juden in Österreich* (4th enlarged edit.; Vienna: Gerold, 1859); Israel Jeiteles, *Die Kultusgemeinde der Israeliten in Wien* (Vienna: L. Rosner, 1873), p. 40–42; Gustav Adolf Schimmer, *Statistik des Judenthums in den in Reichsrathe vertretenen Königreichern und Ländern* (Vienna: Staatsdruckerei, 1872), p. 9; Jakob Thon, *Die Juden in Österreich* (Berlin: Jüdischer Verlag, 1908), p. 15. Comp. Peter Schmidtbauer, "Zur sozialen Situation der Wiener Juden 1857" in *Studia Judaica Austriaca* VI (1978): 57ff.; Ivar Oxaal and Walter R. Weitzmann, "The Jews in Pre-1914 Vienna: An Exploration of Basic Sociological Dimensions," *YBLI* XXX (1985): 395ff.

7. *Österreichische Statistik*, Old Series, I/2, pp. 2–3; XXXII/1, pp. 46–47; LXIII/1, pp. 48–49; New series II, p. 33.

8. Anson G. Rabinbach, "The Migration of Galician Jews to Vienna 1857–1880" in *AHY* IX (1975): 44–54.

9. Schmidtbauer, p. 62; and *Bericht des Burgermeisters* (Vienna: 1884) as quoted in Oxaal and Weitzmann, p. 400. Comp. the contemporary report in *Die Weckstimme* XII, no. 9, p. 22.

10. A. Scott Eddy's reply to Rabinbach in *AHY* IX (1975): 55ff.; and Rozenblit, Op. Cit., pp. 215–16, n. 31.

ABBREVIATIONS USED IN NOTES
AND BIBLIOGRAPHY

AAJRP	*American Academy for Jewish Research. Proceedings*
ADB	*Allgemeine Deutsche Biographie*
AH	*Acta Historica* (Prague)
AHR	*American Historical Review*
AHY	*Austrian History Yearbook*
AJFF	*Archiv für Jüdische Familienforschung*
AKÖGQ	*Archiv für Kunde Österreichischer Geschichts-Quellen*
ARSS	*Actes de la Recherche en Sciences Sociales*
ASS	*Archives de Sciences Sociales*
A/W	*Archiv der Israelitische Kultusgemeinde*
AZJ	*Allgemeine Zeitung des Judentums*
BIISH	*Bulletin of the International Institute of Social History*
BJCC	*Bohemia: Jahrbuch des Collegium Carolinum*
BL	*Biographische Lexicon (Würzbach)*
BLBI	*Bulletin des Leo Baeck Instituts*
ČČH	*Český Časopis Historický*
CEH	*Central European History*
CHR	*Catholic Historical Review*
CI	*Corriere Israelitico*
ČSČH	*Československý Časopis Historický*
CO	*Osterreichisches Central Organ für Glaubensfreiheit*
DÖLG	*Deutsch-Österreichische Literaturgeschichte*
DS	*Dějiny a Součastnost*
ECE	*East Central Europe*
EEQ	*East European Quarterly*
Egy	*Az Egyenlöség*
EJ	*Encyclopaedia Judaica*
GJNB	*Grosse Jüdische National-Biographie*
GuG	*Geschichte und Gesellschaft*
HJ	*Historica Judaica*
HJS	*Hungarian Jewish Studies*
Isr	*Der Israelit*
JCEEA	*Journal of Central and East European Affairs*
JCH	*Journal of Contemporary History*
JEH	*Journal of Economic History*
JFF	*Jüdische Familienforschung*
JGG	*Jahrbuch der Grillparzer Gesellschaft*
JGGJT	*Jahrbuch der Gesellschaft für die Geschichte der Juden in der Tschechos-lowakei*
JIDG	*Jahrbuch des Instituts für Deutsche Geschichte*
JJGL	*Jahrbuch für Jüdische Geschichte und Literatur*
JJLG	*Jahrbuch der Jüdischen Literarischen Gesellschaft*
JJVK	*Jahrbuch für Jüdische Volkskunde*
JMH	*Journal of Modern History*
JSS	*Jewish Social Studies*
JVGSW	*Jahrbuch des Vereines für Geschichte der Stadt Wien*
MAD	*Monatsblatt Adler*
MGJFF	*Mitteilungen der Gesellschaft für Jüdische Familienforschung*

MGWJ	*Monatsschrift für Geschichte und Wissenschaft des Judenthums*
MIÖG	*Mitteilungen des Instituts für Österreichische Geschichtsforschung*
MJVK	*Mitteilungen zur Jüdischen Volkskunde*
MÖSA	*Mitteilungen des Österreichischen Staatsarchivs*
MStK	*Magyar Statisztikai Közlemények*
MZsL	*Magyar Zsidó Lexikon*
MZsO	*Magyar Zsidó Oklevéltár*
MZsSz	*Magyar Zsidó Szemle*
NFP	*Die Neue Freie Presse*
NJM	*Neue Jüdische Monatshefte*
NZ	*Die Neuzeit*
ÖBL	*Österreichisches Biographisches Lexikon*
ÖGL	*Österreich in Geschichte und Literatur*
ÖJB	*Österreichisches Jahrbuch*
Or	*Orient*
ÖRS	*Österreichische Rundschau*
OSN	*Ottuv Slovník Naučný*
ÖSt	*Österreichische Statistik*
ÖW	*Österreichische Wochenschrift*
PHS	*Právně-Historické Studie*
PP	*Past and Present*
PSB	*Polski Slownik Biograficzny*
PSH	*Pražský Sborník Historický*
RA	*Reichsrath Almanach*
RÉJ	*Revue des Études Juives*
RHM	*Revue d'Histoire Moderne*
RMI	*Rassegna Mensile di Israel*
RSR	*Rassegna Storica del Risorgimento*
SEER	*Slavic and East European Review*
SG	*Semigothäisches Genealogisches Taschenbuch, 1913*
SHASH	*Studia Historica Academiae Scientiarum Hungariae*
SJA	*Studia Judaica Austriaca*
SMS	*Statistische Monatschrift*
SODA	*Südostdeutsches Archiv*
SR	*Slavic Review*
TSz	*Történeti Szemle*
UJB	*Ungarn Jahrbuch*
VA	*Verwaltungsarchiv*
VSWG	*Vierteljahrschrift für Sozial- und Wirtschaftsgeschichte*
WGB	*Wiener Geschichtsblätter*
WGT	*Wiener Genealogisches Taschenbuch*
WKZ	*Wiener Kirchenzeitung*
WM	*Wiener Mitteilungen*
WZ	*Wiener Zeitung*
YLBI	*Yearbook of the Leo Baeck Institute*
YVS	*Yad Vashem Studies*
ZDS	*Zeitschrift für Demographie und Statistik*
ZGJT	*Zeitschrift für die Geschichte der Juden in der Tschechoslowakei*
ZNUJ	*Zeszyty Naukowe Universitetu Jagiellonskiego*
ZRGG	*Zeitschrift für Religions- und Geistesgeschichte*
ZVSV	*Zeitschrift für Volkswirtschaft, Sozialpolitik und Verwaltung*

NOTES

ONE. INTRODUCTION

1. Gershom Scholem, *Sabbatai Sevi: The Mystical Messiah, 1626–1676* (Princeton: Princeton University Press, 1973), pp. 461ff., 474–75, and 559–61; and David Kaufmann, *Die letzte Vertreibung der Juden aus Wien und Niederösterreich, ihre Vorgeschichte und ihre Opfer* (Vienna: Carl Konegen, 1889), pp. 91–92.

2. Arthur Ruppin, *Soziologie der Juden* (2 vols., Berlin: Jüdischer Verlag, 1930–31), vol. I, p. 72. Prague, Venice, and Amsterdam were larger with perhaps 10,000, 6,000, and 4,000 Jews respectively. There were larger communities also in the east at Constantinople and Salonika.

3. The classic work on the expulsion is Kaufmann, *Letzte Vertreibung*. The subject was reviewed by Max Grunwald in *Samuel Oppenheimer und sein Kreis* (Vienna: W. Braumüller, 1913), ch. 1, and in his "Geschichte der Juden in Wien, 1625–1740" in Heinrich Zimmermann (ed.), *Geschichte der Stadt Wien* (6 vols., Vienna: Adolf Holzhausen, 1897–1918), vol. V (1914), pp. 65–99. Many relevant documents appear in the classic works on Viennese Jewish history: Alfred Francis Pribram, *Urkunden und Akten zur Geschichte der Juden in Wien* (2 vols, Vienna: W. Braumüller, 1918), vol. I, pp. 197–253; and Israel Taglicht (ed.), *Nachlasse der Wiener Juden im 17. und 18. Jahrhundert* (Vienna: Braumüller, 1917). There are informed briefer accounts in Hans Rotter and Adolf Schmieger, *Das Ghetto in der Wiener Leopoldstadt* (Vienna: Burgverlag, 1926); Ludwig Bato, *Die Juden im alten Wien* (Vienna: Phaidon, 1928), pp. 14ff.; Hans Tietze, *Die Juden Wiens* (1933), pp. 68–77; and Walther Pichler, *Von der Synagoge zur Kirche, Zur Entstehungsgeschichte der Pfarre St. Leopold, Wien II* (Vienna: Dom Verlag, 1974), chs. 2, 3.

4. Josef Fraenkel (ed.), *The Jews of Austria: Essays on their Life, History and Destruction* (London: Vallentine, Mitchell, 1967); Hugo Gold (ed.), *Geschichte der Juden in Österreich. Ein Gedenkbuch* (Tel Aviv: Olamenu, 1971); Harry Zohn, *Österreichische Juden in der Literatur* (Tel Aviv: Olamenu, 1969); and Wolfdieter Bihl, "Die Juden" in Adam Wandruszka and Peter Urbanitsch, *Die Habsburger Monarchie* (4 vols., Vienna: Akademie, 1972-), vol. III/2, pp. 927ff.

5. Arthur Ruppin, *Die Juden der Gegenwart* (Berlin: Jüdischer Verlag, 1920), pp. 32–33, and his *Soziologie der Juden*, vol. I, pp. 90–92.

6. Otto Bauer, *Die Nationalitätenfrage und die Sozialdemokratie* (Vienna: Brand, 1907), esp. pp. 367ff.

7. Saul K. Padover, *Karl Marx on Religion*, vol. V. of his *Karl Marx Library* (New York: McGraw Hill, 1974), pp. 169–93.

8. Werner Sombart, *The Jews and Modern Capitalism* (New York: Collier, 1962; orig. pub. 1913).

9. A solid recent discussion of modernization in Habsburg Europe is David E. Good, *The Economic Rise of the Habsburg Empire, 1750–1914* (Berkeley: University of California Press, 1984). For a discussion of methodologies see Katherine Verdery, *Transylvanian Villagers* (Berkeley: University of California Press, 1983), ch. 1.

10. Oszkar Jászi, *Dissolution of the Habsburg Monarchy* (Chicago: University of Chicago Press, 1961), pp. 170ff.

11. Georg Franz, *Liberalismus* (Munich: Callwey, 1955), pt. II.

12. Bauer, *Die Nationalitätenfrage*, esp. pp. 367ff. For the "self"-denial record of other Jewish socialists, see Edmund Silberner, *Sozialisten zur Judenfrage* (Berlin: Colloquium Verlag, 1962); and Robert S. Wistrich, *Socialism and the Jews* (East Brunswick, N.J.: Associated University Presses, 1982), esp. ch. 8.

13. In the Jewish context self-hatred was given broad currency by the anti-

Semite Theodor Lessing in a collection of character sketches published as *Der jüdische Selbsthass* (Berlin: Mänicke & Jahn, 1930). There are explicatory discussions by Kurt Lewin in an essay originally published in 1941, "Self Hatred among Jews," republished in his *Resolving Social Conflicts: Selected Papers on Group Dynamics* (New York: Harper & Bros., 1948), pp. 186–200; Peter Gay in *Freud, Jews and Other Germans* (New York: Oxford University Press, 1978), pp. 195ff.; Gershom Scholem, "Zur Sozialpsychologie der Juden in Deutschland" in Rudolf von Thadden (ed.), *Die Krise des Liberalismus zwischen den Weltkriegen* (Göttingen: 1978); Hans Dieter Hellige, "Generationskonflikt, Selbsthass und die Entstehung antikapitalisticher Positionen im Judentum" in *GuG* V (1979): 476–518; and Sander L. Gilman, *Jewish Self-Hatred* (Baltimore: Johns Hopkins University Press, 1986). For this theme see also John M. Cuddihy, *The Ordeal of Civility* (New York: Delta, 1974).

14. On the universality of self-hatred see Isaiah Berlin's essay on Disraeli and Marx in *Against the Current* (New York: Viking, 1980), p. 255.

15. Kraus referred to Austria as a *Versuchsstation des Weltunterganges* in his editorial in *Die Fackel* about the assassination of Franz Ferdinand in June 1914: see Heinrich Fischer (ed.), *Gesammelte Werke von Karl Kraus* (14 Vols, Munich: Kösel Verlag, 1952–1967), vol. VIII, p. 418.

16. For the following, comp. Karl W. Deutsch, *Nationalism and Social Communications* (Cambridge, Mass.: The M.I.T. Press, 1953 and 1966); and also the useful essays by John Armstrong and Jeremy Azrael in Jeremy Azrael (ed.), *Soviet Nationality Policies and Practices* (New York: Praeger, 1978), chs. 3 and 12. The importance of borderline study is stressed by Fredrik Barth in his introduction to Fredrik Barth (ed.), *Ethnic Groups and Boundaries: The Social Organization of Cultural Difference* (Boston: Little, Brown, 1969), pp. 15ff. See also the discussion of methodological problems in R. A. Schermerhorn, *Comparative Ethnic Relations* (Chicago: University of Chicago Press, 1978); Anthony D. Smith, *Theories of Nationalism* (New York: Harper & Row, 1971); and Karl W. Deutsch and William J. Foltz (eds.), *Nation Building* (New York: Atherton, 1966), ch. 1.

17. For these problems, see especially Ernst Bruckmüller, *Nation Österreich: Sozialhistorische Aspekte ihrer Entwicklung* (Vienna: Böhlau, 1984); and Peter F. Sugar, "External and Domestic Roots of Eastern European Nationalism" in Peter F. Sugar and Ivo J. Lederer, *Nationalism in Eastern Europe* (Seattle: University of Washington Press, 1969), pp. 3ff.

18. For discussion of assimilation, see Milton M. Gordon, *Assimilation in American Life* (New York: Oxford, 1964); Marsha L. Rozenblit, *The Jews of Vienna, 1867–1914* (Albany: State University of New York, 1983); Peter Hanák, "Problems of Jewish Assimilation in Austria-Hungary in the Nineteenth and Twentieth Centuries" in P. Thane et al (eds.), *The Power of the Past* (Cambridge: Cambridge University Press, 1984), ch. 10; Hanak's "Stages and Types of National Assimilation in Hungary in the 19th Century" (unpub. paper, Budapest, 1983). A radical indictment of the old "melting pot" theory is Walter Connor, "The Ethnopolitical Challenge and Governmental Response" in Peter F. Sugar (ed.), *Ethnic Diversity and Conflict in Eastern Europe* (Santa Barbara, Calif.: ABC-Clio, 1980), pp. 147ff. I have studied the assimilation of Jews in *Jewish Nobles and Geniuses in Modern Hungary* (New York and Boulder, Colo.: Columbia University Press, 1972).

TWO. THE FIRST DECISIONS

Standard accounts of modern Habsburg history are Imre Gonda and Emil Niederhauser, *A Habsburgok* (Budapest: Gondolat, 1977); Adam Wandruszka, *The House of Habsburg* (Garden City, NY.: Doubleday, 1965); R. J. W. Evans, *The Making of the Habsburg Monarchy* (Oxford: Clarendon, 1979); Hugo Hantsch, *Die Geschichte Öster-*

reichs (2 vols., Graz: Styria Verlag, 1959); Friedrich Heer, *Der Kampf um die österreich-ische Identität* (Vienna: Böhlau, 1981); Robert A. Kann, *A History of the Habsburg Empire* (Berkeley: University of California Press, 1974); C. A. Macartney, *The Habsburg Empire, 1790–1918* (London: Weidenfeld and Nicolson, 1968); Victor-L. Tapié, *The Rise and Fall of the Habsburg Monarchy* (New York: Praeger, 1971); Erich Zöllner, *Geschichte Österreichs* (Munich: Oldenbourg Verlag, 1966). For Bohemia's history see in addition Karl Bosel (ed.), *Handbuch der Geschichte der böhmischen Länder* (4 vols., Stuttgart: Anton Hiersemann, 1966–74).

For the history of the Jews, see in general Salo W. Baron, *A Social and Religious History of the Jews* (2nd rev. ed.; 16 vols., New York: Columbia University Press, 1976); Simon Dubnow, *History of the Jews* 4th ed.; 4 vols., New York: T. Yosseloff, 1971); and Bernard Martin, *History of Judaism* (2 vols., New York: Basic Books, 1974).

1. An indispensable guide to the history of the Bohemian Jewry is Otto Muneles, *Bibliografický Přehled Židovské Prahy* (Prague: Orbis, 1952). Valuable for the more distant past is Abraham Stein, *Die Geschichte der Juden in Böhmen* (Brünn: H. Rickl, 1904), and the collection of essays—in effect a survey of Bohemian Jewish history—in Ferdinand Seibt (ed.), *Die Juden in den böhmischen Ländern* (Munich: Oldenbourg, 1983). For the eighteenth and early nineteenth centuries see Ruth Kestenberg-Gladstein, *Neuere Geschichte der Juden in den böhmischen Ländern* (Tübingen: Mohr, 1969); and Hillel Kieval, "The Modernization of Jewish Life in Prague, 1780–1830" in Jakob Katz (ed.), *Toward Modernity: The European Jewish Model* (New Brunswick: Transaction Books, 1986); ill organized and non-analytical but full of interesting data are Hugo Gold (ed.), *Die Juden und Judengemeinden Böhmens* (orig. pub. Brünn: Jüdischer Verlag, 1929; reissued Tel Aviv: Olamenu, 1970); and his *Die Juden und Judengemeinden Mährens* (same data).

2. An overview of eighteenth-century Habsburg Jewry is Meier Kristianpoler, "Die wirtschaftliche Lage der Juden in Österreich in der 2. Hälfte des 18. Jahrhunderts" (unpub. diss., Vienna, 1930). For Hungary, see Lajos Venetianer, *A magyar zsidóság története* (Budapest: Fővárosi nyomda, 1922); and Erno Laszlo, "Hungarian Jewry: Settlement and Demography, 1735–38 to 1910" in *HJS*, vol. I, pp. 61ff.

3. For the following, see Gerson Wolf, "Statistik der Juden in Böhmen, Mähren und Schlesien im Jahre 1754" in *Ben Chananja*, vol. VII (1864), pp. 810–21; and Gustav Otruba's statistical appendix in Seibt (ed.), *Die Juden in den böhmischen Ländern*, p. 324; the detailed statistics on Prague's Jewish population in Wilfried Brosche, "Das Ghetto von Prag" in ibid., pp. 117–19; and Jan Heřman, "The Evolution of the Jewish Population in Bohemia and Moravia, 1754–1953" in U. O. Schmelz et al. (eds.), *Papers in Jewish Demography, 1973* (Jerusalem: Inst. Contemp. Jewry, 1977), pp. 255–64

4. The Czech demographer Otto Placht estimates that there were about 2,160,776 people in Bohemia in 1726 and 900,000 in Moravia, making the Jews about 2% of the total in Bohemia and about 2.5% in Moravia. In Prague he estimates that every fourth inhabitant was Jewish: *Lidnatost a spoločenská skladba českého státu v 16–18 stoletf* (Prague: ČSAV, 1957), pp. 320 and 310.

5. Useful background for the following may be found in William McNeill, *The Rise of the West* (Chicago: University of Chicago Press, 1963); Immanuel Wallerstein, *The Modern World System* (2 vols, New York: Academic Press, 1974–1980); and L. Makkai, "Die Entstehung der gesellschaftlichen Basis des Absolutismus in den Ländern der österreichischen Habsburger," *SHASH* XLIII (Budapest: Akademiai Kiadó, 1960), pp. 6ff.

6. Jerome Blum, "The Rise of Serfdom in Eastern Europe," *AHR* LXII (1957): 807–836; Victor-L. Tapié, *The Rise and Fall of the Habsburg Monarchy*, pp. 72ff.; the parallel essays by László Makkai, William E. Wright, and Béla K. Király in *SR* XXXIV (1975): 225–79; Z. S. Pach, *Agrarian Development in Western Europe and Hungary* (Budapest: Corvina, 1963); R. Rozdolsky, "The Distribution of Agrarian Products in

Feudalism," *JEH* XI (1951): 247–65; and his "On the Nature of Peasant Serfdom in Central and Eastern Europe," *JCEEA* XII (1952–53); 128–39.

7. Tobias Jakubovitz, "Das prager und böhmische Landesrabbinat" in *JGGJT* V (1932), esp. 79–80; Lajos Venetianer, *A zsidóság szervezete az Europai államokban* (Budapest: Franklin Társulat, 1901), pp. 302ff.; the articles on "Bohemia," "Prague," "Moravia," and "Landesjudenschaft" in the *EJ*; and on the general subject of Jewish self-government, Jakob Katz, *Tradition and Crisis* (Glencoe: Free Press, 1961), esp. ch. 13; and S. L. Baron, *The Jewish Community* (Philadelphia: JPSA, 1942).

8. Kestenberg-Gladstein, *Neuere Geschichte*, pp. 6–7; and pt. III/B.

9. William E. Wright, *Serf, Seigneur and Sovereign: Agrarian Reform in 18th Century Bohemia* (Minneapolis: University of Minnesota Press, 1966), chs. 1–3.

10. Comp. Jean Bérenger, *Finances et absolutisme autrichien dans la seconde moitié du XVIIe siécle* (Paris: Imprimerie Nationale, 1975), pp. 306–308.

11. Selma Stern, *The Court Jew* (Philadelphia: JPSA, 1950), ch. 1; Heinrich Schnee, *Die Hoffinanz und der moderne Staat* (6 vols, Berlin: Duncker und Humblot, 1953–1967), pt. 7; and Baron, *Social and Religious History*, vol. XIV, ch. 52.

12. See the reviews of Habsburg administrative reforms in Friedrich Walter, *Österreichische Verfassungs-und Verwaltungsgeschichte, 1500–1955* (Vienna: Böhlau, 1972); and Ernst C. Hellbling, *Österreichische Verfassungs-und Verwaltungsgeschichte* (2nd. ed., Vienna: Springer Verlag, 1974).

13. On the great Jesuit dramas in Vienna, see Joseph Gregor, *Österreichische Theatergeschichte* (Vienna: Donauverlag, 1948), pp. 75ff.; W. Flemming, *Geschichte des Jesuitentheaters in den Ländern deutscher Zunge* (Berlin: Selbstverlag, 1923); and André Tibal, *L'Autrichien: Essais sur la formation d'une individualité* (Paris: Berger-Levrault, 1936).

14. Heer, *Kampf um die österreichische Identität*, ch. 3; and Robert Kann, *A Study of Austrian Intellectual History* (New York: Praeger, 1960), ch. 2.

15. By far the most important study of Oppenheimer is Grunwald's *Samuel Oppenheimer und sein Kreis*; but see also Ferenc Szakály: "Oppenheimer Sámuel müködése különös tekintettel Magyarországi kihatásaira" in *MZsO* XIV (1971): 31–78; Josef Mentschl and Gustav Otruba, *Österreichische Industrielle und Bankiers* (Vienna: Bergland Verlag, 1965), pp. 9–19; the extensive references in Jean Bérenger, *Finances et absolutisme autrichien*; and Michael Wagner, "Zwischen zwei Staatsbankrotten: Der Wiener Finanzmarkt im 18. Jahrhundert" in *WGB* XXXII (1977): 114.

16. See the assessment in Szakály, "Oppenheimer," p. 66; and Bérenger, *Finances et absolutisme*, pp. 203–205, 269, 459.

17. Hantsch, *Die Geschichte Österreichs*, vol. II, p. 94.

18. Ignac Biedermann, *Die Wiener Stadtbank*, in *AKÖGQ* 1858–59: 352–53; and Szakály, "Oppenheimer Samuel," 31–32.

19. For the rise of the Greeks in eighteenth-century central Europe, see especially Trajan Stoianovich, "The Conquering Balkan Merchant," *JEH* XXX (1960): 274ff.; and Georgiou S. Laiou, *Simon Sinas* (Athens: Akademia, 1972). On the Turkish Jews of Vienna, see Rudolf Till, "Geschichte der spanischen Juden in Wien," *JVGSW* V-VI (1946–47): 110ff.; M. Schleicher, "Geschichte der spaniolen Juden in Wien," (unpub. diss., Vienna, 1933); and N. M. Gelber, "The Sephardic Community in Vienna," *JSS* X (1948): 359–89.

20. See J. Bergel, "Die Ausweisung der Juden aus Prag im Jahre 1744" in B'nai B'rith . . . Praga, *Die Juden in Prag. Bilder aus ihrer tausendjährigen Geschichte* (Prague: Bücherstube, 1927), pp. 187–247; and his "Das Exil der Prager Judenschaft," *JGGJT* I (1929): 263–331.

21. This anecdote was reported by Hönig's grandnephew, Ludwig August Frankl, in his *Erinnerungen* (S. Hock, ed., Prague: Josef Koch, 1910), pp. 32–33.

22. Pribram, *Urkunden und Akten*, vol. I, p. 445, my trans.

23. Kristianpoler, "Die wirtschaftliche Lage," p. 47.

24. Pribram, *Urkunden und Akten*, vol. I, pp. 353–59.

25. Schnee, *Hoffinanz*, pt. VII, pp. 234–37; and Makkai, "Die Entstehung der gesellschaftlichen Basis," pp. 38ff.

26. Grunwald, *Oppenheimer*, pp. 217ff.; and David Kaufmann, *Samson Wertheimer, der Oberhoffaktor* (Vienna: Friedrich Beck, 1888).

27. For the following, see Samuel Kraus, *Joachim, Edler von Popper* (Vienna: private, 1925).

28. Kestenberg-Gladstein, *Neuere Geschichte*, esp. p. 109; and Hanns Jäger-Sunstenau, "Die geadelten Judenfamilien im vormärzlichen Wien" (unpub. diss., Vienna, 1950), sub nomine "Hönigsberg," "Hönigshof," and "Henikstein."

29. Christian W. Berghoeffer, *Mayer Amschel Rothschild* (Frankfurt am Main: Englert und Schlosser, 1922), ch. 4.

30. Arnost Klíma. *Manufakturní období v čechách* (Prague: ČSAV, 1955), p. 213.

31. For this thesis, see Heinrich Schnee, "Die Nobilitierung der ersten Hoffaktoren" in *AKG* XLIII (1961): 62–99; and his *Hoffinanz*, vol. IV, pp. 311–45.

32. For the following, see Kieval, "The Modernization," pp. 10ff.; Kestenberg-Gladstein, *Neuere Geschichte*, pp. 118ff.; Mahler, *History of Modern Jewry*, ch. 8; and Guido Kisch, *Die Prager Universität und die Juden* (Moravská Ostrava: Julius Kittl, 1935).

33. Michael A. Meyer, *The Origins of the Modern Jew* (Detroit: Wayne State University Press, 1967), ch. 1.

34. Kieval, "The Modernization of Jewish Life in Prague," pp. 15ff.; Gutmann Klemperer, "The Rabbis of Prague: 1609–1879," *HJ* XIII (1951): 55–74; the essay by Solomon Wind in Leo Jung (ed.), *Jewish Leaders* (New York: Bloch, 1953), pp. 77–98; F. Roubík in *JGGJT* IX (1938): 433–47; and *EJ* X: 1388–91.

35. See Dr. Weil, *Aaron Chorin: Eine biographische Skizze* (Szeged: S. Berger, 1863), chs. 2 and 4.

36. A bibliography of the older literature on Sonnenfels was published in 1931 by Michael Holzman and Max Portheim in *ZGJT* I: 198–207, and II: 60–66. The best older biographies are Wurzbach, *BL* XXXV: 315–17; Franz Kopetzky, *Josef und Franz von Sonnenfels* (Vienna, M. Perl, 1884); and Willibald Müller, *Josef von Sonnenfels* (Vienna: W. Braumüller, 1882). Modern biographies are J. Karniel, "Josef von Sonnenfels," *JIDG* VII (1978): 135ff.; Kann, *A Study of Austrian Intellectual History*, pp. 146–258; and Karl-Heinz Osterloh, *Joseph von Sonnenfels und die österreichische Reformbewegung im Zeitalter des aufgeklärten Absolutismus* (Lübeck: Matthiesen, 1970). There are more or less extensive remarks about Sonnenfels in most works on eighteenth-century Austria; for example in Bernard, *Jesuits and Jacobins*, ch. 2; and Leslie Bodi, *Tauwetter in Wien: Zur Prosa der österreichischen Aufklärung* (Frankfurt am Main: S. Fischer Verlag, 1977), pp. 39–43.

37. Valentin Urfus, "Osvícenství a ekonomická ideologie v Cechách," *PHS* XIV (1969): 201–202. For Sonnenfels's cameralism, see Louise Sommer, *Die österreichischen Kameralisten in dogmatische Darstellung* (2 vols., Vienna: Carl Konegen, 1920), vol. II, ch. 3. For the efforts to formulate a new manufacturing code, see Karl Pribram, *Geschichte der österreichischen Gewerbepolitik, 1740–1860* (Leipzig: Duncker und Humblot, 1907), pp. 535ff.

38. On the contribution to educational reform, see Sigmund Adler, *Die Unterrichtsverfassung Kaiser Leopolds II* (Vienna: Deuticke, 1917), pp. 97ff., and Adam Wandruszka, *Leopold II* (2 vols., Vienna: Herold, 1965), vol. II, pp. 249ff.

39. Sonnenfels, *Gesammelte Schriften* (10 vols., Vienna: Baumeister, 1783–87), vol. III, p. 221.

40. Karniel, "Sonnenfels," pp. 136ff. Several Jewish writers have presented Sonnenfels as totally withdrawn from the Jewish world, and indeed filled with "self hatred": see for example Tietze, *Die Juden Wiens*, pp. 107–109. Karniel seems correct in deprecating such treatments.

41. For example, in the drafting of Joseph II's Toleration Patent, Sonnenfels was consulted and was able to inform the state council about the importance of kosher food for Jews. Later on in 1795 he was named to a government commission for purifying the Talmud: see Pribram, *Urkunden und Akten*, vol. I, pp. 847ff., 494ff.; Majer Balaban, "Herz Homberg in Galizien," *JJGL* 19 (1916): 99. Comp. Alexander Altmann, *Moses Mendelssohn* (University, Alabama: University of Alabama Press, 1973), pp. 502–506, 838–40.

THREE. "SELF"-DENIAL BEGINS

On Galicia and its annexation, see Paul R. Magocsi, *Galicia: a Historical Survey and Bibliographical Guide* (Toronto: University of Toronto Press, 1983), esp. ch. 3; and Stanislaw Grodziski, *Historia ustroju spolecznopolitycznego Galicji 1772–1848* (Wroclaw: Ossolineum, 1971), ch. 1. Comp. the extensive discussions of conditions in post-partition Galicia in Henryk Grossmann, *Österreichs Handelspolitik mit Bezug auf Galizien in der Reformepoche 1772–1790* (Vienna: C. Konegen, 1914), pp. 26ff.

On the Galician Jews, see in general S. M. Dubnow, *History of the Jews in Russia and Poland* (3 vols., Philadelphia: JPSA, 1916), vol. I.; Filip Friedman, "Dzieje Żydów w Galicji; 1772–1914," in Ignacy Schiper, A. Tartakower, and A. Hafftka (eds.), *Żydzi w Polsce Odrodzonej* (2 vols., Warsaw: private, 1932–33), vol. I, ch. 17; Bernard D. Weinryb, *The Jews of Poland* (Philadelphia: JPSA, 1972); Majer Balaban, *Dzieje żydów w Galicji i w Rzeczypospolitej Krakowskiei, 1772–1868* (Lwów: B. Poloniecki, 1914); I. Schiper, "Die galizische Judenschaft in den Jahren 1772–1848 in wirtschaftsstatistischer Beleuchtung," *NJM* II (1918); and Mahler, *A History of Modern Jewry*, pp. 314–41, 495–525, and 587–601.

1. M. Stöger, *Darstellung der gesetzlichen Verfassung der galizischen Juden* (2 vols., Lwow: 1833), vol. I, pp. 60–62; Balaban, *Dzieje Żydów*, pp. 21, 9; and Grodziski, *Historia ustroju*, pp. 99–100.

2. For contemporary observations, see Wolfgang Häusler, *Das galizische Judentum in der Habsburgermonarchie* (Vienna: Verlag für Geschichte und Politik, 1979).

3. Paul von Mitrofanov, *Joseph II* (German trans. by V. von Demelic; 2 vols., Vienna: C. W. Stern, 1910); François Fejtö, *Un Habsbourg révolutionnaire* (Paris: Plon, 1953); Paul Bernard, *Joseph II* (New York: Twayne, 1968); T. C. W. Blanning, *Joseph II and Enlightened Despotism* (London: Longmans, 1970); and Elisabeth Bradler-Rottmann, *Die Reformen Kaiser Josephs II* (Göppingen: Alfred Kämmerle, 1973).

4. Erika Weinzierl, "Der Toleranzbegriff in der österreichischen Kirchenpolitik" in *XIIe Congrès International des Sciences Historiques: Rapports* (Horn-Vienna: Ferdinand Berger, 1965), vol. I, *Grand Thèmes*, pp. 135ff.; Charles H. O'Brien, *Ideas of Religious Toleration at the Time of Joseph II* (Philadelphia: American Philosophical Society, 1969), pp. 22ff.; and the recent collection of conference papers edited by Peter F. Barton, *Im Lichte der Toleranz* and *Im Zeichen der Toleranz* in *Studien und Texte zur Kirchengeschichte*, II/8 and II/9 (Vienna: Protestantverlag, 1981).

5. Pribram, *Urkunden und Akten*, vol. I, pp. 440–42, 476–77. A Jewish *Patent* for Bohemia was issued on 15 October 1781. One followed for Silesia on 15 December, for Lower Austria on 2 January 1782, for Moravia on 13 February 1782, for Hungary on 31 March 1783, for Galicia and the Bukowina on 7 May 1789. No Jewish patents were issued for Styria, Carinthia, or the Tyrol, where in general there were no Jews; or for Trieste, where the Jews preferred their older privileges and persuaded Joseph to confirm these on 1 May 1782. See Joseph Karniel, "Die Auswirkung des Toleranzpatents von 1781" in Peter F. Barton (ed.), *Im Zeichen der Toleranz*, pp. 203–220; and his "Das Toleranzpatent Kaiser Josephs II für die Juden Galiziens und Lodomeriens" in *JIDG* VI (1982): 55–71; both based on his "Hemediniuth klapej ham-

iuthim b'Mamlecheth Habsburg bil'mej Joseph II" (unpub. diss., 2 vols., Tel Aviv, 1980; inaccessible to me); Helene Kohn, "Beiträge zur Geschichte der Juden in Österreich unter Kaiser Joseph II" (unpub. diss., Vienna, 1919); Paul Bernard, "Joseph II and the Jews" in *AHY* IV-V (1968–69): 110ff.; and Wolfdieter Bihl, "Zur Entstehungsgeschichte des josephinischen Patents für die Juden Ungarns" in Heinrich Fichtenau and Erich Zöllner (eds.), *Beiträge zur neueren Geschichte Österreichs* (Vienna: Böhlau, 1979), pp. 282–87.

6. See for example Jacob Allerhand, *Toleranzpolitik und Kulturkampf* (Eisenstadt: Roetzer, 1982), pp. 14ff.

7. Johann Polek, "Josephs II Reisen nach Galizien und der Bukowina und ihre Bedeutung für letztere Provinz" in *Jahrbuch des Bukowiner Landesmuseums*, vol. III (1895); Ludwig Singer, "Zur Geschichte und Bedeutung des Toleranzpatentes vom 2 Jänner 1782" in *B'nai B'rith Mitteilungen für Österreich*, vol. XXXII (1932), p. 8.

8. See Herzberg, *The French Enlightenment and the Jews*, pp. 76–77.

9. Paul Bernard, *Joseph II and Bavaria* (The Hague: M. Nijhoff, 1965). Joseph's concern in May 1781 emerges clearly in Alfred von Arneth, *Joseph II und Leopold von Toscana Ihr Briefwechsel* (2 vols., Vienna: Braumüller, 1872), vol. I, pp. 32ff.

10. Jacob Katz convincingly argues the impossibility of a direct influence by Dohm on Joseph II in *Out of the Ghetto* (Cambridge, Mass.: Harvard University Press, 1973), p. 70.

11. W. Müller, *Sonnenfels*, pp. 28ff.; Pribram, *Urkunden und Akten*, vol. I, p. lxxx; and Hilde Spiel, *Fanny von Arnstein* (Frankfurt am Main: S. Fischer, 1962), pp. 106–108.

12. Meyer, *Origins of the Modern Jew*, ch. 2.

13. For the development of the religion/nation argument at the Vienna court, see Josef Karniel, "Fürst Kaunitz und die Juden" in *JIDG* XII (1983): 15–27. Comp. the minimizing discussion in Kurt Stillschweig, "Die nationalitätenrechtliche Stellung der Juden im alten Österreich" in *MGWJ* LXXXI (1937): 321ff.

14. Major older works on Frank are Heinrich Graetz's *Frank und die Frankisten: Eine Sekten-Geschichte* (Breslau: Grass, Barth und Co., 1868); Alexander Kraushaar, *Frank i Frankiści Polscy, 1726–1816* (2 vols., Cracow: G. Gebethner, 1895); Meir Balaban, *Letoldot ha-tenua ha-frankit* (2 vols., Tel Aviv: Dvir, 1934–35; inaccessible to me); and the favorable Zionist account in Israel Zinberg, *A History of Jewish Literature* (14 vols., trans. and ed. Bernard Martin; New York: KTAV, 1972-), vol. X, ch. 1. Gershom Scholem launched a rehabilition of Frank in 1937, finding him a terrifying but fascinating Jewish mystic: see "Redemption through Sin" in *The Messianic Idea in Judaism* (New York: Schocken, 1971), pp. 78–141; and "Frank, Jacob, and the Frankists" in *EJ*, Vol. VII, pp. 55–72. The polarization of Jewish historians about Frank survives in the contrast between Scholem's version and those of Bernard D. Weinryb, *The Jews of Poland*, ch. 11; and Arthur Mandel, *The Militant Messiah* (Atlantic Highlands, NJ: Humanities Press, 1979). See also Abraham G. Duker, "Polish Frankism's Survival" in *JSS* XXV (1963): 287–333; and "Frankism as a Movement of Polish-Jewish Synthesis" in Bela K. Kiraly (ed.), *Tolerance and Movements of Religious Dissent in Eastern Europe* (Boulder, Colorado; East European Quarterly, 1975), pp. 133–164.

15. See the account in Kraushaar, *Frank i Frankiści Polscy*, vol. I, which is based on chronicles long lost but now published in Hebrew by Hillel Levine (Jerusalem: Academy, 1985).

16. Weinryb, who is less than fond of the Frankists, estimates that about 600 converted: *The Jews of Poland*, pp. 254, 379. Duker, on the other hand, refers to "a few thousand": "Polish Frankism's Duration," pp. 300–301; and some of the older sources speak of "tens of thousands." Ludwik Korwin lists 46 neophyte ennoblements at the coronation Diet of 1764, and another 15 in 1765: see his *Szlachta Neoficka* (Cracow: Styl, 1939). Comp. Kraushaar, *Frank i Frankiści Polscy*, vol. I, ch. 28; and Ludwik Korwin, *Szlachta Mojzeszowa* (Cracow: Styl, 1938).

17. For the following, see Kraushaar, vol. II, chs. 1–5; Gershom Scholem, *Du Frankisme au Jacobinisme* (Paris: Gallimard, 1981); his "Ein Frankist: Moses Dobruschka und seine Metamorphosen" in Hugo Gold (ed.), *Max Brod Gedenkbuch* (Tel Aviv: Olamenu, 1969), pp. 77–99; Oskar K. Rabinowicz, "Jacob Frank in Brno" in Abraham A. Neuman and Salomon Zeitlin (eds.), *Jewish Quarterly Review: The Seventy-Fifth Anniversary Volume*, (Philadelphia: Jewish Quarterly Review, 1967), pp. 429–45; Samuel Krauss, "Schöndl Dobruschka" in Salomon Rappaport and M. Zikier (eds.), *Festschrift Armand Kaminka* (Vienna: Maimonides Institute, 1937), pp. 143–48; Gold (ed.), *Mähren*, p. 148; and Václav Žáček, "Dva Příspěvky k dějinám frankismu v českých zemích" in *JGGJT* IX (1938): 341–98, often cited in a German version.

18. The best evidence that Frank had some sort of high-level protection is the length of his stay at Brno. It can be documented that as early as 1775–76 he was denounced by Moravian rabbis to the Austrian authorities as a crypto-Jew and a heretic; but he was not forced to leave until January 1786 when, as we will see, Joseph II had another sort of reason for expelling him: see Rabinowicz, "Jakob Frank in Brno," for the documents; and also Paul Arnsberg's not always reliable *Von Podolien nach Offenbach. Die jüdische Heilsarmee des Jakob Frank* (Offenbach: W. Wagner, 1965), pp. 23ff.

19. Scholem, *Messianic Idea,* p. 126.

20. H. Jäger-Sunstenau, "Über die unberechtigte Führung von Adelstiteln," *Adler*, vol. V, no. 1–3, pp. 5ff.; his "Geadelte Judenfamilien," p. 71; Heinrich Weiss, "Die Judengesetzgebung der österreichische Regierung in Bezug auf den Realitätenbesitz, Ehe und Taufe vom Jahre 1848–1867" (unpub. diss. Vienna, 1927), p. 200; Gold: *Mähren*, p. 150; and Gerson Wolf, *Judentaufen in Österreich* (Vienna: Herzfeld und Bauer, 1863), p. 80.

21. VA, *Adelsakten* Adlersthal, 1776; Oskar K. Rabinowicz, "Wolf Eibenschütz" in *ZGJT* I (1931): 273; Jakob Katz, *Jews and Freemasons in Europe, 1723–1939* (Cambridge, Mass.: Harvard University Press, 1970), pp. 28, 236 n. 10; and Graetz, *Frank und die Frankisten*, p. 85.

22. Klaus Edel, *Karl Abraham Wetzlar, Freiherr von Plankenstern, 1715–1799* (Vienna: VWGÖ, 1975).

23. Scholem, *Du Frankisme au Jacobinisme*; Samuel Kraus, *Joachim, Edler von Popper*, pp. 75–78; and L. Ruzicka, "Die österreichischen Dichtera jüdischer Abstämmung Franz Thomas und Emanuel von Schönfeld," *MGJFF* IV (1928): 282–89. The servants are mentioned in the petitions for nobility in VA, *Adelsakten* Dobruschka-Schönfeld, 1778, reproduced in Schnee, *Hoffinanz*, vol. V, pp. 226–28.

24. Hermann Broch, *Hofmannsthal und seine Zeit* (Munich: Piperverlag, 1964), pp. 71ff.

25. Duker, "Polish Frankism's Duration," p. 289; and Scholem, "Redemption through Sin," p. 135.

26. Katz, *Jews and Freemasons*, pp. 40, 241 n. 65; Gustav R. Kuess and Bernhard Scheichelbauer, (eds.), *200 Jahre Freimaurerei in Österreich* (Vienna: Kerry, 1959), pp. 65–71; and Rosenstrauch-Königsberg, *Freimaurerei*, pp. 59–62.

27. Arnsberg, *Von Podolien nach Offenbach*, pp. 23–24, 123.

28. Sonnenfels published some autobiographical notes about his youth in Ignaz de Luca, *Das gelehrte Österreich* (2 vols., Vienna: Thom, 1776–78), pp. 143–81. For the following, see J. W. Nagl, Jakob Zeidler, and Eduard Castle, *Deutsch-österreichische Literaturgeschichte* (4 vols., Vienna: Carl Fromme, 1899–1914), vol. II, pp. 257ff.; Gunter Brosche, "Josef von Sonnenfels und das Wiener Theater," (unpub. diss., Vienna, 1962); Kann, *A Study of Austrian Intellectual History*, pp. 208ff.; Karl von Görner, *Der Hans Wurst-Streit in Wien und Joseph von Sonnenfels* (Vienna: Carl Konegen, 1884); and Gregor, *Österreichische Theatergeschichte*, pp. 133–37. On the difference between polyglot eighteenth-century Vienna and northern Germany, see

Leslie Bodi, *Tauwetter in Wien*, pp. 108ff., 29; and Friedrich Heer, *Kampf um die österreichische Identität*, ch. 5, esp. pp. 136ff.

29. Hillel Kieval, *The Making of Czech Jewry: National Conflict and Jewish Society in Prague. 1870–1918* (New York: Oxford University Press, 1987), ch. 2. I am obliged to Kieval for letting me see his book in manuscript form.

30. For the following, see Scholem, *Du Frankisme au Jacobinisme*, p. 56.

31. Bernard, *Jesuits and Jacobins*, pp. 77–79.

32. For the following, see Hans Wagner, "Die politische und kulturelle Bedeutung der Freimaurer im 18. Jahrhundert," in Heinz Ischreyt (ed.), *Beförderer der Aufklärung in Mittel- und Osteuropa* (Berlin: Ulrich Camen, 1979), pp. 79ff.; Edit Rosenstrauch-Königsberg, *Freimaurerei im josephinischem Wien: Aloys Blumauers Weg vom Jesuiten zum Jakobiner* (Vienna: Braumüller, 1975), p. 61; Ludwig Hammermayer, "Zur Geschichte der europäischen Freimaurerei und der Geheimgesellschaften im 18. Jahrhundert: Genese—Historiographie—Forschungsprobleme" in Ischreyt (ed.), pp. 9–68; and Eugen Lennhoff, *Politische Geheimbunden*, (Munich: Amalthea, 1966), pp. 17–109.

33. On the dating, see Katz, *Jews and Freemasons*, p. 222 n. 2. For the following, see pp. 41–42; and Scholem, "Ein verschollener jüdischer Mystiker" in *YLBI* VII (1962): 247–78; as revised in *Du Frankisme au Jacobinisme*, pp. 29–30.

34. Scholem, *Du Frankisme au Jacobinisme*, p. 34.

35. See the poems quoted in *ibid.*, pp. 24–25.

36. *Ibid.*, p. 94ff., which supersedes such older accounts as Egon Erwin Kisch, *Tales from Seven Ghettos* (London: R. Anscombe, 1948), pp. 21–41; Albert Mathiez, *La révolution et les étrangers* (Paris: Renaissance du livre, 1918), pp. 111–19, 142, 166, 176–79; and Mathiez, *Danton et la paix* (Paris: Renaissance du livre, 1919), pp. 179, 201, 217.

FOUR. VIENNA'S BOURGEOISIE

For the new course in Austria's history after 1790, see, apart from the standard general works, Wangermann's *From Joseph II to the Jacobin Trials* (London: Oxford University Press, 1959); Adam Wandruszka, *Leopold II* (2 vols., Vienna: Herold, 1965); Helmut Reinalter, *Aufgeklärter Absolutismus und Revolution* (Vienna: Böhlau, 1980); Victor Bibl, *Der Zerfall Österreichs* (2 vols, Vienna: Rikola Verlag, 1922, 1924); Bibl's *Kaiser Franz* (Leipzig: J. Gunther, 1938); Anton Springer, *Geschichte Österreichs seit dem Wiener Frieden 1809* (2 vols, Leipzig: S. Herzel, 1863, 1865); Heinrich von Srbik, *Metternich: Der Staatsmann und der Mensch* (3 vols., Munich: Bruckmann, 1925–1954). Bibl, in the books just cited, is hostile to Franz I. For favorable assessments, see Walter C. Langsam, *Franz the Good* (New York: Columbia University Press, 1949), ch. 4; Hermann Meynert, *Kaiser Franz I* (Vienna: Alfred Höldner, 1872), pp. 31–38; and Franz Hartig, *Genesis of the Revolution in Austria* in William Coxe, *History of the House of Austria from the Accession of Francis I to the Revolution of 1848* (4 vols.; London: George Bell, 1889), Vol. IV, pp. 11–13.

1. Johann Slokar, *Geschichte der österreichischen Industrie und ihre Förderung unter Kaiser Franz I* (Vienna: F. Tempsky, 1914), pp. 385ff.

2. For the standard works on Vienna Jewry, see ch. I, n. 3 above. Major histories of Vienna are Heinrich Zimmermann (ed.), *Geschichte der Stadt Wien* (6 vols., Vienna: Holzhausen, 1897–1918); and Friedrich Walther, *Die Geschichte einer deutschen Grossstadt an der Grenze* (3 vols., Vienna: Holzhausens Nachfolger, 1940–41). See also Ilse Barea's delightful and penetrating *Vienna* (New York: Knopf, 1967); and Felix Czeike (ed.), *Das grosse Wien Lexikon* (Vienna: Molden, 1974).

3. Pribram, *Urkunden und Akten*, vol. I, pp. liv, lvii, lvvi. For the later development of Vienna's population, see Appendix I.

4. Gustav Gugitz and A. Schlossar (eds.), Johann Pezzl, *Skizzen von Wien* (Graz: Leykam, 1923), ch. 46.

5. Bernard Wachstein, "Die Gründung der Wiener Chevra Kadischa im Jahre 1763," *MJVK* XIII (1910): 9–12. The persons involved may be identified by means of Wachstein's extraordinary notes to his *Die Inschriften des alten Judenfriedhofes in Wien* (2 vols., Vienna: Selbstverlag, 1930).

6. For the following see Pribram, *Urkunden und Akten*, vol. I, pp. 374ff., 608–10, and vol. II, pp. 120–132. The lists attribute professional status to each name, which may be matched with data in Wachstein, *Inschriften*.

7. Hilde Spiel, *Fanny Arnstein*, which unfortunately lacks footnotes; Wachstein, *Inschriften*, vol. II, pp. 294ff., 460ff., 574ff.; Max Grunwald, "Zur Familiengeschichte einiger Gründer der Wiener Chewra Kadischa" in *MJVK* (1910): 1–19; his *Oppenheimer*, pp. 340ff.; Schnee, "Adel aus dem Hoffaktorentum," pp. 328ff., and Renata Komanovitz, "Der Wirtschaftsadel unter Kaiser Franz II (I), in der Zeit von 1792 bis 1815" (unpub. diss., Vienna, 1974).

8. Wachstein, *Inschriften*, vol. II, pp. 358–370; Spiel, *Fanny Arnstein*,; Schnee, "Adel aus dem Hoffaktorentum," p. 331; Franz Putz, "Die österreichische Wirtschaftsaristokratie von 1815–1859" (unpub. diss., 2 vols., Vienna, 1975), vol. II, 366ff.; and A. Wiener, "B. G. Eskeles" in *Illustrierte Monatshefte für die gesamten Interessen des Judentums*, vol. I (1865), pp. 387–94.

9. Wachstein, *Inschriften*, vol. II, p. 461ff.; R. Granichstädten-Czerva in *Wiener Zeitung*, 16 May, 1954; Samuel Baron, *Die Judenfrage auf dem Wiener Kongress* (Vienna: Löwit, 1920), pp. 130ff.; and Leon Ruzicka in *MAD* (1931), pp. 17–31.

10. For the following, see Pribram, *Urkunden und Akten*, pp. civ ff.; Tietze, *Die Juden Wiens*, pp. 13ff.; and Johann Ludwig Ehrenreich, Graf von Barth-Barthenstein, *Politische Verfassung der Israeliten im Lande unter der Ems und insbesondere in der k.k. Haupt- und Residenzstadt Wien* (Vienna: J. B. Wallishaussen, 1821).

11. Franz Baltzarek, "Das territoriale und bevölkerungsmässige Wachstum der Großstadt Wien im 17., 18. und 19. Jahrhundert" in *WGB* XXXV (1980): 9; Stephan Sedlaczek and Wilhelm Löwy, *Wien. Statistische Bericht über die wichtigsten demographischen Verhältnisse* (Vienna: Stat. Amt., 1887), pp. 1–11; and Felix Olegnik, "Historisch-statistische Übersichten von Wien." pt. I, in *Mitteilungen aus Statistik und Verwaltung der Stadt Wien, Sonderheft I* (Vienna: Mimeograph, 1956), pp. 8off. Vienna overtook Prague in the decades after 1683 and Hamburg about 1700, thus becoming for over a century the largest urban conglomeration of the German-speaking world. Brian R. Mitchell, *European Historical Statistics, 1750–1970* (London: Macmillan, 1975), pp. 76–78.

12. Andrea Baryli, "Gewerbepolitik und gewerberechtliche Verhältnisse im vormärzlichen Wien" in Felix Czeike (ed.), *Wien im Vormärz* (Vienna: Jugend und Volk, 1980), pp. 9ff.

13. Walther, *Geschichte einer deutschen Großstadt*, vol. II, pp. 300ff.; Viktor Thiel, "Gewerbe und Industrie" in Zimmermann (ed.), *Geschichte der Stadt Wien*, vol. IV (1911), pp. 411–503; Helene Kuraic. "Die Wiener Niederleger im 18. Jahrhundert" (unpub. diss., Vienna, 1946); Ferdinand Tremel, "Die Griechenkolonie in Wien im Zeitalter Maria Theresia" *VSWG*, vol. LI (1964), pp. 108–115: and N. B. Tomadakis, "Les communautés helléniques en Autriche" in Leo Santifaller (ed.), *Festschrift zur Feier des 200-jährigen Bestandes des Haus-, Hof-, und Staatsarchivs* (2 vols., Vienna: Staatsarchiv, 1951), vol. II, pp. 459ff.

14. Günther Chaloupek, "Wiens Grosshandel in der kommerziellen Revolution" in *WGB* XXXIX (1984): 105–125; Helene Landau, *Die Entwicklung des Warenhandels in Österreich* (Vienna, Leipzig: W. Braumüller, 1906), pp. 6ff.; Franz Baltzarek, "Finanzplatz Wien—Die innerstaatliche und internationale Stellung in historischer

Perspektive," in *Quartalhefte d. Girozentrale* XV (1980): no. 4, p. 22; and Karl Pribram, *Geschichte der österreichischen Gewerbepolitik* (only one volume published; Leipzig: Duncker and Humblot, 1907), pp. 238ff.

15. Hans Novogoratz, "Sebastian Brunner und der frühe Antisemitismus" (unpub. diss., Vienna, 1979), ch. 1.

16. For the following, see Anton Redl, *Adressenbuch der Handlungs Gremien und Fabriken in der KK. Haupt und Residenz Stadt Wien*, 1823 (Vienna: J. P. Sollingen, 1823); Herbert Matis, *Österreichs Wirtschaft 1848–1913* (Berlin: Dunker & Humbolt, 1972), ch. 3; Josef Mentschl, "Das österreichische Unternehmertum" in Wandruschka/Urbanitsch, *Die Habsburger Monarchie 1849–1918*, vol. I, ch. 6; Wolfgang Häusler, "Von der Manufaktur zum Maschinensturm" in Czeike (ed.), *Wien im Vormärz*, pp. 33ff.; and Josef Karl Mayr, *Wien im Zeitalter Napoleons* (Vienna: G. Gistel, 1940), esp. pt. III and pp. 174–77, 188ff.

17. Pezzl, *Skizzen von Wien*, pp. 514–515; and Kuttner, *Reise durch Deutschland*, vol. III, 16th letter, pp. 464–73.

18. Jaeger-Sunstenau, *Geadelte Judenfamilien*, pp. 76–77, 82–83.

19. For the following, see Michael Wagner, "Zwischen zwei Staatsbankrotten," *WGB* XXXII (1977): 115–23; Franz Baltzarek, *Die Geschichte der Wiener Börse* (Vienna: Akademie 1973), pp. 19ff.; his "Finanzplatz Wien," pp. 31–32; and Egon Scheffer, *Das Bankwesen in Österreich* (Vienna: Burgverlag, 1924), pp. 76ff.

20. Adolf Beer, *Die Finanzen Österreichs im XIX Jahrhundert* (Prague: F. Tempsky, 1877); and Scheffer, *Das Bankwesen*, pp. 60ff. The following statistics are conveniently presented by A. F. Pribram, *Materialien zur Geschichte der Preise und Löhne in Österreich* (Vienna: Carl Oberreiten, 1938), pp. 53ff.

21. See Paul Stiassny, *Der österreichische Staatsbankrott von 1811* (Vienna: Hölder, 1912).

22. Siegfried Pressburger, *Österreichische Notenbank 1816–1966* (Vienna: Nationalbank, 1966), ch. 1.

23. Hanns Von Mikoletzky, "Schweizer Händler und Bankiers in Österreich" in *Österreich und Europa, Festgabe für Hugo Hantsch* (Graz-Vienna: Böhlau, 1965), pp. 169ff.; Josef Mentschl and Gustav Otruba, *Österreichische Industrielle und Bankiers*; R. Granichstaedten-Czerva in *WZ*, 4 April 1954, p. 7; and Georgios S. Laios, *Simon Sinas* (Athens: Akademias, 1972), in Greek, but with documents and quotations in the original languages, and exhaustive bibliography.

24. Hellmuth Rössler, *Graf Johann Philipp Stadion* (2 vols., Vienna: Herold, 1966), vol. II, pp. 168ff.; Heinrich Schnee, *Rothschild. Geschichte einer Finanzdynastie* (Göttingen: Musterschmidt Verlag, 1961), pp. 62ff.; the same author's "Adel aus dem Hoffaktorentum," pp. 336–37; and Egon Count Corti's popular *Das Haus Rothschild* (2 vols., Leipzig: Insel Verlag, 1927, 1928), vol. I, pp. 203–205, 221–22. Bertrand Gille, in the most extensive and solidly documented work on the Rothschilds, unfortunately repeats the old legend that Gentz was responsible for the invitation: see *Histoire de la Maison Rothschild* (2 vols., Geneva : Droz, 1965, 1967), vol. I, p. 55. Paul Sweet disproved this long ago in his *Gentz* (Madison, Wisc.: University of Wisconsin Press, 1941), pp. 218–19.

25. Reinhold Lorenz, *Volksbewaffnung und Staatsidee in Österreich* (Vienna-Leipzig: 1926); Emil Karl Blümml (ed.), Caroline Pichler, *Denkwürdigkeiten aus meinem Leben* (Munich: G. Müller, 1914), pp. 197ff., and Josef Bindtner (ed.), J. F. Castelli, *Memoiren meines Lebens* (2 vols., Munich: G. Müller, 1913), vol. I, ch. 5. The patriotism manifest in Vienna in 1797, 1805, and 1809 has been the subject of much debate: see Eduard Winter, "Romantik" in *Revue d'Histoire ecclésiastique* (1927), pp. 81–102; Walter Langsam, *The Napoleonic Wars and German Nationalism in Austria* (New York: Columbia University Press, 1930); André Robert, *L'idée nationale autrichienne et les guerres de Napoléon* (Paris: Félix Alcan, 1933), pp. xix, 155; Winter's *Romantismus, Restauration und Frühliberalismus im österreichischen Vormärz* (Vienna: Europa Verlag,

1968), pp. 27ff., 48ff.; Friedrich Heer, *Kampf um die österreichische Identität*, chs. 5 and 6; and Bruckmüller, *Nation Österreich*, pp. 26ff., 57ff.. 103ff.

26. Edmund Friess, "Die Darlehen der Wiener Grosshändler und Niederleger, Juden und Griechen zum Wiener allgemeinen Aufgebote im Jahre 1797" in *MAD* IX (1921–25): 105–112.

27. For the following, see Joseph Gregor, *Geschichte des österreichischen Theaters*, chs. 5 and 6; and J. W. Nagl, Jakob Zeidler, and Eduard Castle (eds.), *DÖLG*, vol. II, ch. 4.

28. Bauernfeld, in a famous dictum, wrote; "For us (Austrians) the theatre was always a matter of major importance—a life question! In the good old times, when Kaiser Franz went to the Burgtheater every day, the Austrian government was in effect a 'theatocracy.' " Josef Bindtner (ed.), *Eduard Bauernfeld, Erinnerungen aus Alt-Wien* (Vienna: Wiener Drucke, 1923), p. 136. Comp. Frankl, *Erinnerungen*, pp. 142–148; Kuttner, *Reise durch Deutschland*, vol. III, letters 10 and 14, esp. pp. 378ff.; and Robert, *L'idée nationale, pp.* 205ff.

29. Donald E. Emerson, *Metternich and the Political Police* (The Hague: M. Nijhoff, 1968), pp. 150ff., 164ff., Heer, *Kampf*, p. 69, and the report quoted in Ilse Barea, *Vienna*, p. 151.

30. Antal Mádl, *Politische Dichtung in Österreich, 1830–1848* (Budapest: Akademia Kiadó, 1969), p. 12.

31. Karl August Varnhagen von Ense, *Denkwürdigkeiten des eigenen Lebens* (3 vols., Leipzig: F. A. Brockhaus, 1843), pt. I, ch. 16; and Pichler, *Denkwürdigkeiten*, vol. I, pp. 251ff., 579ff.

32. Spiel, *Fanny Arnstein*, pp. 260–61.

33. *Ibid.*, pp. 242, 250, 308, Hannah Arendt, *Rahel Varnhagen* (London: East and West, 1957), pp. 46–52; Hans Eichner, *Friedrich Schlegel* (New York; Twayne, 1970), ch. 3; Michael Meyer, *Origins of the Modern Jew*, ch. 4; Eugen Guglia, "Gesellschaft und Literatur im alten Österreich, 1792–1825" in *ÖRS* I (1883): 714–25, 829–42; and Robert, *L'idée nationale*, ch. 5.

34. Spiel, *Fanny Arnstein*, pp. 310, 313ff., 335ff., 354.

35. Nagl-Zeidler-Castle, *DÖLG*, vol. III, pp. 644ff.; and Andel, "Adelsverleihungen für Wirtschaftstreibende während der Regierungszeit Maria Theresias," pp. 292ff.; Komanovits, "Der Wirtschaftsadel unter Kaiser Franz," pp. 197ff.; and Spiel, *Fanny Arnstein*, pp. 310ff.

36. Meyer, *Origins of the Modern Jew*, pp. 98ff.; Eichner, *S. Schlegel*, ch. 6; Robert, *L'idée nationale*, p. 438ff.; Winter, *Romantismus, Restauration*, pp. 55ff., 61ff. and *passim*.

37. Rudolf Till, *Hofbauer und sein Kreis* (Vienna, Herold, 1951), ch. 5; Meyer, *Origins of the Modern Jew*, p. 97.

38. Spiel, *Fanny Arnstein*, p. 435.

39. Tietze, *Juden Wiens*, pp. 147ff., 162; Wolf, *Geschichte der Wiener Juden* (1876), p. 101; and Eleonore O. Sterling, "Anti-Jewish Riots in Germany, 1819" in *Historia Judaica*, vol. XII (1950), pp. 105ff.

40. Katz, *Out of the Ghetto*, ch. 4.; and the useful review of Katz's work by Stephen M. Poppel in *CEH* IX (1976): 87–90.

41. Heer, *Kampf*, pp. 178–80; Spiel, *Fanny Arnstein*, pp. 242, 260, 292, 308, 504; Auguste de la Garde, *Gemälde des Wiener Kongresses* (2 vols., Munich: G. Müller, 1914), vol. I, p. 389; Varnhagen von Ense, *Denkwürdigkeiten des eigenen Lebens*, vol. II, p. 173; vol. III, p. 237.

42. Obituary of Baron Eskeles in *AZJ* 34 (1839): 134–35; Baron, *Die Judenfrage auf dem Wiener Kongress*, p. 145; and Kestenberg-Gladstein, *Neuere Geschichte*, p. 346. Comp. the rebuttal in Spiel, *Fanny Arnstein*, pp. 446ff.

43. Frances Trollope, *Vienna and the Austrians* (London: R. Bentley, 1838), vol. II, ch. 53, and pp. 213ff.

FIVE. BOHEMIAN BREAKTHROUGH

For the industrialization of Austria, see in general David E. Good, *The Economic Rise of the Habsburg Empire, 1750–1914* (Berkeley: University of California Press, 1984); Aleksander Gerschenkron, *Economic Backwardness in Historical Perspective* (Cambridge, Mass.: Harvard University Press, 1962) and his elegant but violently polemical *An Economic Spurt That Failed* (Princeton: Princeton University Press, 1977); the advocacy of a "leisurely growth" thesis in Eduard März *Österreichische Industrie- und Bankpolitik in der Zeit Franz Joseph I* (Vienna: Europa Verlag, 1968); Richard L. Rudolph, *Banking and Industrialization in Austria-Hungary* (Cambridge: Cambridge University Press, 1976); Nachum T. Gross, "Industrialization in Austria in the Nineteenth Century" (unpub. diss., University of California at Berkeley, 1966); his *The Industrial Revolution in the Habsburg Monarchy, 1750–1914*, vol. V of Carlo M. Cipolla (ed.), *The Fontana Economic History of Europe* (London: Collins, 1972); *AHY* XI (1975): 3–43; Alois Brusatti, *Die wirtschaftliche Entwicklung*, vol. I of A. Wandruszka and P. Urbanitsch, *Die Habsburger Monarchie, 1848–1918* (Vienna: Akademie, 1973); and Heinrich Benedikt, *Wirtschaftliche Entwicklung in der Franz-Joseph-Zeit* (Vienna: Herold, 1958); and Pavla Horská-Vrbová, *Kapitalistická industrializace a středoevropská společnost* (Prague: Academia, 1970).

For the economy of Bohemia, see generally Karel Hoch, *Čechy na prahu moderního hospodářství* (Prague: A. Neubert, 1936); Arthur Salz, *Geschichte der böhmische Industrie in der Neuzeit* (Munich-Leipzig: Duncker und Humblot, 1913); Oldřich Řiha, *Hospodářský a socialně-politický vývoj Československa, 1790–1945* (Prague: Práce, 1946); František Roubík, *Z českých hospodářských dějin* (Prague: Státní Nakladadelství, 1948); *Přehled československých dějin* (3 vols., Prague: ČSAV, 1960).

For the first half of the nineteenth century, see especially Alois Brusatti, *Österreichische Wirtschaftspolitik vom Josephinismus zum Ständestaat* (Vienna: Jupiter, 1965); his "Unternehmungsfinanzierung und Privatkredit im österreichischen Vormärz" in *MIÖG* XIII (1960): 331–79; Slokar, *Geschichte der österreichischen Industrie* (Vienna: F. Tempsky, 1914); and Julius Marx, *Die wirtschaftlichen Ursachen der Revolution in Österreich* (Graz: Böhlau, 1965).

1. For the following see Herman Strach, "Geschichte der Eisenbahnen Oesterreich-Ungarns von den ersten Anfängen bis zum Jahre 1867" in Hermann Strach (ed.), *Geschichte der Eisenbahnen der oesterreichisch-ungarischen Monarchie* (Vienna: K. Prochaska, 1898), vol. I, pp. 94ff.

2. Heinrich Benedikt, *Alexander von Schoeller, 1805–1806* (Vienna: R. Spies, 1958).

3. Marx, *Die wirtschaftlichen Ursachen der Revolution*, pp. 41ff.; and Vera Vomáčková, "Die Bourgeoisie in Böhmen und der deutsche Zollverein im Jahre 1848" in Karl Obermann and Joseph Polišenský (eds.), *Aus 300 Jahren deutsch-tschechoslowakischer Geschichte* (Berlin: Akademie, 1958), pp. 223ff.

4. For the following, see Kieval, "The Modernization of Jewish Life," pp. 20ff.; Ignaz Böhm, *Historische Nachricht von der Entstehung und der Verbreitung des Normalschulinstituts in Böhmen* (Prag: 1784), pp. 139–42; Anton Weiss, "Zur Geschichte der theresianischen Schulreform in Böhmen" in *Beiträge zur österreichischen Erziehungs und Schulgeschichte* XII (1910); Wenzel Žaček, "Zu den Anfängen der Militärpflichtigkeit der Juden in Böhmen," *JGGJT* VII (1935): 268–70; S. M. Dubnow, *Neueste Geschichte des jüdischen Volkes*, vol. I, pp. 27–28; Ludwig Singer, "Zur Geschichte der Juden in Böhmen in den letzten Jahren Josephs II und unter Leopold II," *JGGJT* VI (1934): 230ff.; Altmann, *Mendelssohn*, pp. 487ff.; and Kestenberg-Gladstein, *Neuere Geschichte*, pp. 88ff.

5. Kieval, "The Modernization," esp. p. 32.

6. Kestenberg-Gladstein, *Neuere Geschichte*, pp 133-91.

7. Singer, "Zur Geschichte," p. 214ff.; Kraus, *Popper*, pp. 89-91; Schnee, *Hoffinanz*, vol. V, p. 230.

8. Kestenberg-Gladstein, *Neuere Geschichte*, pp. 337ff.; and the critique of her analysis by Christoph Stölzl, "Zur Geschichte der böhmischen Juden in der Epoche des modernen Nationalismus," *BJCC* XIV (1973): 190.

9. Simon Adler, "Das Judenpatent von 1797," *JGGJT* V (1933): 191-222; and Ludwig Singer, "Die Entstehung des Juden-Systemialpatentes von 1797," *ibid.* VII (1935): 199-263.

10. VA, *Adelsakten* Joel, 1817, 1843; Paul J. Diamant, "Dr. Rafael Joel (1762-1827)," *ZGJT* IV (1934): 10-17; Wurzbach, *BL*, vol. X, p. 224; and Wolf, *Geschichte* (1876), p. 98; comp. Gerson Wolf. *Judentaufen in Österreich* (Vienna: Herzfeld und Bauer, 1867), p. 101.

11. For the following, see Václav Žaček, "Dva příspěvky k dějinám frankismu v českých zemích," pp. 353ff.; Kestenberg-Gladstein, *Neuere Geschichte*, pp. 178ff.; Scholem, "Redemption through Sin," pp. 138ff.; his "A Sabbatian Will from New York," pp. 167ff.; N. M. Gelber, "Napoleons Judenstaatprojekte" in his *Vorgeschichte des Zionismus* (Vienna: Phaidon, 1927), p. 45; his "Zur Geschichte der Frankisten-propaganda im Jahre 1800" in *Aus zwei Jahrhunderten*, pp. 58-69; and S. H. Leiben, "Rabbi Eleazar Flekeles," *JJLG* X (1913): 20ff.

12. Roubík, "Zur Geschichte der Juden in Böhmen," *JGGJT* VII (1935): 365-68; Kieval, "The Modernization," p. 37; Singer, "Systemialpatent," pp. 257ff.; and Mahler, *History of Modern Jewry*, pp. 258ff.

13. František Roubík, "Z počátku spolku pro zlepšení izraelského kultu v Čechách," *JGGJT* IX (1938): 399-427; M. Teller, *Die Juden in Böhmen und ihre Stellung in der Gegenwart* (Prague: Silber und Schenk, 1863), pp. 28ff.; Peter Beer, *Reminiscenzen* (Prague: 1837), pp. 3ff., 27ff.; and Stölzl, "Zur Geschichte," pt. I, p. 195.

14. Michael K. Silber, "The Roots of the Schism in Hungarian Jewry" (unpub. diss. in Hebrew: Jerusalem, 1985), ch. 2. Dr. Silber has generously reviewed some of his work for me.

15. I. Barzilay, *Shlomo Yehuda Rapoport (Shir) and his Contemporaries* (Tel Aviv: Massada, 1969).

16. For the following, see Kieval, *The Making of Czech Jewry*, ch. 1; Kestenberg-Gladstein, "The Jews Between Czechs and Germans" in Hugh Colman (ed.), *The Jews of Czechoslovakia* (2 vols., Philadelphia: The Jewish Publication Society of America, 1968), vol. I, pp. 27ff.; Gary Cohen, "Jews in German Society, 1860-1914," *CEH* X (1977): 28ff.; and Stölzl, "Zur Geschichte der böhmischen Juden, II," *BJCC* XV, (1974): 129ff. For useful statistics, see Thon, *Juden in Österreich*, p. 15; G. A. Schimmer, *Statistik des Judenthums* (Vienna: Staatsdruckerei, 1873), p. 2; and his *Die Juden in Österreich* (Vienna: Hölder, 1881), p. 7.

17. Israel Jeiteles, *Die Kultusgemeinde der Israeliten in Wien* (Vienna: L. Rosner, 1873), p. 54; and Rozenblit, *The Jews of Vienna*, p. 35.

18. For the effects of the educational system on individual Jews, see Gotthilf Kohn, *Abraham Kohn im Lichte der Geschichtsforschung* (Zamarstynow bei Lemberg: Selbstverlag, 1898); and Wolfgang Haüsler, "Hermann Jellinek" in *JIDG* VI (1970): 181-213.

19. Arnošt Klíma, *Manufakturní Obdobi v Cechách*, esp. pp. 71ff.; and his articles "Industrial Development in the Bohemian Lands, 1648-1781," in *PP* XI (1957): 87-99; and "Über die grösste Manufakturen des 18. Jahrhunderts in Böhmen," *MÖSA* XII (1959): 143-61.

20. Siegfried Becher, *Statistische Übersicht der Bevölkerung der österreichischen Monarchie nach den Ergebnissen der Jahre 1834 bis 1840* (Stuttgart: Cotta, 1841), pp. 358-59.

21. For the following, see Bernhard Heilig, "Aufstieg und Verfall des Hauses

Ehrenstamm," in *BLBI* X (1960): 104ff.; Kestenberg-Gladstein, *Neuere Geschichte*, part III; and Kristianpoler, "Die wirtschaftliche Lage der Juden in Österreich in der 2. Hälfte des 18. Jahrhunderts," pp. 50ff., 105ff.; Slokar, *Geschichte*, ch. XVI; and Hermann Freudenberger's case history of a single factory, *The Industrialization of a Central European City: Brno and the Fine Woolen Industry in the 18th Century* (Edington, Wilts.: Pasold Research Fund, 1977).

22. Stölzl, "Zur Geschichte der böhmischen Juden," pt. I, p. 191, n. 60; R. Rürüp, *Emanzipation und Antisemitismus* (Göttingen: Vanderhoeck und Ruprecht, 1975), p. 26; and Jakob Toury, "Der Entritt der Juden ins deutsche Bürgertum" in H. Liebeschütz and A. Paucker (eds.), *Das Judentum in der deutschen Umwelt, 1800–1850* (Tübingen: Mohr, 1977), pp. 200ff.

23. Leopold Kompert in *Jahrbuch für Israeliten, 1847–1848*, pp. 120–144; and the classic works on the tobacco industry, Joseph von Retzer, *Tabakpachtung in den österreichischen Ländern von 1670–1783* (Vienna: Sonnleither, 1784); and Jerome E. Brooks (ed.), *Tobacco: Its History Illustrated by Books, Manuscripts and Engravings in the Library of George Arents Jr.* (5 vols., New York: Rosenback, 1937–1943), vol. III as indexed. For examples of the importance of tobacco contracts to the principal Jewish trading firms of central Europe, see the Presidial Index of the Finance Ministry at the Finanz Archiv in Vienna for 1830 and 1831.

24. Milan Švankmajer, "Simon Lämmel" in *DS* III (1961): 31ff.; Valentin Urfus, "Peněžníci předbřeznové Prahy" in *PHS* VII (1972): 111ff.; and Wurzbach, *BL* XIII, pp. 475ff.

25. J. Klingler, *Über die Unnütz und Schädlichkeit der Juden im Königreiche Böhmens, Mähren, und Österreich* (Prague: 1782), as quoted by Kestenberg-Gladstein, p. 98; Josef Rohrer, *Versuch über die jüdischen Bewohner der österreichischen Monarchie* (Vienna: Kunst und Industrie Comptoir, 1804), pp. 83–84.

26. Freudenberger, *Industrialization*, p. 132. It is clear that Jews played a vital role in the provisioning of the early Moravian textile factories with raw material, in financing them, and in marketing the finished cloth: see B. Heilig, "Die Vorläufer der mährischen Konfektionsindustrie," in *JGGJT* III (1931): 307–448. Only in the late 1840s, however, did Moravian Jews begin to emerge as textile industrialists in any numbers: Kestenberg-Gladstein, p. 106; and Gustav Otruba, "Der Anteil der Juden am Wirtschaftsleben" in Ferdinand Seibt (ed.), *Die Juden in den böhmischen Ländern*, esp. pp. 246–49.

27. Theodor Haas, *Die Juden in Mähren* (Brünn: Jüdischer Buch und Kunstverlag, 1908); and Alfred Willmann, "Die mährischen Landesrabbiner" in Gold, *Mähren*, pp. 45ff.; and Kestenberg-Gladstein, *Neuere Geschichte* pp. 359–61.

28. For the following, see Hoch, *Čechy na prahu*, pp. 117ff.; Jaroslav Purs, "The Industrial Revolution in the Czech Lands" in *Historica*, vol. II, pp. 183–272; Slokar, *Geschichte der österreichischen Industrie*; Herbert Hassinger, "Die Anfänge der Industrialisierung in den böhmischen Ländern" in *BJCC* II (1961): 164–81; and F. W. Carter, "The Industrial Development of Prague, 1800–1850," *SEER* LI (1973): 231ff.

29. VA *Adelsakten* Porges 1841; Wurzbach, *BL*, vol. XXIII, pp. 123–25; Putz, "Wirtschaftsaristokratie," vol. II, pp. 442–43; Moses Porges' obituary in *NZ*, 3 June 1870, p. 249.

30. Otruba, "Der Anteil," pp. 246–47; Kestenberg-Gladstein, *Neuere Geschichte*, p. 101.

31. Dukier, "Polish Frankism's Survival"; and his "Frankism as a Movement of Polish-Jewish Synthesis," in Bela Kiraly (ed.), *Tolerance and Movements of Religious Dissent in Eastern Europe* (Boulder: East European Quarterly, 1975), pp. 133–64.

32. Fritz Mauthner, *Erinnerungen, Prager Jugendjahre* (Munich: G. Müller, 1918), pp. 111–12; and Scholem, "A Sabbatian Will," p. 170.

33. Zdeněk Šolle, "K počátkum dělnického hnutí v Praze" in *ČSČH*, vol. V, pp. 662ff.; and Marx, *Wirtschaftliche Ursachen der Revolution*, pp. 13–15.

34. Cohen, *The Politics of Ethnic Survival*, pp. 76ff.

35. VA, *Adelsakten* Laemmel, 1856; Christoph Stölzl, *Die Ära Bach in Böhmen* (Munich: Oldenbourg, 1971), pp. 72, 80ff.; and Putz, "Wirtschaftsaristokratie," pp. 83ff.

36. Julius von Gomperz, *Jugenderinnerungen* (Brünn: Rohrer, 1902), chs. 1, 2.

37. Karniková, *Vývoj obyvatelstva*, pp. 59, 105.

38. The migration pattern appears clearly in the final list of "toleree" Jews in Vienna, as well as in the contemporary Viennese address books: see Pribram, *Urkunden und Akten*, vol. II, p. 268.

39. For the following, see J. Radimský, "Dělnické bouře v Brně roku 1843" in *Český Lid* XXXVI (1949): 9–13; Friedrich Walter, "Die böhmischen Arbeiterunruhen des Jahres 1844" in *MIÖG* XI, Ergänzungsband (1929): 717–34; Wolfgramm, "Der böhmische Vormärz"; Marx, *Wirtschaftliche Ursachen*, pp. 57ff.; and Theodore S. Hamerow, *Restoration, Revolution, and Reaction: Economics and Politics in German, 1815–1871* (Princeton: Princeton University Press, 1958), pt. 1.

40. Walter, "Böhmische Arbeiterunruhen," pp. 728–29; and Ludwig von Mises, "Zur Geschichte der österreichischen Fabriksgesetzgebung" in *ZVSV* XIV (1905): 256ff.

41. Stanley Z. Pech, *The Czech Revolution of 1848* (Durham, N.C.: University of North Carolina Press, 1969), ch. 12.

42. Walter, "Böhmische Arbeiterunruhen," p. 721; Wolfgramm, "Böhmischer Vormärz," pp. 18off.; comp. George Rudé, *Ideology and Popular Protest* (New York: Pantheon, 1980).

43. For the following, see Joseph F. Zacek, "Nationalism in Czechoslovakia" in Peter F. Sugar and Ivo J. Lederer (eds.), *Nationalism in Eastern Europe* (Seattle: University of Washington, 1969), pp. 175ff.; Peter Brock and H. Gordon Skilling (eds.), *The Czech Renascence of the Nineteenth Century* (Toronto: University of Toronto Press, 1969); Jozef Butvin and Jan Havránek (eds.), *Dějiny Československa* (4 vols., Prague: SNPL, 1965–68), vol. III; Josef Kočí, *České národní obrození* (Prague: Svoboda, 1978); and among older works Jakub Malý, *Naše znovurození* (6 vols., Prague: J. Otto, 1880–84); and Emanuel Rádl, *Der Kampf zwischen Tschechen und Deutschen* (Liberec: Steipel, 1928).

44. See the evaluations of Josef Janáček (ed.), *Dějiny Prahy* (Prague: NPL, 1964), esp. chs. 10 and 11; and Valentin Urfus, "Osvícenství a ekonomická ideologie v Čechách," in *PHS* XIV (1969): 202.

45. Hellmut Diwald, "Deutschböhmen, die Deutschen Prags, und das tschechische Wiedererwachen," in *ZRGG* X (1958): 128–32; and Cohen, *Politics of Ethnic Survival*, pp. 30ff.

46. Miroslav Hroch, "The Social Composition of the Czech Patriots in Bohemia, 1827–1848" in Brock and Skilling (eds.), *The Czech Renascence*, pp. 33ff.; and Malý, *Naše znovurození*, vol. I, pp. 90–91.

47. Pech, *Czech Revolution*, pp. 34–46.

48. For the following, see Karel Havlíček, *Politické spisy* (3 pts. in 5 vols., Prague: J. Laichter, 1900–03), vol. I, pp. 94–95. Comp. Eduard Goldstücker, "Jews Between Czechs and Germans around 1848" in *YLBI* XVII (1972): 17–29; Christoph Stölzl, *Kafkas böses Böhmen* (Munich: Harrassowitz, 1975); Cohen, *Politics of Ethnic Survival*, pp. 81–82; Izrael Olesker, "Der Anteil der Juden in den Nationalitäten-kämpfen in Böhmen im 19. Jahrhundert" (unpub. diss., Vienna, 1934); Michael Riff, "The Assimilation of the Jews of Bohemia and the Rise of Political Anti-Semitism, 1848–1914" (Unpub. diss., London University, 1974); and Hillel Kieval, *Making of Czech Jewry*, ch. 1.

49. Pech, *Czech Revolution*, pp. 92–95; Roubík, *Český Rok, 1848* (Prague: Kunciř, 1931), pp. 170ff.; K. Kazbunda, *České hnutí roku 1848* (Prague: Historický Klub, 1929), pp. 123, 168ff.; and Olesker, "Der Anteil der Juden," p. 50.

50. On the etymology of the word "anti-Semitism," see Rürup, *Emanzipation und Antisemitismus*, ch. 4; and Todd M. Endelman, "Comparative Perspectives on Modern Anti-Semitism in the West" in David Berger (ed.), *History and Hate* (Philadelphia, JPSA, 1986), pp. 95–114. For the French and German origins, see Herzberg, *The French Enlightenment and the Jews*; Katz, *From Prejudice to Destruction*, chs. 4–7; and Sterling, *Judenhass* (Frankfurt am Main: Europäischer Verlag, 1963), ch. 7.

SIX. A JUDEOPHILE REVOLUTION

Standard accounts of 1848 are Eric Hobsbawm, *The Age of Revolution* (New York: New American Library 1962); Peter N. Stearns, *1848: The Revolutionary Tide in Europe* (New York: Norton, 1974); François Fejtö (ed.), *The Opening of an Era: 1848* (2 vols., New York: Grosset and Dunlop, 1948). For events in Austria as a whole, see, apart from the major histories of the monarchy, Joseph Alexander Helfert, *Geschichte der österreichischen Revolution* (2 vols., Vienna: Herdersche Verlagsanstalt, 1907); and Josef Polišenský, *Aristocrats and the Crowd in the Revolutionary Year 1848* (Albany: SUNY, 1980). For the background of the revolution at Vienna, see Felix Czeike (ed.), *Wien in Vormärz* (Vienna: Jugend und Volk, 1980). For the Vienna revolution, see Wolfgang Häusler, *Von der Massenarmut zur Arbeiterbewegung* (Vienna: Jugend und Volk, 1979); Ernst Violand, *Die sociale Geschichte der Revolution in Österreich* (Leipzig: O. Wigand, 1850); Ernst Zenker, *Die Wiener Revolution 1848 in ihren socialen Voraussetzungen und Beziehungen* (Vienna: Hartleben, 1897); and Heinrich Reschauer and Moritz Smets, *Das Jahr 1848: Geschichte der Wiener Revolution* (2 vols., Vienna: Waldheim, 1872). In English are R. John Rath, *The Viennese Revolution of 1848* (Austin: University of Texas Press, 1957), and Josephine Goldmark, *Pilgrims of '48* (New Haven: Yale University Press, 1930).

For the Jews in 1848, see the standard work on religious developments, Josef Alexander Helfert, "Die confessionale Frage in Österreich," a series of long papers in *ÖJB*, vols. VI-XIII (1882–1889), vol. VI, pp. 86–182; Salo W. Baron, "The Impact of the Revolution of 1848 on Jewish Emancipation" in *JSS* XI (1949): 195–248; his "The Revolution of 1848 and Jewish Scholarship" in *AAJRP* XVIII (1948–49): 1–66, XX (1950): 1–100; his "Aspects of the Jewish Communal Crisis in 1848," *JSS* XIV (1952): 99–144; and Reinhold Rürup, "The European Revolutions of 1848 and the Jewish Emancipation," in Werner Mosse, A. Paucker, and R. Rürup (eds.), *Revolution and Evolution: 1848 in German-Jewish History* (Tübingen: Mohr, 1981), pp. 1–54. For the Jews at Vienna in 1848, see Wolfgang Häusler, "Katalog: Die Revolution von 1848 und die österreichischen Juden"; "Konfessionelle Probleme in der Wiener Revolution von 1848"; and "Demokratie und Emanzipation 1848," all in *SJA* I (1974); also Dorothea Weiss, "Der publizistische Kampf der Wiener Juden und ihre Emanzipation" (unpub. diss., Vienna, 1971); and the pedestrian but enthusiastic dissertation of Schmeril Czaczkes-Tissenboim, "Der Anteil der Juden an der Wiener Revolution von 1848" (Vienna, 1927).

1. John Komlos, *The Habsburg Monarchy as a Customs Union* (Princeton: Princeton University Press, 1983), ch. 2.

2. Werner Mosse in Mosse, Paucker, and Rürüp (eds.), *Revolution and Evolution*, pp. 389ff.

3. Heinz Fassmann, "Zur Altersverteilung und Zuwanderungsstruktur der Wiener Bevölkerung um die Mitte des 19. Jahrhunderts" in *WGB* XXXV (1980): 143ff.; and Baltzarek, "Das territoriale und bevölkerungsmässige Wachstum der Großstadt Wien," pp. 1–16.

4. Monika Richarz in Mosse, Paucker, Rürüp, *Revolution and Evolution*, p. 100.

5. Stölzl, "Zur Geschichte. I" p. 216; Violand, *Soziale Geschichte*, pp. 127–28; and Walther, "Die böhmischen Arbeiterunruhen," pp. 721, 725, 729.

6. These names appear either in the toleree lists or in Mayer, *Wiener Juden*, pp. 216ff. Comp. Marx, *Wirtschaftliche Ursachen*, pp. 20–21.

7. Reschauer and Smets, *Das Jahr 1848*, vol. I, pp. 334; Mayer, *Wiener Juden*, pp. 217, 316, 327. For evaluations, see Violand, *Sociale Geschichte der Revolution*, pp 72, 91, 157, 159; Zenker, *Die Wiener Revolution 1848*, p. 95; and Häusler, *Von der Massenarmut zur Arbeiterbewegung, pp. 152–56.

8. Helfert, *Geschichte der österreichischen Revolution*, vol. II, pp. 58ff.; and Werner Blumenberg, "Eduard von Müller-Tellering: Verfasser des ersten antisemitischen Pamphlet gegen Marx," *BIISH* VI (1951): 178–97. There were certainly some anti-Jewish pamphlets published after April at Vienna: see Rath, *The Viennese Revolution*, pp. 102–105; and James E. Walsh (ed.), *1848: Austrian Revolutionary Broadsides and Pamphlets: A Catalogue* (Boston: G. K. Hall, 1976). But both Dorothea Weiss and Wolfgang Häusler, who have studied the very complete collections in the Vienna *Stadtbibliotek*, agree that there was little follow-up to the veritable flood of such literature in March and April: Weiss, "Der Publizistische Kampf," pp. 66ff.; Häusler, "Confessionelle Probleme," pp. 71–72.

9. Renate Banik-Schweitzer and Gerhard Meissl, *Industriestadt Wien. Die Durchsetzung der industriellen Marktproduktion in der Habsburgerresidenz* (Vienna: Deuticke, 1983), pp. 22ff.

10. John W. Boyer, *Political Radicalism in Late Imperial Vienna* (Chicago: University of Chicago Press, 1981), ch. 2; and Andreas Baryli, "Gewerbepolitik und gewerberechtliche Verhältnisse im vormärzliche Wien" in Czeike (ed.), *Wien im Vormärz*, pp. 9–31; Gerhard Meissl, "Industrie und Gewerbe in Wien 1835 bis 1845" in F. Czeike (ed.), *Wien im Vormärz*, pp. 88–102; Zenker, *Die Wiener Revolution*, ch. 2. Comp. Häusler, *Von der Massenarmut*, pp. 25ff.; and Hans Novogoratz, "Sebastian Brunner und der frühe Anti-Semitismus" (unpub. diss., Vienna, 1979), pp. 3ff., 96ff.

11. Mayer, *Wiener Juden*, book II.

12. The following discussion is based on Mayer's data in *Wiener Juden*, and on my own analysis of the toleree list of 1847 in Pribram, *Urkunden und Akten*, vol. II, p. 530, and in particular of the 85 names which were new since 1827. Textile merchants were the largest single group among the new tolerees of 1847—24 out of 85 names. Grain and natural produce merchants comprised the second largest group of newly tolerated Jews in 1847—15 out of 85 names.

13. For the following, see Mayer, *Wiener Juden*, pp. 248ff., 257ff.

14. Mayer, *Wiener Juden*, pp. 228, 231–32, 243, 267.

15. Membership lists appeared in the Vienna address books for the years mentioned. The 1823 National Bank list contained 105 names, of which 17 were great aristocrats, 17 were Jewish (including recent converts), and the rest were identifiably Christian businessmen. The 1836 list contained 97 names, of which 6 were great aristocrats and 37 Jewish. For purposes of this calculation, I have omitted the aristocrats who played on the whole only a decorative role at the bank.

16. Baltzarek, *Die Geschichte der Wiener Börse* (Vienna: Akademie, 1973), pt. I.

17. Hermann von Goldschmidt, *Einige Erinnerungen aus längst vergangenen Tagen* (Vienna: Selbstverlag, 1917); Gille, *Histoire de la Maison Rothschild*, vol. I; Corti, *Haus Rothschild*, vol. I; Jaeger-Sunstenau, "Geadelte Judenfamilien," pp. 95–96; and the sketchy materials in the Vienna *Kultusgemeinde* archive at Jerusalem, A/W 324.

18. Inge and Peter Rippmann (eds.), Ludwig Börne, *Sämtliche Schriften* (5 vols., Düsseldorf: Joseph Melzer, 1964), vol. III, pp. 482–85; Reschauer and Smets, *Das Jahr 1848*, vol. I, pp. 86–87; and Karl Glossy (ed.), *Wien 1840–1848. Eine amtliche Chronik* (2 vols., Vienna: Literarischer Verein, 1917, 1919), vol. I, pp. 121ff., vol. II, pp. 182ff.

19. Max von Kübeck (ed.), *Metternich und Kübeck. Ein Briefwechsel* (Vienna: Carl Gerold, 1910), pp. 36–37.

20. Goldschmidt, *Aus längst vergangenen Tagen*, pp. 62–64.

21. E. J. Hobsbawn, *Primitive Rebels* (New York: Norton, 1959), ch. 7.

22. Dorothea Weiss, "Publizistischer Kampf," pp. 177ff.; and L. A. Frankl, *Erinnerungen*, pp. 314ff.

23. S. Baron, "The Impact of the Revolution of 1848," p. 213; and Rudolf Till, "Der Sicherheitsausschuss des Jahres 1848," in Santifaller, *Festschrift zur Feier des 200-jährigen Bestandes des Haus-, Hof-, und Staatsarchives*, vol. II, p. 121.

24. See my article, "Convert Jews and the Problem of Viennese Jew-Hatred in 1848," *EEQ* XXI (1987): 355–68.); Thomas W. Simons, "Vienna's First Catholic Political Movement: The Guentherians, 1848–1857" in *CHR* LV (July, 1969-Jan. 1970): 173–94, 377–393, 610–625; Rudolf Till, *Hofbauer und sein Kreis*, chs. 5–10; and Eduard Winter, *Die geistige Entwicklung A. Guenthers und seine Schule* (Paderborn: F. Schöningh, 1931).

25. Leo Goldhammer, "Jewish Emigration from Austria-Hungary in 1848–1849" in *YIVO Annual* IX (1954): 332–62; Rürüp, "European Revolutions," pp. 35ff.

26. Indicative of the myth, standard treatments of anti-Semitism in Austria hardly mention 1848: Jakob Katz, *From Prejudice to Destruction* (Cambridge, Mass.: Harvard University Press, 1980), pt. V; Peter Pulzer, *The Rise of Political Anti-Semitism in Germany and Austria* (New York: John Wiley, 1964); and Dirk Van Arkel, "Antisemitism in Austria" (unpub. diss., Leiden, 1966)

27. For the following, see Leib Weissberg, "Die Judenemanzipation und die österreichische Reichsverfasung von 1849" (unpub. diss., Vienna, 1921); Rudolf Leitner, "Die Judenpolitik der österreichischen Regierung in den Jahren 1848–1859" (unpub. diss., Vienna, 1924); and Bihl, "Die Juden," pp. 893ff.

28. For the following, see Pribram, *Urkunden und Akten*, vol. I, Introduction; G. Wolf, *Geschichte* (1876), pp. 110ff.; Tietze, *Juden Wiens*, pp. 151ff.; Bato, *Die Juden im alten Wien*, pp. 70ff., 122ff.; Kopel Blum, "Aufklärung und Reform bei den Wiener Juden" (unpub. diss., Vienna, 1935), chs. 1, 4; and Wolfgang Häusler, "Der Weg des Wiener Judentums von der Toleranz zur Emanzipation" in *JVGSW* XXX-XXXI (1974–75): 84–124.

29. Wurzbach, *BL* IX: 165–69; Wachstein, *Inschriften*, vol. II, pp. 514ff.; his *Mercantilprotokolle*, pp. 292–300; Gerson Wolf, *Vom ersten bis zum zweiten Tempel* (Vienna: W. Braumüller, 1861), pp. 59–69; Arthur Czellitzer, "Die Ahnentafel . . . Hugo von Hofmannsthals," *JFF* V, no 3 (Sept. 1929): 176ff.; Taglicht, *Nachlasse*, pp. 165–66.

30. Wolfgang Häusler, "Das österreichische Judentum zwischen Beharrung und Fortschritt" in Wandruszka and Urbanitsch, *Die Habsburger Monarchie*, vol. IV, pp. 639ff.; Moses Rosenmann, *Isak Noe Mannheimer: Sein Leben und Werken* (Vienna: Löwit, 1922); Blum, "Aufklärung und Reform," ch. 5; Jacob Allerhand, "Die Rabbiner des Stadttempels von I. N. Mannheimer bis Z. P. Chajes," in *SJA* VI, (1978): 9–13; Maximilian Steiner, *Salomon Sulzer und die Wiener Judengemeinde* (Vienna: Österreichische Wochenschrift, 1904); Eric Mandell, "Salomon Sulzer 1804–90," in Fraenkel, *The Jews of Austria*, pp. 221–30; H. Avenary et al., *Kantor Salomon Sulzer und seine Zeit* (Sigmaringen: J. Thorbecke, 1985); Wolf, *Geschichte* (1876), p. 136. Mrs. Trollope visited the temple in 1836 and published an account of its beautiful music that contrasts with her general antipathy for things Jewish: *Vienna and the Austrians*, vol. I, pp. 373–79.

31. S. Husserl, *Gründungsgeschichte der Stadttempel in Wien* (Vienna: Braumüller, 1906), pp. 85ff.; and his "Die israelitische Kultusgemeinde in Wien," *Ost und West* X (1910): 514.

32. Wertheimer, *Die Juden von Österreich* (2 vols., Leipzig: Wigand, 1842). Comp. Gerson Wolf, *Joseph Wertheimer: Ein Leben und Zeitbild* (Vienna: Herz-

feld und Bauer, 1868), pp. 36–42; his *Culturgeschichte*, pp. 147 ff.; and his *Vom ersten bis zum zweiten Tempel*, pp. 172ff.

33. Wurzbach *BL* XLVI: 213–14; the obituary in *NZ* (1866), pp. 332–33; Kann, *Theodor Gomperz*, pp. 45, 48; and Strach, *Geschichte der Eisenbahnen*, vol. I, pp. 132ff.; Castelli, *Memoiren meines Lebens*, vol. II, chs. 24–25; Otto Zausmer, "Die Ludlamshöhle, Glück und Ende," in *JGG* XXXIII (1935): 86–112.

34. Mádl, *Politische Dichtung*, pp. 216–17; Castelli, *Memoiren meines Lebens*, vol. II, ch. 26.

35. Kann, *Theodor Gomperz*, pp. 45ff.; Felicie Ewart (pseud. Emilie Exner), *Zwei Frauenbildnisse* (Vienna: private, 1907), pp. 30ff.

36. For the following, see "Erinnerungen an L. A. Frankl und an sein Haus redigiert von seinem Sohn Dr. Bruno Frankl," Manuscript Collection, Austrian National Library, Cod. Daktyl. 8 (SN 18 229); Frankl's memoir fragments incorporated in the biographical sketch by Dr. Rakonitzky in *Libussa* (Prague), vol. IX (1850), pp. 351ff.; Hock (ed.), *L. A. Frankl, Erinnerungen* (Prague: Josef Koch, 1910); and "Zur Geschichte der Familie Frankl" in *ZGJT* II (1931): pp. 67–80; Anton Schlossar, "Frankl, L. A." *ADB*, vol. XLVIII, pp. 706–712; Gustav Gugitz's note in Pichler, *Denkwürdigkeiten*, vol. II, pp. 579–81; Wurzbach, *BL*, vol. IV, pp. 334ff; Winninger, *GJNB*, Vol. II, pp. 301ff.; Stefanie Dollar, "Die Sonntagsblätter von Ludwig August Frankl, 1842–1848" (unpub. diss., Vienna, 1932); Nikolaus Vielmetti, "Der Wiener Jüdische Publizist Ludwig August Frankl und die Begründung der Lämmelschule" in *JIDG* IV (1975): 167–204; and Eugen Wolbe, *Ludwig August Frankl: Der Dichter und Menschenfreund* (Frankfurt am Main: J. Kaufmann, 1910).

37. Pichler, *Denkwürdigkeiten*, vol. II, pp. 297–98, 304 (herself), 579 (Bauernfeld), and 311 (Lenau).

38. Mádl. *Politische Dichtung in Österreich*, pp. 210ff., cf. pp. 237ff. As so often happens when it comes to Jews in Austria, historians give different evaluations of Frankl's work. A typical "put-down" is Nagl-Zeidler-Castle, *DÖLG*, Vol. II, p. 983. Typical exaggerations are Wolbe, *L.A. Frankl* and Tietze, *Juden Wiens*, pp. 173ff.

39. Ernst Viktor Zenker, *Geschichte der Journalistik in Österreich* (Vienna: Staatsdrückerei, 1900), p. 26; Dollar, *"Die Sonntagsblätter,"* Introduction; Stölzl, "Zur Geschichte der böhmischen Juden. I," pp. 197–98; Friedrich Uhl, *Aus meinem Leben* (Stuttgart: Cotta, 1908), pp. 129–32; and Sigmund Mayer, *Wiener Juden*, pp. 270ff.

40. Franz, *Liberalismus*, pp. 23ff.; and Frankl, *Erinnerungen*, pp. 265ff., 276ff.

41. Richard Charmatz, *Adolf Fischhof* (Stuttgart: Cotta, 1910), pp. 31, 35, 111; B. Frankl, "Erinnerungen an Dr. L. A. Frankl," pp. 488ff.

42. Translation by J. G. Legge as cited in Rath, *The Viennese Revolution of 1848*, pp. 100–101.

43. Josef Alexander Helfert (ed.), *Der Wiener Parnass im Jahre 1848* (Vienna: Manz'sche Buchhandlung, 1882); and Mádl, *Politische Dichtung*, pp. 292–93.

44. Reschauer and Smets, *Das Jahr 1848*, vol. I; and Helfert, *Geschichte der österreichischen Revolution*, vol. I, pp. 264ff.; Weiss, "Der publizistische Kampf," chs. 1 and 2.

45. Weiss, "Der publizistische Kampf," pp. 21ff., 141ff.; Hersch Schächter, "Die Judenfrage in der Publizistik vor dem Jahre und während des Jahres 1848 in Österreich-Ungarn" (unpub. diss., Vienna, 1932), ch. 1, pp. 128ff.; Baron, "The Revolution of 1848 and Jewish Scholarship," pt. II, pp. 33ff.; Wolf, *Culturgeschichte*, pp. 85ff., 130ff.; Käthe Hammer, "Die Judenfrage in den westlichen Kronländern Österreichs im Jahre 1848" (unpub. diss., Vienna, 1948); and Blum, "Aufklärung und Reform," pp. 6off.

46. Wolf, *Culturgeschichte*, p. 31; and Rosenmann, *Mannheimer*, pp. 85–86.

47. Charmatz, *Fischhof*; Heinrich Friedjung, "Adolf Fischhof" in his *Historische Aufsätze* (Stuttgart and Berlin: Cotta, 1919), pp. 362–71; and Robert A. Kann, *The Multinational Empire* (2 vols., New York: Columbia University Press, 1950), vol. II,

pp. 143ff. On Fischhof as a Jew, see Werner Cahnmann, "Adolf Fischhofs jüdische Persönlichkeit und Weltanschauung," in *Kairos* XIV (1972): 110–20; and his "Adolf Fischhof and his Jewish Followers," *YLBI* IV (1959): 111–39.

48. Goldschmidt, *Aus längst vergangenen Tagen*, pp. 62–64. The exact role of the Vertretung cannot be determined, because the protocols of its meetings during the revolutionary months of 1848 are no longer in their place in the Vienna Kultusgemeinde Archive. The relevant volume in Jerusalem (A/W 61.1) contains only the protocols of January and February, and then miscellaneous items from September through December. There is some evidence from late in the year that the Vienna center was very concerned by the activities of its employees, Mannheimer and Frankl, at the parliament, but this only confirms that the center was not in control: see the protocols for 11 Dec., 16 Dec. 1848 in A/W 61–1; and the exaggerated report in *AZJ*, 1910, pp. 56–58.

49. For the following, see Wolfgang Häusler: "Hermann Jellinek im Vormärz. Seine Entwicklung zum revolutionären Demokrat," in Fichtenau and Zöllner (eds.), *Beiträge zur neueren Geschichte Österreichs*, pp. 345–62; and his "Hermann Jellinek (1823–1848): Ein Demokrat in der Wiener Revolution," in *JIDG* V (1976): 125–75; Moses Rosenmann, *Dr. Adolf Jellinek* (Vienna: Josef Schlesinger, 1939), chs. 1–3.

50. Lenore O'Boyle, "The Problem of an Excess of Educated Men in Western Europe, 1800–1850," in *JMH* XLII (1970): 471–95.

51. Häusler, *Von der Massenarmut*, pp. 179ff., 308ff., and 413ff.; and Franz Schuselka, *Das Revolutionsjahr, März 1848–März 1849* (Vienna: Jasper, Hügel & Manz, 1850), pp. 166–67.

52. Ernst Hanisch, *Der kranke Mann an der Donau* (Vienna: Europa, 1978), pp. 117ff.; Herbert Steiner, *Karl Marx in Wien* (Vienna: Europa, 1979); and Häusler, *Von der Massenarmut*, p. 295.

53. Friedrich Unterreuter, *Die Revolution in Wien* (8 vols., Vienna: C. Ueberreuter 1848–49), vol. I, pp. 111–20.

54. Arthur Schnitzler brilliantly dramatizes the consequences of this paradox in his *Der Weg ins Freie* (Berlin: S. Fischer, 1918).

SEVEN. GALICIAN DEADLOCK

For Austria's economic development just after 1848, see, apart from the works noted in chapter V above, especially Carl Czoernig, *Oesterreich's Neugestaltung 1848–1858* (Stuttgart and Augsburg: Cotta, 1858); and Harm-Hinrich Brandt, *Der österreichische Neoabsolutismus: Staatsfinanzen und Politik* (2 vols., Göttingen: Vandenhoeck & Ruprecht, 1979). For statistics, see Josef Hain, *Handbuch der Statistik des österreichischen Kaiserstaates* (2 vols., Vienna: 1852–53); and the useful table compiling nationality statistics for five successive dates between 1848 and 1914 in Wandruszka-Urbanitsch, *Die Habsburger Monarchie*, vol. III/1, opposite page 38.

For political developments, see, apart from the general histories, Josef Redlich, *Das österreichische Staats- und Reichsproblem* (2 vols., Vienna: Reinhold, 1920, 1926); R. Kann, *The Multinational Empire* (2 vols., New York: Columbia University Press, 1950); Heinrich Friedjung, *Österreich von 1848 bis 1860* (2 vols., Stuttgart: Cotta, 1912); Walter Rogge, *Österreich von Vilagos bis zur Gegenwart* (2 vols., Vienna: 1879); and Richard Charmatz, *Minister Freiherr von Bruck* (Leipzig: H. Hirzel, 1916); and on the new Kaiser, Josef Redlich, *Emperor Franz Joseph of Austria: A Biography* (New York: Macmillan, 1928); and Egon Count Corti, *Kaiser Franz Josef* (3 vols., Graz: Styria Verlag, 1952–1955).

For Galicia in the nineteenth century, see, apart from the works cited in chapter III above, the chapters by Stefan Kienkiewicz on the first half of the nineteenth century, and by J. Buszko on the second half, in Tadeusz Manteuffel, *Historia Polski*

(4 vols., in many parts; Warsaw PWN, 1959–65), vol. II; Konstanty Grzybowski, *Galicja 1848–1914*: (Kraków: PAN, 1959); Piotr S. Wandycz, *The Lands of Partitioned Poland* (Seattle: University of Washington Press, 1974); also his "The Poles in the Habsburg Monarchy" in *AHY* III/2 (1967): 261–86; Henryk Wereszycki, "The Poles as an Integrating and Disintegrating Factor" in *Ibid.*, pp. 287–313; and Henryk Batowski, "Die Polen" in Wandruszka-Urbanitsch, *Die Habsburger Monarchie*, vol. III/1, pp. 522–54.

For Galician Jewry, see, apart from earlier cited works, Philip Friedmann, *Die galizischen Juden im Kampf um ihre Gleichberechtigung, 1848–1868* (Frankfurt am Main: J. Kauffmann, 1929). A standard collection of statistics about nineteenth-century Galician Jewry is Rosenfeld, *Die polnische Judenfrage*, pp. 70ff.; but see also the same author's "Die Jüdische Bevölkerung Galiziens von 1772–1862"; "1867–1910"; "In der Städten Galiziens 1881–1910"; and "in Krakau" in *ZDS* X (1914): 138–43; XI (1915): 96–105; and IX (1913): 17–24 and 94–95.

1. Brandt, *Der österreichische Neoabsolutismus: Staatsfinanzen und Politik*, chs. 1–3.

2. For the following, see Aloys von Czedik, *Der Weg von und zu den Österreichischen Staatsbahnen* (3 vols., Teschen: Karl Prechaska, 1913), vol. I., pp. 50ff.; Strach, *Geschichte der Eisenbahnen*, vol. I, pp. 317ff.; Brandt, *Der Österreichische Neoabsolutismus*, vol. I, pp. 319ff.; Karl Bachinger, "Das Verkehrswesen" in Wandruszka-Urbanitsch, *Die Habsburger Monarchie*, vol. I, pp. 282ff.

3. For the following, see especially Fritz G. Steiner, *Die Entwicklung des Mobilbankwesens in Österreich* (Vienna: Carl Konegen, 1913), ch. 5; David Landes, "Vieille banque et banque nouvelle" in *RHM* III (1956): 204–222; Bertrand Gille, *Histoire de la Maison Rothschild*, vol. II, chs. 4–10; and Hiltrud Pichler, "Die Brüder Pereire und die österreichisch-ungarische Monarchie: Unternehmerprojekte als Beitrag zur österreichischen Wirtschaftsentwicklung" (unpub. diss., Vienna, 1974).

4. Pichler, "Die Brüder Pereire," p. 60; Corti, *Haus Rothschild*, vol. II, pp. 381–82.

5. Goldschmidt, *Aus längst vergangenen Tagen*, pp. 71ff.; Anselm Rothschild obituary, *NFP*, 28 July 1874, pp. 1–2, 6; Gille, *Histoire de la Maison Rothschild*, vol. II, pp. 217ff.; März, *Österreichische Industrie und Bankpolitik*, ch. 1.

6. For the following, see Brandt, *Der österreichische Neoabsolutismus*, vol. I, p. 355 n.; Strach, *Geschichte der Eisenbahnen*, vol. I, pp. 301ff., 436ff., 476ff; Czedik, *Der Weg von und zu den österreichischen Staatsbahnen*, vol. I, pp. 78–79ff.; and März, *Österreichische Industrie und Bankpolitik*, p. 75.

7. *NFP*, 14 Oct. 1886, p. 5; H. Benedikt, *Die wirtschaftliche Entwicklung*, pp. 93ff.; Heinrich Pollak, *Dreissig Jahre aus dem Leben eines Journalist* (3 vols., Vienna: A. Holden, 1875, 1898), vol. II, esp. pp. 286ff.; Ludwig Wattmann, *Drei-und-funfzig Jahre* (3 vols., Vienna: Braumüller, 1904), vol. III, pp. 28ff.

8. Mahler, *A History of Modern Jewry, 1780–1815*, pp. 330ff.; M. Lewin, "Die Juden in Galizien zur Zeit Kaiser Josef II" (unpub. diss., Vienna, 1933); and Balaban, *Dzieje żydów w Galicji*, chs. 5–7.

9. Venetianer, *A zsidóság szervezete*, p. 475; and Max Rosenfeld, *Die polnische Judenfrage* (Vienna: Löwit, 1918), pp. 235ff.; and the report by Alfred Stern, Head of the Vienna Jewish Community, to the Jewish Colonization Association in Paris, dated 5 January 1910, in the Jerusalem Archive, A/W-744.1.

10. Mayer Balaban, "Herz Homberg in Galizien," *JJGL* XIX (1916): 189–221; Ludwig Singer, "Die Entstehung des Juden-Systemialpatentes von 1797," *JGGJT* VII (1935): 257ff.; Kestenberg-Gladstein, *Neuere Geschichte*, pp. 57–60; Wolf, *Geschichte* (1876), pp. 121–25; Altmann, *Mendelssohn*, p. 359; and Dubnow, *Neueste Geschichte des jüdischen Volkes*, vol. I, p. 29.

11. N. Gelber, "La police autrichienne et le Sanhédrin de Napoléon," *RÉJ* LXXXIII (1927): 131–33; Balaban, "Herz Homberg in Galizien," pp. 213–15.

12. For the following, see David Ochs, "Die Aufklärung der Juden in Galizien, 1772–1848" (unpub. diss., Vienna, 1937); Balaban, *Dzieje zydów w Galicji*, chs. 5–7; Raphael Mahler, "The Social and Political Aspects of the Haskalah in Galicia" in Joshua A. Fishman (ed.), *Studies in Modern Jewish Social History* (New York: KTAV, 1972), pp. 64–85; and Mahler, *A History of Modern Jewry*, pp. 587–601.

13. Friedmann, *Die galizischen Juden im Kampf um ihre Gleichberechtigung*, p. 43.

14. See Friedmann, *Die galizischen Juden*, pp. 113ff.; Artur Eisenbach, "Das galizische Judentum während des Völkerfrühlings und in der Zeit des Kampfes um seine Gleichberechtigung" in *SJA* VIII (1980): 75ff.; and Menasche Josef Friedler, "Die galizischen Juden vom wirtschaftlichen, kulturellen und staatsbürgerlichen Standpunkt, 1815–1848" (unpub. diss., Vienna, 1923).

15. Raphael Mahler, "The Austrian Government and the Hasidim during the Period of Reaction, 1814–1848" in *JSS* I (1939): 195–240; and Dubnow, *Geschichte der Chassidismus* (1913), ch. 45.

16. Mahler, "The Austrian Government," pp. 222–24.

17. For the following, see the anonymous booklet, *Galizisch-jüdisch Zustände* (Leipzig: Philipp Reclam, 1845), pp. 72ff., 87ff.; Balaban, *Dzieje Zydów*, p. 127; Ochs, "Die Aufklärung," pp. 36–40; and Baron, "The Revolution of 1848 and Jewish Scholarship," pp. 69ff.

18. Gotthilf Kohn, *Abraham Kohn im Lichte der Geschichtsforschung*, p. 33; Ochs, op. cit., pp. 121ff.; Hammer, "Judenfrage in 1848," pp. 71–74.

19. *Galizische Zustände*, pp. 121–29; Friedler, "Die galizischen Juden," pp. 117–20; *CO*, 1848, pp. 169ff.; and Kohn, *Abraham Kohn*, ch. 7.

20. Kohn; *Abraham Kohn*; *CO*, 1848, p. 342; and *Orient*, 1850, pp. 14–15.

21. Gelber, "Zur Geschichte der galizischen Juden in den Jahren 1848–1860" in *Aus zwei Jahrhunderten*, p. 106ff.

22. For the following, see Fr. Bujak, "Rozwój gospodarczy Galicji (1772–1914)" in his *Studia historyczne i spoleczne* (Lwow: Poloniecki, 1917, reprinted), pp. 123–67; and J. Buszko, *Zum Wandel der Gesellschaftsstruktur in Galizien und in der Bukowina* (Vienna: Adademie, 1978).

23. Wandruszka-Urbanitsch, *Die Habsburger Monarchie*, vol. III/1, p. 111.

24. Becher, *Statistische Übersicht*, pp. 358–59.

25. One traveler, who went from Bielitz in Silesia to Lwow in 1844, found the trip took fourteen days: see Gotthilf Kohn, *Abraham Kohn*, p. 33.

26. Eduard Suess, *Erinnerungen* (Leipzig: S. Hirzel, 1916), p. 133; reporting on a journey in 1859.

27. Helena Madurowicz-Urbańska, "Die Industrie Galiziens im Rahmen der wirtschaftlichen Struktur der Donaumonarchie" in *ZNUJ: Prace Historyczne* LVII (1978): 161.

28. For the following, see Friedmann, *Die galizischen Juden*, ch. 2; Balaban, *Dzieje zydów*, ch. 8; Hammer, "Die Judenfrage in den westlichen Kronländern im Jahre 1848," pp. 67ff., 77ff., and 113–16; and Wolfgang Häusler, "Die österreichische Revolution von 1848 und die polnische Frage bis zur Einberufung des Reichstages," in *ZNUJ: Prace Historyczne* LVII (1978): 107–127.

29. Jerzy Zdrada, "Mieses, Rachmiel," *PSB*, vol. XXI, pp. 29–30.

30. F. Ziemialkowski, *Pamietniki* (Cracow: A. Kozianski, 1904), vol. II, pp. 68–69; Baron, "The Revolution of 1848 and Jewish Scholarship," pp. 72ff.; *CO*, 1848, p. 194; and the anonymous "Brief aus Lemberg" advocating Jewish Polonization, ibid., pp. 295–98.

31. For the following, see Peter Brock, "Polish Nationalism" in Sugar and Lederer, *Nationalism in Eastern Europe*, pp. 310ff.; and Grodziski, *Historia ustroju spoleczno-politycznego*, pp. 144ff.

32. Stefan Kieniewicz, *Ruch chlopski w 1846 roku* (Warsaw: Ossolineum, 1951); Arnon Gill, *Die polnische Revolution 1846* (Vienna: Oldenbourg, 1974); and Thomas W. Simons, Jr., "The Peasant Revolt of 1846 in Galicia: Recent Polish Historiography," in *SR* XXX (1971): 795–817.

33. Ivan L. Rudnytsky, "The Ukrainians in Galicia under Austrian Rule," in *AHY* III/2 (1967): 394–429; and Wolfdieter Bihl, "Die Ruthenen" in Wandruszka-Urbanitsch, *Die Habsburger Monarchie*, vol. I, pp. 555–84.

34. Baron, "The Revolution of 1848 and Jewish Scholarship," pt. II, p. 79; Rosenmann, *Mannheimer*, pp. 81, 132ff.; *Orient*, 1848, pp. 215–16; *CO*, 1848, p. 198. For a suggestion that there was Polonism even at Brody, see *CO*, 1848, pp. 296–97, 324; and the report in *Orient*, 1848, p. 119 (23 March).

35. S. Kieniewicz and M. Tyrowicz, "Meisels Dob Beer" in *PSB*, vol. XX, pp. 387–88; Friedmann, *Die galizischen Juden*, pp. 55–56; and Baron, "The Revolution of 1848 and Jewish Scholarship," pt. II, pp. 65–68.

36. Ziemialkowski, *Pamietniki*, vol. II, pp. 68–69; and Leon Sapieha, *Wspomnienia z lat 1803 do 1863* (Lwow: E. Altenberg, 1914), p. 222.

37. *CO*, 1848, pp. 131, 155; Juliusz Starkel, *Rok 1848* (Lwow: Gubrynowicz and Schmidt, 1899), p. 123; and William W. Hagen, *Germans, Poles, and Jews: The Nationality Conflict in the Prussian East, 1772–1914* (Chicago: University of Chicago Press, 1980), pp. 116–17.

38. Balaban, *Dzieje zydów*, pp. 143ff.; and Baron, "The Revolution of 1848 and Jewish Scholarship," II, p. 80.

39. Balaban, *Dzieje zydów*, ch. 6.

40. "Brody," *Evreiskaia Entsiklopediia*, pp. 25–26.

41. Bujak, *Rozwó gospodarczy*, p. 138–39.

42. Heinrich Weiss, "Die Judengesetzgebung," pp. 36–53; and Friedmann, *Die galizischen Juden*, chs. 3 and 4.

43. Report from Lwow, *CO*, 1848, p. 17; and Eisenbach, "Das galizische Judentum während das Völkerfrühlungs," p. 85.

44. Friedmann, *Die galizischen Juden*, pp. 197ff.

45. Ibid., pp. 33–34.

46. Friedman in Schiper, *Zydzi w Polsce Odrodzonej*, vol. I, ch. 17.

EIGHT. HUNGARIAN SUCCESS

The classic essay on the social development of nineteenth-century Hungary is Gyula Szekfü's biased but stimulating *Három Nemzedék* (Budapest: Élet, 1920: reissued Budapest: Egyetemi nyomda, 1935). Recent reconsiderations are in Andrew C. Janos, *The Politics of Backwardness in Hungary: 1825–1945* (Princeton: Princeton University Press, 1982); Zsigmond Pál Pach (ed.), *Magyarország Története* (10 vols., Budapest: Akadémiai kiadó, 1976—), vols. V-VIII. For statistics, see József Kovacsics, *Magyarország történeti demográfijája* (Budapest: Közgazdasági és jógi kiadó, 1963).

For Hungarian Jewry in the nineteenth century, see Lajos Venetianer, *A magyar zsidóság története* (Budapest: Fövárosi nyomda, 1922); Leopold Löw, *Zur neueren Geschichte der Juden in Ungarn* (Budapest: 1874); Sándor Büchler, *A zsidók története Budapesten* (Budapest: Franklin, 1901); Michael Silber, "The Historical Experience of German Jewry and Its Impact on Haskalah and Reform in Hungary" in Katz (ed.), *Toward Modernity* (New Brunswick, N.J.: Transaction, 1986), pp. 107–157; Károly Vörös, "Ungarns Judentum vor der bürgerlichen Revolution" in *Studies in East European Social History* II (1978): 139–56; and Wolfgang Häusler, "Assimilation und Emanzipation des ungarischen Judentums um die Mitte des 19. Jahrhunderts," in *SJA* III (1976): 33–79, which reviews German-language work.

1. For the following, see in general Lajos Venetianer, *A zsidóság szervezete az europai államokban*; also Baron, "Aspects of the Jewish Communal Crisis in 1848" pt. II, *JSS* XIV (1952): 99–144; and Jacob Toury, *Soziale und politische Geschichte der Juden in Deutschland, 1847–1871* (Düsseldorf: Droste Verlag, 1977), ch. 5.

2. Kovács, *A zsidók térfoglalása Magyarországon*, p. 11; Fülöp Grünwald and Sándor Scheiber (eds.), *MZsO*, vol. VII (1963), p. 45. For opposing Hungarian nationalist and Zionist interpretations of the Galician immigration, see Erno Martin, "The Family Tree of Hungarian Jewry," *HJS*, vol. I, esp. p. 57; and on the other, Erno Laszlo, "Hungarian Jewry: Settlement and Demography, 1735–38 to 1910," *ibid.*, pp. 61ff.

3. D. Kaufmann, *Simson Wertheimer*, pp. 174ff.

4. H. Gold (ed.), *Die Juden und die Judengemeinde Bratislava* (Brno: Jüdischer Verlag, 1932; reissued, Tel Aviv: Olamenu, 1965); Fritz Peter Hodik, *Beiträge zur Geschichte der Mattersdorfer Judengemeinde* (Eisenstadt: Burgenländische Forschungen, 1976); and Wolfgang Häusler, "Probleme der Geschichte des westungarischen Judentums in der Neuzeit," in *Burgenländische Heimatsblätter*, vol. XLII, pp. 32–38, 69–100.

5. Ármin Vámbéry, *Küzdelmeim* (Budapest, Franklin, 1905), p. 1.

6. For the following, see Michael K. Silber, "The Roots of the Schism in Hungarian Jewry: Cultural and Social Change from the Reign of Joseph II until the Eve of the 1848 Revolution" (unpub. Hebrew language diss., Jerusalem, 1983), ch. 2. Dr. Silber has kindly summarized his research findings for me. Comp. Jacob Katz, "The Identity of Post-Emancipatory Hungarian Jewry" (unpub. conference paper, Paris, August 1985), pp. 5, 7ff.

7. Schlomo Spitzer, "Der Einfluss des Chatam Sofer und seiner Pressburger Schule auf die jüdischen Gemeinden Mitteleuropas im 19. Jahrhundert," *SJA* VIII (1980): 111–21; Gold, *Bratislava*, pp. 64ff.; and *MZsL*, p. 860.

8. "Teitelbaum," "Szatmàr," and "Sátoraljaújhely" in *EJ* and *MZsL*.

9. For the following, see János Kosa, *Pest és Buda elmagyarosodása 1848-ig* (Budapest: Általános ny. 1937), pp. 93–131; Zsigmond Groszmann, *A magyar zsidók V. Ferdinand alatt* (Budapest: Egyenlöség, 1916); Miksa Grünwald, *Zsidó Biedermeier* (Pécs: Egyetemi könyvny., 1937); Nikolaus Laszlo, *Die geistige und soziale Entwicklung der Juden in Ungarn in der ersten Hälfte des 19. Jahrhunderts* (Berlin: Michel, 1934); and György Szalai, "A hazai zsidóság magyarosodása 1849-ig" in *Világosság* XV (1974): 216–223.

10. B. Mandl, *Das jüdische Schulwesen in Ungarn unter Kaiser Josef II* (Frankfurt am Main: 1903); and his *A magyarországi zsidó iskola a xix. században* (Budapest: 1909).

11. František Roubík "Zur Geschichte der Juden in Böhmen im 19. Jahrhundert" in *JGGJT* VII (1935): 365–68.

12. Dr. Weil (Leopold Löw), *Aaron Chorin: Eine biographische Skizze*.

13. Paul J. Diamant, *Minna Diamant, 1815–1840: Ein Briefwechsel aus der Biedermeierzeit* (Tel Aviv: Olamenu, nd); and Meyer, *Ein jüdischer Kaufmann*.

14. Aron Moskovits, *Jewish Education in Hungary* (New York: Bloch, 1964), p. 38.

15. Elek Fényes, *Statistik des Königreiches Ungarn* (Pest: K. Trattner, 1843), vol. III, p. 109.

16. Venetianer, *A magyar zsidóság története*, pp. 147ff.

17. See for the following Moskovits, *Jewish Education*, ch. 2.

18. The gist of the record is in *MStK*, Vol. V (1907), pp. 510–13, 720–23.

19. Chapter 4, by Gyula Mérei and 6, by Károly Vörös in Pach (ed.), *Magyarország Története*, vol. V/1.

20. Peter Hanák in Pach (ed.), *Magyarország Története*, vol. IX/1, pp. 480–81.

21. Becher, *Statistische Übersicht der Bevölkerung der österreichischen Monarchie*, pp. 358–59; Fényes, *Statistik des Königreiches Ungarn*, vol. I, p. 136.

22. Ferenc Eckhardt, *A bécsi udvar gazdaságpolitikája Magyarországon* (2 vols., Budapest: 1922 and 1958); and the chapter by Kálmán Benda in Pach (ed.), *Magyarország Története*, vol. V/1.

23. For the following, see Moritz Csáky, *Von der Aufklärung zum Liberalismus* (Vienna: Akademie, 1981); George Barany, *Stephen Szechenyi and the Awakening of Hungarian Nationalism* (Princeton: Princeton University Press, 1968); and chapter 8, by András Gergely, and chapter 10, by Károly Vörös in Pach (ed.), *Magyarország Története*, vol. V/1.

24. Venetianer, *A magyar zsidóság története*, pp. 58ff.; Henrik Marczali, *Hungary in the 18th Century* (Cambridge: The University Press, 1910), pp. 120ff.; and Béla Király, *Hungary in the Late Eighteenth Century* (New York: Columbia University Press, 1969), pp. 25ff.

25. S. Stojanovich, "The Conquering Balkan Merchant" in *JEH* (1960): 237ff.; and Ferenc Eckhardt, "Kereskedelmunk közvetitöi a 18-ik században" in the *Századok* (1918), pp. 359ff.

26. For the following, see Steven Bela Vardy, "The Origins of Jewish Emancipation in Hungary" in *UJB* VII (1976): 144–47; László Simon, *A zsidók a magyar reformkorban* (Debrecen: Vertok Lajos kiadása, 1936); Venetianer, *A magyar zsidóság története*, pt. II; George Barany, "Magyar Jew or Jewish Magyar?" in Bela Vagó (ed.), *Jews and Non-Jews in Eastern Europe* (Jerusalem: Keter, 1974), pp. 65ff.; and Häusler, "Assimilation und Emanzipation," pp. 43ff.

27. Imre Sándor, "Ballagi Mór," *Akadémiai Emlékbeszédek* (Budapest: Akademia, 1893); and McCagg, *Jewish Nobles and Geniuses in Modern Hungary*, pp. 80–83.

28. For the following, see Istvan Deak, *The Lawful Revolution* (New York: Columbia University Press, 1979), ch. 2; Béla Bernstein, *A negyvennyolcas magyar szabadságharc és a zsidók* (2nd ed., Budapest: Hungária, 1939); Zsigmond Groszmann, *A magyar zsidók a XIX század középen, 1849–1870* (Budapest: Egyenlöség, 1917); Salomon Stern, "Die politischen und kulturellen Kämpfe der Juden in Ungarn vom Jahre 1848–1871" (unpub. diss., Vienna, 1932), pp. 130ff.; and Jenö Zsoldos (ed.), *1848–1849 a magyar zsidóság életében* (Budapest: Neuwald Illes, 1948).

29. McCagg, "Jewish Conversion in Hungary" in Todd Endelmann (ed.), *Jewish Apostasy in the Modern World* (New York: Holmes and Meier, 1987), pp. 142-64; Venetianer, *A magyar zsidóság története*, p. 149; and Groszmann, *A magyar zsidók V Ferdinand alatt*, p. 15.

30. Bernstein, *A negyvennyolcas magyar szabadságharc*, ch. 2; Stern, "Die politischen und kulturellen Kämpfe," pp. 130ff.

31. J. Einhorn, *Die Revolution und die Juden in Ungarn* (Leipzig: Carl Geibel, 1851), pp. 81ff.; Büchler, *A zsidó története Budapesten*, pp 447ff.; Bernstein, op. cit., ch. 2.

32. See the contemporary assessment in *Orient* I (1840): 123; and August Fournier, *Erinnerungen*, chs. 1–2.

33. McCagg, *Jewish Nobles and Geniuses*, chs. 4, 5.

34. For the following, see Gusztav Gratz, *A Dualizmus Kora* (2 vols., Budapest: Magyar Szemle Társaság, 1934), chs. 3. 5.

35. Venetianer, *A zsidóság szervezete*, pp. 483ff.

36. Jeiteles, *Die Kultusgemeinde der Israeliten in Wien*, p. 55; and Kovács, *A zsidók térfoglalása*, pp. 57, 60.

37. For the following, see N. M. Gelber, "Ignaz Deutsch" in *Aus zwei Jahrhunderten* (Vienna: R. Löwit, 1942), pp. 145–77; G. Wolf's pseudonymous *Beitrag zur Geschichte jüdische Tartuffe* (Leipzig: C. G. Naumann, 1864); and Wolfgang Häusler, " 'Orthodoxie' und 'Reform' im Wiener Judentum in der Epoche des Hochliberalismus," in *SJA* VI (1978): 35ff.

38. G. Wolf, *Zur Culturgeschichte*, pp. 121ff.

39. Moskowitz, *Jewish Education*, pp. 36.

40. Friedmann, *Die galizischen Juden*, p. 42.

41. Büchler, *A zsidók története Budapesten*, pp. 490ff.; McCagg, *Jewish Nobles and Geniuses*, pp. 91–94.

42. Venetianer, *A magyar zsidóság története*, pp. 142ff.; and *NZ* I (1861): 159; II (1862): 74, 86; III (1863): 27, 161–63, 187–89, 194ff.; McCagg, *Jewish Nobles and Geniuses*, esp. pp. 131–134; and the chapter by György Szabad in Pach (ed.), *Magyarország Története*, vol. Vi/1, pt. II.

43. Venetianer, *A magyar zsidóság története*, p. 277.

44. On the problem of the Magyarization of later nineteenth-century Hungary, see Kosa, *Pest és Buda elmagyarosodása*; Peter Hanák, "Problems of Jewish Assimilation in Austria-Hungary" in P. Thane et al. (eds.), *The Power of the Past* (Cambridge: Cambridge University Press, 1984), ch. 10; Hanák, "Polgárosodás és asszimiláció Magyarországon a XIX században" in *TSz* XVII (1974): 513–36; Ludwig von Gogolák, "Zum Problem der Assimilation in Ungarn in der Zeit von 1790 bis 1918" in *SODA* IX (1966): 1–44; Éva Windisch, "A Magyarországi német nemzetiségi mozgalom elötörténete" in *Századok* XCVIII (1964): 648ff.; McCagg, *Jewish Nobles and Geniuses*, chs. 4 and 5; Barany, "Magyar Jew or Jewish Magyar," pp. 75ff., esp. p. 84; and Gyula Farkas's insightful but anti-Semitic *Az assimiláció kora a magyar irodalomban* (Budapest: Franklin, nd).

45. For the following, see Venetianer, *A magyar zsidóság története*, pp. 273–95; Thomas Domjan, "Der Kongress der ungarischen Israeliten 1868–1869" in *UJB* I (1969): pp. 139–62; and Nathaniel Katzburg, "The Jewish Congress in Hungary" in *HJS*, vol. I, pp. 1–33.

46. The numerical strength of Orthodox and Neologs at this time is impossible to measure: one can only trace the rapidly rising percentage of Magyar-speakers— 58.5% in 1880, 77.8% in 1910. See Katz, "The Identity of Post-Emancipatory Hungarian Jewry," pp. 7ff.

47. Moskovits, *Jewish Education in Hungary*, pp. 75ff.

NINE. VIENNA CONFUSED

On Vienna in the Ausgleich era, see Zeisberg et al. (eds.), *Wien 1848–1888* (2 vols., Vienna: Carl Konegen, 1888); Felix Czeike (ed.), *Wien in der liberalen Ära* (Vienna: VGSW, 1978); Baltzarek, Hoffmann, Stekl (eds.), *Wirtschaft und Gesellschaft der Wiener Stadterweiterung* (Wiesbaden: Steiner, 1975): Hans Bobek and Elizabeth Lichtenberger, *Wien: Bauliche Gestalt und Entwicklung seit der Mitte des 19. Jahrhunderts* (Vienna: Böhlau, 1966); R. Till, *Geschichte der Wiener Stadtverwaltung* (Vienna: Jugend und Volk, 1957); Franz, *Liberalismus*; Karl Eder, *Liberalismus in Altösterreich* (Vienna: Herald, 1955); Rogge, *Österreich von Világos bis zur Gegenwart*; and Boyer, *Political Radicalism in Late Imperial Vienna*. For the culture of the *Ringstrasse*, see Elizabeth Springer, *Geschichte und Kulturleben der Wiener Ringstrasse*; Klaus Eggert, *Der Wohnbau der Wiener Ringstrasse im Historismus* (Wiesbaden: Steiner, 1976); and the catalogue, *Hans Makart: Triumph einer schönen Epoche* (2 vols., Baden-Baden: 1972). An outstanding modern study of the Vienna Stock Exchange boom is Annalies Rohrer, "Die Wiener Effektenbörse und ihre Besucher in den Jahren 1867 bis 1875" (unpub. diss., Vienna, 1971). See also Benedikt, *Die wirtschaftliche Entwicklung*, pp. 88ff.; Baltzarek, *Die Wiener Börse*, pp. 71ff.; and the older accounts by Josef Neuwirth, *Die Speculationskrise von 1873* (Vienna: 1874); Moritz Lindner, *Die Asche der Millionen* (Vienna: 1884).

1. Hannes Stekl, "Rathaus Jubiläum 1973—Wirtschaftlicher und sozialer Hintergrund" in *WGB* XXVII (1973): 184ff.; and Baltzarek, Hoffmann, and Stekl, *Wirtschaft und Gesellschaft*, chs. 1, 2.

2. Gustav Otruba and L. S. Rutschka, "Die Herkunft der Wiener Bevölkerung in den letzten hundertfünfzig Jahren" in *JVGSW* XIII (1957–58): 230.

3. Rohrer, "Wiener Effektenbörse," pp. 59ff.; Baltzarek, *Die Wiener Börse*, pp. 57ff.; and Rogge, *Oesterreich seit der Katastrophe Hohenwart-Beust* (2 vols., Leipzig: F. A. Brockhaus, 1879), vol. I, p. 149.

4. Jaeger-Sunstenau, "Die geadelten Judenfamilien," pp. 74, 76.

5. Heinrich Benedikt, "Friedrich von Schey," *ÖBL*, vol. XXII, pp. 130ff.; Wurzbach, *BL*, vol. XXII, pp. 246–48; Rohrer, "Wiener Effektenbörse," pp. 71ff.; and Lindner, *Die Asche der Millionen*, p. 75.

6. Ludwig Speidel, "Theater" in Zeisberg et al. (eds.), *Wien 1848–1888*, vol. II, p. 373ff.

7. Eduard Hanslick, "Musik" in ibid., pp. 312ff.; and Peter Gay, *Freud, Jews and Other Germans* (New York: Oxford, 1978), chs. 5 and 6.

8. See the record of the politically important and culturally involved Auspitz-Gomperz-Lieben family, J. Winter, *50 Jahre eines Wiener Hauses* (Vienna: 1927).

9. For the following, see Appendix I, below.

10. Israel Jeiteles, *Die Kultusgemeinde der Israeliten in Wien*, pp. 67–73, 100.   See for the following the basic older works: G. Wolf, *Vom ersten bis zum zweiten Tempel* (1861); his *Geschichte* (1876); and his *Zur Culturgeschichte* (1888); also Häusler, " 'Orthodoxie' und 'Reform' im Wiener Judentum in der Epoche des Hochliberalismus" in *SJA* VI (1978): 29–56; and his "Das österreichische Judentum zwischen Beharrung und Fortschritt" in Wandruszka-Urbanitsch, *Die Habsburger Monarchie*, vol. IV, pp. 633–69.

11. Wolf, in his *Geschichte* (1876), p. 139, compared the toleree lists of 1787 and 1847, and found only 10 names out of the 66 on the first list still present in 1847. He erroneously perceived this as a sign of great instability among the tolerees. Had he used another eighteenth-century list, that of 1789, he would have found the names of 33 out 70 individuals cited still represented as Jews by their descendents in 1847—almost 50%. This is a rather high percentage for name continuity within a modern big city elite group.

12. Peter Schmidtbauer, "Zur sozialen Situation der Wiener Juden im Jahre 1857" in *SJA* VI (1978): 63–67; and Jeiteles, *Kultusgemeinde*, pp. 61, 71ff., 164ff.

13. Schmidtbauer, "Zur sozialen Situation," p. 62; and Jeiteles, *Kultusgemeinde*, pp. 53–55, 100–101. In both cases there was a smallish percentage of foreigners to the Habsburg dominions. In the 1857 case, there was a large number of unknowns.

14. Wolf, *Wertheimer*, p. 253; L. A. Frankl in A/W, 92.1, vol. II, pp. 5–7; and Wolf, *Culturgeschichte*, pp. 87–90. These Hungarian "German" Jews should be distinguished from the "German" Jews in Galicia, who were modernists and derived their name from their assertive use of modern (i.e., German) clothing: see Anonym, *Galizische Zustände*, p. 86.

15. Wolf in *NZ* (1868), p. 155.   Comp. "Verzeichnis der wählbaren Mitglieder . . . der isr. Kultusgemeinde in Wien," (Vienna: Jacob Schossberg, 1870).

16. Kieval, *Making of Czech Jewry*, pp. 6ff.

17. Wandruszka-Urbanitsch, *Die Habsburger Monarchie*, vol. III/1, opp. p. 38; and Thon, *Die Juden in Österreich*, p. 8.

18. For the following, see Blum, "Aufklärung und Reform," pp. 85ff.; Rozenblit, *The Jews of Vienna*, p. 40.

19. Comp. George Clare, *Last Waltz in Vienna* (New York: Holt, Rinehart, 1982), p. 67.

20. Rozenblit, *The Jews of Vienna*, p. 44.

21. Clare, *Last Waltz*, p. 31; and the numerous anecdotal examples in Adolf Dessauer, *Grossstadt Juden* (Vienna: Braumüller, 1908).

22. Husserl, "Die Entstehungsgeschichte des ersten definitiven Statutes der israel. Kultusgemeinde Wien" in A/W 732.2, pp. 10ff.   The Vorstand drew up a

temporary statute between 1849 and 1851, but was unable to gain the approval of the government for a permanent statute until 1867.

23. The following derives from a reading of the Vorstand meeting protocols for the 1850s: A/W 69.2 and 3. For the background, see Wolf, *Zur Culturgeschichte*, p. 91.

24. A/W 69.3, records of 9 Aug. 1854 and 18 December Vorstand meetings.

25. For the following, see N. M. Gelber, "Ignaz Deutsch" in his *Aus zwei Jahrhunderten*, pp. 145–77; (Gerson Wolf), *Beitrag zur Geschichte jüdische Tartuffe*; Wolf, *Josef Wertheimer*, pp. 259ff.; his *Zur Culturgeschichte*, pp. 120ff.; and Häusler, " 'Orthodoxie' und 'Reform,' " pp. 35ff.

26. Weissberg, "Die Judenemanzipation und die österreichische Reichsverfassung von 1849" (unpub. diss., Vienna, 1921); Wolf, *Culturgeschichte*, p. 121.

27. A/W 69.3, record of 5 Apr. 1855 meeting. Compare the report from Vienna in *AZJ* (1855), p. 59.

28. A/W 69.3, record of 17 Feb. 1856 meeting.

29. A/W 69.3, record of 4 Sept. 1856 meeting.

30. Peter Leisching, "Die römisch-katholische Kirche in Cisleithien" in Wandruszka-Urbanitsch, *Die Habsburger Monarchie*, vol. IV, pp. 25–34; Rogge, *Österreich von Világos bis zur Gegenwart*, vol. I, pp. 356ff.; and the alarmed discussion recorded in A/W, 69.2, meeting 6 Jan. 1852.

31. This ignorance of the enemy underlay the entire struggle with Deutsch. One may observe it especially clearly in the Vorstand's negotiations with the Vienna Orthodox just before and after the community election of December 1861. Until the voting revealed the real weakness of the foe, the Vorstand was conciliatory; afterwards it was arrogant: see A/W 69.4, negotiation session 12 Dec. 1861; plenary session 13 Jan. 1862; negotiating sessions of 19 and 22 Jan. and 9 Feb. 1862.

32. Blum, "Aufklärung und Reform," pp. 101ff.; Wolf, *Josef Wertheimer*, pp. 260ff.; Wolf, *Culturgeschichte*, p. 56; Tietze, *Die Juden Wiens*, p. 223; and Häusler, "Orthodoxie und Reform," p. 38.

33. Jaques's obituary, *NFP*, 26 Jan, 1894, p. 5; *ÖBL*, vol. III, p. 78.

34. See A/W 70, pp. 229–30, record of 20 Apr. 1859 meeting. The petition was submitted anyway, and was subsequently published by Jaques as *Denkschrift über die Stellung der Juden in Österreich* (Vienna: C. Gerold, 1859).

35. Max Letteris in *Wiener Mitteilungen*, vol. XXII (1860), esp. pp. 12, 81–85; *AZJ*, 1860, pp. 56, 342; and Bihl, "Die Juden," pp. 89off.

36. Baltzarek, Hoffmann, and Stekl, *Wirtschaft und Gesellschaft*, ch. 2 and table 8.

37. On Kuranda, see Wurzbach, *BL*, Vol. XIII, pp. 407–16; O. Doublier in *ADB*, Old Series, vol. LI, pp. 445–50; Winninger, *GJNB*, vol. III, pp. 554–55; A. Kohut in *AZJ* LXXVI (1913): 273–75, 282–84, 292–94; M. Landau in *EJ*, vol. X; S. Husserl in A/W 3133.2; Margarete Baumgarten, "Kurandas 'Ostdeutsche Post' und die deutsche Frage von 1859 bis 1863" (unpub. diss., Vienna, 1947), esp. ch. 1; Francis L. Loewenheim, "Ignaz Kuranda, *Die Grenzboten*, and Developments in Bohemia, 1845–1849," in Brock and Skilling (eds.), *The Czech Renascence*, pp. 146–175; W. Angerstein, *Österreichs parlamentarische Grossen* (Leipzig: Luckhardt, 1872), pp. 31–36; E. von Plener, *Erinnerungen* (2 vols., Stuttgart: Deutsch Verlagsanstalt, 1911–1921), vol. II, pp. 100ff.; Joseph S. Bloch, *Erinnerungen aus meinem Leben* (Vienna: Löwit, 1922), vol. I, pp. 142–45; and Kuranda's autobiographical sketch in *Die Grenzboten* (1845), pp. 345ff. Further bibliography is in Gold: *Mähren*, p. 109.

38. Plenary Vorstand meeting of 5 May 1861; School Committee meeting of 24 Oct. 1861, both in A/W 69.4. The records of 1862 and 1863 show the reformers to have become much less brash and pushy.

39. Fight between Kuranda and Königswarter recorded in A/W 69.4, meeting of 5 May 1861. The frustration among the lesser and more liberal Vorstand members

emerges from A/W 71.1, record of School Committee, 22 Sep. 1864. Comp. the records of the Finance Committee meetings in A/W 69.4 and 71.1.

40. Obituary sketch by Husserl in A/W 3133.2.

41. Angerstein, *Österreichs parlamentarische Grossen*, pp. 31–36.

42. *Wiener Kirchenzeitung*, 4 Feb. 1871, p. 1.

43. The following reflects the organization records in A/W 732.13.1.

44. *Die Presse*, 12–21 July, 1869.

45. Rohrer, "Wiener Effektenbörse," pp. 143ff.

46. Adolf von Sonnenthal, *Fünfzig Jahre im Wiener Burgtheater, 1856–1906* (Vienna: 1906); Ludwig Eisenberg, *Adolf Sonnenthal. Eine Künstlerlaufbahn* (Dresden: Pierson, 1896, 1900); Speidel, "Theater," pp. 375ff.; Springer, *Geschichte und Kulturleben*, pp. 523–24, 533ff.; and Theophila Wassilko, *Fürstin Pauline Metternich* (Vienna: Geschichte und Politik, n.d.), pp. 177ff.

47. For the following, see Schorske, *Fin de siécle Vienna*, esp. ch. 3; William J. McGrath, *Dionysian Art and Populist Politics in Austria* (New Haven: Yale University Press, 1974), ch. 6; his *Freud's Discovery of Psychoanalysis* (Ithaca: Cornell University Press, 1986); and Jonny Moser, "Von der Emanzipation zur antisemitischen Bewegung. Georg von Schönerer und Heinrich Friedjung" (unpub. diss., Vienna, 1962), pp. 78ff.

TEN. IMPERIALISM AND ANTI-SEMITISM

On Austrian politics after 1867, see, apart from the standard histories cited elsewhere, Arthur J. May, *The Hapsburg Monarchy, 1867–1914* (Cambridge, Mass.: Harvard University Press, 1960); and the monographs: William A. Jenks, *Austria under the Iron Ring* (Charlottesville: University Press of Virginia, 1965); his *The Austrian Electoral Reform of 1907* (New York: Columbia University Press, 1950); his *Vienna and the Young Hitler* (New York: Columbia University Press, 1960); Andrew Whiteside, *Austrian National Socialism before 1914* (The Hague: Nijhoff, 1962); his *The Socialism of Fools* (Berkeley: University of California Press, 1975); and Vincent J. Knapp, *Austrian Social Democracy, 1889–1914* (Washington: University Press of America, 1980).

The most extensive history of Trieste is Attilio Tamaro, *Storia di Trieste* (2 vols., Rome: Stock, 1924; republished with a critical introduction by G. Cervani at Trieste in 1976). See also Aldo Stella, "Il Comune di Trieste" in Giuseppe Galasso (ed.), *Storia d'Italia* (17 vols., Turin: UTET, 1979), vol. XVII, pp. 609–695; Ferruccio Fölkel and Carolus Cergoly, *Trieste, provincia imperiale: Splendore e tramonto del porto degli Asburgo* (Milan: Fabbri-Bompiani, 1983); Alfred Escher, *Triest und seine Aufgaben im Rahmen der österreichischen Volkswirtschaft* (Vienna: Manzsche Verlag, 1917); and the relevant parts of Umberto Corsin, "Die Italiener" in Wandruszka-Urbanitsch, *Die Habsburger Monarchie*, vol. III/2, pp. 839–79; Theodor Veiter, *Die Italiener in der österreichisch-ungarischen Monarchie* (Vienna: Geschichte und Politik, 1965); and Hans Kramer, *Die Italiener unter der österreichisch-ungarischen Monarchie* (Vienna: Böhlau, 1954).

For the Bukowina, see Keith Hitchins, "Die Rumänen" and Wolfdieter Bihl, "Die Ruthenen" in Wandruszka-Urbanitsch, *Die Habsburger Monarchie*, vol. III, chs. 6 and 7; and Erich Prokopowitsch, *Die rumänische Nationalbewegung in der Bukowina und der Dako-Romanismus* (Graz: Böhlau, 1965).

For Bohemia, see Cohen, *The Politics of Ethnic Survival*; Stanley B. Kimbal, *Czech Nationalism: A Study of the National Theatre Movement, 1845–83* (Urbana: University of Illinois Press, 1964); and Bruce M. Garver, *The Young Czech Party, 1874–1891* (New Haven: Yale University Press, 1978). On Bohemia's economic development, see, apart from the economic histories cited elsewhere, Pavla Horská-Vrbová, "Pražský prumsysl v druhé polovině 19. stoleti" in *PSH*, vol. V (1969–70): 52-69; Bernard

Michel, *Banques et banquiers en Autriche au début du 20e siècle* (Paris: FNSP, 1976); and Rudolph, *Banking and Industrialization in Austria-Hungary*, chs. 1–2.

1. Fritz Stern, *Gold and Iron*, esp. pp. 372–81; and N. M. Gelber, "The Intervention of the German Jews at the Berlin Congress, 1878," in *YLBI* V (1960), pp. 223ff.

2. Jakob Katz, *From Persuasion to Destruction*, ch. 21; R. Rürüp, *Emanzipation und Antisemitismus*, ch. 4; and Pulzer, *The Rise of Political Anti-Semitism in Germany and Austria*, chs. 9–20.

3. Judit Kubinsky, *Politikai antiszemitizmus Magyarországon, 1875–1890* (Budapest: Kossuth könyvkiadó, 1976), chs. 3, 5.

4. Chapter by Zoltán Szász in Pach (ed.), *Magyarország története*, vol. VI/II, ch. V/5; and Victor Karady and István Kemény, "Les juifs dans la structure des classes en Hongrie: Essai sur les antécédants historiques des crises d'antisémitisme du XXe siècle" in *ARSS* no. 22 (June 1978), pp. 25–59.

5. Jeanine Verdès-Leroux, *Scandale financier et antisémitisme catholique* (Paris: Centurion, 1969); Jean Bouvier, *Le krach de l'Union Générale, 1878–1880* (Paris: PUF, 1960); H. Benedikt, *Wirtschaftliche Entwicklung*, pp. 109–118; "Labienus," *Wiener geharnischte Briefe: Taaffe und Bontoux* (Vienna: Wiener Zeitung, 1880); and Wattmann, *53 Jahre*, vol. III, pp. 36ff.

6. A. Joshua Sherman, "The Nordbahn Controversy in Austrian Politics, 1884–1885" (Unpub. masters essay, Columbia University, 1967).

7. Vienna, calculated for modern city limits: Baltzarek, "Das territoriale und bevölkerungsmässige Wachstum" in *WGB* (1980), p. 13. Budapest: I. Lajos Illyesfalvi, *A székesföváros multja és jelene számokban* (Budapest: Stat. Hiv., 1934), p. 95. Prague, calculated for modern city limits: Havránek, "Demografický vývoj Prahy" in *PHS* 1969–70, p. 73. Trieste (land, not city) and Cernauti: earlier figures from Tamaro, *Storia di Trieste*, vol. II, pp. 157, 206, 396; and Raimund F. Kaindl, *Geschichte von Czernowitz* (Czernowitz: H. Pardini, 1908), p. 186; later figures from Wien, Statistische Zentralamt, *Vorläufige Ergebnisse der Volkszählung von 31 Dez. 1900* (Vienna: A. Hölden, 1901), pp. xviii, xxvi; *Öst. Stat. Handbuch* 1912, pp. 4, 14.

8. Israel Zoller, "La Comunità israelitica di Trieste: Studio di demografia storica" in *Metron* (Ferrara), vol. III, pp. 521–55 (also separately reprinted).

9. Kristianpoler, "Die wirtschaftliche Lage der Juden in Österreich," pp. 45ff., 101ff.; Colbi, "Note di storia ebraica," pp. 65–66. A *Hofkanzlei* discussion in 1776 made the following distinction between Triestine and northern Jews: "Weder die Görzer noch Triester jüdischen Handelsleute sind mit den grossen Häusern des übrigen erbländischen Juden-Gesindels, die sich weitaus nur auf Schwarz- und Schleichhandel verleget, zu vermengen": see *Hofkammer Archiv, Kommerz, Niederösterreich*, 1754–1812, fasc. 70, pp. 474–75.

10. Giulio Cervani and L. Buda, *La comunità israelitica di Trieste nel secolo XVIII* (Udine: del Bianco, 1873); Paolo S. Colbi, "Note di storia ebraica a Trieste nei secoli xviii e xix," in *RMI*, serie 3, vol. XXXIII (1970), pp. 59–73; A. V. Morpurgo, "Gli israeliti di Trieste," in *Corriere Israelitico*, vol. II (1862), pp. 8–11, 30–32, 63–65, and 125–28; and Ricardo Curiel, "Gli ebrei di Trieste nel secolo XVIII" in *RMI*, vol. XII (1938), p. 241.

11. Stella, "La comune di Trieste," pp. 655–66; Liana de Antonellis Martini, *Porto Franco e comunità ethico-religioso nella Trieste settecentesco* (Milano: Guffre, 1968); Giovanni Volli, "La nazione ebrea a Trieste" in *RMI*, serie 3, vol. XXIV (1958), pp. 206–314; Fabio Cusin, "Trieste e il Risorgimento," in *La Porta Orientale*, vol. VIII (1938), pp. 416ff.

12. Carlo Schiffrer, *Le origini dell'irredentismo triestino* (Udine: Del Bianco, 1978; orig. pub. 1937), p. 47.

13. Fölkel-Cergoly, *Trieste Provincia Imperiale*, p. 123.

14. Cervani-Buda, *La comunità israelitica*, pp. 45ff.; Altmann, *Moses Mendelssohn*, p. 477.

15. Mario Stock, "Giuseppe II d'Austria el l'emancipazione ebraica" in *RMI*, vol. XXXIX (1973), p. 371.

16. Giovanni Quarantotti, *Trieste e l'Istria nell'età napoleonica* (Florence: le Monnier, 1954); Giuseppe Stefani, "Bonapartisti triestini" in *La Porta Orientale*, vol. II (1932), no. 6–7; Curiel, "Gli ebrei di Trieste," pp. 253–54; and Cervani-Buda, *La communità israelitica*, pp. 92ff.

17. Tamaro, *Storia di Trieste*, vol. II, pp. 213–14.

18. For the following, see Giulio Cervani, *La borghesia triestina nell'età del Risorgimento* (Udine: Del Bianco, 1969), pp. 74–75; Cervani-Buda, *op. cit.*, p. 151; and Stella, "La commune di Trieste," pp. 664ff.; Israel Zoller, "Das Seeversicherungswesen und die Juden in Trieste" in *Freie jüdische Lehrstimme* VI: 3–4 (15 May 1917), pp. 45–47; Francesco Basilio, *Le assicurazione marittime a Trieste* (Trieste: 1911); and Giuseppe Pella (ed.), *L'assicurazione in Italia fino all'unità*, (Milano: A. Giuffre, 1975), esp. pp. 155ff.

19. Colbi, "Note di storia ebraica," p. 65; and Angelo Scocchi, "Gli ebrei di Trieste nel Risorgimento italiano" in *RSR*, vol. 7 (1951), p. 644ff.; and the report in *CO*, 1848, pp. 213–14.

20. Josef Wertheimer, "Die Triester Cultusgemeinde" in *Jahrbuch für Israeliten*, *1855–56* (Vienna: Knöpfelmacher, 1855), pp. 224–25; and Zoller, "La communità israelitica," pp. 536–37.

21. Giuseppe Stefani, "Le origini del' Lloyd Triestino" in *La Porta Orientale*, vol. I (1931), pp. 627–54; and Benedikt, *Die wirtschaftliche Entwicklung*, pp. 81ff.

22. *CO*, 1848, pp. 309–310; Schiffrer, *Le origini*, ch. 5; Baron, "The Revolution of 1848 and Jewish Scholarship," pt. I, pp. 50ff.; Cusin, "Trieste e il Risorgimento," pp. 434–37.

23. The principal Trieste Jewish confessional publication *Il Corriere Israeltico*, founded in 1862, was very heavily reoccupied with west European and Italian, as opposed to Austrian, Jewish affairs. Comp. Baron, "The Revolution of 1848 and Jewish Scholarship," pp. 54–55.

24. Bruno Cocceani, *Trieste della belle époque* (Trieste: Universitas, 1971), pp. 57–68; Mario Alberti, *L'irredentismo senza romanticismo* (Como: Cavalleri, nd; repub. 1938), pp. 277–82; and Colbi, "Note di storia," pp. 71–72.

25. Eduardo Morpurgo, *La Famiglia Morpurgo di Gradisca sull'Isonzo, 1585–1885* (Padua: SCT, 1909); Cervani-Buda, *La comunità israelitica*; Colbi, "Note di storia ebraica," pp. 65ff.; VA, *Adelsakten* Morpurgo, 1853 and 1867; Wurzbach, *BL*, vol. XVI.

26. Scocchi, "Gli ebrei di Trieste nel Risorgimento italiano," p. 654; Tamaro, *Storia di Trieste*, p. 435.

27. *Öst. Stat*, NF I/2 (1914), p. 53; Colbi, "Note di storia ebraica," p. 72.

28. Wandruszka-Urbanitsch, *Die Habsburger Monarchie*, vol. III/1, table I.

29. Fölkel, *Trieste*, p. 125; and H. Stuart Hughes, *Prisoners of Hope* (Cambridge, Mass.: Harvard University Press, 1983), pp. 39–40.

30. N. M. Gelber, "Geschichte der Juden in der Bukowina, 1774–1914" in H. Gold (ed.), *Geschichte der Juden in der Bukowina* (2 vols., Tel Aviv: Olamenu, 1958, 1962), vol. I, pp. 26–27, 46; Bihl, "Die Juden," p. 882. For background, see Kaindl, *Geschichte von Czernowitz*.

31. S. J. Schulsohn, "Die Rabbinerhöfe in Sadagora und Bojan" in Gold (ed.), *Juden in der Bukowina*, vol. I, pp. 85–89; and N. M. Gelber, "Die Wiznitzer Dynastie," ibid., pp. 83–84.

32. Gelber, "Geschichte," p. 49ff., 51; Hermann Sternberg, "Zur Geschichte der Juden in Czernowitz" in Gold (ed.), *Juden in der Bukowina*, vol. II, pp. 32ff.

33. Gelber, "Geschichte," p. 63, 40ff.; and Sternberg, "Zur Geschichte," pp. 32ff.

34. Hitchins, "Die Rumänen," p. 617.

35. For the following, see *Öst. Familienarchiv*, vol. III, pp. 138–43.

36. Fritz Mauthner, *Lebenserinnerungen*.

37. VA, *Adelsakten* Mauthner/Mautstein, 1850; Wurzbach, *BL*, vol. XVII, pp. 156–58; and Julius L. Pagel, *Biographisches Lexikon hervorragender Ärzte des 19. Jahrhunderts* (Vienna: Urban u. Schwarzenberg, 1901), p. 1107.

38. VA, *Adelsakten* Mautner/Markhof, 1872; *Haus-, Hof-, und Staatsarchiv, Kabinets-Kanzlei*, 1490; *GIO* 1898, vol. V; and J. Mentschl, *Österreichische Wirtschaftspionieren*, pp. 63–67.

39. VA, *Adelsakten* Mauthner, 1902; and *NFP*, 29 Dec. 1904 (Ab), p. 8.

40. VA, *Adelsakten* Mauthner, 1887; and obituaries in *Allg. Jur. Ztg.*, vol. X (1887), p. 409; and *NFP*, 29 Nov. 1887, p. 8.

41. VA, *Adelsakten* Mauthner, 1884; *NFP*, 20 May 1902, p. 6; *Publizistische Blätter*, 2 Feb. 1880.

42. Max Brod, *Der Prager Kreis* (Stuttgart: Kohlhammer, 1966), pp. 39ff.; and Johnson, *The Austrian Mind*, pp. 196ff.

43. McCagg, *Jewish Nobles and Geniuses*, pp. 186–88.

44. Bihl, "Die Juden," p. 882.

45. W. Brosche, "Das Ghetto von Prag," in Seibt (ed.), *Die Juden in den böhmischen Ländern*, p. 119.

46. Karel Kazbunda, *České hnutí roku 1848*, pp. 123, 168ff.; Stölzl, *Kafkas böses Böhmen*, ch. 1; Michael Riff, "The Assimilation of the Jews in Bohemia and the Rise of Political Anti-Semitism, 1848–1914" (unpub. diss., University of London, 1974); and Olesker, "Der Anteil der Juden an den Nationalitätenkämpfe," esp. ch. 4.

47. Kieval, *Making of Czech Jewry*, chs. 1, 2; Christoph Stölzl, "Zur Geschichte der böhmischen Juden," pt. II; Gary Cohen, "The Jews in German Society: Prague, 1860–1914," in *CEH* X (1977), pp. 28ff.; and Olesker, "Nationalitätenkämpfe," chs. 2 and 3.

48. Wolf, *Culturgeschichte*, pp. 113ff.; Teller, *Juden in Böhmen*, p. 81; *NZ*, 1861, p. 40. Comp. *AZJ*, 1865, p. 775; Olesker, "Nationalitätenkämpfe," p. 115.

49. Cohen, *Politics of Ethnic survival*, pp. 76ff.

50. Whiteside, *Austrian National Socialism*, chs. 1–2.

51. Albert Kohn (ed.), *Die Notabellenversammlung der Israeliten Böhmens* (Prague: 1852); Kieval, *Making of Czech Jewry*, ch. 1. pp. 22ff.

52. *Dějiny českožidovského hnutí* (Prague: 1932); Egon Hostovský, "The Czech Jewish Movement" in Coleman (ed.), *The Jews of Czechoslovakia*, vol. II, pp. 148–54; and Olesker, "Nationalitätenkämpfe," ch. 3.

53. Quoted from Häusler, *Von der Massenarmut*, p. 285.

54. Ernst Rychnovsky (ed), *Thomas G. Masaryk and the Jews* (New York: 1941), pp. 148–234; and František Červinka, "The Hilsner Affair" in *YLBI* XIII (1968), pp. 142–57.

55. Emil Brix, *Die Umgangssprache in Altösterreich zwischen Agitation und Assimilation* (Vienna: Böhlau, 1982), pp. 381ff.; Kieval, *Making of Czech Jewry*, ch. 2.

56. Oskar K. Rabinowicz, "Czechoslovak Zionism: Analecta to a History," in Coleman (ed.), *Jews of Czechoslovakia*, vol. II, pp. 72ff., esp. p. 76; Max Brod, *Streitbares Leben* (Munich: 1960), pp. 60ff.

57. Coleman (ed.), *Jews of Czechoslovakia*, vol. I, p. 449, 485; František Langer, *Byli a bylo* (Prague: Č. Spisovatel, 1963), pp. 10–28.

ELEVEN. THE CRISIS

On prewar Galicia, see, apart from the works cited in chapters 3 and 7 above, H. Batowski, "Die Polen" and W.-D. Bihl, "Die Ruthenen" in Wandruszka-Urbanitsch, *Die Habsburger Monarchie*, vol. III/1, pp. 522–54; 555–84; Madurowicz-Urbanska, "Die Industrie im Rahmen der wirtschaftlichen Struktur der Donaumonarchie" in *ZNUJ, Prace Historyczne* 57 (1978), pp. 158–73; and H. Matis/ K. Bachinger, "Österreichs industrielle Entwicklung" in Brusatti, *Die wirtschaftliche Entwicklung*, ch. 4.

On prewar Hungary, see especially Gusztáv Gratz, *A dualizmus kora* (2 vols., Budapest: Magyar Szemle Társaság, 1934); Janos, *The Politics of Backwardness*, chs. 3 and 4; and Péter Hanák, "Magyarország társadalma a századforduló idején" in Pach (ed.), *Magyarország Története*, vol. VII, 1, pp. 424ff.

On prewar Vienna, see, apart from works cited in chapter 9 above, Kurt Skalnik, *Dr. Karl Lueger* (Vienna: Herold, 1954); and Adam Wandruszka, "Österreichs politische Struktur" in Heinrich Benedikt (ed.), *Geschichte der Republik Österreich* (Vienna: Gerold, 1954; repr. 1977), pt. II.

1. Gerald Stourzh, "Die Gleichberechtigung der Volksstämme" in Wandruszka-Urbanitsch, *Die Habsburger Monarchie*, vol. III/2, pp. 1171–98.

2. Adalbert Rom, "Der Bildungsgrad der Bevölkerung Österreichs" in *Stat. MS, NF*, vol. XIX (1914), pp. 595ff.

3. Hans Chmelar, *Höhepunkte der österreichischen Auswanderung* (Vienna: Akademie, 1974).

4. According to the census the Poles had 58% of the Galician population, but Batowski, after subtracting the Jews, estimates their real strength as 50%: "Die Polen," pp. 527–28.

5. S. R. Landau, *Unter jüdische Proletarier* (Vienna: L. Rosner, 1898); Leo Herzberg-Fränkel, *Polnische Juden* (Stuttgart: C. Grüningen, 1888); Rosenfeld, *Polnische Judenfrage*, esp. pp. 70ff.; and Siegfried Fleischer, "Enquête über die Lage der jüdischen Bevölkerung Galiziens" in Alfred Nossig (ed.), *Jüdische Statistik* (Berlin: Jüdischer Verlag, 1903), pp. 203–231.

6. Frank Golczewski, *Polnisch-jüdische Beziehungen, 1881–1922* (Wiesbaden: Steiner, 1981), chs. 2 and 4.

7. Raphael Mahler, "The Economic Background of Jewish Emigration from Galicia to the United States," *YIVO Annual* VII (1952), pp. 255–67; Chmelar, *Höhepunkte der österreichischen Auswanderungen*, pp. 93ff.; and Rozenblit, *The Jews of Vienna*, pp. 21ff.

8. Rosenfeld, *Polnische Judenfrage*, pp. 74ff.; and Celia S. Heller, *On the Edge of Destruction* (New York: Columbia University Press, 1977), ch. 6.

9. Tietze, *Die Juden Wiens*, pp. 243–45; Joseph S. Bloch, *Erinnerungen aus meinem Leben* (2 vols., Vienna: Löwit, 1922); his *Der nationale Zwist und die Juden in Österreich* (Vienna: M. Gottlieb, 1886, orig. pub. as a series of editorials in the *Österreichische Wochenschrift*, 1884–1885); and the criticism of his ideas in Rosenfeld, *Polnische Judenfrage*, pp. 155ff.

10. Moses Landau, "Geschichte des Zionismus in Österreich" (unpub. diss., Vienna, 1932); Ezra Mendelsohn, "Jewish Assimilation in Lvov: The Case of Wilhelm Feldman," *SR* XXVIII (1969): 577–90; his "From Assimilation to Zionism in Lvov: The Case of Alfred Nossig," *SEER* XLIX (1971): 521–34; and S. L. Landau, *Sturm und Drang im Zionismus* (Vienna: Neue National-Zeitung, 1937), pp. 30ff.; and Rozenblit, *The Jews of Vienna*, pp. 168 and 243, n. 100.

11. Jacob Bross, "The Beginnings of the Jewish Labor Movement in Galicia," *YIVO Annual* V (1950), pp. 55ff.; Schiper et al. (eds.), *Zydzi w Polsce Odrodzonej*, vol. I, pp. 399–410; Hertz, *Austrian Social-Democracy*, p. 90; Jonathan Frankl, *Prophecy*

and Politics (Cambridge: Cambridge University Press, 1981), pp. 177, 310; McCagg, "The Assimilation of the Jews in Austria," pp. 132ff.; and Rosenfeld, *Polnische Judenfrage*, pp. 162–63.

12. Frankel, *Prophecy and Politics*, p. 370; and Rosenfeld, *Polnische Judenfrage*, p. 161.

13. For the following, see Kurt Stillschweig, "Nationalism and Autonomy among Eastern European Jewry," in *Historia Judaica* VI (1944): 27–68; his "Die nationalitätenrechtliche Stellung der Juden im alten Österreich," *MGWJ*, Vol. LXXXI (1937), pp. 321–340; and "Zur neueren Geschichte der jüdischen Autonomie," *MGWS* LXXXIII (1939): 509–532; and Max Rosenfeld, "Die nationale Autonomie der Juden in Österreich" in *Heimkehr* (Berlin, 1912), pp. 30–69.

14. Rosenfeld, *Polnische Judenfrage*, pp. 156ff.; and Brix, *Umgangssprache*, pp. 355ff.

15. Frankel, *Prophecy and Politics*, p. 159.

16. J. Fraenkel, "Rozwoj chasidyzmu" in Schiper et al. (eds.), *Zydzi w Polsce Odrodzonej*, vol. I, pp. 504–517; and Rabinowicz, *A Guide to Hassidism* (New York: Yoseloff, 1960), pp. 95–96.

17. Gerson Bacon, "Agudath Israel in Poland, 1916–1938" (unpub. diss., Columbia, 1979), pp. 129ff.

18. These and following statistics are from Hanák, "Magyarország társadalma a századforduló idején," pp. 424ff.

19. Gusztáv Thirring (ed.), *Budapest félszázados fejlödése* (Budapest: Statisztikai Hivatal, 1925), pp. 20–21; László Katus, "A nemzetiségi kérdés" in Pach (ed.), *Magyarország története*, vol. VII/2, p. 1010; and R. W. Seton-Watson, *Racial Problems in Hungary* (London: Constable, 1908).

20. *Magyar Zsidó Szemle* (1911), pp. 1–2; (1912), p. 1; Laszlo, "Hungarian Jewry: Settlement and Demography," pp. 75, 85, 99; and Laszlo, "Hungarian Jewry: A Demographic Overview, 1918–1945," in *HJS*, vol. II, p. 150.

21. Bihl, "Die Juden," p. 907.

22. Péter Hanák, "Polgárosodás és asszimiláció Magyarországon a XIX században," in *Társadalmi Szemle* (1974), pp. 513–36; Harriet Freidenreich, *The Jews of Yugoslavia* (Philadelphia: JPSA, 1979), chs. 1 and 2.

23. *Budapest statisztikai évkönyv*, vol. XII (1913), pp. 30–31. For the following comparisons, see my article, "Vienna and Budapest about 1900" in György Ránki (ed.), *Hungary and European Civilization* (Budapest: Akadémia, 1988).

24. McCagg, *Jewish Nobles*, p. 89.

25. Iván Berend and György Ránki, "Ungarns wirtschaftliche Entwicklung" in Wandruszka-Urbanitsch, *Die Habsburger Monarchie*, vol. I, pp. 514ff.

26. McCagg, *Jewish Nobles*, pp. 39ff., 152ff.

27. Szekfü, *Három nemzedék*, pp. 242–47; and McCagg, "The Role of the Magyar Nobility in Modern Jewish History," in *EEQ* XX (1986), no. 1, 41–531.

28. Péter Hanák, *Jászi Oszkár dunai patriotizmusa* (Budapest: Magvetö, 1985); and Zoltán Horváth, *Magyar századforduló* (Budapest: Gondolat, 1961).

29. "Zsidó autonomia" in *MZsL*, p. 896; the annual reports in *MZsSz* for 1910–14; and the materials cited in McCagg, *Jewish Nobles*, pp. 200–201.

30. McCagg, *Jewish Nobles and Geniuses*, pp. 199–208; and Venetianer, *A magyar zsidóság története*, pp. 417ff.

31. Livia Bitton, "Jewish Nationalism in Hungary" (unpub. diss., New York University, 1968), chs. 1–3; R. L. Braham, "Zionism in Hungary," in R. Patai (ed.), *Encyclopedia of Zionism and Israel*, vol. I, pp. 523–27; and the articles "Magyar Cionista Szövetség" and "Mizrachi" in *MZsL*, pp. 548–49, 608–609.

32. Janos, *Politics of Backwardness*, pp. 186ff.; McCagg, "Jews in Revolutions: The Hungarian Experience" in *JSS* V (1972): 176–92; and the articles on Mezöfi and Frankel in *MZsL*.

33. Mary Gluck, *Georg Lukacs and His Generation* (Cambridge, Mass.: Harvard University Press, 1985).

34. Hanák, *Jászi*, ch. 1; and McCagg, *Jewish Nobles*, p. 105.

35. Rozenblit, *The Jews of Vienna*, ch. 8; Arthur Mahler, "Jüdische Politik" in *Ost und West* (1910), pp. 546ff.; "—B—SZ," "Adolf Stern und die Wiener Kultus-gemeinde" in *Österreichische Wochenschrift*, 15 Nov. 1918, pp. 724–26; and Robert Stricker, *Jüdische Politik in Österreich* (Vienna: *Wiener Morgen Zeitung*, 1920).

36. These remarks are based on an attempt to card and count the Jews and non-Jews in the directorships of the leading Austrian business institutions between 1860 and 1918. The intent was to parallel the card collections analyzed in *Jewish Nobles and Geniuses in Modern Hungary*, ch. 6. There was no difficulty for the early sample years 1870 and 1880. For 1890, 1900, and 1910, however, the difficulties in distinguishing true wealth-holders from straw men, "Jews" from "non-Jews," and "representative" institutions frustrated the entire project.

37. Obituary in *NFP*, 18 Aug. 1910, p. 11; and Eva Holleis, *Die sozialpolitische Partei* (Vienna: Geschichte und Politik, 1978), pp. 77ff.

38. Franz Kobler, "The Contribution of Austrian Jews to Jurisprudence" in Fraenkel, *The Jews of Austria*, pp. 32–33; and Rozenblit, *The Jews of Vienna*, pp. 181ff.; Holleis, *Sozialpolitische Partei*, p. 22; Alfred Stern correspondence re Redlich candidacy of 1911 in A/W 744.1.

39. Kobler, "Contribution," pp. 31–32; McCagg, "The Assimilation of Jews in Austria," pp. 130ff.

40. Sander Gilman, *Jewish Self-Hatred*, pp. 188ff.; Robert Wistrich, *Socialism and the Jews: The Dilemmas of Assimilation in Germany and Austria-Hungary* (Rutherford, N.J.; Fairleigh Dickinson University Press, 1982), chs. 1, 8; and his *Revolutionary Jews* (London: G. Harrap, 1976), chs. 1, 5, 6.

41. Alex Bein, *Theodor Herzl* (Philadelphia: JPSA, 1940); Henry J. Cohn, "Theodore Herzl's Conversion to Zionism" in *JSS* XXXII (1970): 101–110; Jacques Kornberg, "Theodor Herzl: A Reevaluation" in *JMH* LII (1980): pp. 226–52; and Andrew Handler, *Dori* (University, Ala.: University of Alabama Press, 1983).

42. Rozenblit, *The Jews of Vienna*, pp. 185ff., 243 n. 109, and esp. 192; Landau, *Sturm und Drang im Zionismus*, ch. 18.

43. David Vital, *The Origins of Zionism* (London: Oxford University Press, 1975), p. 222ff.; Landau, *Sturm und Drang*, ch. 4; and Rozenblit, *The Jews of Vienna*, pp. 170ff.

44. Emanuel S. Goldsmith, *Architects of Yiddishism at the Beginning of the Twentieth Century* (Rutherford, N.J.: Fairleigh Dickinson University Press, 1976), pp. 99–119; S. A. Birnbaum, "Nathan Birnbaum and National Autonomy," in Fraenkel, *The Jews of Austria*, pp. 131–46; and Gelber, "Geschichte der Juden in der Bukowina," pp. 60–63.

45. See, for the following, Rozenblit, *Jews of Vienna*, ch. 1 and conclusions.

TWELVE. THE COLLAPSE

This chapter expands a paper delivered at the conference, "Contemporary Issues of Central European Jewry," at the Maison de l'Homme in Paris, August 1985. I am obliged to the participants in the conference for comments and criticisms.

On the collapse of the Habsburg Empire, see, apart from the general histories listed elsewhere, Richard G. Plaschka, Horst Haselsteiner, and A. Suppan, *Innere Front* (2 vols., Vienna: Geschichte und Politik, 1974); R. G. Plaschka and K. H. Mack (eds.), *Die Auflösung des Habsburger Reiches* (Vienna: Geschichte und Politik, 1970); and Arthur J. May, *The Passing of the Hapsburg Monarchy* (2 vols., Philadelphia: University of Pennsylvania Press, 1966).

1. For the state-by-state trend, see Ignac Schiper et al. (eds.), *Zydzi w Polsce Odrodzonej*; Joseph Marcus, *Social and Political History of the Jews in Poland, 1919–1939* (Amsterdam: Mouton, 1983); Agnes Heller, *On the Edge of Destruction*; Josef Fraenkel, *The Jews of Austria*; R. Braham (ed.), *Hungarian Jewish Studies*; H. Colman et al. (eds.), *The Jews of Czechoslovakia*; and Ezra Mendelsohn, *The Jews of East Central Europe Between the World Wars* (Bloomington, Ind.: Indiana University Press, 1985), p. 259, n. 3.

2. *Die Juden im Kriege* (Den Haag: Poale Zion, 1915); and Schiper (ed.), *Zydzi*, vol. I, pp. 413ff.

3. A. Böhm, *Die zionistische Bewegung* (2 vols., Tel Aviv: Hozaah Ivrith, 1935–37), vol. I, p. 630.

4. Contrast the figures in Thon, *Juden in Österreich*, pp. 10–11; or *ÖSt, NF*, vol. I, table 4, with the Polish *Annuaire Statistique* III (1924), pp. 16–17. The Jewish population rose during the war in only nine Galician *Kreise*, but these included seven of the eight most urban. The flight from small town to city was underway well before the war, but not on the same scale as during 1914–1920.

5. Golczewski, *Polnisch-jüdische Beziehungen, 1881–1922*, pp. 185ff.; and A. Reiss, "The Jews of Eastern Galicia in the Rebirth of Poland" (Hebrew) in Arieh Tartakower (ed.), *World Federation of Polish Jews: Yearbook*, vol. III (1970), pp. 33–122.

6. Essay on Slovakia by Livia Rothkirchen in Colman (ed.), *Jews of Czechoslovakia*, vol. I, pp. 85ff.; the documents in ibid., vol. I, pp. 223ff.; and the Nazi chronicle by Klaus Schickert, *Die Judenfrage in Ungarn* (Essen: Essener Verlag, 1937), pt. III.

7. L. Goldhammer, *Die Juden Wiens* (Vienna: Löwit, 1927), p. 9.

8. M. Heshel, "The History of Hassidism in Austria" in Fraenkel, *The Jews of Austria*, p. 354.

9. A. Kovács, *A Csonkamagyarországi zsidóság a statisztika tükrében* (Budapest: EKNL, 1938), p. 60.

10. The Belz Rebbe tried to stay in Czechoslovakia after the war, returning finally to Galicia only after a fight with the Mukačevo Rabbi in 1921, and settling again at Belz only in 1923: see *EJ*, vol. IV, pp. 452–53; and H. Rabinowicz, *Guide to Hassidism* (New York: Th. Yoseloff, 1960), ch. 8.

11. Moritz Rosenfeld, *Oberrabbiner H. P. Chajes: sein Leben und sein Werk* (Vienna: J. Rabinowitsch, 1933), ch. 4.

12. See for the following Gershon Bacon, "Agudath Israel in Poland, 1916–1938" (unpub. diss., Columbia, 1979); Rabinowicz, *Guide to Hassidism*, ch. 8; and Fraenkel, *Jews of Austria*, pp. 347ff.

13. Bacon, "Agudath Israel," vol. I, pp. 24, 116–19; and E. Mendelsohn, "The Politics of Agudas Yisroel in Inter-War Poland" in *Soviet Jewish Affairs* II (1972), no. 2, p. 58.

14. Gertrude Hirschler in Colman (ed.), *Jews of Czechoslovakia*, vol. II, esp. pp. 161–62.

15. Contrast the Polish *Annuaire Statistique* III (1924), pp. 16–17, with the prewar statistics usefully compiled in Wandruschka-Urbanitsch, *Die Habsburger Monarchie*, vol. III/1, table 1. The 1921 Polish census asked nationality, not language, so this contrast may exaggerate; but the 1931 census, which did ask language, revealed a similarly pronounced trend away from prewar figures.

16. *Statistisches Handbuch der čechoslovakischen Republik*, vol. II (1925), pp. 368, 379.

17. Ibid.; and *Anuarul Statistic al Romaniei*, 1922, pt. 3, table 12 as contrasted with the 1910 Hungarian figures reported in Kovács, *A zsidók térfoglalása*, pp. 63–65. It is clear that the introduction of Yiddish in the census in both Bohemia and Transylvania detracted heavily from the formerly strong German and Magyar po-

sitions, but not from those of the Czechs and Rumanians who now held power, and who both grew.

18. Max Rosenfeld, *Die polnische Judenfrage*, pp. 155ff.; and Mendelsohn, *Jews of East Central Europe*, pp. 49–51.

19. S. J. Agnon, *Nur wie ein Gast zur Nacht* (Frankfurt am Main: Fischer Verlag, 1964).

20. Thon, *Juden in Österreich*, pp. 118ff.; Kovács, *A zsidóság térfoglalása*, tables 6, 7; Jacob Lestchinsky, "The Industrial and Social Structure of the Jewish Population in Interbellum Poland" in Joshua A. Fishman (ed.), *Studies in Modern Jewish History* (New York: YIVO, 1972), pp. 254ff.

21. Tamar Bermann, *Produktivierungsmythen und Antisemitismus* (Vienna: Europaverlag, 1973), pp. 17–34, 65–71; Friedmann, *Die galizischen Juden*, pp. 17ff.; Marcus, *Social and Political History*, pp. 51ff.

22. Berman, *Produktivierungsmythen*, pp. 97–141; Philip L. Utley, "Siegfried Bernfeld's Jewish Order of Youth, 1914–1922" in *YLBI* XXIV (1979): 349–68; Elkana Margalit, "Social and Intellectual Origins of the Hashomer Hatzair Youth Movement, 1913–1920" in *JCH* IV: 2 (April 1969), pp. 25–46 (also published in German); and Walter Laqueur, *History of Zionism*, pp. 297–301.

23. *ÖSt, NF*, vol. III/1, table 26; and then in each of the ensuing crownland *Hefte*, table 6; *MStK, Új Sorozat*, vol. LXIV, pp. 216 and 280–281; and vol. LVI, tables 6 and 91;

24. Goldhammer, *Die Juden Wiens*, p. 57.

25. Rosenfeld, *Polnische Judenfrage*, pp. 122–23; and Marcus, *Social and Political History*, pp. 53ff.

26. Goldhammer, *Die Juden Wiens*, p. 68; Marcus, *Social and Political History*, pp. 204ff.; *ÖSt, NF*, Vol. III/1, table 27.

27. *ÖSt, NF*, vol. III/1, Table 26.

28. Discussion in Marcus, *Social and Political History*, ch. 3.

29. Rozenblit, *Jews of Vienna*, ch. 4, esp. pp. 75ff. and p. 226, n. 33.

30. E. Mendelsohn, *Class Struggle in the Pale* (Cambridge: Harvard University Press, 1970), pp. 10ff.; Zwi Gitelman, *Jewish Identity and Soviet Politics* (Princeton: Princeton University Press, 1972), ch. 1; and John Bunzl, *Klassenkampf in der Diaspora* (Vienna: Europaverlag, 1975), pp. 29ff.

31. Robert Wistrich, "Austrian Social Democracy and the Problem of Galician Jewry, 1890–1914" in *YLBI* XXVI (1981): 89–124; Jonathan Frankl, *Prophecy and Politics*, pp. 169ff.; and Wistrich, *Revolutionary Jews*, ch. 7.

32. Bruno Frei, *Jüdisches Elend in Wien* (Vienna: Löwit, 1920); Marcus, *Social and Political History*, pp. 43ff. and ch. 10.

33. McCagg, "Jews in Revolutions: The Hungarian Experience" in *Journal of Social History* VI (1972): 78–105; "The Assimilation of Jews in Austria" in Bela Vago (ed.), *Jewish Assimilation in Modern Times* (Boulder: Westview, 1981), pp. 127–40; and Christoph Stölzl, "Die 'Burg' und die Juden" in K. Bosl (ed.), *Die 'Burg'* (Munich: Oldenbourg, 1974), pp. 79–110.

34. Robert Schwarz, "Antisemitism and Socialism in Austria, 1918–1962" in Fraenkel, *Jews of Austria*, pp. 446ff.

35. Andrew C. Janos, *The Politics of Backwardness*, esp. pp. 176ff. and ch. 6.

36. Gold (ed.), *Geschichte der Juden in der Bukowina*, vol. I, pp. 67ff.; vol. II, pp. 1–27.

37. Margalit, "Social and Intellectual Origins," pp. 31ff.

38. Bunzl, *Klassenkampf*, pp. 119ff.; and F. Werfel's Roman à clef, *Barbara oder die Frommigkeit*.

39. McCagg, *Jewish Nobles and Geniuses*, p. 206, n. 37; O. Rabinowicz, "Czechoslovak Zionism" in Colman (ed.), *Jews of Czechoslovakia*, vol. II, pp. 76ff.; F. B. M. Fowkes, "Origins of Czechoslovak Communism," in Ivo Banac (ed.), *The Effects of World War I: The Class War after the Great War; The Rise of Communist Parties in East*

Central Europe, 1918–1921 (New York and Boulder, Col.: *EEQ*, 1983), pp. 71, 76; Marcus, *Social and Political History*, pp. 274ff.; Mendelsohn, *Jews of ECE*, pp. 46–53; A. Hafftka in Schiper (ed.), *Zydzi*, vol. II, pp. 270ff.; and Tadeusz Szafar, "The Origins of the Communist Party of Poland" in Banac, pp. 42–43, n. 49.

40. Michael Löwy, "Messianisme juif et utopies libértaires en Europe (1905–1923)" in *ASS* LI/1 (Jan. 1981): 5–47; William McGrath, *Freud's Discovery of Psychoanalysis: The Politics of Hysteria*, pp. 20–24; and McCagg, "Jews in Revolutions" present these arguments.

41. Walter B. Simon, "The Jewish Vote in Austria," *YLBI* XVI (1971): 117ff.; Rabinowicz, "Czechoslovak Zionism," pp. 78ff.

42. Rozenblit, *Jews of Vienna*, p. 51; and Ivor Oxaal, "The Jews of Pre-1914 Vienna" (unpub. mimeograph, Hull, 1981), pp. 111ff.

43. *MStK, US*, vol. LXIV, table 102. In 1900 the Jewish "manager" proportion in Budapest had been only 48.6%!

44. Peter Gay, *Freud, Jews and Other Germans* (New York: Oxford, 1978), Introduction.

45. Bihl, "Die Juden," pp. 940ff.

46. István Bibó wrote in 1948: "But perhaps in no other central and eastern European country was the inner world of the assimilating Jewish community so incoherent, and the course of Jewish assimilation so burdened with lies and contradictions, as in Hungary," *Harmadik Út* (London: CEH, nd), p. 317. Comp. the even more devasting remarks on p. 318.

47. Gold, *Bukowina*, vol. I, pp. 67–68.

48. See in general Wolfgang von Weisl, "Die Juden in der Armee Österreich-Ungarns" (Tel Aviv: Olamenu, 1971); and Erwin A. Schmidl, "Jews in the Austro-Hungarian Army" (mimeograph conference paper, Jerusalem, Oct. 1984). Officially 501 Jewish officers died in the war, comprising 6.78% of all the K.u.K. and Landwehr officers: see M. Paul-Schiff, "Teilnahme der österreichisch-ungarischen Juden am Weltkrieg" in *JJVK* XXVI-XXVII (1924–1925): 151–56. Prof. István Deák of Columbia University tells me that there were actually 732 Jewish and Cisleithanian officers killed or missing; and that in addition 270 Hungarian *Honvéd* officers were killed (a third of all the lost *Honvéd* officers). For the allegedly "sub-standard" non-officer Jewish war-death toll, see *MZsL*, "Világháború" and Kovács, *Térfoglalása*, pp. 23–25.

49. Victor Karady and István Kemény, "Antisémitisme universitaire et concurrence de classe" in *ARSS* 22 (1978): 25–60, and 34 (1980): 67–96.

50. Valentine Sobotka's *Ways and Issues Retraced* (Berkeley: private, 1980); and Joseph Pick, "The Economy" in Colman (ed.), *Jews of Czechoslovakia*, pp. 359ff.

51. The conversions were announced by such journals as the *Österreichische Wochenschrift* at Vienna and the *Egyenlöség* in Budapest. Comp. Michael A. Riff, "Assimilation and Conversion in Bohemia" in *YLBI* XXVI (1981): 78–79; and my "Jewish Conversion in Hungary," in Todd Endelmann (ed.), *Jewish Apostasy in the Modern World* (New York: Holmes & Meier, 1987), pp. 142-164.

52. Robert Weltsch, "Österreichische Revolutionschronik" in *Der Jude*, vol. XII (1919), pp. 350–58.

53. Albrecht Hellmann, "Die Geschichte der Österreichisch-jüdische Kongressbewegung," *Der Jude*, vol. V (1920–21), pp. 204–214, 389–95, 634–45, 685ff.; Stillschweig, "Nationalism and Autonomy," pp. 44ff., 52ff.; Anonym. "Adolf Stern" in *ÖW*, 15 Nov. 1918, pp. 724–726; Robert Stricker, *Jüdische Politik in Österreich*.

THIRTEEN. CONCLUSIONS

1. Compare my "On Habsburg History and Its Disappearance," in Jonathan Frankl (ed.), *Studies in Contemporary Jewry* IV (1987): 172-96.

BIBLIOGRAPHY

To list all the works consulted in preparing this book or even just those cited in the notes, would consume a great deal of space. It would also duplicate the analytical "general notes" at the head of each chapter, and would be redundant since half a dozen partial bibliographies are readily available in print. The following is, therefore, simply a report on the more important raw materials which form the foundation of the book—first unpublished and published documents, statistical and topographical works, and writings of eye-witnesses; then unpublished dissertations; finally, for readers' convenience, selected monographs. In this last list, I have leaned toward recent works which readers may not find in older bibliographies.

UNPUBLISHED MATERIALS

JERUSALEM

Central Archives of the Jewish People
    Archiv der israelitischen Kultusgemeinde, Wien (A/W)
        Vertreter Protokollen, 1798–1867
        Vorstand Protokollen, 1868–1890
        Wahlakten
        Personalien
        Jahrbuch für das Jahr 1911 (collection of
            statistical and institutional data)
        Totenanzeigen
        Antisemitica (clipping collection, 1881–1911)
        Steuerkartei
        Austritte Korrespondenz
        Historical manuscripts (S. Husserl, M. Brunner,
            B. Wachstein, M. Grunwald, A. F. Pribram,
            L. Frankl

VIENNA

Haus-, Hof-, und Staatsarchiv
    Kabinets-Kanzlei, files on ennobled citizens
Verwaltungsarchiv (VA)
    Adelsarchiv, files on ennobled Jews
Hofkammer Archiv
    Kommerzienakten. Judensachen 1700–1825
Stadtarchiv
    A. Wiesinger Clipping Collection
    Leon Ruzicka Card Collection of converted Jews
Österreichische National-Bibliothek
    Manuscript Collection (Frankl Biography, CD.8 SN18229)
Österreichische National-Biographie
    Personalities Card File

MUNICH

Neue deutsche Biographie
    Personalities Card File
Collegium Carolinum, Munich
    Personalities Card File

NEW YORK

Leo Baeck Institute, New York
Collection of unpublished memoirs

NEWSPAPERS

I have used the following journals extensively for the periods noted. For other
journals consulted, see Abbreviations.

Allgemeine Zeitung des Judentums (1840–1875)
Corriere Israelitico (1863–1890)
Deutsche Wochenschrift (1883–1887)
Az Egyenlöség (1870–1920)
Der Israelit (1860–1875)
Der Jude (1910–1920)
Die Neue Freie Presse (1864–1938)
Die Neuzeit (1860–1910)
Der Orient (1840–1850)
Österreichische Wochenschrift (1884–1914)
Österreichisches Central-Organ für Glaubensfreiheit (1848)
Wiener Kirchenzeitung (1868–1873)
Wiener Mitteilungen (1859–1865)

PUBLISHED DOCUMENTS AND PRIMARY SOURCES

Barth-Bartenstein, Johann Ludwig Ehrenreich, Graf von. *Politische Verfassung der
    Israeliten im Lande unter der Ems und insbesondere in der k.k. Haupt- und Residenz-
    stadt Wien.* Vienna: J. B. Wallishaussen, 1821.
Glossy, Karl (ed.). *Wien 1840–1848. Eine amtliche Chronik.* 2 vols. Vienna: Literar-
    ischer Verein, 1917, 1919.
Helfert, Joseph A. (ed.), *Der Wiener Parnass im Jahre 1848.* Vienna: Manz'sche Buch-
    handlung, 1882.
Iggers, Wilma. *Die Juden in Böhmen und Mähren* (Munich: Beck, 1986).
Pribram, Alfred Francis (ed.). *Urkunden und Akten zur Geschichte der Juden in Wien.*
    2 vols. Vienna: W. Braumüller, 1918.
Redl, Anton. *Addressenbuch der Handlungs Gremien und Fabriken in der KK. Haupt und
    Residenz Stadt Wien, 1823.* Vienna: J.P. Sollingen, 1823.
Taglicht, Israel (ed.). *Nachlasse der Wiener Juden im 17. und 18. Jahrhundert.* Vienna:
    Braumüller, 1917.
Wachstein, Bernard. "Die Gründung der Wiener Chevra Kadischa im Jahre 1763."
    MJVK XIII (1910): 9–12.
———. *Die Inschriften des alten Judenfriedhofes in Wien.* 2 vols. Vienna: Selbstverlag,
    1930.
———. *Merkantilprotokolle. Der Anteil der Wiener Juden an Handel und Industrie.* Vi-
    enna: Selbstverlag, 1936.
———. *Randbemerkungen zu meinen 'Inschriften. . . .'* Vienna: Selbstverlag, 1936.
Walsh, James E. (ed.). *1848: Austrian Revolutionary Broadsides and Pamphlets: A Cata-
    logue.* Boston: G. K. Hall, 1976.

STATISTICAL AND TOPOGRAPHICAL WORKS

Baltzarek, Franz. "Das territoriale und bevölkerungsmässige Wachstum der Gross-
    stadt Wien." *WGB* XXXV (1980): 1–16.

——, A. Hofmann, and H. Stekl. *Wirtschaft und Gesellschaft der Wiener Stadter-weiterung.* Wiesbaden: Steiner, 1975.

Becher, Siegfried. *Statistische Übersicht der Bevölkerung der österreichischen Monarchie nach den Ergebnissen der Jahre 1834 bis 1840.* Stuttgart: Cotta, 1841.

Czoernig, Carl. *Oesterreichs Neugestaltung 1848–1858.* Stuttgart and Augsburg: Cotta, 1858.

Fényes, Elek. *Statistik des Königreiches Ungarn.* Pest: K. Trattner, 1843.

Goldhammer, Leo. *Die Juden Wiens.* Vienna: Löwit, 1927.

Hain, Josef. *Handbuch der Statistik des österreichischen Kaiserstaates.* 2 vols. Vienna: 1852–53.

Heřman, Jan. "The Evolution of the Jewish Population in Bohemia and Moravia, 1754–1953." In U. O. Schmelz et al. (eds.), *Papers in Jewish Demography 1973.* Jerusalem: Inst. Contemp. Jewry, 1977.

——. "The Evolution of the Jewish Population of Prague, 1969–1931." In U. O. Schmelz et al. (eds.), *Papers in Jewish Demography 1977.* Jerusalem: Inst. Contemp. Jewry, 1980.

Illyesfalvi, I. Lajos. *A székesföváros multja és jelene számokban.* Budapest: Stat. Hiv., 1934.

Jeiteles, Israel. *Die Kultusgemeinde der Israeliten in Wien.* Vienna: L. Rosner, 1873.

Kárníková, Ludmila. *Vývoj obyvatelstva v českých zemí 1754–1914.* Prague: ČSAV, 1965.

Kovács, Alajos. *A zsidóság térfoglalása Magyarországon.* Budapest: private, 1922.

——. *A csonkamagyarországi zsidóság a statisztiká tükrében.* Budapest: private, 1938.

Kovacsics, Josef, *Magyarország történeti demogràfiája.* Budapest: K. J. Kiadó, 1963.

K.-k. Statistische Central-Commission. *Österreichische Statistik: Neue Folge.* Vols. I-III (1912–1917).

Magyar Kir. Központi Statisztikai Hivatel. *Magyar Statisztikai Közlemények. Új Sorozat.* No. 64 (1924).

Nossig, Alfred (ed.). *Jüdische Statistik.* Berlin: Jüdischer Verlag. 1903.

Olegnik, Felix, "Historisch-statistische Übersichten von Wien." *Mitteilungen aus Statistik und Verwaltung der Stadt Wien Sonderheft I.* Vienna: mimeograph, 1956.

Placht, Otto. *Lidnatost a společenská skladba českého státu v 16–18 století.* Prague: ČSAV, 1957.

Rohrer, Josef. *Versuch über die jüdische Bewohner der österreichischen Monarchie.* Vienna: Kunst und Industrie Comptoir, 1804.

Schimmer, G. A. *Die Juden in Österreich.* Vienna: Hölder, 1881.

——. *Statistik des Judenthums.* Vienna: Staatsdruckerei, 1873.

Schwarzer, Ernst von. *Geld und Gut in Neu-Österreich.* Vienna: Wallishauser, 1857.

Sedlaczek, Stephan and Wilhelm Löwy. *Wien: Statistischer Bericht über die wichtigsten demographischen Verhältnisse.* Vienna: 1887.

Slokar, Johann. *Geschichte der österreichischen Industrie und ihre Förderung unter Kaiser Franz I.* Vienna: F. Tempsky, 1914.

Thirring, Gusztáv. *Budapest félszázados fejlödése.* Budapest: Stat. Hiv., 1925.

Thon, Jakob. *Die Juden in Österreich.* Berlin: Louis Lamm, 1908.

COMPENDIA

Allgemeine Deutsche Biographie. 56 vols. Leipzig: Duncker and Humblot, 1875–1912.

Benda, Kálmán (ed.). *Magyarorság Történeti Kronológiája.* 4 vols. Budapest: Akadémia, 1983.

Czeike, Felix (ed.). *Das grosse Wien Lexikon.* Vienna: Molden, 1974.

Dějiny Československa v Datech. Prague: Svoboda, 1968.

Encyclopedia Judaica. Jerusalem: Ency. Jud., 1960.

Frühling, Moritz. *Biographisches Handbuch der in der österreichisch-ungarischen Armee . . . Offiziere . . . jüdischen Stammes.* Vienna: 1911.

Graeffer, Franz (ed.). *Jüdischer Plutarch.* 2 vols. Vienna: Klopf, 1848.

Granichstädten-Cerva, Rudolf, J. Mentschl, and G. Otruba (eds.). *Altösterreichische Unternehmer.* Vienna: Bergland, 1969.

Kleindel, Walter. *Österreich. Daten zur Geschichte und Kultur.* Vienna: Überreuther, 1978.

Knauer, Oswald. *Österreichs Männer des öffentlichen Lebens.* Vienna: Manz, 1960.

Mentschl, Josef and Gustav Otruba, *Österreichische Industrielle und Bankiers.* Vienna: Bergland Verlag, 1965.

Muneles, Otto. *Bibliografický Přehled Židovské Prahy.* Prague: Orbis, 1952.

Nagl, J. W., J. Zeidler, and Eduard Castle. *Deutsch-österreichische Literaturgeschichte.* 4 vols. Vienna: Carl Fromme, 1899–1914.

Neue Deutsche Biographie. Berlin: Duncker & Humblot, 1955–.

Österreichisches Biographisches Lexikon, 1815–1950. Graz: Böhlau, 1950–.

Polski Slownik Biograficzny. Cracow and Warsaw: various publishers, 1935–.

Portheim, Max von, and M. Holzman. "Materialen zu einer Bibliographie über die österreichischen Juden." In *Jüdisches Archiv,* I: 3, 4/5, 6; II: 1/2, 5/7.

Semigothäisches Genealogisches Taschenbuch. Munich: Kyffhäuser, 1912, 1913.

Stöger, M. *Darstellung der gesetzlichen Verfassung der galizischen Juden.* 2 vols. Lwow: 1883.

Sturm, Herbert (ed.). *Biographisches Lexikon zur Geschichte der böhmischen Länder.* Munich: Oldenbourg, 1974–.

Újváry, Péter (ed.). *Magyar Zsidó Lexikon.* Budapest: Zsidó Lexikon, 1927.

Winninger, Salomon (ed.). *Grosse jüdische National-Biographie.* 7 vols. Cernauti: Arte, 1925–1932; reprint, Liechtenstein: Nendelen, 1980.

Wurzbach, Constantin von (ed.). *Biographisches Lexicon des Kaisertums Österreich.* 60 vols. Vienna: Manz, 1856–1891.

CONTEMPORARY ACCOUNTS

Angerstein, Wilhelm. *Die Corruption in Österreich.* Leipzig: Luckhardt, 1872.

———. *Österreichs parlamentarische Grossen.* Leipzig: Luckhardt, 1872.

———. *Volkswirthschaftliche Zustände.* Leipzig: Luckhardt, 1871.

Bauer, Otto. *Die Nationalitätenfrage und die Sozialdemokratie.* Vienna: Brand, 1907.

Bauernfeld, Eduard. Ed. Josef Bindtner. *Erinnerungen aus Alt-Wien.* Vienna: Wiener Drucker, 1923.

Beer, Peter. *Reminiscenzen.* Prague: 1837.

Benedikt, Heinrich. *Damals im alten Österreich.* Vienna: Amalthea, 1979.

Benedikt, Moritz. *Aus meinem Leben.* Vienna: C. Konegen, 1906.

Bloch, Josef Samuel. *Erinnerungen aus meinem Leben.* 2 vols. Vienna: Löwit, 1922.

———. *Der nationale Zwist und die Juden in Österreich* (Vienna: M. Gottlieb, 1886).

Braunthal, Julius. *In Search of the Millennium.* London: V. Golanz, 1945.

Brod, Max. *Streitbares Leben.* Munich: Herbig, 1969.

Castelli, J. F. Ed. Josef Bindtner. *Memoiren meines Lebens.* 2 vols. Munich: G. Müller, 1913.

de la Garde, August. *Gemälde des Wiener Kongresses.* 2 vols. Munich: G. Müller, 1914.

de Luca, Ignaz. *Das gelehrte Österreich.* 2 vols. Vienna: Thom, 1776–78.

Dessauer, Adolf. *Grossstadtjuden.* Vienna: Braumüller, 1908.

Einhorn, J. *Die Revolution und die Juden in Ungarn.* Leipzig: C. Gerbel, 1851.

Ewart, Felicie (pseud, Emilie Exner). *Zwei Frauenbildnisse.* Vienna: private, 1907.

Frankl, Ludwig August. *Erinnerungen.* Ed. S. Hoch. Prague: J. Koch, 1910.

Frei, Bruno. *Jüdisches Elend in Wien.* Vienna: Löwit, 1920.

Galizisch-jüdische Zustände. Leipzig: Philipp Reclam, 1845.

Goldschmidt, Hermann von. *Einige Erinnerungen aus längst vergangenen Tagen*, Vienna: Selbstverlag, 1917.

Gomperz, Julius von. *Jugenderinnerungen*. Brünn: Rohrer, 1902.

Gutmann, Wilhelm. *Aus meinem Leben*. Vienna: Gerold, 1911.

Jaques, Heinrich. *Denkschrift über die Stellung der Juden in Österreich*. Vienna: Gerold, 1859.

Kohn, Gotthilf. *Abraham Kohn im Lichte der Geschichtsforschung*. Zamarstynow bei Lemberg: Selbstverlag, 1898.

Kompert, Leopold. "Israel Hönig." In *Jahrbuch für Israeliten*, 1847–1848.

Küttner, Carl G. *Reise durch Deutschland*. 3 vols. Leipzig: 1804.

Landau, S. R. *Sturm und Drang im Zionismus*. Vienna: Neue National-Zeitung, 1937.

———. *Unter jüdische Proletarier*. Vienna: L. Rosner, 1898.

Langer, František. *Byli a bylo*. Prague: Č. Spisovatel, 1963.

Löw, Leopold. *Zur neueren Geschichte der Juden in Ungarn*. Budapest: L. Aigner, 1874.

———. (Dr. Weil, pseud.). *Aaron Chorin: Eine biographische Skizze*. Szeged: S. Berger, 1863.

Mauthner, Fritz. *Erinnerungen, Prager Jugendjahre*. Munich: G. Müller, 1918.

Mayer, Sigmund. *Ein jüdischer Kaufmann*. Leipzig: Duncker & Humblot, 1911.

———. *Die Wiener Juden*. Vienna: Löwit, 1917.

Meissner, Alfred. *Schwarzgelb*. Leipzig: Grunow, 1971.

Pezzl, Johann. *Skizzen von Wien*. Ed. Gustav Gugitz and A. Schlossar. Graz: Leykam, 1923.

Pichler, Caroline. *Denkwürdigkeiten aus meinem Leben*. Munich: G. Müller, 1914.

Pollak, Heinrich. *Dreissig Jahre aus dem Leben eines Journalisten*. 3 vols. Vienna: A. Hölden, 1875, 1898.

Retzer, Josef von. *Tabakpachtung in der österreichischen Ländern von 1670–1783*. Vienna: Sonnleither, 1784.

.Rogge, Walter. *Österreich von Világos bis zur Gegenwart*. 3 vols. Leipzig: F. A. Brockhaus, 1879.

———. *Österreich seit der Katastrophe Hohenwart-Beust*. 2 vols. Leipzig: F. A. Brockhaus, 1879.

Roth, Josef. *Radetzkymarsch*. Berlin: Kiepenhever, 1932.

Schnitzler, Arthur. *Jugend in Wien*. Vienna: Molden, 1968.

———. *Der Weg ins Freie*. Berlin: S. Fischer, 1918.

Schuselka, Franz. *Das Revolutionsjahr, März 1848-März 1849*. Vienna: Jasper, Hügel & Manz, 1850.

Sieghart, Rudolf. *Die letzten Jahrzehnte einer Grossmacht*. Berlin: Ullstein, 1932.

Sonnenthal, Adolf von. *Fünfzig Jahre im Wiener Burgtheater*. Vienna: 1906.

Springer, Anton. *Geschichte Österreichs seit dem Wiener Frieden 1809*. 2 vols. Leipzig: S. Herzel, 1863, 1865.

Suess, Eduard. *Erinnerungen*. Leipzig: S. Hirzel, 1916.

Szekfü, Gyula. *Három nemzedék*. Budapest: Élet, 1922; republished Egyetemi nyomda, 1935.

Teller, M. *Die Juden in Böhmen und ihre Stellung in der Gegenwart*. Prague: Silber und Schenk, 1863.

Trollope, Frances. *Vienna and the Austrians*. London: R. Bentley, 1838.

Uhl, Friedrich. *Aus meinem Leben*. Stuttgart: Cotta, 1908.

Vámbéry, Ármin. *Küzdelmeim*. Budapest, Franklin, 1905.

Varnhagen von Ense, Karl August. *Denkwürdigkeiten des eigenen Lebens*. 3 vols. Leipzig: F. A. Brockhaus, 1843.

Wattmann, Ludwig. *Drei-und-fünfzig Jahre*. 3 vols. Vienna: Braumüler 1904.

Weisl, W. Wolfgang von. *Die Juden in der Armee Österreich-Ungarns*. Tel Aviv: Olamenu, 1971.

Werfel, Franz. *Barbara oder Die Frömmigkeit*. Berlin: P. Zsolnay, 1929.

Wertheimer, Josef. *Die Juden von Österreich.* 2 vols. Leipzig: Weigand, 1842.
Winter, J. *Fünfzig Jahre eines Wiener Hauses.* Vienna: Braumüller, 1927.
Wolf, Gerson. *Geschichte der Juden in Wien, 1156–1876.* Vienna: Hölden, 1876; reissued Vienna: Geyer, 1974.
————. *Joseph Wertheimer. Ein Leben und Zeitbild.* Vienna: Herzfeld und Bauer, 1868.
————. *Vom ersten bis zum zweiten Tempel.* Vienna: Braumüller, 1861.
————. *Zur Culturgeschichte in Österreich-Ungarn, 1848–1888.* Vienna: A. Hölden, 1888.
————. *Beitrag zur Geschichte jüdische Tartuffe.* Leipzig: D. G. Naumann, 1864.
Zeisberg et al. (eds.). *Wien 1848–1888.* Vienna: C. Konegen, 1888.
Zweig, Stefan. *Die Welt von Gestern.* Stockholm: Berman-Fischer, 1942.

UNPUBLISHED DISSERTATIONS

Andel, Brigitte. "Adelsverleihungen für Wirtschaftstreibende während der Regierungszeit Maria Theresias." Vienna: 1969.
Bacon, Gershon. "Agudath Israel in Poland, 1916–1939." Columbia University: 1979.
Baumgartner, Margarete. "Kurandas Ostdeutsche Post und die deutsche Frage von 1859 bis 1863." Vienna: 1947.
Bitton, Livia. "Jewish Nationalism in Hungary." New York University: 1968.
Blum, Kopel. "Aufklärung und Reform bei den Wiener Juden." Vienna: 1935.
Brosche, Gunter. "Joseph von Sonnenfels und das Wiener Theater." Vienna: 1962.
Czaczkes-Tissenboim, Shmeril. "Der Anteil der Juden an der Wiener Revolution von 1848." Vienna: 1927.
Dollar, Stephanie. "Die Sonntagsblätter von Ludwig August Frankl, 1842–1848." Vienna: 1932.
Friedler, Menasche Josef. "Die galizischen Juden vom wirtschaftlichen, kulturellen und staatsbürgerlichen Standpunkt, 1815–1848." Vienna: 1923.
Gross, Nachum T. "Industrialization in Austria in the Nineteenth Century." University of California at Berkeley: 1966.
Hammer, Käthe. "Die Judenfrage in den westlichen Kronländern Österreichs im Jahre 1848." Vienna: 1948.
Jäger-Sunstenau, Hans. "Die geadelten Judenfamilien im vormärzlichen Wien." Vienna: 1950.
Kohn, Helene. "Beiträge zur Geschichte der Juden in Österreich unter Kaiser Joseph II." Vienna: 1919.
Komanovitz, Renata. "Der Wirtschaftsadel unter Kaiser Franz II (I), in der Zeit von 1792 bis 1815." Vienna: 1974.
Kristianpoler, Meier. "Die wirtschaftliche Lage der Juden in Österreich in der 2. Hälfte des 18. Jahrhunderts." Vienna: 1930.
Kuraic, Helene. "Die Wiener Niederleger im 18. Jahrhundert." Vienna: 1946.
Landau, Moses. "Geschichte des Zionismus in Österreich." Vienna: 1932.
Leitner, Rudolf. "Die Judenpolitik der österreichischen Regierung in den Jahren 1848–1859." Vienna:1924.
Lewin, M. "Die Juden in Galizien zur Zeit Kaiser Josef II." Vienna: 1933.
März, Eduard. "The Austrian Economy in Transition." Harvard: 1948.
Moser, Jonny, "Von der Emanzipation zur antisemitischen Bewegung. Georg von Schönerer und Heinrich Friedjung." Vienna: 1962.
Novogoratz, Hans. "Sebastian Brunner und der frühe Antisemitismus." Vienna: 1979.
Obergruber, Rudolf. "Die Zeitschriften für jüdische Kulturinteressen im 19. Jahrhundert in Wien." Vienna: 1941.
Ochs, David. "Die Aufklärung der Juden in Galizien, 1772–1848." Vienna: 1937.

Olesker, Izrael. "Der Anteil der Juden an den Nationalitätenkämpfe in Böhmen im 19. Jahrhundert." Vienna: 1934.
Pichler, Hiltrud. "Die Brüder Pereire und die österreichisch-ungarische Monarchie. Unternehmerprojekte als Beitrag zur österreichischen Wirtschaftsentwicklung." Vienna: 1974.
Putz, Franz. "Die österreichische Wirtschaftsaristokratie von 1815–1859." Vienna: 1975.
Rechberger, Walther. "Zur Geschichte der Orientbahnen." Vienna: 1958.
Riff, Michael. "The Assimilation of the Jews of Bohemia and the Rise of Political Anti-Semitism, 1848–1914." London University: 1974.
Rohrer, Annalies. "Die Wiener Effektenbörse und ihre Besucher." Vienna: 1971.
Schächter, Hersch. "Die Judenfrage in der Publizistik vor dem Jahre und während des Jahres 1848 in Österreich-Ungarn." Vienna: 1932.
Schleicher, M. "Geschichte der Spaniolen Juden in Wien." Vienna: 1933.
Simons, Thomas W. "Sebastian Brunner, or The Biedermeier Day in Vienna." Harvard: 1963.
Stern, Salomon, "Die politischen and kulturellen Kämpfe der Juden in Ungarn vom Jahre 1848–1871." Vienna: 1932.
Sznajdman, Johann. "Die Zeit der Aufklärung und die Juden in Österreich unter der Regierung Joseph II." Vienna: 1934.
Van Arkel, Dirk. "Antisemitism in Austria." Leiden: 1966.
Weiss, Dorothea. "Der publizistische Kampf der Wiener Juden und ihre Emanzipation." Vienna: 1971.
Weissberg, Leib. "Die Judenemanzipation und die österreichische Reichsverfassung von 1849." Vienna: 1921.

MODERN MONOGRAPHS AND
FREQUENTLY-CITED WORKS

Altmann, Alexander. *Moses Mendelssohn.* University, Alabama: University of Alabama Press, 1973.
Avenary, H. et al. *Kantor Salomon Sulzer und seine Zeit.* Sigmaringen: J. Thorbecke, 1985.
Balaban, Mejer. *Dzieje Żydów w Galicji i w Rzeczypospolite Krakowskiei, 1772–1868.* Lwow: B. Polniecki, 1914.
———. "Herz Homberg in Galizien." In *JJGL,* vol. XIX (1916).
Baltzarek, Franz. *Die Geschichte der Wiener Börse.* Vienna: Akademie, 1973.
Baron, Salo W. "Aspects of the Jewish Communal Crisis in 1848." In *JSS* XIV (1952): 99–144.
———. "The Impact of the Revolutions of 1848 on Jewish Emancipation." In *JSS* XI (1949): 195–248.
———. "The Revolution of 1848 and Jewish Scholarship." In *AAJRP* XVIII (1948): 1–66; and XX (1950): 1–100.
Bato, Ludwig. *Die Juden im alten Wien.* Vienna: Phaidon, 1928.
Benedikt, Heinrich. *Wirtschaftliche Entwicklung in der Franz-Joseph-Zeit.* Vienna: Herold, 1958.
Bihl, Wolfdieter. "Die Juden." In Wandruszka/Urbanitsch, *Die Habsburger Monarchie,* vol. III/2, pp. 927ff.
Brix, Emil. *Die Umgangssprache in Altösterreich.* Vienna: Böhlau, 1982.
Brod, Max. *Der Prager Kreis.* Stuttgart: Kohlhammer, 1966.
Boyer, John W. *Political Radicalism in Late Imperial Vienna.* Chicago: University of Chicago Press, 1981.
Broch, Hermann. *Hofmannsthal und seine Zeit.* Munich: Piperverlag, 1964.
Charmatz, Richard. *Adolf Fischhof.* Stuttgart: Cotta, 1910.

Cohen, Gary. "Jews in German Society." In *CEH* X (1977): 28–54.

―――. *The Politics of Ethnic Survival; Germans in Prague, 1861–1914.* Princeton: Princeton University Press, 1981.

Colman, Hugh (ed.). *The Jews of Czechoslovakia.* 2 vols. Philadelphia: The Jewish Publication Society of America, 1968.

Czeike, Felix (ed.). *Wien im Vormärz.* Vienna: Jugend und Volk, 1980.

Edel, Klaus. *Karl Abraham Wetzlar, Freiherr von Plankenstern.* Vienna: VWGÖ, 1975.

Fraenkel, Josef (ed.). *The Jews of Austria: Essays on their Life, History and Destruction.* London: Vallentine, Mitchell, 1967.

Frankl, Jonathan. *Prophecy and Politics.* Cambridge: Cambridge University Press, 1981.

Franz, Georg. *Liberalismus.* Munich: Callwey, 1955.

Fuchs, Albert. *Geistige Strömungen in Österreich.* Vienna: Globus, 1949.

Gelber, N. M. *Aus zwei Jahrhunderten.* Vienna: R. Löwit, 1932.

Gille, Bertrand. *Histoire de la Maison Rothschild.* 2 vols. Geneva: Droz, 1965, 1967.

Golczewski, Frank. *Polnisch-jüdische Beziehungen, 1881–1922.* Wiesbaden: Steiner, 1981.

Gold, Hugo (ed.). *Geschichte der Juden in der Bukowina.* 2 vols. Tel Aviv: Olamenu, 1962.

―――. *Geschichte der Juden in Wien. Ein Gedenkbuch.* Tel Aviv: Olamenu, 1971.

―――. *Die Juden und Judengemeinden Böhmens.* Brno: Jüdischer Verlag, 1934; republished Tel Aviv: Olamenu, 1970.

―――. *Die Juden und die Judengemeinde Bratislava.* Brno: Jüdischer Verlag, 1932; republished Tel Aviv: Olamenu, 1965.

―――. *Die Juden und Judengemeinden Mährens.* Brno: Jüdischer Verlag, 1929; republished Tel Aviv: Olamenu, 1970.

Good, David E. *The Economic Rise of the Habsburg Empire, 1750–1914.* Berkeley: University of California Press, 1984.

Gregor, Josef. *Österreichische Theatergeschichte.* Vienna: Donauverlag, 1948.

Grunwald, Max. "Geschichte der Juden in Wien, 1625–1740." In vol. 5 of Heinrich Zimmermann (ed.), *Geschichte der Stadt Wien.* 6 vols. Vienna: Adolf Holzhausen, 1897–1918.

―――. *Samuel Oppenheimer und sein Kreis.* Vienna: 1913.

Hanák, Péter. *Jászi Oszkar dunai patriotismusa.* Budapest: Magvetö, 1985.

―――. "Problems of Jewish Assimilation in Austria-Hungary." In P. Thane et al. (eds.), *The Power of the Past.* Cambridge: Cambridge University Press, 1984.

―――. *Zsidókérdés asszimiláció antiszemitizmus.* Budapest: Gondolat, 1984.

Haüsler, Wolfgang. "Demokratie und Emanzipation 1848." In *SJA* I: 92–112.

―――. "Katalog: Die Revolution von 1848 und die österreichischen Juden." In *SJA* I (1974): 5–64.

―――. "Konfessionelle Probleme in der Wiener Revolution von 1848." In *SJA* I (1974): 64–78.

―――. " 'Orthodoxie' and 'Reform' im Wiener Judentum in der Epoche des Hochliberalismus." In *SJA* VI (1978): 35ff.

―――. "Das österreichische Judentum zwischen Beharrung und Fortschritt." In Wandruszka/Urbanitsch, *Die Habsburger Monarchie,* vol. IV.

―――. *Von der Massenarmut zur Arbeiterbewegung.* Vienna: Jugend und Volk, 1979.

―――. "Der Weg des Wiener Judentums von der Toleranz zur Emanzipation." In *JVGSW* XXX-XXXI (1974–75): 84–124.

Heer, Friedrich. *Der Kampf um die österreichische Identität.* Vienna: Böhlau, 1981.

Hoch, Karel. *Čechy na prahu moderního hospodářství.* Prague: A. Neubert, 1936.

Husserl, Sigmund. *Gründungsgeschichte der Stadttempel in Wien.* Vienna: Braumüller, 1906.

―――. "Die israelitische Kultusgemeinde in Wien." In *Ost und West* X (1910): 514.

Jászi, Oszkar. *Dissolution of the Habsburg Monarchy*. Chicago: University of Chicago Press, 1961.

Johnston, William M. *The Austrian Mind*. Berkeley: University of California Press, 1972.

Kann, Robert. *A Study of Austrian Intellectual History*. New York: Praeger, 1960.

———. *Theodor Gomperz. Ein Gelehrtenleben*. Vienna: Akademie, 1974.

Karady, Victor, and Istvan Kemeny. "Les juifs dans la structure des classes en Hongrie." In *ARSS* 22 (1978): 26–60.

Karniel, Joseph. "Josef von Sonnenfels." In *JIDG* VII (1978): 135ff.

———. "Fürst Kaunitz und die Juden." In *JIDG* XII (1983): 15–27.

———. "Das Toleranzpatent Kaiser Josephs II für die Juden Galiziens und Lodomeriens." In *JIDG* VI (1982): 55–71.

———. "Zur Auswirkung des Toleranzpatents von 1781." In Peter F. Barton (ed.), *Im Zeichen der Toleranz*. Vienna: Protestantenverlag, 1981.

Katz, Jakob. *Jews and Freemasons*. Cambridge, Mass.: Harvard University Press, 1970.

———. *Out of the Ghetto*. Cambridge, Mass.: Harvard University Press, 1973.

———. *From Prejudice to Destruction*. Cambridge, Mass.: Harvard University Press, 1980.

Katz, Jakob (ed.). *Toward Modernity: The European Jewish Model*. New Brunswick, NJ: Transaction Books, 1987.

Kaufmann, David. *Letzte Vertreibung der Juden aus Wien und Niederösterreich, ihre Vorgeschichte und ihre Opfer*. Vienna: Carl Konegen, 1889.

———. *Die Familie Simson Wertheimers*. Vienna: F. Beck, 1888.

Kestenberg-Gladstein, Ruth. *Neuere Geschichte der Juden in den böhmischen Ländern*. Tübingen: Mohr, 1969.

Kieval, Hillel. "The Modernization of Jewish Life in Prague." In Katz (ed.), *Toward Modernity*.

———. *The Making of Czech Jewry*. New York: Oxford University Press, 1988.

Kopetzky, Franz. *Josef und Franz von Sonnenfels*. Vienna: M. Perl, 1884.

Kraus, Samuel. *Joachim Edler von Popper*. Vienna: private, 1925.

Laios, Georgios S. *Simon Sinas*. Athens: Akademias, 1972.

Laszlo, Erno. "Hungarian Jewry: Settlement and Demography." In *HJS* I: 61–136.

Macartney, C. A. *The Habsburg Empire, 1790–1918*. London: Weidenfeld and Nicolson, 1968.

März, Eduard. *Österreichische Industrie- und Bankpolitik in der Zeit Franz Joseph I.* Vienna: Europa Verlag, 1968.

Mahler, Raphael. *A History of Modern Jewry, 1780–1815*. New York: Schocken, 1971.

Marcus, Joseph. *Social and Political History of the Jews in Poland*. Amsterdam: Mouton, 1983.

Mayr, Josef Karl. *Wien im Zeitalter Napoleons* (Vienna: G. Gistel, 1940).

McCagg, William O., Jr. *Jewish Nobles and Geniuses in Modern Hungary* (New York and Boulder, Colorado: Columbia University Press, 1972; reissue with new Preface, 1986).

———. "The Assimilation of Jews in Austria" in Béla Vágó (ed), *The Assimilation of Jews in Modern Times* (Boulder, Colorado: Westview, 1981), pp. 127–140.

———. "The Role of the Magyar Nobility in Modern Jewish History" in *East European Quarterly* XX (1986): 41–53.

———. "On Habsburg Jewry and Its Disappearance" in Jonathan Frankl (ed.), *Studies in Contemporary Jewry* IV (1987): 172–96.

———. "Convert Jews and the Problem of Viennese Jew-Hatred in 1848" in *East European Quarterly* XXI (1987): 355–68.

———. "Jewish Conversion in Hungary in Modern Times" in Todd Endelmann (ed.), *Jewish Apostasy in the Modern World* (New York: Holmes and Meier, 1987).

———. "Vienna and Budapest about 1900: The Problem of Jewish Influence" in

Gy. Ránki (ed.), *Hungary and European Civilization* (forthcoming, Budapest: Akadémiai könyvkiado, 1988).

————. "The Jewish Position in Interwar Central Europe: A Structural Study of Jewry at Vienna, Budapest and Prague" in Victor Karady and Yehuda Don (eds.), *Social and Economic History of Central European Jewry*. New Brunswick, N.J.: Transaction Press, 1989.

————. "Austria's Jewish Nobles, 1741–1918," forthcoming in YLBI XXXIV (1989).

McGrath, William J. *Dionysian Art and Populist Politics in Austria*. New Haven: Yale University Press, 1974.

————. *Freud's Discovery of Psychoanalysis*. Ithaca: Cornell University Press, 1986.

Mendelsohn, Ezra. *The Jews of East Central Europe between the Wars*. Bloomington: Indiana University Press, 1983.

Meyer, Michael. *The Origins of the Modern Jew*. Detroit: Wayne State University Press, 1967.

Mosse, Werner. A. Paucker, and R. Rürüp (eds.). *Revolution and Evolution: 1848 in German-Jewish History*. Tübingen: Mohr, 1981.

Osterloh, Karl-Heinz. *Joseph von Sonnenfels und die österreichische Reformbewegung*. Lübeck: Matthiesen, 1970.

Pulzer, Peter. *The Rise of Political Anti-Semitism in Germany and Austria*. New York: John Wiley, 1964.

Rosenfeld, Max. *Die polnische Judenfrage*. Vienna: Löwit, 1918.

Rosenmann, Moses. *Isak Noe Mannheimer. Sein Leben und Werken*. Vienna: Löwit, 1922.

————. *Dr. Adolf Jellinek. Sein Leben und Schaffen*. Vienna: J. Schlesinger, 1931.

Rozenblit, Marsha. *The Jews of Vienna: Assimilation and Identity, 1867–1914*. Albany: SUNY, 1983.

Rürüp, Reinhold. *Emanzipation und Antisemitismus*. Göttingen: Vanderhoeck und Ruprecht, 1975.

Ruppin, Arthur. *Die Juden der Gegenwart*. Berlin: Jüdischer Verlag, 1920.

————. *Soziologie der Juden*. 2 vols. Berlin: Jüdischer Verlag, 1930–31.

Schiper, Ignacy, A. Tartakower, and A. Haffta (eds). *Zydzi w Polsce Odrodzonej*. 2 vols. Warsaw: private, 1932–33.

Schnee, Heinrich. *Rothschild. Geschichte einer Finanzdynastie*. Göttingen: Musterschmidt Verlag, 1961.

————. *Die Hoffinanz und der moderne Staat*. 6 vols. Berlin: Duncker und Humblot, 1953–1967.

Scholem, Gershom. *Du Frankisme au Jacobinisme*. Paris: Gallimard, 1981.

————. *The Messianic Idea in Judaism and Other Essays*. New York: Schocken, 1971.

————. *Sabbatai Sevi: The Mystical Messiah 1626–1676*. Princeton: Princeton University Press, 1973.

Seibt, Ferdinand, ed. *Die Juden in den böhmischen Ländern*. Munich: Oldenbourg, 1983.

Silber, Michael. "The Historical Experience of German Jewry and its Impact on Haskalah and Reform in Hungary." In Katz (ed.), *Toward Modernity*.

Spiel, Hilda. *Fanny von Arnstein*. Frankfurt am Main: S. Fischer, 1962.

Stillschweig, Kurt. "Nationalism and Autonomy among Eastern European Jewry." In *HJ* VI (1944): 27–68.

————. "Zur neueren Geschichte der jüdischen Autonomie." In *MGWJ* LXXXIII (1939): 509–532.

Stölzl, Christoph. *Die Ära Bach in Böhmen*. Munich: Oldenbourg, 1971.

————. *Kafkas böses Böhmen*. Munich: Harrassowitz, 1975.

————. "Zur Geschichte der böhmischen Juden in der Epoche des modernen Nationalismus," part I: "Vormärz und Revolution." In *BJCC* XIV (1973): 179–221. Part II: "Neoabsolutismus und Liberalismus." In *BJCC* XV (1974): 129–157.

Tietze, Hans, *Die Juden Wiens*. Vienna: Tal, 1933.
Vágó, Béla. *Jewish Assimilation in Modern Times*. Boulder, Colorado: Westview, 1981.
Venetianer, Lajos. *A magyar zsidóság története*. Budapest: Fövárosi ny., 1922.
———. *A zsidóság szervezete az Europai államokban*. Budapest: Franklin, 1901.
Wandruszka, Adam, and Peter Urbanitsch. *Die Habsburger Monarchie. 1848–1918.*
    Vols. I, II, III/1, III/2, IV. Vienna: Akademie, 1973, 1978, 1980, 1985.
Winter, Eduard. *Romantismus, Restauration und Fruhliberalismus im österreichsichen
    Vormärz*. Munich: Oldenbourg, 1966.
Wistrich, Robert. "The Modernization of Viennese Jewry." In Jacob Katz (ed.),
    Toward Modernity.
———. *Socialism and the Jews: The Dilemmas of Assimilation in Germany and Austria-
    Hungary*. Rutherford: Fairleigh Dickinson University Press, 1982.

INDEX

Abraham a Sancta Clara, 17
Adler, Victor, 157, 212
Agnon, S. J., 206
Albrecht (archduke of Austria), 143
Alexander II (emperor of Russia), 163
Amsterdam Jews, 233n.2
Anti-Semitism: by Jews, 217; origins of, 163–
  64. *See also specific headings*
Arnstein, Fanny, 60–62, 63
Arnstein, Nathan, 40, 50, 62
Arnsteiner, Adam Isaak, 50
Arnsteiner, Isaak, 50
Arnsteiner, Nathan Adam, 50
Ashkenazim, 27
Assimilation of Jews. *See specific headings*
Austrian Jews: as agriculturalists, 207; anti-
  Semitism against, 163, 212, 224; assimila-
  tion of, 224; in business, 209; as Frankists,
  34, 35; proletariat of, 212. *See also* Viennese
  Jews; *specific Jews*
Austrians, defined, 7

Baal Shem Tov, 32–33
Badeni, Kasimir Felix, 178
Balkan wars, of Joseph II, 55
Ballagi, Mór. *See* Bloch, Moritz
Banet, Mordekai Ben Abraham, 74, 112, 126,
  128
Barbara oder die Frömmigkeit (Werfel), 219
Bassevi, Jakob, 20
Bauer, Otto, 198; politics of, 2, 4, 185, 212,
  214
Bauerle, Anton, 93
Bauernfeld, Eduard von, 93, 94
Baumgartner, Andreas, 105, 106–7
Becher, Anton, 98
Beer, Peter, 70–71, 127
Beethoven, Ludwig van, 59, 60
Berger, Johann, 98
Berlin Congress (1878), 163
Berlin Jews, 54, 166. *See also* German Jews;
  specific Jews
BEShT. *See* Baal Shem Tov
Bettelheim, Samuel, 194
Biedermann, Josef, 152
Biedermann, M. L., 91
Biedermann, Simon, 153
Birnbaum, Nathan, 199, 200
Bismarck, Otto von, 163
Bloch, Joseph Samuel, 157, 184, 193, 198–99
Bloch, Moritz, 133
Bohemian Jews: in business, 14, 209; demo-
  graphics of, 11–12, 27, 176, 177; education
  of, 67, 82, 109, 178; elite of, 20–22; emigration of, 11, 71, 100, 125, 147; as financiers,
  177; as Frankists, 34–35, 69; Germanization
  of, 177–78; as industrialists, 100, 177; and
  industrial revolution, 71, 73, 74, 176–77; Judeophobia against, 77, 78, 79, 87, 100, 177,
  223; language of, 177–79, 217, 269n.17;
  marriage and residence restrictions on,
  120, 125; modernization of, 15, 82, 124, 147,
  224; Orthodox Jews, 179, 202; politics of,
  206, 223; proletariat of, 27–28, 208, 215;
  unity and disunity of, 14, 178, 179, 180;
  Zionism of, 208. *See also* Prague Jews; *specific Jews*
Bolshevik Jews, 214, 216
Borkenau, Moritz von. *See* Pollak, Moritz
Börne, Ludwig, 88
Borochov, Ber, 185
Brahms, Johannes, 144
Brandeis, Jakob, 152
Brno Jews: demographics of, 176–77; elite of,
  76–77; as industrialists, 74; and industrial
  revolution, 176–77; origins of, 22; politics
  of, 179. *See also* Moravian Jews; *specific Jews*
Brody, Zsigmond, 191
Brody Jews, 116, 118, 119, 120. *See also* Gali-
  cian Jews; Polish Jews; *specific Jews*
Bruck, Karl Ludwig, 105, 107, 168–69
Bruckner, Anton, 144
Buber, Martin, 213
Budapest Jews: anti-Semitism against, 221;
  assimilation of, 193; as Bolsheviks, 214;
  community organization of, 192; demographics of, 191, 204; elite of, 217, 271n.43;
  Neologs, 191, 192, 193; Orthodox Jews, 202;
  proletariat of, 208; and World War I, 219;
  Zionism of, 214, 221. *See also* Hungarian
  Jews; *specific Jews*
Bukowina Jews: as agriculturalists, 207; anti-
  Semitism against, 173, 212; demographics
  of, 171–72; education of, 172–73; Hasidim,
  172, 173, 202; language of, 172–73, 174;
  Maskilim of, 172, 173; nationalism of, 173–
  74, 184, 187, 194; Orthodox Jews, 202; politics of, 200; proletariat of, 208; Zionism of,
  179, 180. *See also* Cernauti Jews; *specific Jews*

Carl, Carl, 94
Castelli, Ignaz Franz, 92, 94
Catherine II (empress of Russia), 30
Cernauti Jews, 173, 174, 178, 219–20. *See also*
  Bukowina Jews; *specific Jews*
Chajes, Z. P., 205
Chajzes, Avram, 89, 98, 99
Chorin, Aaron, 23, 127–28, 133